First Women

ALSO BY KATE ANDERSEN BROWER

The Residence: Inside the Private World
of the White House

First Women

THE GRACE AND POWER
OF AMERICA'S
MODERN FIRST LADIES

★

KATE ANDERSEN BROWER

HARPER

NEW YORK • LONDON • TORONTO • SYDNEY

TO THE FIRST LADY IN *OUR* FAMILY, MY MAGNIFICENT
MOTHER, VALERIE ANDERSEN.

AND TO MY EXTRAORDINARY FATHER,
CHRISTOPHER ANDERSEN.

There is no way in the world to figure out what it's like to live here.

—HILLARY CLINTON ON LIFE IN THE WHITE HOUSE

CONTENTS

FIRST WOMEN

JACQUELINE KENNEDY	1961–1963
LADY BIRD JOHNSON	1963–1969
PAT NIXON	1969–1974
BETTY FORD	1974–1977
ROSALYNN CARTER	1977–1981
NANCY REAGAN	1981–1989
BARBARA BUSH	1989–1993
HILLARY CLINTON	1993–2001
LAURA BUSH	2001–2009
MICHELLE OBAMA	2009–2017

First Women

Both women were wearing sunglasses. One looked glamorous even in a baseball cap with her hair tied back in a ponytail; the other looked a little less regal in a straw hat with a black bow, her hair blown by the salty wind. Both were beaming as the President of the United States snapped their photograph.

It was August 24, 1993, and Hillary Clinton was posing for a photo with Jacqueline Kennedy Onassis on board the *Relemar*, a seventy-foot, sleek white yacht owned by the former first lady's longtime companion, diamond dealer Maurice Tempelsman. Jackie had invited the Clintons, who had moved into the White House just seven months before, for a five-hour cruise on the brilliantly sunny day along Vineyard Sound, heading toward the red clay bluffs of Gay Head at the western end of Martha's Vineyard island. Jackie owned a four-hundred-acre estate nearby but the Clintons were far less familiar with the patrician elite who dominate the Vineyard in the summer. It was more than just a joyride; Jackie Kennedy was one of six former first ladies alive at the time, and she wanted to give Hillary advice on how to survive life in the White House. Jackie knew that Hillary was concerned about her daughter Chelsea's well-being, and, as a member of the elite sorority of former first ladies, she wanted to explain how she had raised the well-adjusted Caroline and JFK Jr. in the spotlight. Months before, Hillary had had a private lunch with Jackie at her elegant New York apartment at 1040 Fifth Avenue. At the meeting they discussed how to keep Chelsea shielded from the press.

Lisa Caputo, Hillary's press secretary in the White House, remembers how Jackie and her children talked to both Hillary and the President about "how you can grow up and have a sense of normalcy. That was really important to both the President and Mrs. Clinton at the time." In a letter to Betty Ford, another member of the exclusive sorority, Hillary said the trip "gave us the change of pace our family really needed for a few days." It was one of several meetings between Jackie and Hillary that solidified their profound bond. Jackie was happy that she could help Hillary, not only with parenting advice, but also by guiding her through the complicated social world of old-money Martha's Vineyard. Jackie made sure to introduce Hillary to her wealthy friends and encouraged her to make entertaining a priority in the White House. (She felt that some of her successors—especially Lady Bird Johnson, Pat Nixon, and Rosalynn Carter—could have done more to bring entertainers to the White House and expose the country to the arts.)

Jackie, who was sixty-four years old at the time, took a particular liking to the Clintons, in part because of Bill Clinton's adulation of President Kennedy, whom he referred to as his hero. She especially liked seeing the famous photo of a teenage Bill Clinton shaking President Kennedy's hand in the Rose Garden during a visit he made with a civic organization to Washington, D.C. (The Clintons were not shy about their admiration of the Kennedys. On the eve of the 1993 inauguration, they laid white roses at President Kennedy's grave and the grave of his brother, Robert, at Arlington National Cemetery.) No other Democratic president—not President Johnson or President Carter—had been quite so devoted to JFK's legacy. And no other first couple had been able to develop a real rapport with Jackie. The meeting that day between Hillary, a new first lady struggling to find her own voice, and Jackie, a former first lady who seemed so self-possessed, would have a deep impact on how Hillary raised her teenage daughter during the eight years of her husband's presidency.

At first, the always camera-shy Jackie stayed belowdecks while her brother-in-law Senator Ted Kennedy greeted the Clintons. "Hello, welcome to Massachusetts!" Senator Kennedy called out as the Clintons arrived, the President in preppy salmon-colored pants and Hillary in shorts. "Glad to be here!" the President shouted back as he climbed aboard. A forty-eight-foot boat trailed the presidential party, carrying White House Press Secretary Dee Dee Myers and dozens of reporters and photographers all hoping to catch a glimpse of the famous passengers. Jackie sat next to Hillary at one point and Hillary beamed, but Jackie, who had lived most of her life in the spotlight, seemed to resent the intrusion of the press.

The yacht sailed out into Buzzards Bay, beyond Vineyard Sound, and stopped in a quiet, sun-drenched cove for three hours in the middle of the day while the guests, including Chelsea Clinton and Caroline Kennedy, ate lunch and dived into the cold water from a thirty-foot diving board, the highest diving board on the yacht. When it was Hillary's turn, she climbed to the top and stood there, terrified.

"Jump!" President Clinton yelled. "Don't be a chicken, Hillary! JUMP!" Other male members of the intrepid Kennedy clan joined in until suddenly Hillary could hear a woman's voice rise above the rest from down below, in the water—it was Jackie's.

"Don't do it, Hillary! Don't do it! Just because they're daring you, you don't have to!"

Hillary paused a moment, considering Jackie's advice, and turned around to climb down to a less frightening height. No other woman in the world could understand Hillary's feeling of vulnerability better than Jackie. From there, Hillary leapt into the cold blue water.

————

IN A LETTER to First Lady Betty Ford, a Texas woman wrote, in all seriousness: "You are constitutionally required to be perfect." So much is expected of these women while so little is defined about the role they play. Lady Bird Johnson said a first lady needs to be a "showman and a salesman, a clotheshorse and a publicity sounding board, with a good heart, and a real interest in the folks" from all over the country, rich and poor. No easy feat.

When I covered President Obama's administration for Bloomberg News, I was invited to a luncheon for fewer than a dozen reporters who were assigned to follow First Lady Michelle Obama. At the lunch, which was supposed to be about her campaign to end childhood obesity, the First Lady mentioned that her husband had kicked his smoking habit. Any kernel of information about the first families travels fast and the news quickly became a big story, eclipsing anything about her healthy-eating campaign. I wondered how she felt sharing such personal information with the world, and whether she had come to accept her life as a global celebrity.

No one has written about the relationships between the first ladies and how these fascinating women turn to each other in times of joy and in times of sorrow. For this book, I interviewed more than two hundred people, including chiefs of staff to the first ladies, press secretaries, and other top political advisers, along with the first ladies' close friends and family members, to discover what life is really like in the White House. Their children shared revealing stories about their mothers' personal struggles and their ultimate resilience.

From Jackie Kennedy to Michelle Obama, each of these women has carved out her own path, all while raising her children, serving as her husband's greatest protector and confidante, and negotiating the fraught relationship between her staff in the East Wing and her husband's advisers in the West Wing. Those responsibilities are punctuated by the constant fear these women share for their families' safety.

Never-before-published letters between the first ladies reveal just how deeply they empathize with each other, and offer a window into the complexities of their relationships and into their own private worlds. Just as presidents are part of a lifelong club, so too are first ladies: presidents are members of the world's most selective fraternity, and first ladies are members of the world's most elite sorority. Staffers who have never spoken with a reporter before, including White House butlers, maids, ushers, chefs, and florists whom I interviewed for my first book, *The Residence*, have spoken with me about their unique relationships with these remarkable women. For this book I was able to interview more staffers who would not agree to talk with me before. It is the residence staffers who work in the White House who see the first families during their most private moments. I also had candid conversations with Rosalynn Carter (whom I interviewed twice) and Barbara and Laura Bush that helped build the foundation for this book.

These women's lives are shaped by history. Betty Ford's son, Steve, remembers coming home from elementary school in 1963 and finding his mother alone and crying in their family room. "Why are you crying, Mom?" he asked her. "President Kennedy has been killed," she told him softly. Nancy Reagan was driving down San Vicente Boulevard in Los Angeles when she first heard the news over her car radio that Kennedy had been shot. Neither Betty nor Nancy knew then that they would become part of this small sorority of first ladies and that both of their husbands would one day be the targets of assassination attempts.

Ten first ladies have lived in the White House since 1961, from Jackie Kennedy to Michelle Obama. They were married to five Republicans and five Democrats, and they are all incredibly different women. What makes them so compelling is their shared humanity, their imperfection. "My mom," Steve Ford says proudly, "always thought she was an ordinary woman in an extraordinary time." These women aren't "perfect," and that is what makes them so captivating.

The Political Wife

★

What first lady is understood? It's the king. It's not the queen.
—Connie Stuart, chief of staff and press
secretary to First Lady Pat Nixon

First ladies are modern women with modern problems, joys, careers, doubts, insecurities, and crises. They are wives, working mothers, and political advisers who are transformed into international celebrities simply because of whom they chose to marry. They are often beloved, sometimes vilified, and they are almost always their husbands' most trusted advisers. While it takes a nation to elect a president, "we were elected by one man," Laura Bush says. Their position is not enshrined in the Constitution, and the role of the unpaid spouse seems incredibly anachronistic in today's world, especially since these women helped get their husbands elected and are then confined to the East Wing. But Rosalynn Carter understood decades ago the covert power a first lady wields. "I have learned," she said, "that you can do anything you want to."

The title of first lady comes with a thorny combination of intense scrutiny, an incredible platform, and no official mandate. Yet it is vital to the American presidency, and these women embody American womanhood and American motherhood. But they aren't always happy about it. Martha Washington called herself a "state prisoner." Jacqueline Kennedy proclaimed: "The one thing I do not want to be called is 'First Lady.' It sounds like a saddle horse." And Michelle Obama says that living in the White House is like living in a "really nice prison." Nancy Reagan, however, proudly put "First Lady" as her occupation on her income tax forms—she had worked hard for it. She told her press secretary, Sheila Tate, "I thought, well, my husband has been governor of the great big state of California. We've had a lot of experience, maybe being in the White House will be fifty times harder. You know what, it's a thousand times harder." They all cope with the singular pressure-filled position in their own ways, some more successfully than others. Some envy each other, some hate each other, and some help each other navigate life in the White House. Behind every great president there has been a great woman.

The relationships these women share with each other are complicated and often surprising, and they have much more to do with the personalities of the individual women than with the political parties or policies their names are identified with. There are unlikely rivalries, like that between Nancy Reagan and Barbara Bush, and surprising friendships, like the one between Laura Bush and Michelle Obama, and lifelong bonds, like the friendship forged between Lady Bird Johnson and Betty Ford. And there are relationships fraught with hurt feelings and resentment, like that between Hillary Clinton and Michelle Obama. Looking through their private correspondence reveals the complexity of their relationships with each other: they commiserate about the deaths of their parents, their husbands, their friends, and even, in some particularly tragic situations, the loss of their own children. These women go through the entire human experience while living in the fishbowl of the White House surrounded by a pack of intimidating men and women wearing earpieces and staring blankly ahead. "There is no way in the world to figure out what it's like to live here," Hillary Clinton said in a 1995 interview. It can be surprisingly claustrophobic. Betty Ford referred comically to the White House, a 132-room, six-floor building with two hidden mezzanine levels, as her "one-bedroom apartment" because she was essentially living on the second floor, where she worked out of a dressing room adjacent to the President and First Lady's bedroom. Life changes quickly for these women. Rosalynn Carter remembers how startled she was when, shortly after she and her family moved in, she picked up the phone and asked a White House operator to be connected to "Jimmy." There was a pause and the operator said, "Jimmy who?" From then on she had to remind herself to refer to her husband as "the President" in certain circumstances. Their lives had changed forever, and there was little time to adjust.

On April 12, 1945, when President Franklin Delano Roosevelt died at his cottage in Warm Springs, Georgia, First Lady Eleanor Roosevelt was hard at work back in Washington. When she learned of her husband's death she immediately called their four sons, who were all on active military duty, and changed into a black mourning dress. It was Eleanor who told Vice President Harry Truman the news. "Harry," she said calmly, "the President is dead." Stricken, Truman asked her if there was anything he could do to help. She shook her head and said, "Is there anything we can do for *you*? For you are the one in trouble now."

———

IN THE NINETEENTH century a woman's name was to appear in writing on only three occasions: upon her birth, her marriage, and her death. Originally, the president's spouse was expected to be only a hostess, and the unofficial title was not even used until President James Buchanan's niece, Harriet Lane, began accompanying him to events. Buchanan was the only lifelong bachelor to be president. In 1858, *Harper's Weekly* referred to Lane as "Our Lady of the White House," and two years later, in *Frank Leslie's Illustrated Newspaper*, her picture was printed with this caption: "The subject of our illustration . . . may be justly termed the first lady in the land." By the time Mary Todd Lincoln moved into the White House in 1861, the term "first lady" was ensconced in the American lexicon. (She was sometimes called "Mrs. President" by her husband and his advisers.) When the Civil War hero General Ulysses S. Grant was elected president in 1868, women reporters were eager to cover his wife, Julia, even though many of them would write under a pen name because being a reporter was considered a highly unladylike occupation in the nineteenth century. (Julia loved to entertain—she threw twenty-nine-course dinners—but she came under blistering attacks for her appearance: she was cross-eyed and would pose for portraits in profile to try to disguise it.)

The president's wife has always wielded a subtle but effective power. Mary Todd Lincoln made sure some of her allies were part of her husband's Cabinet, and Edith Bolling Galt Wilson, President Woodrow Wilson's second wife, is thought to have actually assumed many of the duties of the presidency after her husband's stroke in 1919, eighteen months before he left the White House. For twelve years, from 1933 to 1945, Eleanor Roosevelt challenged the expectations the public had of a first lady by working tirelessly as an activist for human rights and women's rights. Eleanor was such a force that, veteran White House correspondent Sarah McClendon wrote, "she set a standard that all the first ladies who have followed her must measure themselves against." Between

Eleanor and the glamorous Jackie Kennedy were Bess Truman and Mamie Eisenhower. Bess Truman hated Washington (she and her husband and daughter all called the White House the "Great White Jail") and went back to their home in Independence, Missouri, as often as possible, and never gave interviews. She was terrified that the press would reveal her father's suicide of many years earlier. When reporters tried to interview her, Bess replied, "You don't need to know me. I'm only the President's wife and the mother of his daughter." Mamie Eisenhower was the embodiment of the charming 1950s housewife and loving mother, but she was aware of her influence. She had such an aversion to the controversial Republican Senator Joseph McCarthy of Wisconsin, who became famous for his committee on un-American activities, that she made sure he was excluded from certain White House dinners. Her surreptitious use of power is fascinating given that her public comments about womanhood were so formal. "Being a wife is the best career life has to offer a woman," she said, adding that she had "only one career, and his name is Ike."

————

Jacqueline Kennedy lived in the White House for a little more than a thousand days, from January 20, 1961, until shortly after her husband's assassination on November 22, 1963. John Kennedy was forty-three years old when he became president—the youngest man ever elected to the office. At thirty-one, Jackie was the third-youngest first lady in U.S. history and the first first lady to be the mother of a baby since the turn of the century. She transformed the role of first lady and became a global superstar. She undertook a massive restoration of the White House and became singularly focused on making it the "most perfect house" in the country. Jackie was a patrician woman who grew up in a twenty-eight-room Victorian mansion in Newport, Rhode Island, and was educated at Miss Porter's School in Farmington, Connecticut. But she made an incredibly egalitarian decision when she opened up the White House to anyone who had access to a television during her tour of the mansion on February 14, 1962. The broadcast was watched by an unprecedented 56 million viewers and contributed to her celebrity status.

Jackie's greatest legacy, however, was how bravely she mourned her husband's death. As the years passed she came to resent being a vessel for the shared grief of Americans and desperately wanted to live a private life. When she returned to Washington to go to Arlington National Cemetery to visit her husband's grave and the grave of their two young children—Patrick, who died two days after his premature birth; and their stillborn daughter, Arabella—she asked her driver to avoid getting near the White House, a house she had once so lovingly restored. She did not want to see the place that held so many bittersweet memories for her and her two young children, Caroline and John F. Kennedy Jr.

Lady Bird Johnson came into a White House in mourning, with black cloth hanging over chandeliers, windows, and doorways, and devastated Kennedy staffers walking shell-shocked through the mansion's hallways. The last woman who had assumed the title of first lady under such dark circumstances was Theodore Roosevelt's wife, Edith, who replaced Ida McKinley after President William McKinley's assassination in 1901. But Ida, who was not often seen in public and who suffered from epileptic seizures, was no Jackie Kennedy, and Lady Bird was coming in at the dawn of the television era, when first ladies could no longer maintain the kind of relative privacy that someone like Ida McKinley enjoyed. Lady Bird worked hard to distinguish herself from her glamorous predecessor, but, she sighed, "People see the living and wish for the dead." Nonetheless, Lady Bird, who was almost two decades older than Jackie and who was not as glamorous, became a powerful first lady who was a critical part of her husband's victory in the 1964 presidential election.

Pat Nixon was prepared to be a first lady in 1960, when her husband ran against Jack Kennedy and lost, but she had absolutely no desire for him to run again in 1968. By then she had seen Richard Nixon through seven political campaigns over more than twenty years. In the White House she was nicknamed "Plastic Pat" because she was simply exhausted playing the role of political wife. She stood by her husband through their most difficult years as the Watergate scandal brought down his presidency and he became the only president in history to resign. The day they left the White House in disgrace, the Nixons sat in silence in the helicopter as it took off from the South Lawn and began its journey over the National Mall. Pat murmured to herself, "It's so sad. It's so sad." Her private suffering struck a nerve, and in 1990, sixteen years after she left the White House, she was number six on *Good Housekeeping*'s list of Most Admired Women, coming in right before the legendary actress Katharine Hepburn. It was her twentieth year in the top ten.

Betty Ford escorted her friend Pat to the helicopter on the Nixons' last day in the White House. As the wife of Nixon's Vice President, Gerald Ford, Betty had grown fond of Pat and felt deeply sorry for her. That day, Betty put her arm around her friend's small waist. "My heavens, they've even rolled out the red carpet for us, isn't that something," Pat said to Betty ruefully. "You'll see so many of those . . . you'll get so you hate them." While Pat was suffering, Betty was consumed with anxiety about her sudden ascendance to the White House. The night before, Betty and her husband held hands and prayed together. As they walked from the presidential helicopter, Marine One, back to the

White House after seeing the Nixons off, President Ford reached for his wife's hand and whispered, "We can do it."

The residence may not have been draped in black as it had been after President Kennedy's assassination, but the mood when the Fords moved in was almost as somber. Betty could not say anything to ease Pat's pain and humiliation, but once she became a first lady she quickly discovered the power of her newfound celebrity. For the next two and a half years she weathered two assassination attempts on her husband, voiced her support for the Equal Rights Amendment, and helped to remove the stigma attached to breast cancer when she revealed her own diagnosis. She spoke more freely than any of her predecessors, and though she was a registered Republican, after her husband left office she sometimes voted Democrat. It was after she left the White House, however, that Betty made her greatest contribution with her stunning admission that she had an addiction to alcohol and prescription pills, a revelation that transformed her private pain into healing for so many others.

Rosalynn Carter was a shrewd politician whose syrupy southern drawl belied her personal ambition. During her four years in the White House, she sat in on Cabinet meetings and was a crucial player in the Camp David Accords, the first peace treaty between Israel and one of its Arab neighbors, which was agreed upon after a thirteen-day summit in 1978 at the presidential retreat. She helped her husband decide how to approach Egyptian President Anwar Sadat and Israeli Prime Minister Menachem Begin when the deal seemed stalled. On the campaign trail she realized that she could interact with people in a way her husband could not. When he was running for governor of Georgia and later for president she would slip out of the crowd surrounding him and talk to supporters. People felt comfortable talking to her about their problems. "One of the roles that she played during the campaign and played as first lady and continues to play now is as the eyes and ears for her husband," said Rosalynn's White House projects director, Katherine Cade. Aides say she was a better judge of character than her husband. During Jimmy Carter's 1980 reelection campaign, Rosalynn came back from a solo campaign trip and updated her husband. "The governor's really good, isn't he?" the President asked her cheerfully.

"Why do you think he's so good?" she shot back.

"Well, when I went there he really turned people out."

"Right, when *you* come there, anybody can turn the people out," she said. "He isn't organized at all, I could tell. The event was no good."

Rosalynn is still bitter about her husband's loss to Ronald Reagan—nearly forty years later the stigma of a one-term presidency has stayed with her. When asked decades after leaving Washington what she misses most about living in the White House, she replied, "I miss having Jimmy in the Oval Office taking care of our country. I have never felt as safe as I did when he was there." But President Carter has had the longest post–White House career of any president, and Rosalynn has been a crucial part of his success. She cofounded the Carter Center with her husband and has helped eradicate diseases and monitor elections around the world.

Nancy Reagan, who passed away at the age of ninety-four, was first lady from 1981 to 1989. "She was the human resources department," says Reagan political consultant Stuart Spencer, weighing in on Nancy's involvement in deciding who would be in her husband's Cabinet. Nancy was not particularly close with any of the other first ladies, and she was deeply traumatized by the assassination attempt during her husband's first year in office, which brought him much closer to the brink of death than anyone knew at the time. She was a self-described worrier and a perfectionist who sometimes made impossible demands of the residence staff at the White House. (She even assigned someone to guard her pink chiffon dress on the trans-atlantic flight to Prince Charles and Lady Diana's 1981 wedding.) But she understood the symbolic power of the executive mansion in a way that no other first lady, with the exception of Jackie Kennedy, ever had. When Soviet president Mikhail Gorbachev and his wife, Raisa, made their historic visit to Washington in 1987, Nancy made it clear to the residence staff that she wanted the White House to look its best. Her most lasting legacy was her deep devotion to her husband, whom she stood by in his last years as he suffered from Alzheimer's disease.

Nancy passed away in March 2016. Her funeral was held at her husband's presidential library in Simi Valley, California, a library that she was deeply devoted to and that she helped build. Not surprisingly, she planned every detail of the service down to the guest list which blended her love of Washington with her love of Hollywood. It included then–First Lady Michelle Obama, Hillary Clinton, Tom Selleck, Arnold Schwarzenegger, and Caroline Kennedy. Former Canadian Prime Minister Brian Mulroney read a moving letter written by President Reagan and addressed to "Mrs. R" on Christmas Day 1981. In it Reagan wrote to his wife: "There could be no life for me without you."

Barbara Bush died at ninety-two in April 2018, and shares the distinction with Abigail Adams of having had a husband and a son elected president. She was the matriarch of a Republican dynasty and had many nicknames: her family called her Bar, Mother, Ganny, the Silver Fox, and the Enforcer. She had six children, seventeen grandchildren, and seven great-grandchildren.

Much has been made of the romance between the Reagans, but at her private funeral service at St. Martin's Episcopal Church in Houston, the Bushes' seventy-three years of marriage was celebrated. The two met at a dance in Greenwich, Connecticut, in

1941, not long after the attack on Pearl Harbor, when she was six-teen and he was seventeen; they had the longest presidential mar-riage in history. During his emotional remarks, the Bushes' son Jeb read a love letter his father wrote to his mother on their wed-ding anniversary more than thirty years ago. "'Will you marry me? Oops, I forgot we did that forty-nine years ago. I was very happy on that day in 1945, but I'm even happier today. You have given me joy that few men know. You have made our boys into men by balling them out and then right away, by loving them. You've helped Doro be the sweetest, greatest daughter in the whole world,'" Bush said, reciting his father's letter. "'I've climbed per-haps the highest mountain in the world, but even that cannot hold a candle to being Barbara's husband. Mom used to tell me, now George, don't walk ahead. Little did she know I was only trying to keep up, keep up with Barbara Pierce from Rye, New York, I love you.'" Weeks before she died, Barbara, who was known for her sharp tongue and dry sense of humor, said she was "still old" and "still in love" with her husband. "I married the first man I ever kissed," she said during the first year of George H. W. Bush's presidency. "When I tell this to my children, they just about throw up." She died holding her husband's hand.

Fifteen hundred people attended her funeral service, includ-ing four of the five living former presidents and three former first ladies—Michelle Obama, Laura Bush, and Hillary Clinton—along with current First Lady Melania Trump, who sat next to the Obamas. Barbara was buried in a family plot at the George Bush Presidential Library and Museum at Texas A&M Univer-sity in College Station. She was buried near their daughter Robin, who died of leukemia at three years old.

When she was the wife of then–vice president George H.W. Bush, she had a difficult relationship with Nancy Reagan, who barely mentioned Barbara in her memoir and whom she said she never got to know. That might be because the Bushes were rarely invited to the second and third floors of the residence. When Barbara lived in the White House from 1989 to 1993, she was beloved by the butlers and maids who work there, but her cutting remarks sometimes offended presidential aides. She said that there is something wrong with a first lady if she does not embrace the "big opportunity" that's handed to her to make a real difference in people's lives. But even Barbara Bush recognized how daunting the job is when she said, "I'd like to go back and live there [in the White House] and not have the responsibility."

Hillary Clinton is the only first lady to run for office. She served as a senator and as secretary of state, and she waged two failed bids to get back in the White House. She was first lady from 1993 to 2001 and attempted unsuccessfully to redefine the role by having her office in the West Wing and by playing an active and unapologetic part in major policy decisions. Scandals swirled around the Clintons during their entire eight years in the White House, and at a 1994 press conference Hillary was pelted with questions from reporters for more than an hour. The questions ranged from cattle futures trades that she made while her husband was Arkansas governor to their Whitewater real estate venture to suggestions that documents were removed from Deputy White House Counsel Vince Foster's office after Foster's suicide. "I can't really help it if some people get up every day wanting to destroy instead of build," she said. In that same press conference she referred to herself as a "transition" figure who has worked her entire life and who was surprised by how uncomfortable people were with her ambitious approach to being first lady.

Hillary greatly admires Eleanor Roosevelt, and in the White House she had imaginary conversations with her "to try to figure out what she would do in my shoes," she said. "She usually responds by telling me to buck up or at least to grow skin as thick as a rhinoceros." In the wake of the failure of her health-care plan and after the Democrats lost the House and the Senate in the 1994 midterm elections, Hillary was walking by her office on a gray November morning. She had just finished meeting with her husband in the Oval Office, and a framed photograph of Eleanor she had displayed on a table caught her eye. She asked herself, *What would Eleanor do?* She loved living in the house where Eleanor had once lived. Hillary especially liked how much consternation Eleanor caused a member of FDR's administration who said she should stay out of her husband's business and "stick to her knitting." Eleanor's advice, Hillary thought, would be to press on and not get bogged down by setbacks. Hillary blamed herself for the failure of her health-care proposal and knew she played some role in the disastrous midterm election results. She had emboldened "the enemy," she wrote in her memoir *Living History*.

Roosevelt's great-granddaughter Anna Fierst, who as a young girl knew Eleanor and remembers her holding court at the dinner table at her cottage in New York's Hudson Valley, does not think that Eleanor would naturally take to Hillary. "I think she'd be a little weary of Hillary Clinton. Hillary kind of has a hard edge to her, which is okay. It's not a criticism, it's just her personality." Hillary concedes that she has a tough veneer and has said of herself, "I'm probably the most famous person you don't really know." Aides insist she can be "soulful" and "warm," and when she was first lady, they say, there were many times when she was brought to tears visiting sick children in hospitals.

Hillary wanted to have more influence than Nancy Reagan or Eleanor Roosevelt; she wanted a seat at the table, and her husband was eager to give it to her. When she was first lady a large photograph of herself speaking at a podium hung in her West Wing office, with an

inscription from her biggest booster: "You are so good, Love, Bill."
Hillary shared more than just ambition and intellect with Eleanor—
she shared the painful bond of marriage to an unfaithful husband,
a point that was ironically made by Monica Lewinsky herself. In a
letter, Lewinsky, who had an affair with President Clinton when
she was a twenty-one-year-old White House intern, wrote to him
on September 30, 1997, and pleaded with the President to meet her.
"Oh, and Handsome [her nickname for Clinton], remember FDR
would never have turned down a visit with Lucy Mercer [President
Roosevelt's longtime mistress]!" In 1992, when Bill Clinton was running for his first term and unselfconsciously advertising himself and
Hillary as "buy one, get one free," he said that he saw Hillary playing a far greater role than her idol. "If I get elected president, it will
be an unprecedented partnership, far more than Franklin Roosevelt
and Eleanor. They were two great people, but on different tracks. If
I get elected, we'll do things together like we always have."

Laura Bush speaks in a sweet and thoughtful way and approached the role of first lady in a much more traditional manner
than her predecessor. When asked about her relationship with her
mother-in-law, Barbara, Laura says, "I think George and I had a
huge advantage moving into the White House, having stayed there
so many times with his parents and having seen them as President and First Lady; that was a huge advantage for us. The only
other family that had that were John Quincy and Louisa Adams."
Barbara Bush had reason to like Laura. She famously got her son
George W. to quit drinking, something that Barbara and her husband, George H. W. Bush, had always been grateful to her for. "I
let him know that I thought he could be a better man," Laura said.
Laura's chief of staff in the White House, Anita McBride, said the
elder Bushes "look at Laura as somebody that they never really
had to worry about." She was so good for their son, and they knew

that without her he could not have become president. Barbara said her daughter-in-law followed "a great philosophy in life—you can either like it or not, so you might as well like it." But their relationship is more complicated than that. Once, when Barbara Bush was walking through the residence, she made a comment about new leopard-printed upholstery on a piece of furniture. "You had your time," Laura told her. "This is my house now."

After the terrorist attack of September 11, 2001, Laura had the grim task of talking to victims' families and serving as a symbol of hope in the wake of devastation. She found a new voice after 9/11 and turned her attention to the treatment of women and girls in Afghanistan and other parts of the world. But she left the White House under a dark cloud of criticism because of her husband's handling of the Iraq War.

Michelle Obama occupies a unique place as the country's first African American first lady. Growing up in a working-class family on Chicago's South Side, she struggled to find her identity at the predominantly white Princeton University, where she graduated cum laude in 1985, and at Harvard Law School, where she graduated three years later. In the White House, friends say, she feels that critics are waiting to pounce on her for one misstep. "She was a working mother, a professional mother. Hillary Clinton worked but she was also the governor's wife. She had a huge infrastructure. Michelle Obama's infrastructure was her mother," says former White House communications director Anita Dunn.

Michelle has more closely followed in the footsteps of Laura Bush than of Hillary Clinton. She came into the White House describing herself as a J.Crew–wearing mom-in-chief, and her devotion to the Obamas' two daughters has remained her top priority. "When people ask me how I'm doing," Michelle says, "I say, 'I'm only as good as my most sad child.'" She doesn't enjoy politics; in fact she hates glad-handing and raising money. She does not wear her emotions on her sleeve, and her older brother and her mother both say that she has never once called them in tears. She is most comfortable in a room full of students from diverse backgrounds whom she views as reflections of herself and her husband. "Maybe you feel like your destiny was written the day you were born, and you ought to just rein in your hopes and scale back your dreams. But if any of you are thinking that way, I'm here to tell you, stop it. Don't do that," she told 158 seniors graduating from an Anacostia high school considered one of the worst schools in Washington, D.C. "Don't ever scale back your dreams." And she has a way of speaking to these mostly African American students, some of whom were raised in poverty or became parents as teenagers, with none of the saccharine qualities of politicians who insist that they can relate but obviously cannot. "You can't just sit around," she told them. "Don't expect anybody to come and hand you anything. It doesn't work that way." But the political climate in Washington and the constant demands of the presidency have made her battle-hardened. She thought a California college student summed up the role of first lady well when she called it "the balance between politics and sanity." Again and again, Michelle has put her foot down in an effort to carve out some semblance of normalcy for herself and her daughters. The fight has been exhausting.

These women each faced the loss of privacy coupled with mounting personal and, oddly enough, financial pressure when they moved into the White House. Rosalynn Carter said she was stunned to learn that first families have to pay for their own food. She remembers when the chief usher, who runs the executive mansion, showed her her family's food bill for their first month in the White House. "The bill was six hundred dollars, which doesn't sound like very much, but that was enormous to me back then because this was 1976. We had a lot of company with my family, Jimmy's family and friends, and then I got a six-hundred-dollar bill. I was shocked." To save money, Rosalynn would ask the chef to serve leftovers some nights when it was just the family eating. Jackie Kennedy reorganized her staff and put someone new in charge of housekeeping because the food bill had gotten so high. Barbara Bush, however, had spent eight years as the wife of the Vice President and knew that her family would be expected to pay for their food and toiletries. "If they [other first ladies] were shocked, there's something wrong with them," she said sternly. "We had lots of guests, as did George W., and we paid for those private guests. But the bill would come and it would say, 'One egg: eighteen cents.' Mrs. So-and-So had an egg and a piece of toast. It's cheaper to eat at the White House."

While there are enormous perks that come with the job, the family doesn't get to keep any gifts over a certain amount. When the Carters were in the White House they could not accept anything that cost more than one hundred dollars. Their daughter, Amy, tearfully had to give up a carved coral head of Christ that Pope John Paul II had given her when she visited him at the Vatican, and a small gold bracelet inscribed with her name (and valued at $150) given to her by President Sandro Pertini of Italy. Rosalynn said they weren't allowed to purchase the items, even at retail price. Occasionally, the First Lady got around the rules—while giving a tour of the Carters' home in Plains, Georgia, she told the interviewer about a little bowl that was given to them by Emperor Hirohito on a state visit to Japan. "They valued that at ninety-nine dollars and I was able to keep it," she said happily. President Carter quickly interjected, "One of the few things we ever kept, by the way."

The complete lack of privacy is a common complaint. Rosalynn Carter recalls first moving into the White House and being surprised to discover a Secret Service agent posted in the stairwell outside the door to the family's private quarters, another at the foot of the stairs, and "plenty" on the ground floor. "We thought, 'This isn't home!' so Jimmy had the one outside our door removed." White House Usher Chris Emery remembers his first week on the job during the Reagan years when the panic alarm went off in the residence. He thought, *Oh, God, the President's having a heart attack!* Emery was sitting at his desk in the Usher's Office and he saw Secret Service officers gathering at the door. An agent said, "Chris, you're really supposed to respond first before we go up there. Mrs. Reagan's not going to like us walking in her room." So Emery went running up the stairs and knocked on the First Lady's door. "Mrs. Reagan, it's Chris from the Usher's Office." When he did not get a response he opened the door to find the First Lady in bed with cold cream on her face and Vaseline under her eyes. "Mrs. Reagan, I'm really sorry but the panic alarm went off and I just want to be certain that everything's all right." She said, "Everything's fine," and could offer no explanation. When he left, all he could think of were reports of the First Lady's tirades. But no one ever said a thing about the incident—not even Nancy Reagan could demand complete privacy in the White House.

While Nancy was happy that her husband had emerged as an important historical figure, she did not appreciate candidates, on the right or the left, using his legacy for their own political ends. "She didn't see any of them as being the reincarnation of her husband," the Reagans' son Ron says. And she did not hesitate to call friends and offer her opinion on the state of the Republican Party. Ron said that his mother had a definite opinion of Donald Trump. During the 2016 presidential campaign, he said, she thought Trump was "silly."

Nancy was more protective of her husband than any other first lady. She rejected two official portraits of President Reagan by famed artist Aaron Shikler, who was commissioned by the White House Historical Association to paint the couple. (One portrait was scrapped altogether and the other one hung only briefly in the White House.) The Reagans enlisted Everett Raymond Kinstler, who had painted several portraits of President Ford, to try again. When Kinstler showed them four sketches, "[t]here was no question," he says, "*she* was the one I had to please." And at first Nancy was not happy. She did not like one preliminary sketch of her husband in a brown suit and asked Kinstler worriedly, "What are you going to do about his shoulders?" When the President finally sat for his official portrait, Nancy sat behind Kinstler for three hours as he painted, something Betty Ford had never done. "It was terribly distracting," he recalled. When Kinstler asked Nancy if she would rather go sit in the living room, she replied, "No, I really would like to stay here while you work."

———

The Associated Press Stylebook advises that "first lady" is always lowercase because it is not an official title. When her husband leaves office, he will always be called "president" for the rest of his life but she will always be referred to as "former first lady." Expectations for first ladies change as women's roles in society evolve; the only constant is their lifelong central role as their husbands' chief protectors. "If they made a mistake it was in loving their husbands," says Tony Fratto, who served as deputy press secretary in President George W. Bush's White House. "None of them are perfectly cast for the job, or at least what our expectations of the job are."

The East Wing is where the first lady's office is located, along a quiet corridor on the second floor next to the calligraphers, who write elegant invitations to formal White House events. Pat Nixon and Nancy Reagan preferred working out of their offices in the private family quarters on the second floor of the residence rather than their formal offices in the East Wing, which Michelle Obama uses. For Michelle, working from her East Wing office helps keep her work life separate from her family life in the residence.

There is a battle between the East Wing staff, made up mostly of women who are loyal to the first lady, and the West Wing staff, which is still predominantly male. No administration is without this old-fashioned conflict. In the Obama White House, when Michelle officially launched her "Let's Move" healthy-eating campaign, it conflicted with a televised statement that the President was scheduled to make about health care. When East Wing aides called the West Wing to request that the President's schedule be tweaked, the President's advisers acted like they were being inconvenienced. Former White House Press Secretary Robert Gibbs tried to avert a potential public relations nightmare when a book published in France claimed that Michelle told then–French First Lady Carla Bruni-Sarkozy that living in the White House was "hell." After effectively quashing the story, Gibbs allegedly cursed the First Lady at a meeting when he was told that she was not happy with his handling of the situation. The First Lady was not present at the meeting but aides were stunned by his reaction. The tension between the First Lady and Gibbs, who had worked for the president for more than six years, was said to have contributed to his resignation in 2011. Things got so bad that a consultant was even brought in to lead a retreat at Blair House, the official guesthouse across the street from the White House, to discuss the East Wing staffers' resentment of the West Wing.

Michelle can do very little without the consent of her husband or his staffers. Social Secretary Desirée Rogers left fourteen months after the Obamas took office, in part because of controversy after two people managed to sneak into the Obamas' first state dinner. But before then she was close with Michelle and she had made it clear that she did not care for Executive Chef Cristeta Comerford. Comerford was the first woman appointed to the prestigious post of executive chef, by Laura Bush in 2005. Because Michelle was surrounded by only a handful of people, she listened to Rogers's opinion of Comerford and let it color her own, according to a former residence staffer who spoke on the condition of anonymity. This staffer was called into a meeting with the First Lady and Rogers in the family's private living quarters on the second floor. "Cris is not capable," Michelle told the staffer flatly. "Tell her she is on a six-month probation." Michelle wanted to replace Comerford with the Obamas' longtime Chicago friend and personal chef, Sam Kass.

Historically, new first families have brought in new executive chefs, as Hillary Clinton did when she replaced French chef Pierre Chambrin with the younger American chef Walter Scheib. But Comerford is a beloved member of the residence staff and she is not only the first woman, she is the first person of color—she is Filipino—to serve in the highly esteemed post. "The look on her face ripped me apart," the staffer said, recalling how Comerford took the news of her probation. "Desirée just had it out for her." Five months later the staffer was called back to the second floor to meet with the First Lady and Rogers again. Rogers told him, "Cris is not cutting it."

"I was practically on my knees," the staffer said. Comerford had been working harder than ever, often staying until midnight to clean the kitchen and prepare for the next day's meals. A moment later, the First Lady chimed in. "I talked to Barack, and he told me that this isn't a good thing to do." The President was rightly concerned that firing Comerford would look bad in the press. Michelle paused, turned to the staffer, and said, "I guess you won on this one." Even though first ladies have the most direct authority over the residence staff, Michelle was powerless to make any changes.

The conflict between the East Wing and the West Wing was never more pronounced than during Pat Nixon's five-and-a-half-year tenure. Richard Nixon's trusted chief of staff, H. R. "Bob" Haldeman, sneeringly called First Lady Pat Nixon "Thelma" behind her back. ("Thelma Catherine Ryan" was Pat's given name, but she adopted "Pat," the nickname her Irish father gave her because she was born on the eve of St. Patrick's Day.) In a diary entry for November 4, 1970, Haldeman wrote, "On flight back to DC, Pat Nixon blasted me and P [Haldeman refers to President Nixon as "P" throughout his diary] about West Wing interference in social operations. Feels we override Lucy [Pat Nixon's social secretary, Lucy Winchester] and slow down decisions, etc. Wants all control in East Wing." The fight between the men of the West Wing and the women of the East Wing was particularly pronounced during the Nixon administration in part because Pat was adored by the women who worked for her. When the men of the West Wing communicated with Pat Nixon's staff they would say, "Tell Mrs. Nixon." The standard East Wing retort was "We don't *tell* Mrs. Nixon anything, we *ask* Mrs. Nixon." The President's advisers wanted to have a book written about Pat ahead of the 1972 reelection campaign to soften her image. A reporter came to the White House and met with her several times, but Pat abruptly called the project off when it was halfway finished. She did not like the attention and hated talking about herself.

Pat's staff called her the "Minute Man" because she never kept anybody waiting and operated with military precision. (This was very different from her successor, Betty Ford, who was jokingly referred to as "the late Mrs. Ford" by her staff because she was never on time.) "I love team sports and that's what I thought it was going to be," Pat Nixon's social secretary, Lucy Winchester, said. "I was stunned when it turned out *not* to be a team sport." But Pat put up a strong defense. Winchester said, "She was an absolute rock-ribbed woman."

Since no woman has been president, vice president, or even White House chief of staff (a position that was created in 1946), the first lady is the most visible office in the White House held by a woman. Residence staffers are just as protective of the first ladies as their East Wing staffers are. Within the private quarters, when staffers say that a decision comes from "the second floor," they mean it's coming directly from the first lady. Residence staffers deal directly with the first lady and her social secretary. They watch elections closely; in 2004 their greatest fear was that John Kerry would win and that they would have to deal with Teresa Heinz Kerry, who was called "a loose cannon" during the campaign. Christine Limerick, who was head housekeeper on and off from 1979 to 2008, said, "If the first ladies were happy, I was happy." When she was working upstairs in the residence and noticed Nancy Reagan lying on her bed with her legs crossed chatting with one of her close girlfriends (she was often on the phone with her friend and confidante Betsy Bloomingdale), Limerick was relieved. "She'd be on the phone like a teenager. And when we saw that, we knew she was at peace, everything was good with her." When Hillary was laughing with Chelsea, or Laura Bush's daughters were home from college, the residence staff knew things were all right. So much of life in the White House is claustrophobic and anxiety-filled that these lighter moments take on new meaning. "That's when we knew they were as close to having a normal life as possible and that's what we tried to help them accomplish," says Limerick.

EVERY FIRST LADY is her husband's ultimate protector. She will sniff out anyone who she thinks could jeopardize his career.

Nancy Reagan most famously helped get her husband's chief of staff, Don Regan, fired. Jackie Kennedy was well aware of her husband's plans to get rid of FBI director J. Edgar Hoover. Betty Ford did not care for her husband's hard-charging speechwriter Robert Hartmann. Laura Bush was not a fan of Bush's senior adviser and campaign guru Karl Rove. And Michelle Obama did not mesh well with her husband's first chief of staff, Rahm Emanuel. Emanuel, who is notoriously irascible and, as one former Obama staffer put it, "cultivates an asshole vibe," wanted Michelle, whose approval ratings surpassed her husband's (on the road during the 2008 campaign, people ran up to Obama campaign staffers excitedly and asked them, "Have you ever met Michelle?"), to make more political appearances than she was willing to do. But she does not like campaigning. According to a former White House official, Michelle said that during the 2008 campaign she was assigned a small and uncomfortable plane compared with her husband's. "Typical, isn't it, how women get treated?" she said.

Michelle's Chicago-based hairstylist, Michael "Rahni" Flowers, remembers how annoyed she was that every detail of her appearance was obsessed over. She used to have highlights before the campaign, Flowers said, but campaign aides decided they were "too racy." Michelle's frustration grew with each superficial critique. At a 2013 summit in Africa with Laura Bush, Michelle talked about the power that comes with being first lady and the absurdity of all the attention placed on trivial things, like her decision to get bangs in 2013. (There was even a backlash when her long bangs got in her eyes during a speech at the G8 Summit and the hashtag #bangsfail quickly popped up on Twitter.) "While people are sorting through our shoes and our hair and whether we cut it or not . . . whether we have bangs . . . We take our bangs and we stand in front of important things that the world needs to see, and eventually people stop looking at the bangs and they start looking at what we are standing in front of."

In the end, the First Lady would not allow Emanuel to bully her. She resented some Senate Democrats for not supporting her campaign to end childhood obesity and she was not about to go out of her way to help them. "She doesn't particularly like politics, which is why you rarely see her on the trail campaigning for Democratic candidates. She doesn't love doing the fund-raisers or events, even for the President," said one former Obama aide. Hillary Clinton, however, campaigned hard for Democrats in the midterm elections in 1998, visiting about twenty states, while Michelle Obama visited only a handful in 2014.

Getting the first lady on the campaign trail to support her husband and other important elected officials from his party has long been par for the course. Though Hillary was more willing to campaign for fellow Democrats, she had a similarly strained relationship with Emanuel. When he was working for her husband as a senior adviser she was furious when Emanuel booked her to appear at a last-minute dinner with members of Congress without consulting with her office first. She had plans for that evening and simply refused to go. She called Emanuel to make her displeasure known, and when he promised her that it would not happen again, and added that she was needed just this once, she relented. (Hillary came to dislike Emanuel's abrasive style so much that she tried to have him fired from her husband's administration.)

Barbara Bush was so popular that in 1992 she was sent to New Hampshire to file the papers for her husband's second candidacy, and she spent more time campaigning in the state than her husband did. Her loyalty to her husband had always been reciprocated: when George H. W. Bush first ran for president in 1980 a group of supporters strongly suggested that Barbara start dyeing her hair. Her hair had started turning white when she was twenty-eight years old and their toddler daughter, Robin, was diagnosed with leukemia. The stress of staying by Robin's hospital bedside and watching their three-year-old daughter endure rounds of transfusions and painful surgeries was written all over Barbara's face, and eventually it began to turn her dark hair silver. She had given up the chore of dyeing her hair in 1970, when she was in her mid-forties. Bush refused to bring it up with her, and he threw out the relative who had been given the unenviable task of going to his office to deliver the suggestion.

———

PART OF THE bargain some of these women strike with their husbands is to keep quiet about infidelity. Jackie Kennedy and Hillary Clinton are the most famous examples of this kind of compartmentalization, and in many ways they were the perfect matches for their husbands: intelligent, witty, and above all, discreet. The complicated Kennedy and Clinton marriages are not entirely unique. President Johnson made no secret of his affairs and would often try to corner the prettiest girl in the room at a party. By the end of the evening he'd have lipstick marks on his face. Lady Bird would sometimes be in the same room and would plead with him to stop embarrassing her. "You're wanted over there, Lyndon," she would tell him. "You're neglecting some of your friends." Traphes Bryant, who was a White House electrician and also cared for the first family's dogs, said Johnson had "inherited" two female reporters from President Kennedy. "He would mention one or the other to me as 'all woman' or 'a lot of woman' and even accord them the ultimate compliment he ordinarily reserved for his favorite dog, Yuki, telling me they were 'pretty as a polecat.'"

Lady Bird knew that her husband desperately wanted a son,

and she went through four miscarriages in an attempt to give him one (the Johnsons had two daughters: Lynda, born in 1944; and Luci, born in 1947). She was particularly hurt to see him with younger women, who she worried would be able to give him what she could not. Long after the Johnsons left the White House and after her husband had died, Lady Bird appeared on the *Today* show, where anchorwoman Barbara Walters asked her directly about LBJ's womanizing. She laughed and gave an off-the-cuff but shrewd response: "Oh, Lyndon was a people lover. And that certainly did not exclude half the people of the world, women."

Some first ladies were willing to put up with incredible and recurring betrayals so that they could be part of their husbands' lives. Jackie told her friend Adlai Stevenson II, the U.S. ambassador to the United Nations, "I don't care how many girls [Jack sleeps with] as long as I know he knows it's wrong, and I think he does now. Anyway, that's all over, for the present." Sir Alastair Granville Forbes was a close friend of Jack and Jackie and in 1956 staged a sort of intervention with Kennedy, warning him to be less flagrant in his philandering if he wanted to pursue the presidency. "Jack was very, very attracted to women who were very attracted to him," Forbes said of Kennedy. Because both Jack and Jackie were Catholic, and did not believe in divorce, they did not think they needed to work as hard on their marriage, Forbes argued.

JFK approached his private life as if he were in wartime, acting with reckless abandon as though any moment could be his last. Kennedy's friend Charles Spalding said that the President's chronic back problems and poor health gave him a great perspective on life: "Most of us don't realize how fast time is passing, and he did." (It's no surprise that the always loyal Spalding abruptly stopped an oral history interview for the Kennedy Library when he was asked, "Is there anything about his [President Kennedy's] attitude towards sex in American life that stands out in your mind?")

Forbes was more candid. "I think he was very conscious that he was marrying in a way which was suitable in the sense that he was marrying a very pretty girl who was also Catholic. His family was pleased," Forbes said. "I think that he was infatuated with Jackie, but I think that he also was aware that he was taking on somebody basically incompatible." Jackie knew about his cheating and was deeply disturbed. Referring to the intervention he staged with Kennedy before he pursued the presidency, Forbes said, "He did express surprise that his slip was showing to that extent."

Betty Ford was less accommodating than Jackie. The Fords had a loving marriage, and there is no evidence that President Ford cheated on Betty, but he was a flirt. Once, when Mexican American singer Vikki Carr came to perform at a state dinner, Betty seethed when she saw the two giggling together. At the end of the evening, she watched as the President escorted Carr out of the White House and overheard the singer ask Ford what his favorite Mexican dish was. When she heard her husband's reply— "You are"—it was too much for her. "That woman will *never* get into the White House again," she declared.

Each of these first ladies, from Jackie Kennedy to Michelle Obama, has had complete and utter devotion to her husband, and at a cost to her own career, each has been unswervingly loyal to the man she married. When Bill Clinton met Hillary he was in awe of her intellect, and mutual friends warned him to be careful about his womanizing. Susan Thomases, an old friend of both Clintons, told him to give up any hope of marrying Hillary. "She's too good for you," she said. "She's so nice, and she's so brilliant, and she's so straight." But their political partnership worked because Hillary fell in love with Bill and was completely devoted to him. During the 1992 presidential campaign, Thomases issued a warning similar to the one Forbes gave to JFK thirty-six years earlier: "You're stupid enough to blow this whole presidential thing over your dick. And if that turns out to be true, buddy, I'm going home, and I'm taking people with me." Thomases says President Clinton didn't cheat on Hillary during the campaign because he "knew that I would land on his neck with both feet."

But Clinton's past came back to haunt him in the White House. One overnight White House guest of the Clintons remembers hearing the phone ring in the hallway of the second-floor residence around midnight. The President picked it up, and after a moment slumped over and yelled, "Oh *shit!*" and slammed the phone down. Clinton straightened himself up and continued entertaining his guests well into the early-morning hours, as though nothing had happened. The next morning the houseguests—there were always houseguests during the Clinton years—got up and went to the sunny Solarium, with its floor-to-ceiling windows overlooking the Washington Monument and the Mall, to have a quiet breakfast. The *Washington Post*, the *New York Times*, and the *Wall Street Journal* were laid out on a table and right away the guests could see what had upset the President the night before: Paula Jones had just filed a formal lawsuit accusing him of making an unwanted sexual advance toward her when he was governor of Arkansas.

It was just the beginning. Unlike Jackie, Hillary had no choice but to address her husband's philandering in a very public way. His affair with Monica Lewinsky, which occurred between November 1995 and March 1997 and was finally revealed to the public in January 1998, shook their marriage to its core. It was "a near crisis in their relationship," according to Thomases. He had humiliated Hillary, but in the end she would not leave him. Like Pat Nixon during Watergate, she stopped reading the newspapers at the height of the barrage and blamed others, in this case Republicans, for trying to bring her husband down. "She worked out a resolution that worked for her," Thomases said. "It was important for her to keep their marriage together." Shirley Sagawa, who was Hillary's deputy chief of staff when she was first lady, said that Monica Lewinsky was a "terrible distraction" and that members of Hillary's inner circle were all "very angry at the time. . . . It was a very complicated time and she handled it all with such grace." It took a heavy toll on Hillary, especially knowing that their daughter, Chelsea, had read the Starr Report detailing her husband's transgressions. Chelsea was the glue that bound them together, and the day after the President admitted the affair to the country, it was Chelsea who held hands with both of them as they crossed the lawn to Marine One for their annual Martha's Vineyard summer vacation. For the first time, Bill sought help for his reckless behavior when counselors were smuggled into the White House.

Hillary's aversion to divorce stemmed in part from years of witnessing its effects among her friends. Rumors flew that she had hyperventilated when she discovered Bill's cheating back in Arkansas. When an old friend told her that she was considering getting a divorce, Hillary said, "You need to be prepared. . . . If you are not prepared to stand on your own, the man gets the deal and you'll get the shaft." She then recited a list of their mutual girlfriends who had gotten a divorce and had struggled financially ever since.

With divorce off the table, Hillary transferred much of her anger and frustration to what she called "the vast right-wing conspiracy." In a 1999 interview published in *Talk* magazine, Hillary does not object when the reporter calls her husband's cheating "an addiction." But when asked if she agrees that it is indeed an addiction, she replies, "That's your word. I would say 'weakness.' Whatever it is, it is only part of a complex whole." She makes excuses for him, saying that the Lewinsky affair occurred at a difficult time after the deaths of his mother, her father, and their friend Vincent Foster. She considered her husband's cheating a "sin of weakness" not a "sin of malice." She even compared their situation to when Peter betrayed Jesus three times. "Jesus knew it but loved him anyway."

In the living quarters of the White House there was deep pain. Hillary had been through this before, even carefully choreographing camera angles during her first *60 Minutes* interview in 1992, when she sat beside her husband, who was asked difficult questions about his alleged twelve-year affair with Arkansas state employee and cabaret singer Gennifer Flowers. The biggest headline of the interview was not anything he said, however; it was when Hillary broke from the script. "I'm not sitting here, some little woman standing by my man like Tammy Wynette." She had known about his cheating and she wasn't about to let it stand in the way of their chance to win the presidency. But six years later, she was less forgiving. "That Monica Lewinsky thing really tore her up," said former White House Maître d' George Hannie. Hillary herself said that the problem was that her husband hadn't gone "deep enough" or worked "hard enough" when he had tried to change ten years before Monica. Usher Worthington White recalled the tension in the White House during that time and said that he felt like a kid whose parents almost got divorced. "There were a lot of tough times, but those times when mom and dad were fighting we don't talk about. That's how we all felt; we all tried to make them smile. All in our desperate way trying to inject a little humanity." Life went on inside the White House—even as Independent Counsel Kenneth Starr was deposing the President, the staff was setting afternoon tea.

One of the women in Hillary's inner circle was overheard complaining about the double standard. "If *she* had done that [cheated on Bill] she would have been the bitch of the universe!" For the six butlers who work on the second and third floors of the White House and pride themselves on their discretion, it was a stressful time. "We never uttered a word about that," Hannie says. "You didn't know what to say." Hannie was even interviewed by Starr and, according to the investigation, confirmed that he saw White House intern Lewinsky in the West Wing during the time of her affair with President Clinton. Joni Stevens worked in the Military Office, across the hall from the First Lady's office, during the Clinton administration and remembers a friend of hers who was working in the West Wing. One day she wasn't working at the White House anymore. "Where did she go?" Stevens asked a colleague. "She got transferred to another department. She caught the President in the family theater with an intern." This was in the fall of 1996, about a year after Clinton first began his affair with Lewinsky. "The Military Office always kept our mouths shut," Stevens says.

But Hannie remembers happier times with the Clintons. On Inauguration Day in 1993, he told Hillary Clinton some alarming news. "Mrs. Clinton, there's a white man downstairs in a wheelchair in the Yellow Oval Room asking me for some Ronald Reagan souvenirs. He said he's a Republican, not a Democrat." The new First Lady laughed. "Yeah, I know, George, that's my dad." Hugh Rodham never gave up hope that his son-in-law would join him in the Republican Party. (Hillary supported Republican Barry Goldwater for president when she was in high school, and even owned a cowboy outfit and straw hat with the slogan "Au H_2O"—the chemical symbols for "gold" and "water" worn by his most enthusiastic supporters—etched on it. As a freshman at Wellesley College she was president of the Young Republicans Club, but by 1968 she had left her father's party and was volunteering for Democrat Eugene McCarthy's campaign.)

Hillary was often the only one who could focus her husband and it was Hillary who believed that her husband could win the presidential election in 1992, before he was even convinced of it. Because Hillary's East Wing staffers knew how loyal she had been to him throughout his political career, most of them never fully forgave the President for his affair with Lewinsky. "At the White House correspondents' dinner he joked about why [the Monica Lewinsky scandal] hadn't made the association's list of top fifty stories of last year, and Hillary was right there," said former Hillary spokeswoman Marsha Berry. "How was she supposed to feel?" The dozen or so women who make up Hillaryland, a nickname created by a Clinton campaign aide in 1992 and one that members of the close-knit circle seem eager to encourage, are incredibly loyal. "My staff prided themselves on discretion, loyalty, and camaraderie, and we had our own special ethos," Hillary said, adding that her husband's aides "had a tendency to leak" while "Hillaryland never did." Hillary's former press secretary Neel Lattimore says, "I think it's very telling that to date no member of 'Hillaryland' has written a book about their experiences." Hillary's friends are surprised that she wants to go through another campaign. If President Clinton becomes the first man to be the president's spouse, they say she would likely dispatch him as an envoy to a hot spot somewhere around the world, like the Middle East. They also say that if Hillary is elected she would choose a very experienced social secretary and chief of protocol who could make most of the decisions about dinner menus and flowers, since it's unlikely that Bill would be interested in those more traditional assignments. Since there's no blueprint for what a first spouse should do, they say, there's no reason why he should feel confined. Hillary herself has said that she has "ruled out" her husband when it comes to selecting china for state dinners and choosing floral arrangements. She has said that, if elected, she would "send him on special missions because he's just unique in the world in being able to do things for our country." Chelsea is also expected to take over some of the first lady's traditional duties. The last time the White House had a hostess who was not the president's spouse was a hundred years ago, after President Woodrow Wilson's first wife, Ellen, died and their daughter, Margaret, took on the role until her father remarried.

At the 2007 Aspen Ideas Festival, Bill Clinton joked about breaking new ground. "Scottish friends of mine have suggested I should be called the 'First Laddie.' That would be the easiest to relate to the previous." (Because "Laddie" sounds like "Lady.") A member of Hillaryland, Lissa Muscatine, who was a speechwriter for Hillary in the White House and her chief speechwriter and a senior adviser when she was secretary of state, says that she thinks Bill Clinton will love being first gentleman. "He'll make it work. . . . He just connects with people so instinctively and so instantly," she said. "I'm sure she'll have an East Wing staff that takes care of a lot of the social side. He's not going to sit there and pick the flowers for a dinner, obviously."

Bill Clinton's hearing has gotten so bad that he has taken to reading lips, but that has not slowed him down and he is expected to play a formidable role in a Hillary Clinton administration. Still, a First Gentleman would be unprecedented (it's not even clear that that would be his official title) and Clinton is a unique character. Former Vice President Walter Mondale, who is a friend of the Clintons, mused in an interview, "How's this going to work? . . . Bill is somewhat *unorganizable*. . . ."

———

EVEN AFTER FIRST ladies leave Washington, politics is never far behind them, and it's true not only for Hillary Clinton. Republican or Democrat, they all share a unique understanding of what the others have been through: excruciating campaigns; long days watching their husbands struggle with crises; the terrible and strange loneliness that comes from living in the world's most public private home; and the intense desire to protect and preserve their families' place in history. Nothing is done publicly without some political calculation and internal debate about whether it will help or hurt their husbands' legacies.

There's no job description for first ladies, and the very title is anachronistic in the twenty-first century, when most women work and would balk at the notion of giving up their jobs simply because of their husbands'. But to say that the job is outdated and that these women are throwbacks to the nineteenth century would be to not understand them at all. Even though not all of them get along, they all share an undeniably unique experience that binds them together. They all know what it's like to live every day with the fear that their husbands may not come home. (White House Doorman Preston Bruce said that even before President Kennedy's assassination the residence staff knew when they saw the President's helicopter depart from the South Lawn that they might never see him again.) After President Obama's election there was a spike in threats, but the number has since leveled off and has been consistent with threats to his predecessors, according to the Secret Service. Michelle Obama, like the first ladies before her, also knows what it's like to live with deep concern for her own life and the lives of her children. On at least one occasion, body bags were loaded onto a first lady's plane during a foreign trip. Several residence staffers say they worry about the safety and security of the first family, even when they are in the White House.

Most will not admit it publicly, but all of these women realize their power, especially once they see their poll numbers eclipsing their husbands'. Putting their heads down every night on the pillow next to the president's, they can sometimes influence policy. Once, at a small dinner party, President Ford reminisced about an old girlfriend who was a member of the family that owned Steelcase, a furniture company based in his hometown of Grand Rapids, Michigan. "Well now, Jerry, just think, if you'd married Mary Pew, you could've been the President of Steelcase instead of the President of the United States," Betty told him with a twinkle in her eye. Without the strength, support, and sheer star power of their wives, these men could not have reached the pinnacle of American politics.

Sisterhood of 1600

★

There's a reason people like her. It's because she doesn't, sort of,
you know, add fuel to the fire.
—MICHELLE OBAMA ON LAURA BUSH

There's a sense of profound empathy among the first ladies that is very apparent in the letters they send to one another in times of hardship, in the aftermath of resignations, and during battles with illnesses. Many of these notes have "DO NOT ANSWER!" written in the margin so that there's no obligation on the part of the recipient to write back. After the devastating losses of parents, husbands, and even, most tragically, children, they are there for each other. There are hundreds of these letters—many of which have never been seen by outsiders before—that show how their relationships evolve after they leave the White House and how they cut across political party lines. In an age when email is nearly ubiquitous, it's fascinating to see the thoughtful letters these women wrote to each other and how they reveal universal truths about being first lady, whether serving as a Democrat or as a Republican. They also show the responsibilities they share as modern women who are wives, mothers, daughters, sisters, and friends. Some of these letters are intensely personal and shockingly candid, and they offer a window into the private thoughts of these very public women.

The relationships between them last long after the White House years, with many letters inquiring about each other's "grands" and "great-grands," joking about aging (Lady Bird Johnson wrote to Laura Bush, "I don't even buy green bananas anymore!"), and celebrating the openings of their husbands' presidential libraries. They sympathize with each other about their exhausting schedules even after their husbands leave office, cheer each other on after television interviews, and donate to each other's favorite causes (over the years Lady Bird donated thousands of dollars to the Betty Ford Center, a world-renowned addiction treatment center started by her friend Betty). In a 1983 letter, Lady Bird told Betty, "Not long ago I came across a mutual friend of ours who told me quite straight-forwardly that she decided to face up to a drinking problem and to overcome it. She is so much more fun to be around these days!" Betty was active raising money for the center and would invite very wealthy donors to the Fords' house, sometimes taking her husband aside and declaring, "This is mine, not yours."

Each came into office during a different time in the country's history, and each was limited by the evolving perspectives on women's rights and the role of the first lady. Protesters at Hillary Clinton's alma mater, the all-women's Wellesley College in Massachusetts, objected to having Barbara Bush as their commencement speaker in 1990 because, they said, her accomplishments were tied solely to her marriage. During Bill Clinton's 1992 presidential campaign, stay-at-home mothers were furious when Hillary Clinton made the famous quip, "I suppose I could have stayed home and baked cookies and had teas, but what I decided to do was to fulfill my profession." It seems they draw fire from either side no matter what they do. But small acts of kindness, like the Carters' invitation to Luci Baines Johnson to see the papal inauguration in the Vatican—a trip that meant so much to the Johnsons' younger daughter because she had converted to Catholicism—and invitations to the White House, demonstrate a special and enduring bond among these families. Rosalynn Carter and Betty Ford grew so close that Betty's daughter, Susan, sits on an advisory committee at the Carter Center in Atlanta.

Upon the opening of the Kennedy Library in 1979, Lady Bird Johnson, who was seated in the front row with Jackie at the ceremony dedicating the library, wrote to her recognizing the complicated emotions of the day: "This has to be both a proud day and an emotionally exhausting day for you. . . . Do remember that there are so many people wishing you happiness and contentment. Count me among them." Barbara Bush begged Pat Nixon to bring her children and grandchildren back to the White House in a 1990 note: "It would be *so* nice if you would bring Julie and Tricia and all their children back to the White House for lunch one day and then they could, with your help, give the grandchildren a tour. It would be such a treat for all." In another private note, Barbara told Pat that she thought of her often, especially when she passed her White House portrait. "You are a shining example to us all of grace and graciousness both." They even sent each other silly Hallmark cards, including a politically themed birthday card from Barbara Bush to Betty Ford in 1998 with a bunch of animals in party hats on the front. "We started out to get a signature for each of your birthdays and before we knew it—It turned into a petition drive—you're now eligible to run for office in 23 states!!!" Barbara signed the card, telling Betty, "You'll always be First Lady to us! Happy Birthday, with Respect and Love, Barbara B."

Some of them use their former titles and friendships with each other to help personal friends. Lady Bird Johnson wrote an impassioned plea to President Clinton asking him to pardon her friend, Texas banker Ruben Johnson (no relation), who was convicted in 1989 of bank fraud. "To use an old-fashioned word, Ruben is very much a gentleman," she wrote. Clinton obliged and Ruben Johnson's was part of a slew of pardons he granted during the final days of his presidency (the pardon erased $4.56 million Johnson owed in court-ordered penalties).

These remarkable women are more than ceremonial figures—they play key roles in diplomacy, smoothing out rough edges and soothing hurt feelings. At countless formal dinners they are seated next to key political figures and have to communicate the administration's agenda and, with any luck, sway their dinner partners. Often they report back to their husbands that night, or the next morning. During the Cold War, Pat Nixon was seated next to the cantankerous Soviet political leader Alexei Kosygin, whom she deftly handled throughout the dinner. She was a hard-liner when it came to the Soviets, according to her press secretary, Connie Stuart, "but she also felt that talking is better than not talking." A Voice of America broadcaster who served as their translator during the dinner kept a record of their conversation. Kosygin asked the First Lady how many women served in the Senate and then said, "Women careerists in the U.S. are arrogant, ambitious, merciless, whereas in the Soviet Union, women deputies, who make up one-third of the total number, are serious, studious, and reasonable officials." He went on to deride the American press, especially women reporters, whom the First Lady defended. But by the end of their conversation Pat had turned him around by expressing sympathy for the Russian people, who she noted had suffered terribly during World War II, and added that she was especially sorry for the Russians who had died because of the German blockade of Leningrad. Kosygin's demeanor changed almost completely. "I was there," he said softly. "It was dreadful."

They understand the weight of the presidency better than anyone else. Betty Ford's personal assistant, Nancy Chirdon Forster, remembers how Betty would call Lady Bird Johnson on quiet evenings. "And Lady Bird would call her sometimes, especially if there was something in the press and Mrs. Johnson thought she could be of help." When asked if any former first ladies offered her support during the Iran hostage crisis, Rosalynn Carter said, "Lady Bird Johnson often reached out with concern." Lady Bird was the grande dame of the first ladies and wrote beautiful letters. She wrote to Barbara Bush on June 5, 1991, while the Bushes were in the White House, saying, "I've been thinking of you with so much empathy and warmth. I hope you've been able to prevail upon the President not to let the all-pervasive duty of that Office devour completely his time and energies." When Barbara Bush was First Lady she thanked Betty Ford for installing the outdoor pool on the south side of the West Wing. The pool, she wrote, "has saved my life." When Laura Bush gave Michelle Obama her first tour of the White House, she was eager to assure Michelle that a life could be made there for her daughters. She wanted the tour to be special and private, even though Michelle had brought along a staffer. "This is really for Michelle and I," Laura told Michelle's aide. "You can meet with my staff, but this is a private visit for us." Unlike the president, who leaves a note behind with advice for his successor, the first lady does not leave a letter behind but instead uses the tour of the second and third floors to impart words of wisdom. When asked if she left a note behind for Nancy Reagan, Rosalynn Carter said, "I did not leave her a note.

I didn't think about it. Betty Ford didn't leave me one." Laura Bush did not leave a note behind for Michelle Obama, either.

———

EACH OF THESE women, from Jackie Kennedy through Laura Bush, seemed to genuinely enjoy aspects of being first lady. Even Jackie Kennedy, though she hated seeing photographs in the press of her two small children, grew to love life as first lady. The only one who stands out is Michelle Obama. (Though Pat Nixon was unhappy in the White House, she enjoyed traveling, and reporters who covered her said she shone during trips away from Washington.) In dozens of interviews, friends and political aides say that Michelle is deeply unhappy in the White House. She's not part of the Washington social scene that the Clintons embraced, and she mostly socializes with the same people she was friends with in Chicago, including the Whitaker and Nesbitt families, who have children close in age to the Obamas' daughters, Sasha and Malia, and who live close to their house in Chicago's Hyde Park neighborhood. (When they decided to run, the Obamas asked their longtime friends to promise that they would be there for them no matter what, win or lose.) Former Head Butler George Hannie was serving the new President and First Lady in the family's private living quarters after the inauguration and told them, "You guys are going to be on the ride of a lifetime. Your whole life is changing today. You don't have to wait for no more airplanes, you don't have to do anything but just show up. Everything is right there ready for you." Michelle's eyes got big and she smiled, but Hannie got the sense that she had not fully understood how much their lives were about to change.

Now she cannot wait to leave. "They're ready, they're done!" says President Obama's former communications director Anita

Dunn. During one of her first meetings with Chief Usher Admiral Stephen Rochon, Michelle told him, "Please, call me Michelle." He replied, "I can't do that, Mrs. Obama." It wasn't only his military training; it was his allegiance to the presidency that would not allow him to drop the formality. But Michelle longs to be treated like a private person again. In a September 2015 interview on *The Late Show with Stephen Colbert*, Michelle said she was counting down the days until she could escape the intense and watchful eye of the Secret Service. "I also want to do little things like, you know, open a [car] window," she said. "One day as a treat, my lead agent let us have the windows open on the way to Camp David. It was like five minutes out and he was like, 'The window's open. Enjoy it!' I was like, 'Thanks, Allen.'" It is the simple, everyday things that she misses. She still makes time at night to unplug, however, and especially likes watching *The Real Housewives of Atlanta* on Bravo after a long day.

Hillary can relate. In a 1995 column she wrote, "On a recent trip to Arkansas, I had a sudden impulse to drive. I jumped behind the wheel of a car and, much to the discomfort of my Secret Service detail, drove myself around town." Such a simple act had become "extraordinary for me," she said. Sometimes Hillary would throw on a baseball hat and walk through Georgetown, desperate to escape the White House. On the rare occasion when someone stopped her to say she looks like Hillary Clinton, she would smile and reply, "So I've been told." Betty Ford's press secretary, Sheila Rabb Weidenfeld, remembers getting a call from a White House reporter who said, "What is she doing in New York?" Weidenfeld said, "Mrs. Ford is not in New York. She's upstairs in her bedroom." The reporter replied, "No, she's not. She was spotted on Seventh Avenue." Betty had taken off shopping with her close friend Nancy Howe. "All right, let me check,"

Weidenfeld said, annoyed. Like a small child who had been caught with her hand in the cookie jar, Betty promised she would not let it happen again. Betty's personal assistant, Nancy Chirdon Forster, remembers how sad Betty was when, for fear of being spotted, she couldn't go out in New York during scheduled trips and enjoy the evening. "So we'd just go back to the suite and we'd go to bed."

Michelle Obama's East Wing office is not forthcoming with information. "It's harder than ever to get access to the First Lady!" said the exasperated veteran CBS News correspondent Bill Plante, who began covering the White House in 1981. "Requests to the First Lady's office for an interview are normally politely declined." The First Lady's staff looks for any signs of self-promotion within the White House and makes sure to quash it. Friends and advisers say one reason for the hard line from her office is Michelle's deep unhappiness as first lady.

Hairstylist Michael "Rahni" Flowers and his business partner Daryl Wells own Van Cleef hair salon, which is located in a refurbished church in downtown Chicago and caters to wealthy African American clients. Flowers first started doing Michelle's hair when she was a teenager and she would come in with her mother, Marian Robinson. "Knowing her the way that we know her, this was nothing that she wanted," Rahni said. Michelle is a "no-nonsense" woman who does not take herself too seriously, he adds. There was a casual atmosphere in the salon. Rahni remembers how he and the future first lady would talk about their shared love of bacon ("We're bacon people," she admitted in a 2008 interview on ABC's *The View*), and Wells used to call her "Boo." After her husband was elected president, Wells teased her, "Should I call you 'First Lady Boo'? I'm going to call Marian 'First Boo Mom.'" Now her whole world is different and her friends cannot get a message through to her directly. After her husband won the presidential election and Flowers and Wells wanted to make an announcement that she was at their salon, she asked them not to. "I'm just here to get my hair done," she said. "I don't want people standing up and clapping."

When Michelle moved her young family into the White House, it was the first time that she'd been unemployed in her adult life. Before she started scaling back her schedule at the University of Chicago Medical Center, where she was vice president of external affairs, to campaign for her husband, she was earning almost $275,000 a year. She was forty-five when she became first lady, the youngest woman to hold the position since Jackie Kennedy. "Remember, she was his mentor to begin with," Bill Plante noted, referring to her work as an associate at the corporate law firm Sidley & Austin in Chicago and her assignment, at age twenty-five, to mentor Obama, who was a twenty-seven-year-old summer associate. (She rejected his requests to take her on a date because she thought it would be "tacky" if "the only two black people" at the law firm started dating, but she admits she fell in "deep like" with him when they first met.) She knew that the responsibility of transitioning their daughters, Malia and Sasha, who were ten and seven when they moved into the White House, would fall squarely on her shoulders. In an August 2008 interview with *Ladies' Home Journal* she said, "They'll be leaving the only home that they've known. Someone's got to be the steward of that transition. And it can't be the President of the United States. It will be me." Her first chief of staff, Jackie Norris, said, "I think there were a lot of people saying no to her in the beginning, 'No, I'm sorry, you can't do this. No, I'm sorry, you can't do that.' Like going out for a walk, or 'I just want to go to Target' or 'I just want to drive my kids to school.' That's pretty hard when you first come into an environment and have so many restrictions put on you and such high scrutiny. It was even higher than on the campaign trail."

Michelle took a lavish trip to Spain in 2010 with daughter Sasha and family friends that came during the economic recession. The four-day vacation cost taxpayers almost half a million dollars due to the high cost of paying for the large Secret Service contingent and the cost of sending the First Lady's traveling staff to accompany her on the trip. The Obamas paid for hotel expenses and the equivalent of first-class airfare. A New York *Daily News* headline blared, "A Modern Day Marie Antoinette." A year later, in 2011, Michelle did get to take that trip to Target. She was photographed at a Target department store in suburban Alexandria, Virginia, where a photographer from the Associated Press shot photos of her casually dressed in a button-down floral shirt, a Nike baseball cap, and sunglasses. The trip was not as simple as it appeared, however, with Secret Service agents arriving at the store thirty minutes before the First Lady walked in. The First Lady's office would not discuss how the lone AP photographer happened to be positioned to take shots of Michelle checking out, but the images were used to help diffuse the uproar about her expensive taste.

Michelle spoke much more bluntly than she ever had before about her frustrations with public life during Tuskegee University's commencement in Tuskegee, Alabama, in May 2015. She told the graduating class of mostly African American students, "Back when my husband first started campaigning for president, folks had all sorts of questions of me: What kind of first lady would I be? What kinds of issues would I take on? Would I be more like Laura Bush, or Hillary Clinton, or Nancy Reagan? . . . But, as potentially the first African American first lady, I was also the focus of another set of questions and speculations; conversations sometimes rooted in the fears and misperceptions of others. Was I too loud, or too angry, or too emasculating? Or was I too soft, too much of a mom, not enough of a career woman?" She was angry about personal attacks against her husband, especially by those who persisted in questioning his citizenship. During the 2000 campaign, George W. Bush attacked Bill Clinton's ethics. But the Clintons and the Bushes, unlike the Obamas, are veterans of the bruising games of politics. "Things that were said about President Obama were taken very personally because it's hard to hear someone talk about someone you love," said Laura Bush's chief of staff, Anita McBride. "The Bushes and the Clintons have been at this for so long, they know they have to brush it off." In fact, twelve days after her husband was sworn in as governor of Texas, Laura was invited to the White House for a luncheon with governors' spouses as part of the annual National Governors Association meeting. She was not surprised to find herself seated next to Rhea Chiles, the wife of Florida's governor, Lawton Chiles, who had run and won a heated race against her brother-in-law Jeb the previous fall. "Whether the seating was intentional or accidental," Laura Bush wrote in her memoir, "Rhea and I were forced to make polite conversation."

Michelle is not always comfortable in the transactional world of politics, and friends say she finds it hard not to take some things personally. She has confessed to sleepless nights agonizing over how people were seeing her, people whom she would never meet in person but who had formed opinions about her through the media. The *New Yorker* spoof of her with an Afro in combat boots and a Kalashnikov slung over her shoulder while fist-bumping her husband in the Oval Office was meant to show the outlandishness of her critics, but it wounded her. "You are amazed sometimes at how deep the lies can be," she said in the *New York Times*. She told the students in Tuskegee that, eventually, she had to ignore the criticism. "I realized that if I wanted to keep my sanity and not let others define me, there was only one thing I could do, and that was to have faith in God's plan for me."

Reggie Love, Obama's former personal assistant—who is known as his "body man" and is like a third child to the Obamas—says that he thinks the President is a hopeless optimist about the political system and his wife is a realist. She says she's "Eeyore" and the President is "Mr. Happy." Ever since Obama burst onto the national stage after he delivered the keynote address at the 2004 Democratic National Convention, Michelle has been tamping down expectations that he can fix everything that's wrong with Washington, though she made the case on the campaign trail in 2007 that "there is a specialness to him." Unlike Hillary Clinton, Michelle rejects any comparisons of her young husband to President Kennedy, and of her style to Jackie Kennedy's, even though she is the only other first lady to rival Jackie as a style icon. "Camelot to me doesn't work," Michelle said, referring to Jackie's romanticized description of her family's thousand days in the White House. "It was a fairy tale that turned out not to be completely true because no one can live up to that. And I don't want to live like that."

Michelle is frustrated in the White House, in part because she had to give up her career. "She can't get up and leave and take a job in Europe or Chicago," Love says, "so if there was something that was really appealing to her somewhere else she can't do it." She also doesn't mask her feelings well. When she wrote emails to Alyssa Mastromonaco, who was in charge of the President's schedule, to voice her concerns, she did it so bluntly that Mastromonaco asked for advice from colleagues about how to respond. (In the White House, staffers usually keep anything in an email innocuous, knowing that it could one day become public.)

President Obama knows that his wife is unhappy. In a 2013 *Vogue* interview the President spoke about Michelle, revealing a tinge of guilt. "She is a great mom. What is also true is Michelle's had to accommodate"—here he pauses—"a life that"—another pause—"it's fair to say was not necessarily what she envisioned for herself. She has to put up with me. And my schedule and my stresses. And she's done a great job on that. But I think it would be a mistake to think that my wife, when I walk in the door, is, *Hey, honey, how was your day? Let me give you a neck rub.* It's not as if Michelle is thinking in terms of, *How do I cater to my husband?*" The President told *New York Times* reporter Jodi Kantor that his staff "worries a lot more about what the first lady thinks than they worry about what I think," a sentiment echoed by Love. "He's the leader of the free world and she's his wife. I think even the leader of the free world has to figure out how to keep everyone happy." Michelle is a cut-to-the-chase working mother who "doesn't hold stuff back," Love says. And if anyone wants to challenge her, she says simply, "I'm not running for anything." She does not get angry at criticisms of her husband's policies, but she becomes infuriated by personal attacks, a current Obama administration official said on the condition of anonymity. She also abhors leaks, and at the beginning of her husband's first term, when stories leaked out about infighting, she wanted explanations. "How could this happen?" she wanted to know. "We could say it's just the way Washington works," the Obama official said, "but she has a way of letting you know that that is no excuse."

Michelle is keenly aware of what's going on in her husband's administration. One Obama staffer says that he worked for years in a less senior position, but when he got a much bigger job that brought him into daily contact with the President, he figured he had to introduce himself to the First Lady. "Oh, I know you," she said, and rattled off five things about him. According to former White House Deputy Press Secretary Bill Burton, Michelle watches MSNBC's *Morning Joe* when she works out (ninety minutes, up to five times a week) and talks with the Obamas' closest friend and adviser in the White House, Valerie Jarrett, often. "She's plugged in," Burton said. "She's a consumer and knows what's going on." (Michelle introduced her husband to Jarrett, who has been instrumental in his political career.)

When her husband was a senator she dismissed the idea of leaving her girls, and her high-powered job, to fly to Washington for a luncheon with other Senate wives honoring then–First Lady Laura Bush. She still does not want to do anything without a specific purpose. When she became first lady she demanded that, in exchange for spending four hours at the annual Congressional Club luncheon—a tradition that began in 1912 in honor of the first lady—the well-to-do attendees commit to a day of volunteer work. "Whether it's a food bank or a homeless shelter, there's so much need out there," she told the congressional wives clad in Lily Pulitzer dresses. During staff meetings, when advisers suggest she attend certain events, she will ask, "But why? I don't want to just show up to show up." She has always been absolutely clear to her staff that she is not Hillary Clinton. She laughs at the suggestion that she run for office herself one day, and she did not relish the battle to secure health-care reform and the fight to pass the President's stimulus package. Unlike Hillary, whose feminism is so much a part of her identity, Michelle has said that while she agrees with much of the feminist agenda, she is "not that into labels" and would not identify herself as a feminist.

For Michelle, it's always been about her husband's personal exceptionalism and not about party loyalty. In a way, she is like

Nancy Reagan, who had little interest in getting to know other Republican first ladies and even had a bad relationship with Barbara Bush during the eight years that the latter was the wife of President Reagan's vice president. Sometimes Michelle's advisers forget that she is part of a much larger tradition. The Obamas held a mental health summit at the White House in 2013, but Rosalynn Carter, who brought about the passage of mental health legislation in 1980 and made it her signature issue as First Lady, was left off the guest list. "I got really mad," a former Carter aide said. He called a friend who had worked for the Obamas and told her about the oversight. She then called the First Lady's chief of staff, Tina Tchen, who responded, "Oh God, I forgot." According to President Carter's aide, Rosalynn did not believe them and felt intentionally excluded. When asked in an interview if Hillary Clinton had sought her input when crafting health-care legislation, or if either Michelle Obama or President Obama asked for her advice when developing the health-care overhaul because of her extensive work on mental-health issues, Rosalynn said simply: "The answer to both of these questions is no."

When they first moved into the White House the Obamas were overwhelmed, and it took them a long time to get used to a hundred-person staff. The day after his inauguration, President Obama came into the East Room and introduced himself to the residence employees. Both the President and the First Lady looked surprised when they met the staff separately, former White House Florist Bob Scanlan recalled. "They didn't realize that there were that many people just in the house to take care of the house. At the time it doesn't sink in that you have maybe two plumbers, three carpenters, you have gardeners, and you have eight housekeepers, because they're not cleaning just the private quarters, they're cleaning from the bottom up. Half those housekeepers are everywhere else in the house but the private quarters." When the Obamas' predecessors, George and Laura Bush, moved in, they knew exactly what to expect and they enjoyed reconnecting with butlers, maids, and others who affectionately referred to Bush's father, George H. W. Bush, as "Old Man Bush."

Michelle Obama is surrounded by a team of women who insulate her from the press. It is easier for her handlers to go around traditional media and control the way she is perceived through posts on social media and selective interviews, often on late-night television. Her remove from her predecessors has been a source of frustration to the families of some of the women who came before her. Bob Bostock, who worked for the Nixons in the post-presidency and later worked for the Nixon Presidential Library and Museum, was thrilled after the associate director of the library, Richard "Sandy" Quinn, met with a member of the First Lady's staff about honoring the late Pat Nixon's one-hundredth birthday in 2012 by dedicating the Spring 2012 Garden Tour in her honor. Pat had started the tradition of opening up the White House gardens to the public twice a year in 1972. He suggested a brief ceremony with Julie Nixon Eisenhower and Tricia Nixon Cox and their children, and a short dedication to Mrs. Nixon in the brochure. "Perhaps a photograph of Mrs. Nixon from that first spring tour could also be included," Quinn offered. "I know that Mrs. Nixon's daughters would be deeply gratified if you were to honor their mother in this way. They know, as few do, the enormous demands on the First Lady and on the President's family." A curt response from the First Lady's deputy chief of staff, Melissa Winter, arrived two months later, thanking Quinn for the note and telling him that Mrs. Obama is "proud to continue the tradition of seasonal White House garden tours" but rejecting the idea of a ceremony. "It is not the practice of our office to dedicate

White House tours," she said. "We appreciate the thoughtful nature of your request." The Nixon Library staff felt completely blown off and deeply disappointed. It's not known whether Michelle ever saw Quinn's original request or Winter's response.

Hillary Clinton, on the other hand, read voraciously about her predecessors, in whom Michelle had expressed limited interest. When she was working on health care she sought advice from Betty Ford, who had worked tirelessly to get more funding for addiction. She invited Betty to a meeting with her and Vice President Al Gore's wife, Tipper. In a letter dated March 24, 1993, she thanked Betty for her advice and wrote that she hoped her health-care proposal would reflect "a new commitment to the problems of substance abuse."

Hillary's closest relationship was with Jackie Kennedy, but the stresses of the job make for unlikely allies. According to her White House press secretary, Neel Lattimore, Hillary, who did not have much in common with Nancy Reagan, told her staff that she thought it was unfair that Nancy had been criticized for spending $200,000 (in private donations) on a new set of china for the White House. Nancy's image as an imperial first lady—she was referred to contemptuously in the press as "Queen Nancy"—was amplified by the purchase (and not helped by revelations that she spent $25,000 on her inaugural wardrobe and $10,000 on a single gown). But when the Clintons first came to the White House and Hillary had to decide what china to use for state dinners, the Reagan china was the only complete set available. (Nancy had been unapologetic about her decision to purchase new china. "We haven't got enough china to serve a state dinner so we got china. The White House had to have china for heaven's sake.") As a young lawyer Hillary had worked on the House Judiciary Committee's impeachment investigation of President Nixon, and she began to sympathize with the quiet suffering of Nixon's wife, Pat, and the brave face she put on every day. Somebody on Hillary's staff said something unkind about Pat when she passed away five months after the Clintons moved into the White House, and Hillary shot back, "That's not true, you have to appreciate what Pat Nixon did in this White House." (Neither Clinton, however, attended Pat's funeral.) As first lady, Pat had created special tours for the blind and the disabled, so that blind visitors could touch some of the furniture, and she opened the White House to the public at night so that working people could visit more easily.

Hillary could identify with Pat's humble childhood and her stoicism during her husband's humiliating resignation. In a 1979 interview, Hillary made it clear that she empathized with political spouses and said, "I think that people who are married to politicians are under a tremendous strain, because unless you have a pretty strong sense of your own self-identity, it becomes very easy to be buffeted about by all the people who are around your husband. People who are advising him, people who want favors from him, people who want to do things with him, for him, or to him, and very often those people are not anxious to have the politician's wife or family members around because that's then competition for their time."

Hillary's friend and former speechwriter Lissa Muscatine says that Hillary believes strongly that women need to be given the freedom to make the right choices for their own lives, whether it's working or staying home with their families. "She felt the same way about the first lady's role, that the first ladies are different and they have different needs and interests and different experiences. They just need the freedom to be in that position in a way that works for them and their husbands and the presidency," she said, adding, "This is not a defined job, so let people define it the way that they need to define it." After the 2000 election, Hillary advised Laura Bush not to let the responsibilities of her new role cloud her decision making. Hillary had once turned down an invitation from Jackie Kennedy to go to the ballet in New York with Chelsea because she said she was too busy. She had always regretted it because Jackie passed away just a few months later.

When Hillary gave Laura the customary tour of the residence, they stood together in the first lady's dressing room and Hillary said, "Your mother-in-law stood right here and told me that from this window you can see straight down into the Rose Garden and also over to the Oval Office." Eight years later, when Michelle Obama came for her first tour of the White House, Laura showed her the exact same spot where so many first ladies have stood discreetly in the shadows, watching their husbands at work.

Surprisingly, Michelle is closer to Laura than she is to Hillary. Even though they are on different sides of the political spectrum, Laura and Michelle have personalities that mesh. During the 2008 presidential campaign, Michelle was heavily criticized for a remark she made during a speech in Milwaukee. "For the first time in my adult life," she said, "I am proud of my country because it feels like hope is finally making a comeback." Though she didn't plan to say it, it became the most-talked-about quote from her time on the campaign trail. Laura Bush defended Michelle in an interview four months later. She had flown all night from Afghanistan, where she was visiting U.S. troops, to Slovenia, where she was joining President Bush for an annual summit. When she got to Slovenia she and her aides had a couple of hours to sleep and shower before an interview with ABC News's Jon Karl. Laura had not anticipated being asked about Michelle's remarks from several months earlier, but she immediately came to her defense. "I think she probably meant I'm 'more proud,' you know, is what she really meant," she said sympathetically. "You have to be very careful in what you say. I mean, I know that, and that's one of the things you learn and that's one of the really difficult parts both of running for president and for being the spouse of the president, and that is, everything you say is looked at and in many cases misconstrued."

A week later, in an interview on *The View*, Michelle said she was "touched" by what Laura said. "There's a reason people like her," she said. "It's because she doesn't, sort of, you know, add fuel to the fire." Laura had grown accustomed to the rough-and-tumble world of presidential politics and remembered four years earlier when Teresa Heinz Kerry, the wife of then–presidential candidate John Kerry, told a newspaper that she didn't know if Laura Bush had ever had "a real job," forgetting that Laura had worked in Texas public schools as a librarian and a teacher from 1968 to 1977. Michelle and Laura clearly had a rapport as they praised one another at a conference promoting women's rights in September 2015. "I think it's also a great example for the world to see that women of different political parties in the United States agree on so many issues," Laura said. "We're in the midst of a political campaign now, as everyone knows, a presidential race coming up and when you watch television you think that everyone in the United States disagrees with everybody else, but in fact we as Americans agree on so many more things than we disagree on." Michelle added, "It has made my transition to this office so much easier having somebody like Laura and her team. . . . It's not just Laura and I, it's not just President Bush and President Obama, but it's our staffs. My chief of staff continues to talk to Laura's former chief of staff on a very regular basis and it's that kind of sharing that prevents us from re-creating the wheel, allows us to build on the things that are already working so that the country gains as we transition from one party to the next."

Michelle's first chief of staff, Jackie Norris, says that she will "never forget the intense camaraderie and loyalty that the first ladies and members of the first ladies' staffs have for each other." After President Obama's election, Norris sat down in Laura Bush's office with Laura's East Wing team, including Laura's chief of staff, Anita McBride. Michelle's staff was given what amounted to a blueprint, as Laura's staff told them what missteps they had made along the way, which parties and luncheons were important, and which could be safely skipped. "What they wanted was to completely set aside politics and to help us succeed and to help Michelle Obama succeed as first lady. They were all in this unique position to understand just how hard her role would be." When Hillary Clinton's former chief of staff, Melanne Verveer, was running a nonprofit specializing in global women's rights, she brought a group of Afghan women to meet Laura Bush. After their meeting, Laura escorted the women out through the Diplomatic Reception Room. But Verveer lagged behind them, lost in conversation with Laura's chief of staff. Laura approached them. "Oh, I'm sorry," Verveer said, realizing that she had to leave, "but we belong to a small club." "I completely understand," Laura said with a smile. "I belong to a small club, too."

———

PAT NIXON TOOK Connie Stuart, her chief of staff and press secretary, aside on a quiet day in February 1971 and whispered, "Jackie is coming. Nobody is to know and I'm only telling a few people; she is coming tomorrow." Pat had invited Jackie and her children, Caroline and John-John, to visit the White House for the official unveiling of the President's and the former First Lady's portraits by Aaron Shikler. It was tradition for the former first family to attend such unveilings, but Jackie had not been back to the White House since her husband's assassination. In response to an earlier invitation to return from Pat, she had told her that she wasn't ready yet but that she knew that "time will make things easier, and that one day, when they and I are older, I must take Caroline and John back to the places where they lived with their father." She had left the White House behind when she moved to New York shortly after the assassination, and she felt guilty about serving on the Committee for the Preservation of the White House and never showing up for meetings. "I'm still in mourning," she told one reporter who asked for an interview a year after President Kennedy's assassination. Jackie's former social secretary and lifelong confidante Nancy Tuckerman sent her a memo on April 13, 1964, not yet five months after the assassination, asking her if she wanted to see a movie the navy had made of her husband's funeral. "Could I wait a bit," Jackie wrote at the bottom of the note. Jackie had been through so much pain in her life and Pat Nixon understood, telling her that she knew a public unveiling of the portraits would be too emotional. Pat promised that it would be absolutely private.

The Nixons and the Kennedys had known each other for years—the men's offices were across the hall from each other when Richard Nixon was President Dwight Eisenhower's vice president and John Kennedy was a senator. The Nixons were even invited to the Kennedys' 1953 wedding (though they did not attend). After Pat wrote to Jackie that the portraits were ready to be hung in the White House, she must have been surprised by the letter she received, hand-delivered by Tuckerman. Jackie would come, but on her own terms. "I really do not have the courage to go through an official ceremony, and bring the children back to the only home they both knew with their father under such traumatic conditions." She wanted to keep the press out of "their little lives" but said she was open to the idea of a private viewing. Immediately, Pat asked Tuckerman to call Jackie and schedule a time. A week later Jackie set foot in the house she had so lovingly restored and in which she had spent so many happy days with her husband.

If Jackie had had even the slightest sense that the press knew about her visit, she would never have come. (Veteran United Press International White House correspondent Helen Thomas somehow found out about the visit, and when she threatened to write a story she was promised an exclusive interview with Pat if she agreed to keep quiet.) During the top-secret meeting, the White House was on lockdown. There was no traffic between the normally bustling corridors connecting the East and West Wings. Most people on the staff did not know who was coming because it wasn't noted on the President's and First Lady's calendars. Even their social secretary, Lucy Winchester, didn't know what was happening. Only four staffers were told about the visit, and they had to pledge absolute secrecy.

On February 3, 1971, the Nixons sent a plane to pick up Jackie, ten-year-old John-John, and thirteen-year-old Caroline in New York for the trip to Washington. The Nixons quietly welcomed the Kennedys in the Diplomatic Reception Room, and Pat, knowing how much the White House restoration had meant to Jackie, showed her an English Regency chandelier she had added to the room. The Nixons' two daughters—Tricia, twenty-four; and Julie, twenty-two—brought Caroline, who was wearing her school uniform, and John-John to the Solarium, which was once Caroline's kindergarten, to see the panoramic view of the National Mall. Then the Nixon daughters stood in the hallway outside the

Oval Office to let the Kennedys have a private moment inside. It was the place where their father had spent so many hours, and where two-year-old John-John had poked his head out from underneath his father's desk in one of the most iconic photographs from the Kennedy White House. When they came to President Kennedy's portrait in the Cross Hall, Jackie was quiet and simply thanked Pat for displaying it so prominently. The Nixon daughters dreaded showing the portrait to Caroline and John-John, but were relieved when the Kennedy children told their mother how much they liked it. Tricia and Julie continued the tour with three dogs in tow, including the Nixons' beloved two-year-old Irish setter, King Timahoe.

The two families had dinner in the Family Dining Room on the second floor, and President Nixon joined them. Jackie, who wore an elegant long-sleeved black dress, told Pat that every first family should leave its own mark on the White House, and she complimented her on adding more antiques to the state rooms. (In a note later she told Pat, "I have never seen the White House look so perfect.") There was an awkward moment when Jackie mused, "I always live in a dream world." But John-John spilled his milk and lightened the mood considerably. The day after the visit, he wrote to the Nixons a heartbreakingly sweet, handwritten letter in childish scrawl on stationery with the imposing monogram JOHN KENNEDY in big block letters on the bottom right. "I can never thank you more for showing us the White House. I really liked everything about it," he wrote. "You were so nice to show us everything. I don't think I could remember much about the White House but it was really nice seeing it all again." He said that when he sat on Lincoln's Bed, where his father had slept, he made a wish and it was that he would do well in school. "I really really loved the dogs, they were so funny. As soon as I came home my dogs kept on sniffing me. Maybe they remember the White House." He ended the note saying that he had "never tasted anything as good as the soufflé."

Caroline wrote her thank-you note on hot-pink paper with a lowercase monogram on the bottom right: "Your Swiss chef is the best thing that ever came out of Switzerland, except maybe the chocolate." She was five days shy of her sixth birthday when her father was killed, and remembered slightly more about the residence than her little brother. "It was so nice to see it all again," she wrote, and thanked Julie and Tricia for being so nice to her. She also remembered to thank Butlers Eugene Allen and Charles Ficklin in her note. Caroline would recall that dinner years later as an adult, saying the visit helped her mother open up and share more of her White House memories with them. "I think she really appreciated Mrs. Nixon's thoughtfulness in the sense that there are family values and a dedication to politics and patriotism that go beyond any disagreement on issues or party. One of the things you learn, having lived in the White House, is that there really are these common experiences and what we share is so much larger than what divides us."

Jackie's mother-in-law, Rose Kennedy, sent Pat a touching note after Jackie called her to give the details of the evening. "Your warm-hearted welcome to her [Jackie] and my grandchildren on a day which might have been most difficult for all of them, moved me deeply. . . . And so, dear Mrs. Nixon, you brought joy to many who are near and dear to me and I thank you from my heart."

The most poignant letter came from Jackie herself, written in her signature spidery handwriting on her sky blue stationery. "Can you imagine the gift you gave us to return to the White House privately with my little ones while they are still young enough to rediscover their childhood," she wrote. "The day I always dreaded turned out to be one of the most precious ones I have spent with my children. May God bless you all. Most gratefully, Jackie."

———————

AFTER PRESIDENT KENNEDY's assassination, the transition to the Johnson administration was difficult and emotional. Jackie politely declined all of Lady Bird Johnson's invitations to come back to the White House. Phone calls between President Johnson and Jackie in the days following the assassination show just how much he wanted her to stay close after she moved out. After her incredible poise at her husband's funeral, her popularity had risen to mythic heights and it was important that the Johnsons appear to have her support. In the calls LBJ tells her how much he loves her and how she gave him "strength," and he all but begs her to come visit them. President Johnson even shamelessly had four reporters listen in on a call he made to her over Christmas 1963, in an attempt to show how close they were. But Jackie was not swayed. In 1965, Lady Bird renamed the elegant East Garden, with its boxwood and topiary trees and lavender and rosemary, after Jackie, but she never could get her to visit the White House. Jackie sent her mother, Janet Lee Bouvier Auchincloss, to attend the dedication of the Jacqueline Kennedy Garden. "I explained to her [Lady Bird] in writing and on the telephone that it was really difficult for me and I didn't really ever want to go back," Jackie recalled.

Jackie and Lady Bird were bound forever by the assassination. Lady Bird was haunted by that day too, and would often refer to Jackie as "that poor young woman." Rumors had been flying in late 1963 that Lyndon Johnson might be dumped from the Democratic ticket in 1964, so Lady Bird had gone to Texas a week earlier to prepare for the Kennedys' scheduled stay at the Johnson ranch near Austin after they visited Dallas. She made sure the President's favorite Ballantine's Scotch was available and that champagne (champagne on the rocks was Jackie's drink of choice) and Salem and L&M cigarettes (for Jackie) were on hand. Lady Bird even laid out terry-cloth hand towels because she had heard that the First Lady had an aversion to linen ones. Because of the President's bad back, Lady Bird had procured a horsehair mattress like the one he used in the White House, and a Tennessee walking horse was available should Jackie want to ride. The smell of pecan pies cooling in the kitchen wafted through the air as technicians from the Signal Corps furiously installed secure phone lines for the President. Lady Bird reminded everyone to have the Kennedys come through the front door, instead of the kitchen door.

Leaving the rest of the preparations to the Johnsons' social secretary, Bess Abell, Lady Bird went to Dallas to help her husband campaign. Abell remembers talking with a Secret Service agent outdoors about the entertainment they had set up for the Kennedys, including a man who would have a gun and a whip and a lasso for an act he was to perform. Suddenly someone ran down to the riverbank saying that the President had been shot. "Everybody was just in shock," she said. "We all wanted to know, *What can I do?*" The Secret Service agents who had been waiting for the President's arrival crammed around the television set in the kitchen, and in a panic Abell called her husband, Tyler, who would later become Johnson's chief of protocol. He told her, "Bess, you've just got to buck yourself up and get yourself together. You're in charge, now make something happen."

Lady Bird was with her husband two cars behind the President's limousine when the fatal shots were fired. She later stood dutifully beside him as he took the oath of office in the executive suite of Air Force One. Bess Abell did not see her until the next day when she went to the Johnsons' Washington home, the

Elms. Lady Bird was sitting in a small room off the foyer, a room she loved because of its privacy. Lady Bird put her arms around her friend. "Oh Bess, what you've been through," she said. Abell laughs at the memory now—here was a woman who saw first-hand the devastation in Dallas, but she was worried about someone else. "She always thought about somebody else. She was just in control, she was moving forward."

After her husband's death, Jackie wrote a letter to LBJ and recounted good times they had all shared together. "We were friends, all four of us. All you did for me as a friend and the happy times we had. I always thought, way before the nomination, that Lady Bird should be the First Lady—but I don't need to tell you here what I think of her qualities—her extraordinary grace of character—her willingness to assume every burden. She assumed so many for me and I love her very much." Jackie ended the note with a sad and needless apology: "It cannot be very much help to you your first day in office to hear children on the lawn at recess," she wrote, referring to Caroline's kindergarten in the White House Solarium. "It is just one more example of your kindness that you let them stay—I promise they will soon be gone."

When President Johnson died, Jackie called Lady Bird to express her condolences. Lady Bird, after all, had been there for her during the most difficult time in her life. "These have been emotion packed days, but there is still a certain feeling of insulation from the deep sadness I am sure must come," Lady Bird wrote to Jackie, thanking her for her phone call. "You know all too well how the responsibilities come crowding in." In the 1990s Jackie and Lady Bird met occasionally in Martha's Vineyard, where they both vacationed. Lady Bird loved Jackie's house on the island, and as a nature enthusiast she told Jackie, "It sits on the Island so 'at home' with its surroundings, almost as if it grew out of the land!" She agonized over news that Jackie had cancer and tried to boost the spirits of the woman she shared such an incredible history with. "Do know that you have an *army* of friends—known and *unknown*—who care very much about you."

Letters between Jackie and Lady Bird show this lifelong feeling of sympathy Lady Bird had for her predecessor and what she called "the shadow of grief" that hung over the Kennedy family. Two remarkable letters from Lady Bird to Caroline Kennedy— one a week after Jackie's death in 1994, the other after John Jr.'s death in 1999—show the depth of her feeling for the Kennedys and the enduring bond that they shared. Lady Bird had wept for Caroline three decades before, after President Kennedy's death, and she cried for her again when she attended Jackie's funeral at St. Ignatius Loyola Church on Park Avenue in New York. "As I looked at the faces of the crowds—and they were deep everywhere along the streets—I felt the keen edge of their sorrow," she wrote to Caroline. She recalled a lunch with Jackie at her Martha's Vineyard home the August before her death. "She seemed happy and contented and that is how I shall keep her in my thoughts—full of life, serene, and so justly proud of her beautiful family." Five years later, Lady Bird wrote to Caroline again, after the plane John was piloting plunged into the Atlantic Ocean with his wife, Carolyn Bessette-Kennedy, and her sister, Lauren Bessette, on board. The tragedy, Lady Bird wrote, "has cast a shadow over these long days. It is particularly painful for me thinking of all the suffering your family has had to bear." It must have been surreal for Lady Bird to write about the man she knew best as a playful two-year-old little boy. "Mere words cannot erase, or even lessen—although I dearly wish they could—the enormous burden that lays so heavily upon you," she told Caroline. "Surely you will be strengthened by the love and pride you feel for John, as so many of us did. He was the 'nation's child,' too, universally admired and respected—a promising life too early ended."

Presidents and first ladies, in and out of office, felt protective of the Kennedy children, who had endured so much. In 1996, John F. Kennedy Jr., by then the head of a major political magazine, *George*, and already named *People*'s "Sexiest Man Alive," was at the Republican convention in San Diego to interview Gerald Ford for his magazine. After the interview, Ford, who was widely regarded as the nicest and most gracious of the former modern presidents, told him, "You know, John, I knew your dad fairly well. Is there anything you'd like to know about him?" Susan Ford was there and recalls that her father spoke privately with John. Her father never told her what Kennedy asked him. "He felt that was very much between him and John."

Laura and Barbara Bush said that Lady Bird, a fellow Texan, is their favorite first lady. Aside from each other, of course. The Bushes and the Johnsons had a surprisingly strong relationship built over years of shared political ambition. In the 1950s, Lyndon Johnson was in the Senate with Prescott Bush, George H. W. Bush's father, before divisive partisanship engulfed Washington. When Johnson, a Democrat, told George H. W. Bush, a Republican, how much he respected his father, Bush said he was happy to hear that from such a loyal Democrat. "Your father and I don't like to be thought of as Republican or Democrat, rather as good Americans!" Johnson replied. George H. W. Bush was the first Republican congressman to represent the Houston area, and he voted for President Johnson's Civil Rights Act of 1968, even though it cost him political support. Bush left the inaugural celebration for Johnson's Republican successor, Richard Nixon, to say goodbye to the Johnsons at Andrews Air Force Base, an act of kindness that Lady Bird always remembered. Barbara and George Bush also visited the Johnsons at their Texas ranch after they left Washington. Johnson took the Bushes for one of his famous high-octane, furiously fast drives around his 330-acre spread (Lady Bird called it their "own Serengeti") and gave the young Republican congressman advice. The trip was a time for Barbara, a future first lady, and Lady Bird, a former first lady, to bond. Barbara summed up the families' bipartisan friendship in a 1998 letter to Lady Bird: "All Bushes love the Johnsons."

Lady Bird came back to the White House when Barbara's daughter-in-law, Laura, was first lady. The two had met in 1973, but Lady Bird would not have known it. Laura had joined thousands of others to pay tribute to LBJ at his presidential library, where his flag-draped casket was brought to lie in state. Lady Bird and her daughters, Lynda and Luci, stood at the door of the library and shook people's hands as they walked in, and Laura, then a young student, was among the mourners. Lady Bird was in her nineties by the time she visited Laura at the White House and had suffered a stroke. She could not speak and had to use a wheelchair, but when her car pulled up to the South Portico of the White House and Doorman Wilson Jerman, who had been maître d' when the Johnsons lived there, greeted her the two shared an unforgettable moment together. "He and I are at the door," Laura Bush later told Lady Bird's two daughters, "and he literally falls into your mother's arms." When Laura Bush showed Lady Bird the official portrait of her husband, whom she had survived by decades, the former first lady raised her arms lovingly toward his face. So many years had passed since his death, but it was clear how much she loved him still.

———

JACKIE KENNEDY'S APPRECIATION for Hillary Clinton surprised her close friend the historian Arthur Schlesinger Jr. Before he had met Hillary himself, he told Jackie that he was sure she would be "humorless." Jackie quickly corrected him: "You couldn't be more wrong," she told him.

No other president had been able to develop a real rapport with Jackie. After the Clintons arrived on Martha's Vineyard in August 1993, Jackie attended two private dinners for them with guest lists that included the celebrated writers William Styron and David McCullough and former Secretary of State Henry Kissinger. She also organized a luncheon for Hillary, and before the 1992 New Hampshire primary she and her son, John Jr., donated the maximum amount to Clinton's campaign. Much has been made about President Bill Clinton's worship of President Kennedy, but not much is known about the powerful friendship forged between Hillary Clinton and Jackie Kennedy.

Hillary asked Jackie how she had managed to raise her children to be such wonderful adults, all in the public eye. "That time together was extremely valued," said Melanne Verveer during an interview in her small office in the back of a Georgetown townhouse. Verveer was Hillary's chief of staff when she was first lady and remembers how important these conversations were to both women. "Nobody else can relate to this, there are so few women who've lived this existence. . . . No matter what differences they had among them, they shared that abiding understanding of the role that they played."

Jackie had always tried to make sure that her children—John-John was the youngest child to live in the White House in the twentieth century—were respectful. She insisted that they call Doorman Preston Bruce, an African American who became like family to the Kennedys, "Mr. Bruce" instead of his nickname. "She was not about to have them say 'Bruce,'" said Curator Jim Ketchum, who worked closely with Jackie on the redecoration of the White House. It was all about respect for the White House and its staff. "If you allow them," Jackie told Hillary, "the White House staff will do anything for these kids. They will go out of their way for them and spoil them rotten." She added, "You're going to have to put your foot down, you're going to have to make sure they have as normal a life as possible."

Once, Chelsea had some of her classmates from her expensive private school, Sidwell Friends, over for a movie in the White House's small private theater. "The kids made a real royal mess of the theater, there was popcorn everywhere," Verveer recalled. Hillary saw it and was furious. "Nobody leaves the theater until every kernel is cleaned up," she told them. There was also a real effort by the Clintons and the press to give Chelsea privacy. "As a mom you get to know another mom," Verveer says. "And here's a woman whose husband was assassinated, who went through horrors, all of that you accumulate." Jackie thought that the identities of many of the other first ladies were too wrapped up in their husbands', and she respected Hillary for cultivating her own image. Jackie herself had carefully done the same, even practicing her handwriting to make sure that it was distinct.

Jackie passed away on May 19, 1994, less than a year after that cruise off Martha's Vineyard. The Clintons were heartbroken by the news of her death, Hillary most of all. She and Jackie had spoken on the phone in Jackie's final days, and both Clintons received constant updates on her condition. When Jackie succumbed to cancer, the first couple spoke to the press from the Jacqueline Kennedy Garden on the east side of the White House.

"She's been quite wonderful to my wife, to my daughter, and

to all of us," the President said. As he stepped away from the microphone, reporters started shouting questions. He cut them off. "I'd like for Hillary to say a word first, please."

Unlike her husband, who was the picture of composure, the normally self-controlled Hillary Clinton was close to tears. "She was a great support to me personally when I started talking with her in the summer of 1992 about the challenges and opportunities of being in this position and how she had managed so well to carve out the space and privacy that children need to grow into what they have a right to become. She will always be more than a great first lady; she was a great woman and a great friend"—here her voice breaks—"and all of us will miss her very much."

Hillary went to Jackie's funeral Mass in New York City and flew back to Washington with members of the Kennedy family and Jackie's close friends for her burial at Arlington National Cemetery. She was buried beside President Kennedy, their premature son, Patrick—who died shortly after his birth—and their stillborn daughter, Arabella. Two weeks later, John F. Kennedy Jr. wrote the Clintons a handwritten note about what their friendship had meant to his mother: "Since she left Washington I believe she resisted ever connecting with it emotionally—or the institutional demands of being a former First Lady. It had much to do with the memories stirred and her desires to resist being cast in a lifelong role that didn't quite fit. However, she seemed profoundly happy and relieved to allow herself to reconnect with it through you."

Hillary may have idolized Jackie, but she did not embrace the role of being first hostess and was not as sophisticated as Jackie, who left detailed instructions about minute details with the waitstaff, including what kind of champagne should be served. Hillary never forgot her middle-class roots. One evening, Vernon Jordan, a friend and powerful Clinton ally, went out to the West Sitting Hall, a living room on the second floor of the White House, and said, "Hillary, I got the wine." She looked at the bottle—it was eight hundred dollars. "Oh no, you don't have that one." She took it and put it back. But Hillary's old friend Mary Ann Campbell remembers how much had changed once she was in the White House. Campbell naïvely thought she could drop by casually and see Hillary. "One of her assistants said to come to this certain gate and she [Hillary] received me in the Diplomatic Reception Room. We sat in two antique chairs; a photographer came and took a picture of us." Campbell could not fully comprehend the change in Hillary until she walked into the room. "For the first time in my life I was starstruck. I couldn't say anything." But the minute the photographer and Hillary's aides walked out of the room, the First Lady leaned in conspiratorially and asked about their old Arkansas friends, local gossip, and who was getting a divorce.

JACKIE KENNEDY AND Nancy Reagan developed an unlikely friendship that began with a 1981 visit that Rose Kennedy made to the White House, the first time she had been back since her son John's death. The Reagans had a delightful time with Rose and later attended a 1985 fund-raiser at Senator Ted Kennedy's house in McLean, Virginia, to help raise money for the John F. Kennedy Presidential Library. "He was a patriot who summoned patriotism from the heart of a sated country," Reagan told the crowd of wealthy donors on that summer night. "Which is not to say I supported John Kennedy when he ran for president, because I didn't. I was for the other fellow. But you know, it's true: when the battle's over and the ground is cooled, well, it's then that you see the opposing general's valor." The Reagans tried to greet every member of the Kennedy family they could, and after his remarks, Jackie approached President Reagan and said, "That was Jack." The next morning a letter arrived from Ted Kennedy thanking the President: "Your presence was such a magnificent tribute to my brother. . . . The country is well served by your eloquent graceful leadership Mr. President."

The day after Ted Kennedy died in 2009, Nancy Reagan did a telephone interview with Chris Matthews on MSNBC's *Hardball*. "We were close," she said of the Kennedys, "and it didn't make any difference to Ronnie or to Ted that one was a Republican and one a Democrat." Jackie didn't care much if Nancy was a Republican or a Democrat, either; she had a genuine respect for her. Nancy could also relate to Jackie's trauma because she had almost lost her husband to an assassination attempt. Most of all, Jackie appreciated Nancy for her interest in fashion and for inviting icons like Ella Fitzgerald and Frank Sinatra to perform at the White House. "She [Jackie] didn't agree with them politically, but with Nancy she had a great appreciation for what she was trying to do to bring glamour back, because it's the people's house," said a Kennedy family friend, Gustavo Paredes, the son of Jackie's personal assistant Providencia Paredes.

Nancy had the same horrified reaction to the White House when she first saw it that Jackie had two decades earlier. "It really looked awful, the wooden floors, the painting, everything needed to be done to make it look the way it should have looked," she said. Nancy raised $800,000 in private donations for its redecoration, with most of the money going to a face-lift for the second-floor residence. Nancy knew how her spending was perceived, and she wrote candidly in her memoir that she "won the unpopularity contest" among the other first ladies "hands down." The Reagans' son Ron was happy to hear that Jackie appreciated his mother's sense of style. "I know that my mother admired Jackie Kennedy because she rewrote the book on first ladies; she was the first glamorous first lady and I think my mother was fascinated by that."

Even though Jackie's politics were more in line with the Carters', she deplored their folksiness. Rosalynn Carter was well aware of Jackie's opinion: "There is a bias against southerners, there was. . . . You had to keep proving yourself over and over. It didn't matter what you did. . . . I wasn't supposed to be sophisticated enough or something. But, you know, who wants to be sophisticated?!" In an interview, she mentioned a *Washington Post* cartoon that depicted her and her family with straw in their teeth and wearing straw hats. She sounded annoyed when asked if she sewed her and daughter Amy's clothes in the White House, likely because of the criticism she had gotten for being a country bumpkin. She said she hadn't made clothes for herself "since Jimmy was in the navy." Unlike Jackie, who had the help of world-renowned decorator and socialite Mrs. Henry Parish II, known as Sister Parish, and Henry Francis du Pont, an heir to his family's fortune, the Carters were decidedly less worldly. One of the only changes they made to the White House was paneling a wall on the third floor with wood from a barn from Rosalynn's grandfather's farm.

———

THE PRIVATE CORRESPONDENCE between the first ladies provides a fascinating window into the true nature of their relationships. There are the pro forma thank-you notes (like the one from Lady Bird to Rosalynn Carter thanking her for an invitation to a White House dinner and mentioning the tablecloths with their "green lattice work and pink roses and the charming centerpieces of roses in antique baskets") and the Christmas cards and small gifts (Texas pecan praline candy from Lady Bird Johnson, tchotchkes from Pat Nixon, and almond toffee from the Fords). One year, after Barbara Bush received her annual package of Texas pralines, she thanked Lady Bird with her usual self-deprecating sense of humor: "Only someone who lived in the White House would know that, although the food is the best in the world, the cupboard is bare in the upstairs kitchen. For someone who always fights a losing weight battle, this is not all bad." There are also touching notes offering support after President Nixon's resignation and after September 11, 2001, and letters to Nancy Reagan as she cared for her husband and dealt with the devastating effects of his Alzheimer's disease.

They all share a deep and abiding loyalty to their husbands, perhaps none as great as what Nancy Reagan felt for Ronald Reagan. She told Mike Wallace in a 1975 interview: "My job is being Mrs. Ronald Reagan." Does she ever see herself as her own person? "No, I never do. Always as Nancy Reagan. My life began with Ronnie." Every year the President left a love note on her breakfast tray on March 4, the date of their wedding anniversary. In 1981 he told her that he would "scooch" down at his desk in the Oval Office just so that he could see the window in the West Sitting Hall where she would sometimes be sitting. He wrote that he "feels warm all over just knowing she is there." In 1983 the two were apart on their anniversary and he wrote to her from their California ranch: "You know I love the ranch—but these last two days made it plain I only love it when you are there. Come to think of it that's true of every place every time. When you aren't there I'm no place, just lost in time and space." Nancy Reynolds, a Reagan press aide and family friend, said, "He really didn't function very well for a couple of days if she wasn't around. Once she was there everything was all right. . . . He wanted her there every minute." Nancy's press secretary, Sheila Tate, remembered how the President would call her in her office early in the mornings as the Reagans were having coffee in bed. "Sheila, it's President Reagan," he'd say. "Mommy [the President's nickname for Nancy] wants to speak to you," and he'd pass the receiver over to Nancy because the phone was on his side of the bed.

Five years after President Reagan's death, Nancy told *Vanity Fair* correspondent Bob Colacello that she hadn't been to church in a while but that she asked preacher Billy Graham if she would be with her "Ronnie" again one day. "Just tell me that and I'll be okay."

"You are," he told her.

"Okay," she said, feeling as though she could go on, knowing that. She said when she woke up in the middle of the night she would sometimes see her late husband and talk to him. "It's not important what I say. But the fact is, I *do* think he's there. *And I see him.*"

Lady Bird Johnson praised Nancy for making the Reagans' long goodbye public. "It will be a comfort to others," she wrote to her, "whose families have been afflicted, to know that it [Alzheimer's] is no respecter of fame or importance." Lady Bird wrote to Nancy again on January 16, 2001, after the President broke his hip. "I hear news on the television since my limited vision and the newspapers have parted company. Some of the Secret Service agents on my detail also keep me informed." She heard the news when she was listening to a set of tapes called *Great Presidents* and she was deep into the Reagan presidency. After President Reagan revealed he was suffering from Alzheimer's in a moving letter to the nation, Betty Ford called Nancy several times. The two had not been close, but they both shared the experience of having been first lady and a deep love for their husbands. And their husbands had both been targets of assassination attempts. "She felt very bad for her because she realized what a lonely life Nancy had ahead of her," Betty Ford's daughter, Susan, says. On June 5, 2004, President Reagan died. Right before his death, Nancy said, he turned to look directly at her, something that he had not done in more than a month. "Then he closed his eyes and went. And that was a wonderful gift." Even though Nancy was not particularly close with any first lady, the deep and lasting grief they all suffer after the deaths of their husbands binds them together. Ron Reagan said that although his mother is "not in a state of grief all the time" over his father's death, "it's not something you get over."

―――――

FIRST LADIES BELONG to the world and get pleading letters and requests for help from people they know and from complete strangers. "Life as a first lady is to be in touch with the hard reality of other people's lives," says Hillary Clinton's former chief of staff, Melanne Verveer. "Going across the country there are constant pleas to a first lady for help. She doesn't escape those stories, she doesn't live in a bubble." Verveer watched Hillary meet with a group of working-class women, one of whom said to her, "You know, Mrs. Clinton, I look up at the wall and when it's three o'clock I freeze every day because I know my child's getting out of school at three o'clock. I have no idea what's happening to him from the moment he walks out of school until he gets home." Hillary turned to Verveer after the meeting and said, "Can you imagine not being able to know until after you left your job hours later if your child is okay?" Decades earlier, when a residence staffer's child was born with a disability, Mamie Eisenhower asked the mother and child to move into the White House. During Christmas she handed out Mamie dolls to the staffers, saving them some money on Christmas shopping. A couple of years later, when the Kennedys were in the executive mansion, White House Electrician Larry Bush asked Jackie if she would sell him her 1961 Mercury Colony Park, the car she often drove for long weekends in the Virginia countryside, because he knew that Jackie got a new car every year. She called him one day and said, "I heard my new car will be ready in two weeks. Do you still want my old one?" He bought it and drove it for ten years. Jackie donated many of the toys that were sent to her children to nearby orphanages. In a June 18, 1990, letter from First Lady Barbara Bush to former First Lady Betty Ford, the two are working together to help a young girl: "I do not know whether there is hope for little Diana Mowsesjan, but I will forward it to the appropriate office with the hope that maybe there can be." According to the Ford Library, Mowsesjan was a Soviet child who needed help. Neither Betty Ford nor Barbara Bush wanted to publicize what they were doing to help this little girl, and there's something dignified about their quiet efforts. In a similar way, Betty sent information about Pressley Ridge, a child advocacy organization, to Laura Bush in 2005, hoping that her office could do something to support its work. When Lady Bird Johnson found out that a butler's wife was battling cancer she called two of the top oncologists in New York and that same day they landed at Washington's National Airport to examine her. Before a trip to Korea, Nancy Reagan was told about two Korean children who badly needed heart surgery. Nancy started working the phones, and by the time the Reagans were flying back home on Air Force One, they had asked some staff to fly commercial so that the children could fly back with them. Both of the surgeries went well, and the children visited the White House when they were teenagers to thank the First Lady at the end of the administration. The son of one White House butler said it best: "The first lady can pick up the telephone and change your life."

———

DURING THE 1976 presidential campaign, Rosalynn Carter was on her way to pay her respects to Lady Bird Johnson, whose husband had been the most recent Democratic president. The day before their meeting, Jimmy Carter's embarrassing *Playboy* interview was published. In it, he said that he had "looked on a lot of women with lust" and had "committed adultery in my heart many times." Carter's campaign aides scrambled to repurpose a television ad featuring Rosalynn chatting with a bunch of women around a punch bowl and saying, "Jim has never had any hint of scandal in his personal life or his public life." But the worst part, at least at that moment for Rosalynn, was what her husband had said in the interview about President Johnson: "I don't think I would ever take on the same frame of mind that Nixon or Johnson did—lying, cheating and distorting the truth." Merely mentioning Johnson and Nixon in the same breath, so close to Nixon's resignation, was anathema to Democrats. Rosalynn turned to an aide who was close with the Johnsons. "What does Mrs. Johnson think about the interview? What should I say about it?"

"You don't say anything, Mrs. Carter," the aide said. "You're a southern lady just like Mrs. Johnson; it won't be brought up. You're two lovely southern ladies; just be yourself." And that's exactly what happened. No one understood the embarrassing position Rosalynn was in better than Lady Bird Johnson.

Profiles in Courage

★

Once it's done, put it behind you and go on with your life.
—BETTY FORD TO A WOMAN ABOUT TO UNDERGO
BREAST CANCER SURGERY

Two first ladies who were in the White House during different decades and married to men from different political parties demonstrated incredible grace under pressure. One was willing to sacrifice her life for her husband and the other fought for her life on the national stage.

Jacqueline Kennedy was lying in the sun, breathing in the crisp, fresh country air at Glen Ora, the four-hundred-acre estate that the Kennedys rented in Virginia's horse country. She had just arrived there after an hour-and-a-half car ride from the White House with her two children, five-year-old Caroline and two-year-old John-John. They whined for most of the ride and had just been put down for naps. Jackie was relieved to have a moment to herself, and she was happy to finally relax and get away from the tension of the White House. Then the phone rang.

"I'm coming back to Washington this afternoon. Why don't you come back there?" President Kennedy said, telling his wife, rather than asking her. Jackie stopped herself before she suggested, "Well, why don't you come down here?" President Kennedy knew how much his wife enjoyed being in the country and away from the claustrophobic White House. According to her Secret Service agent, Clint Hill, between the summer of 1961 and the summer of 1962, the First Lady spent nearly four months away from Washington. She often left on Thursday afternoon or Friday morning and would not return until Monday afternoon or even Tuesday morning. In the summers she went to the Kennedy family compound in Hyannis Port, Massachusetts, and to her family's Hammersmith Farm home in Newport, Rhode Island—where the Kennedys were married in 1953—and she escaped to Palm Beach, Florida, for Christmas and Easter, but these very long weekends were usually reserved for Virginia.

"I could tell from his voice something was wrong, so I didn't even ask," she recalled during an interview with historian Arthur Schlesinger Jr. Still, she wanted to know what was happening that would be worth her sacrificing one of her coveted weekends out of town, where she would have picnics with her children and enjoy the rare opportunity of tucking them into bed herself.

"Why?" she asked him.

"Well, never mind," the President said, his voice persistent and strained. "Why don't you just come back to Washington?"

Though she was frustrated, Jackie woke Caroline and John-John up from their naps and dutifully drove back to the White House with her Secret Service detail, still not knowing what awaited her there. She said to herself, *That's why you're married, you do things for the other person when you sense that they need you, even if you don't know why they need you.*

It was Saturday, October 20, 1962, and the President wanted his wife to be by his side during the agonizing thirteen-day standoff between the United States and the Soviet Union that would come to be known as the Cuban Missile Crisis. Photos taken by a U.S. U-2 spy plane revealed that during the summer of 1962, Soviet Premier Nikita Khrushchev had reached a secret deal with Cuban dictator Fidel Castro to place Soviet nuclear missiles in Cuba that could reach the United States in less than four minutes. The forty-two Soviet medium- and intermediate-range ballistic missiles were each capable of hitting the United States with a nuclear warhead twenty or thirty times more powerful than the bomb that hit Hiroshima.

The President convened ExComm, a nickname for his Executive Committee, composed of his closest advisers, including his brother Attorney General Robert Kennedy, Secretary of State Dean Rusk, and National Security Adviser McGeorge "Mac" Bundy. Day and night the haggard advisers gathered around the long conference table in the Cabinet Room or in Undersecretary of State George Ball's conference room, which became known as the "think tank." JFK was facing a possible nuclear war and wanted his wife by his side.

"From then on, it seemed there was no waking or sleeping," Jackie recalled of the days after she returned to the White House. The President clung to her for strength during the loneliest time of his presidency; he asked her to join him on long walks on the South Lawn, where the two talked through the complicated options laid before him. Kennedy told her everything: he told her about his tense meeting with Soviet Foreign Minister Andrei Gromyko, in which he did not let on just how much he knew about the Soviets' deal with Cuba; he told her about Khrushchev's angry telegram sent in the middle of the night during the agonizing final weekend of the crisis; and he confessed to her his anguish about the criticism he was getting from some of his more hawkish advisers, who did not think he was being strong enough. ("Those trigger-happy so-and-sos want me to knock Cuba off the map. We can do that. But we'd be bullies. They could be right or they could be dead wrong.") *Time* magazine's White House correspondent, Hugh Sidey, said that over dinner the President "would tell her everything that was happening." This woman, who is so often recognized only for her expensive taste in clothes, often knew exactly what was going on in her husband's administration.

When he did not tell her himself, she took to eavesdropping during meetings with the President's top advisers in the Yellow Oval Room on the second floor in the family's private quarters. The President had a general aversion to women in positions of power; his friend Charles Spalding said he was "much more comfortable with Secretary [of Defense Robert] McNamara than he would have been with [former U.S. Labor Secretary Frances] Perkins. It just seemed incongruous to him that a woman would have to appear at a Cabinet meeting." But Jackie knew about the political landscape he was operating in because of her proximity to power and her intelligent maneuvering.

The Cuban Missile Crisis engulfed the lives of both Kennedys. Once, during those tense days, late at night, Jackie came into the President's bedroom in her nightgown to find him lying on the bed. She did not see National Security Adviser "Mac" Bundy sitting out of sight, on the phone. As she walked over to Kennedy, he waved her away, saying, "Get out! Get out!" Bundy held his hands over his eyes. Other days, Bundy would be standing at the foot of their bed to wake the President up in the early-morning hours. Jackie would later cherish this tense time, when the country stood at the brink of war, because it was then that she felt valued in her husband's life. "That's the time I've been the closest to him, and I never left the house or saw the children, and when he came home, if it was for sleep or for a nap, I would sleep with him." She'd walk by the Oval Office to see if he needed a break; the two held what she described as a sort of "vigil."

The White House was shrouded in secrecy during the crisis. The President's advisers agonized over how to respond to the Soviet action and what the Soviets' motivation truly was. One group argued for a naval quarantine of Cuba and another insisted that the United States launch an air strike targeting the missile sites. The discovery was being kept secret until the President could decide on a response. In an oral history, Undersecretary of State Ball described the top-secret meetings and how much ExComm members dreaded any leaks to the press before they could devise a plan. Ball recalled ushering Secretary of Defense Robert Mc-Namara into the State Department through his private elevator so that the press would not see them. Attorney General Robert Kennedy, the President's most trusted adviser, showed up for one Oval Office meeting in his riding clothes so that it would look as though he was working during an otherwise carefree weekend, and once all of the President's other advisers piled into one car so as not to arouse suspicion from the press.

Jackie heard that the wives of Cabinet officials were preparing to leave Washington, knowing that it would be a target in the event of war. She would have none of it. "Please don't send me anywhere. If anything happens, we're all going to stay right here with you," she told her husband. "Even if there's no room in the bomb shelter in the White House . . . Please, then I just want to be on the lawn when it happens—you know—but I just want to be with you, and I want to die with you, and the children do too— than live without you." The President promised her that he would not send her anywhere. Their relationship had grown closer in the White House than it had ever been before. The President's personal doctor, Janet Travell, remembered seeing Kennedy walk from the West Wing to Marine One on the South Lawn shortly before the crisis began, trailed by his loyal aides. Then something strange happened. "The President reappeared in the doorway and descended the steps alone. *How unusual*, I thought. Then I saw why. Jackie, her hair wild in the gale of the rotors, was running from the South Portico across the grass. She almost met him at the helicopter steps and she reached up with her arms. They stood motionless in an embrace for many seconds."

During a private meeting with her Secret Service agent, Clint Hill, Hill reached out to Jackie and gently touched her elbow. "You know about the bomb shelter here, under the White House. I know that [Chief Usher] J. B. West gave you a brief tour of the facility a few months ago. . . . In the event . . . a situation develops . . . where we don't have time to leave the area, we would take you and the children into the shelter for protection." But Jackie had already made up her mind and she would not be told what to do. She abruptly pulled her arm away. "Mr. Hill, if the situation develops that requires the children and me to go to the shelter, let me tell you what you can expect." She lowered her already soft, sweet voice into an even deeper whisper and said, "If the situation develops, I will take Caroline and John, and we will walk hand in hand out onto the south grounds. We will stand there like brave soldiers, and face the fate of every other American."

Hill was stunned. "Well, Mrs. Kennedy, let's just pray to God that we will never be in that situation."

For the first time ever, the U.S. Strategic Air Command was placed on DEFCON (Defense Condition) 2, meaning there was an immediate threat of war. It was the closest the country has ever come to launching nuclear missiles. If one wrong move was made, one miscalculated comment or misguided message between advisers in the so-called ExComm and Soviet advisers hunkered down in the Kremlin, it could mean complete and utter devastation. Usher Nelson Pierce, who began working at the White House just a year before the crisis, said he was the most frightened he had ever been in his life. "You knew that those missiles were aimed right at us," he recalled, shivering at the memory of walking through the White House's Northwest Gates on Pennsylvania Avenue, knowing he was walking into a bull's-eye. "You knew that if you heard that something [a missile] was on the way, you had to get the first family out, or to a safe place, and you were there regardless. You'd be the last one to leave," he paused, "if you left at all."

Part-time Butler Herman Thompson was called in to work during the crisis and served drinks to the President's advisers who gathered day and night at the White House. "I was scared to death. I went to bed that night and didn't sleep," Thompson recalled, having heard the men talk. Unfurled maps, half-eaten sandwiches, and old coffee cups littered the usually pristine Oval Office.

Jackie took charge and, never missing a detail, realized she had to begin the delicate process of canceling a dinner planned for the Maharajah and Maharani of Jaipur, who had graciously hosted her during a whirlwind trip to India. Before the crisis took hold of the White House, Jackie's memos to the man who ran the residence, Chief Usher J. B. West, were so thoughtful and detailed that she instructed him, ahead of the visit, to paint a chest of drawers black in the Queens' Dressing Room and to put her fur rug on a daybed in the Lincoln Sitting Room along with "some green and yellow pillows" to make her guests more comfortable. There was no time for such things now; everything had changed once the missiles were detected. That Sunday, October 21, 1962, Jackie woke West up at his Arlington, Virginia, home, just as he and his wife, Zella, were enjoying a rare morning of sleeping in.

"Could you please come to the White House right away, Mr. West, but come up through the kitchen elevator so nobody will know you're here."

"I'll be there in twenty minutes," he told her. He noticed more cars than usual in the White House driveway, and when he stepped off the elevator he saw Jackie with no makeup on, wearing bright Pucci pants and loafers and sitting on a sofa in the West Sitting Hall beneath its dramatic half-moon window as sunlight flooded into the room. She seemed enveloped in a halo, a bright light during a very tense, dark time.

"Thank you for coming, Mr. West," she said apologetically. "There's something brewing that might turn out to be a big catastrophe—which means that we may have to cancel the dinner and dance for the Jaipurs Tuesday night." West was surprised; it was rare to cancel an event so suddenly. "Tell me when the Jaipurs are set to arrive and make sure they are assigned the best maid, Wilma, and the best valet at Blair House," she told him, cool and calm under unimaginable pressure.

"Could you please handle the cancellation for me? This is all very secret," she told him, "and I'm afraid Tish [Social Secretary Letitia Baldrige] would get all upset and rant and rave—*you* know—and I think you could do it more calmly." Jackie and her social secretary were often at odds. Baldrige had been three years ahead of her at Miss Porter's and Vassar, and at the White House she always wanted Jackie to do more, to host more teas, to have more luncheons with deserving groups. But all Jackie wanted was to have more privacy and rest.

Mary Boylan, a secretary in the East Wing, remembers the

flurry of activity that weekend as she sat in her office across the hall from the Military Office. On October 22 the President explained the crisis to the nation in a prime-time televised address. That morning Baldrige walked into the East Wing and, as Jackie had predicted, she was anything but calm. She commanded everyone's attention: "I have an announcement to make." The room full of well-dressed young women grew silent. "All of you should start praying like you never prayed before. Tonight you're going to hear some news that's going to be very shocking, and none of us know what the outcome is going to be."

Press aide Barbara Coleman remembers getting a call at home through the White House switchboard from Press Secretary Pierre Salinger, who was with the President aboard Air Force One on the way back from a campaign trip to Chicago. "He wanted me to be on hand at the White House as soon as they landed," she said. Salinger said the President had a cold and needed to come home on doctor's orders. Salinger did not tell her the real reason for the President's abrupt return, but he suggested something was amiss when he told her to cancel any plans she had for the weekend.

"It was soon that I became aware that something was happening," she said. "I didn't know what it was; I knew it had something to do with Cuba." Throughout the crisis there was always someone in the press office, and some aides even brought clothes to the White House and slept in the bomb shelter.

In his televised address the President spoke from the Oval Office and announced the naval quarantine of Cuba. "Nuclear weapons are so destructive and ballistic missiles are so swift, that any substantially increased possibility of their use or any sudden change in their deployment may well be regarded as a definite threat to peace," he declared, crystallizing the essential dilemma of the Cold War. "It shall be the policy of this nation to regard any nuclear missile launched from Cuba against any nation in the Western Hemisphere as an attack by the Soviet Union on the United States, requiring a full retaliatory response upon the Soviet Union."

Finally, on October 28, Khrushchev issued a statement that the Soviet missiles would be removed from Cuba. Jackie watched surveillance video showing Soviet ships approaching the U.S. blockade and turning back, and she breathed a sigh of relief. If the crisis had gone on for just two more days, a Kennedy adviser told her, the outcome could have been different because everyone was reaching total exhaustion and maybe irrational decisions would have been made.

Throughout those tension-filled days, Jackie retained her faith in her husband and in her own ability to calm and center him. "I always thought with Jack that anything, he could make—once he was in control, anything, all the best things would happen. In this childish way, I thought, 'I won't have to be afraid when I go to sleep at night or wake up.'" She wept when her husband presented her with the same sterling-silver Tiffany calendar that he gave to the members of ExComm, with those thirteen frightening days highlighted in bold. Her initials were engraved next to his, "J.B.K." and "J.F.K."

Less than two weeks after her husband's assassination, on December 1, 1963, Jackie penned one of the last letters she would ever write on White House stationery. It wasn't to a close family friend or to one of her husband's many political advisers. It was to the man who her husband said had committed a "clandestine, reckless, and provocative threat to world peace" and in turn gave her a distinct and powerful role to play in the White House. During those thirteen days she was more than a beautiful, devoted wife; she was a partner. She recognized that one of

her husband's greatest triumphs was breaking through to Soviet
Premier Khrushchev and saving the world from nuclear war.
"You and he were adversaries, but you were allied in a determination that the world should not be blown up. You respected each
other and could deal with each other," Jackie wrote. "While big
men know the needs for self-control and restraint—little men are
sometimes moved more by fear and pride. If only in the future the
big men can continue to make the little ones sit down and talk,
before they start to fight."

———

THERE IS SEEMINGLY nothing out of the ordinary about the black-
and-white White House photograph taken on September 27, 1974.
First Lady Betty Ford is giving a tour of the President's bedroom
to Lady Bird Johnson, who had been first lady five years before
her. Joining them are Lady Bird's two daughters, Lynda and Luci;
and Lynda's husband, Charles Robb, who had come to Washington for the dedication of the Grove, President Johnson's memorial
park along the Potomac River. In the photograph, Betty Ford leans
in toward Luci as though listening to a question; Luci's hand is
outstretched, pointing at something out of the camera shot. Betty,
playing the role of gracious hostess, smiles serenely. The only clue
that something is amiss lies at the foot of the satin tufted bed—it is
a small black suitcase. The suitcase is there because Betty Ford was
just told the day before the Johnsons' visit that she likely had breast
cancer. She would leave for Bethesda Naval Hospital as soon as her
guests departed. Betty never said a word about her condition to her
guests; she did not want to ruin their special day.

"You were so calm and hospitable to us last Friday that it
shocked the four of us even more than the rest of the nation when
we heard the news that you had gone to the hospital," Lady Bird

wrote in a handwritten note delivered to Betty's hospital room. Luci, the Johnsons' younger daughter, remembers rushing to catch the six o'clock news that night to see if there was anything about the dedication ceremony earlier that day. She was shocked to see images of Betty Ford, with that small black suitcase in her hand, leaving the White House. "All of our collective mouths dropped. We were dumbfounded." Because they had spent more than five years in the White House themselves and were all too familiar with the grueling schedule, the Johnsons of all people would have understood if the First Lady had wanted to cancel the tour. "I just think there was such a strong sense of communion. They felt this was Mother's big day, Daddy was gone, and they weren't going to do anything to take away from that," Luci says. "I think it was very much who Betty Ford was."

Betty Ford did not become a public person until she was fifty-six years old but she embraced the role completely. She was a dedicated mother and housewife when her husband was in Congress for twenty-five years. Steve Ford, the third of the Fords' four children, says, "As kids, we just watched our mother blossom when she was given the chance after all those years of bringing up us kids. It was a wonderful thing to see." When Betty was a little girl she went to a fortune-teller who told her that one day she would meet kings and queens, which she took to mean that she would become a great dancer. And she did—she had been a modern dancer with Martha Graham's prestigious company. When she married Gerald Ford, she said, she thought she was marrying a lawyer and that they would raise a family in Grand Rapids, Michigan. But in 1955 the Fords settled in a four-bedroom, two-bathroom redbrick colonial on Crown View Drive in Alexandria, Virginia, across the Potomac from the White House. They even lived there when Ford unexpectedly became vice president in 1973. Their phone number was listed in the phone book, and Betty Ford could be found most days with a pot of tea on the stove and wearing a long housecoat.

In early August 1974, days before President Nixon resigned, the Fords were getting ready to move into the official vice presidential residence at One Observatory Circle, less than three miles from the White House. But just before Vice President Ford and his wife arrived at the beautiful Victorian-style house to talk with interior decorators, he learned that President Nixon would be resigning and he would be taking over. Somehow, Ford managed to sit calmly through a series of meetings about décor with Betty by his side. Finally, when they had a moment alone he whispered to her, "Betty, we are never going to live in this house."

Less than two months after she and her husband were thrust into the White House, and only eighteen days after the President's controversial pardon of President Nixon, the new First Lady was being told the devastating news that she might have breast cancer. The day before the Johnsons' visit, on September 26, Betty spontaneously decided to accompany her close friend Nancy Howe to see a doctor. Howe was having a routine checkup and Betty thought she might as well have her six-month appointment then, too. When the doctor performing Betty's mammogram excused himself to bring in the chief of surgery, Betty thought nothing of it. "Doctors had been checking portions of my anatomy for so long . . . I could take quite a bit of poking and prodding and hearing murmurs of 'Mmmmm,' and go right on wondering when I was going to be able to attack the huge pile of mail which was waiting on my desk." This time the news was not good.

Around noon the President's doctor, William Lukash, made the unusual request for the President to meet him at seven that evening in his ground-floor office at the White House. Lukash had called in the chairman of surgery from George Washington University Medical School and had asked the new First Lady to come down a few minutes before seven for another breast exam. When Lukash sat down with the President and the First Lady, he told them they had found a lump that could be cancer. "Well, you can't operate immediately. I have a full day tomorrow," Betty said. Her response was unusual but, Lukash told her, surgery could wait for a day or two. Their seventeen-year-old daughter, Susan, had red-rimmed eyes when she came in for dinner in the second-floor private living quarters that evening. She had heard the news before her parents did. She had stopped by Dr. Lukash's office looking for some cold medicine earlier that day. "He pulled me in and sat me down, and I thought, *What have I done wrong now?*" Lukash told her, "Your mother has a lump in her breast, there's a good chance it's cancer, and she doesn't know, so hush, hush, don't say anything to anybody." Susan was so scared that she might lose her mother. The next day, Betty kept a harrowing schedule: she went to the groundbreaking of the Grove, made a speech at a Salvation Army luncheon, and hosted the afternoon tea and White House tour for the Johnsons. Her car pulled up to the hospital at 5:55 p.m. and at 6:00 p.m. her illness was broadcast around the world.

At the time, cancer was referred to as the "C" word, almost as if it were contagious, and it was usually not discussed at all. And no one said "breast." Ever. Even though beloved child star and diplomat Shirley Temple Black had disclosed her mastectomy in 1972, it was Betty Ford who brought national attention to the importance of early detection. At a state dinner, after Betty's mastectomy, Black and Betty shared a private moment. Black, with tears welling up in her eyes, put her arms around the First Lady and whispered something. "Yes, we understand," Betty replied. Over the next few weeks, more than fifty thousand letters poured into the First Lady's office. Many of the letters were from women who credited the First Lady with saving their lives, and some were from men who wanted her to know that they found their wives beautiful after their mastectomies. Happy Rockefeller, the wife of Ford's vice president, Nelson Rockefeller, had a breast exam after hearing about Betty's cancer and discovered a lump and had surgery. Like so many others, Happy credited Betty with saving her life. (When President Reagan had colon cancer surgery years later, Happy sent a single red rose to Nancy Reagan. Among all the cards and flowers it was the only thing Nancy took upstairs to the residence with her that evening.)

Betty was a brave patient who was determined to beat the disease. She checked into the presidential suite at Bethesda Naval Hospital and had a quiet dinner there with her family before the surgery that was scheduled for the next morning. She told them she would be fine, to go home and get some rest. President Ford, who was deeply committed to his wife, told her he was never lonelier than that evening on his way back to the White House. Before he left her, they held hands and prayed. Unlike the Nixons, the Fords were very affectionate and they were the first presidential couple to openly share a bedroom since the Coolidges. In a note President Ford wrote to his wife before surgery he said, "No written words can adequately express our *deep, deep* love. We know how *great* you are and we, the children and Dad, will try to be as strong as you. Our Faith in you and God will sustain us. Our total *love* for you is everlasting."

For Betty, it was one in a string of challenges that she knew she would overcome. When she was just sixteen years old her father died in an apparent suicide. (He was an alcoholic, and died of carbon monoxide poisoning.) "I faced the situation rather matter-of-factly," she wrote of her cancer diagnosis in her memoir. "This is one more crisis, and it will pass." If the biopsy showed that the lump was benign, there would be no need for the mastectomy, but she knew in her heart that she had cancer as they wheeled her into the operating room. It was the Fords' daughter, Susan, who first learned that the lump was cancerous. "Susan, they had to go ahead," Dr. Lukash told her as her knees buckled. "But she's all right." When the President found out that the lump was malignant he broke down in tears in the Oval Office.

The President's political advisers had told Betty that she didn't have to go public with such a personal matter, but she insisted. Once she found out the number of women who were dying from the disease, she told staffers that if it was cancer they should release a statement while she was on the operating table saying that she was having a mastectomy, instead of something amorphous like she was dealing with a "health issue." When President Ford and his son Mike flew on Marine One to visit Betty after the surgery, Mike got on his knees with his father and they prayed in the aisle for her recovery. After the surgery, Betty wrote a letter to Lady Bird explaining why she had not told her the news. "I wanted you to enjoy your visit as much as I did." She added a bit of levity and thanked Lady Bird for the pink robe she had sent her in the hospital. "I just loved the design and color. As a matter of fact, I chose it for my first public picture after my operation."

Years later, after Betty left the White House, her unflinching honesty about her own addiction to pain pills and alcohol would help remove the stigma from another disease. She opened the now world-famous Betty Ford Center in 1982, on fourteen acres in Rancho Mirage, California. The center has treated more than one hundred thousand people. Her recognition of her own struggle with alcoholism and her addiction to painkillers has saved an untold number of lives. She visited the center regularly and would go to local Alcoholics Anonymous meetings and stand up in the middle of the room and introduce herself. "I'm Betty, and I'm an alcoholic," she'd say. Long after she left rehab herself, she would meet regularly with a group of women who had graduated from the program. "I had had breast cancer and I had survived that and now I was confronted with addiction, and by golly I made up my mind I was going to survive that, too," she said.

After her mastectomy, she urged other women who were facing breast cancer surgery to "go as quickly as possible and get it done."

"Once it's done," she said, "put it behind you and go on with your life."

Though she approached the surgery with unflinching hero-ism, her recovery was not easy. Afterward she woke up to see her family surrounding her, some in tears. "If you can't look happy, please go away," she told them from her hospital bed. "I can't bear to look at you." Betty did exercises to try to strengthen her right arm after part of the muscle was removed, and it was a small vic-tory when she could finally gain enough strength to pick up a cup of tea with her right hand. Susan remembers those tough times. "There were days she would walk in her closet and say, 'Well, I can't wear *that* dress anymore. Everybody will look at my scar.'" Betty never got reconstructive surgery and was often worried that during formal dinners she would bend over in an evening gown and her gel prosthetic would fall out. Sometimes she had pads sewn into her clothes.

Betty hit the campaign trail as her husband sought the presi-dency in 1976. His advisers considered her a potent weapon and were astounded to find that her candor led to approval ratings as high as 75 percent, even while her husband's presidential approval rating dipped below 50 percent. At almost every campaign event there were women wearing buttons saying "Keep Betty in the

White House" and "Betty's Husband for President." Still, Ford lost to Jimmy Carter. When Ford could not read his concession speech because his voice was weak, it was Betty Ford who read it. "She supported him wholeheartedly from beginning to end," says Susan. "And he supported her from beginning to end, through her breast cancer and her drug and alcohol issues. They were true soul mates." Betty Ford's bravery earned her the Presidential Medal of Freedom in 1991, an astounding eight years before her husband was awarded his own medal. On the tenth anniversary of her founding of the Betty Ford Center, President Ford said, "When the final tally is taken, her contributions to our country will be bigger than mine." And that was just fine with him.

Motherhood

★

If you bungle raising your children, I don't think whatever else
you do well matters very much.
—JACKIE KENNEDY

Having children in the White House brings a sense of fun to the executive mansion's formal halls, especially for the butlers, maids, and chefs who tend to the needs of the first families, and for the reporters who cover them. When a reporter asked three-year-old Caroline Kennedy, "Where's your daddy?" she replied, "He's upstairs with his shoes and socks off, doing nothing." Caroline always wanted her door open a crack when she lived at the White House because she was scared by the size of her room and the height of the ceilings.

Presidential children have a way of grounding the rich and famous, and no one did it quite like Caroline and John-John. World-renowned composer Leonard Bernstein was frequently invited by Jackie Kennedy to the small dinner parties she organized to entertain her husband. One evening Bernstein asked Jackie if he could watch the first few minutes of a TV program that he was on before dinner. She showed him into Caroline's room, where the little girl was getting ready for bed with her nanny, Maud Shaw. Bernstein sat holding hands with Caroline, who was mesmerized by the program featuring very adult classical music. "I thought she was all wrapped up in it, and suddenly she looked up at me with this marvelous clear face and said, 'I have my own horse.' I thought now that does it for me, you know, that really brought one so down to earth that I was grateful to her for it because I realized that I was being horrid for watching my own show on television and not being with the guests. So at that moment I turned off the set and rejoined the others."

White House Electrician Larry Bush remembers Jackie asking him to put some blocks on the pedals of the tricycle that Caroline got for Christmas because her legs weren't yet long enough to reach them. A few months later, the First Lady needed another favor. "She's grown so much, can you please take the blocks off?" Jackie asked him. "She was just so in love with those children. And she showed it," Bush recalled. It also made for some scary moments for the young Kennedys. Caroline and John-John used to love to accompany their father in the White House elevator and walk with him to the Oval Office in the morning. "Come on! We've got to get to work!" John-John would shout, still in his pajamas. One morning when Caroline and the President stepped off the elevator, dozens of flashbulbs exploded. The President had forgotten that he had arranged to have the press trail him that day. Caroline was so scared that JFK swept her back into the elevator and asked the doorman to take her back upstairs to the residence. President Kennedy's doctor, Janet Travell, was riding with them in the elevator that morning and remembers a startled Caroline crying, wanting to see her father but frightened by the sheer number of photographers gathered around to catch a glimpse of her. "She ran out of the elevator and under the sofa," Travell recalled. "It took all of Miss Shaw's coaxing to get her out."

The Kennedys had different views of how to raise their toddler son John-John and their kindergartner Caroline, and their staffs—both on the political side and on the residence side—had to try to meet both parents' demands. Jackie liked John-John's hair to be long but the President preferred it short. "You know, sir," Maud Shaw told the President, "I have to look along the corridor and see who's coming. If Mrs. Kennedy comes, I comb his hair frontways, if you come along, I give him a part." Both wanted to make their children's abnormal life in the White House as normal as possible. The day they moved into the White House, Jackie asked the gardener to make a giant snowman near the driveway at the South Portico with a carrot for its nose and an apple for its mouth. Caroline was thrilled.

At times Jackie and JFK disagreed about how much exposure their children should have to the media. President Kennedy's friend Charles Spalding said that when photographers got a shot of Caroline riding her pony, Macaroni, on the South Lawn, the President knew the political value of that one photo. The President loved roughhousing with his kids and did not talk down to them. He had a special bond with Caroline. Gustavo Paredes, the son of Jackie's personal assistant Providencia, was close to the Kennedy children and was a constant playmate of John-John. He remembers the assassination hitting Caroline the hardest, and not just because she was older. "Fathers always love their daughters and mothers always love their sons. They kind of divvied it up, so Caroline felt the most loss, a tremendous loss." A week after the assassination, Jackie said simply, "I'm going to bring up my son. I want him to grow up to be a good boy. I have no better dream for him." She mused that he might become an astronaut one day "or just plain John Kennedy fixing planes on the ground." She did everything she could to give her children as normal a life as possible. After the assassination she took them to Palm Beach for Christmas and hung up the familiar stockings. When they moved into an eighteenth-century Georgetown townhouse she asked her decorator to replicate the bedrooms the children had had in the White House.

Before she moved out of the White House, she asked Chief Usher J. B. West, whom she considered a friend, to accompany her to the Oval Office one last time. The model ships and books, and the President's beloved rocking chair, were all being carted away before her eyes. "I think we're probably in the way," she murmured. She and West walked the short way to the Cabinet Room, where they sat at a long mahogany table. "My children. They're good children, aren't they, Mr. West?"

"They certainly are."

"They're not spoiled?"

"No, indeed."

"Mr. West, will you be my friend for life?" West could only nod. He was afraid that if he spoke the floodgates would open and his own personal grief and sympathy for the young widow would overwhelm him.

Jackie saw a therapist in New York for years and would never completely heal from the trauma of sitting next to her husband during the violent end of his life. Recounting the horror of November 22, 1963, she told journalist Theodore H. White, "His [President Kennedy's] last expression was so neat; he had his hand out, I could see a piece of his skull coming off; it was flesh colored not white—he was holding out his hand—and I can see this perfectly clean piece detaching itself from his head; then he slumped in my lap." She was tormented in the spring of 1964 and kept asking herself, *Why hadn't I insisted on a bubbletop?* She had trouble sleeping and would take long naps in the afternoon. She mused that it would have been better if her husband had not been killed by a lone gunman with communist beliefs; it would have offered her some solace if he had died for a bigger cause at the hands of someone who was angered by his support of civil rights or someone who was part of a larger conspiracy. In an interview, she said, "I should have known that it was asking too much to dream that I might have grown old with him and see our children grow up together . . . so now he is a legend when he would have preferred to be a man."

Maud Shaw had been with the family since Caroline was eleven days old, and she was the one who fed, bathed, and clothed the children, but Jackie was a surprisingly hands-on mother and a disciplinarian. ("John was in the know absolutely. When any lady walks into the room, you stand up," John Kennedy Jr.'s longtime friend Gustavo says.) Jackie would not tolerate tantrums. "If you have a tantrum, you bring it to me," she'd tell her son if she found him crying with Shaw or a member of the White House residence staff. "Don't take it out on the staff."

Jackie took charge of her children's education, setting up a kindergarten for Caroline in the Solarium, a sort of family room on the third floor of the residence. She asked the parents of friends from a playgroup Caroline was part of in Georgetown if they'd like to join the White House school. Fourteen children came to the White House two mornings a week, filling the hallways with laughter. Jackie even designed a playground for them on the South Lawn. The first year it was actually a cooperative nursery school with all the mothers, including the First Lady, pitching in as teachers and aides. Gradually they hired professional teachers and made it more formal. Jackie and the President would stop by every week and check on the class, and the President would play with the children on the South Lawn. "The house was full of children morning, noon, and night," recalled Social Secretary Letitia Baldrige. "You never knew when an avalanche of young people would come bearing down on you—runny noses, dropped mittens in the hall, bicycles. . . ." At recess they lined up to head outside and once the doors to the South Lawn were opened the children exploded out, running after puppies and careening toward the playground.

Jackie asked Caroline's French teacher, Jacqueline Hirsh, to take her daughter out on Mondays so that she could have a normal outing. Going with her famous mother was too fraught. "Just take her anywhere. Just anywhere." Hirsh ended up taking her on bus rides so that she could get fresh air and see people outside her small circle. One time they were on an old bus on Pennsylvania Avenue and all the seats were occupied, so Caroline sat on her teacher's lap clutching a stuffed rabbit. A bunch of teenagers got on and one of them said, "You know, I think I'm sitting next to Caroline Kennedy." Their friend snapped back, "Oh, don't be silly. What would she be doing on a bus like this?" Sometimes they went grocery shopping or to museums; once they even picked up Hirsh's son and watched his school's football game. "It was very difficult for Mrs. Kennedy to take her out and not be recognized and it spoiled the fun," Hirsh recalled. The President joined Caroline in trying to learn French to surprise Jackie. When Jackie returned from Greece in 1963, he watched proudly as Caroline exclaimed, "I'm so happy you're back" ("Je suis contente de te revoir"). Jackie didn't know about his French lessons (he had taken four classes before he was killed) until Hirsh told her. "After the funeral I mentioned it," Hirsh said. "I thought, as a gift, you know, I would tell her that her husband had thought of giving her a surprise, that obviously she was on his mind."

The White House was a lively place when the Kennedys

were in residence and the President delighted in all kinds of pets. They had five dogs, two parakeets, two hamsters, one rabbit, one canary, and one cat. The White House residence staffers took care of the pets, with Electrician Traphes Bryant serving as the dog minder. Jackie enjoyed the happy chaos wrought by their children and their ever-expanding slew of pets, and she had a sense of fun rarely seen by the public. "Let's go kiss the wind," she would whisper to Caroline when they went outside to play on the South Lawn.

The President, like many fathers of his generation, was mostly there for the fun times and was not the primary disciplinarian. Doorman Preston Bruce fondly recalled seeing the President on all fours crawling around his office with Caroline on his back. He even witnessed the President bump his head as he was playing with them. "I made a quick retreat out of sight," he said, not wanting to embarrass the President. The children would run into the President and First Lady's bedroom while they were eating breakfast and they would turn on the television so they could watch cartoons, and story time was a real favorite. One of Caroline's favorite stories, about a white shark, was one the President usually reserved for when they were on his beloved yacht, the *Honey Fitz*. This shark, JFK told her, ate only socks. When Caroline asked him where the white shark went he'd tickle her and say, "I think he is over there and he's waiting for something to eat." Once he teased one of Caroline's friends, "Give him your socks. He's hungry." In a panic the young boy threw his socks overboard and Caroline looked on with great interest, waiting for the shark to appear. The President showed a softer side to his daughter when she rushed to the Oval Office with one of their pet birds who had died. "He was really upset," Spalding said in an interview for the JFK Library. "He insisted that she get it out of his sight." Spalding wondered whether the President's reaction was in some way an intimation of his own death.

Jackie was fiercely protective of her children. She resented the press's insatiable appetite for photos of her family. After she had an emergency C-section for John-John's birth, her husband, then president-elect, obligingly stopped at an X mark that photographers had taped on the floor of the lobby of Georgetown University Hospital. Jackie, in a wheelchair, bristled, "Oh, Jack, please keep going!" In one memo to her close friend and personal secretary Pamela Turnure, she went after a comedian on *The Ed Sullivan Show* named Vaughn Meader, who had done a sketch with a girl name Caroline. She told Turnure to call Meader and let him know that the First Lady considered him to be "a rat." The actress Grace Kelly remembered Jackie's dismay that her children were being harassed by a voracious press that treated them like American royalty. Kelly, who was an actual princess after marrying Prince Rainier III of Monaco, remembered her daughter, also named Caroline, watching a ceremony on television showing the Kennedy children standing outside the White House. "She saw Jackie Kennedy's Caroline peering out from behind a curtain and asked, 'Mummy, why is Princess Kennedy's house white?'"

Assistant White House Press Secretary Christine Camp said that Jackie made it clear that she did not want any photographers using long-range lenses to capture images of the children playing on the South Lawn—she had tall rhododendron bushes planted along the fence to block their view. But the rules were constantly changing. "Mrs. Kennedy, of course, in her great glorious way, would forget her own rule and take the kids out in a sleigh on the South Lawn and be kind of mad that there weren't any pictures," Camp said. Press aide Barbara Gamarekian said there was a general understanding that when Jackie and her children were playing together on the South Lawn, the photographers would respect their privacy. Gamarekian remembers one shot of Caroline playing with a friend on the White House swing set. The picture won a prize from the White House Correspondents' Association, but Jackie was furious when she saw it in the papers. White House Press Secretary Pierre Salinger was instructed to call up the wire photographer who took the photo and ream him out, but two days later Jackie asked Salinger to get a print of the photo for herself because she liked it so much.

Salinger had a good relationship with the First Lady and knew that he would have to patiently wait to get her blessing for access to the children. He gently brought up a request from *Look* magazine once a month for six months, but each time the First Lady resisted. President Kennedy told Salinger, "Now, you tell *Look* magazine that I'll reconsider it. . . . Why don't you ask me the next time Mrs. Kennedy goes out of town?" Not long after that, Jackie took Caroline on a trip and the President saw his opportunity. He stuck his head into the press office. "Is there a *Look* photographer around?" Within ten minutes, photographer Stanley Tretick was there and got the iconic shots of John-John poking his head out from under the President's desk in the Oval Office. Kennedy said he would take the blame when his wife came back, and when she did "all hell broke loose," recalled Camp. Jackie told the President, "You tell *Look* magazine to never publish a picture." She knew exactly what had happened. Laura Bergquist Knebel, the reporter who was assigned to write the accompanying story for *Look*, said that when Jackie found out she came to her and said, "Stan and Jack were like two sneaky little boys. The minute I left town, they would let you in to do these things that I didn't particularly want done." Jackie had the final word on the matter and the photos were held back until after Kennedy's assassination, when she had a change of heart. The photos became a bittersweet glimpse at this loving father-and-son relationship and ran in the magazine's Father's Day issue.

Caroline was better able to understand that her father was gone than her little brother. "For a while there it was very rough. She just looked ghastly. She looked so pale and her concentration . . ." Caroline's teacher Jacqueline Hirsh remembered in an interview for the JFK library, her voice trailing off at the thought of those terrible months. The first time Hirsh took her out after the assassination, photographers hounded them. "Hi, Caroline!" they shouted. Caroline hid in the backseat of the car and asked Hirsh, "Please tell me when nobody's looking." Jackie's and Caroline's red-rimmed eyes were the only signs to those around them that they were reeling from the enormous loss.

Jackie Kennedy sought counseling from the Reverend Richard McSorley, a Jesuit priest who taught at Georgetown University. On the morning of JFK's state funeral he received a call from Jackie asking him to come and talk with her. A few weeks later, Jackie asked him if he would give her tennis lessons. McSorley had won tennis tournaments in seminary, but he knew from the start that there was more to her request than just tennis—she was seeking spiritual guidance and not help with her backhand. The two met at noon every day at Robert Kennedy's estate, Hickory Hill in McLean, Virginia. Jackie was such a seasoned tennis player that there was no point in even keeping score as they played. Instead she asked him existential questions and whether God knew what was going to happen to her husband, and if he did, why he would take her son Patrick from her just weeks before. Jackie asked McSorley penetrating questions about life and death and the Resurrection and he would go back to his office at Georgetown and consult different texts and theologians and report back the next time they met.

In late 2000, writer Thomas Maier interviewed McSorley for a book about the Kennedys' Irish Catholic heritage. He asked the priest, who died in 2002, whether Caroline and John-John had ever wanted to know why, "if there's a loving God, why . . . this could happen to somebody like the President?" McSorley replied, "The children never asked me. Jackie Kennedy asked me." According to Maier, Jackie confided in McSorley that she was so distraught that she had even contemplated suicide. The two were so close that members of the extended Kennedy clan asked McSorley to urge her to move her family to New York when they saw how unhappy she was in Georgetown, where she couldn't escape from the tragedy of what had happened. After she moved her two young children to New York she asked him to visit them, and over time McSorley became a strong male presence in John Jr.'s life. The two took strolls in Central Park with a Secret Service agent trailing not far behind.

The depth of the Kennedy children's loss was too much to bear at times, even for the priest who had seen so much suffering. McSorley recalled that one night after dinner with Jackie and her children, Jackie told her son, "You get ready for bed, and maybe Father will come in to say good night." A few minutes later the priest walked into John-John's bedroom as Jackie stood in the doorway. Jackie asked him in a soft voice, "Do you know 'Danny Boy'? His father used to sing it to him just before he went to sleep. He used 'Johnny' instead of 'Danny.'" McSorley dutifully sang as the young boy stared up at him in rapt attention. "Jackie stood silently in the doorway looking at us," he said. "I was in tears as I left the room." After he left, Jackie walked over to her son's bedside, said a prayer with him, and gave him a kiss good night.

Jackie told McSorley that she hoped her move to New York would help her stop "brooding." Ultimately, it was her children who saved her. "If you want to know what my religious convictions are now," she wrote to McSorley after the move, "they are: to keep busy and to keep healthy so that you can do all you should for your children. And to get to bed very early at night so you don't have time to think."

―――――

SOME OF THE first ladies struggled with motherhood and were honest about the isolation that sometimes comes during the first few months with a baby at home. Almost every afternoon, Lady Bird Johnson escaped to the small blue sitting room overlooking the Rose Garden that had been Jackie Kennedy's dressing room and Eleanor Roosevelt's bedroom in previous incarnations. She dutifully taped a note to the door: "Mrs. J at work!" Here she sat on a blue velvet sofa and recorded the day's events into her tape recorder. She locked the tapes away, and the only person to hear them (until her secretary transcribed them a month before she left the White House) was Chief Justice Earl Warren. He requested her recording from November 22, 1963, for the commission investigating President Kennedy's assassination. Her diligent effort produced a comprehensive diary offering insight into day-to-day life in the White House.

In her diary, she recalled feeling panicked when, as the wife of a congressman, she was alone with baby Lynda Bird: "I give myself small plaudits for knowing how to handle children," she said. "I remember the absolute horror I felt on the day when it was finally this lady's [Lynda Bird's nanny's] day off and I saw her disappearing down the street growing smaller and smaller in the distance. And there was that squirming red infant in that bassinet that I was totally responsible for." A congressman's wife, she jumped at an invitation to christen a submarine in Portsmouth, New Hampshire. "It was a marvelous break from a vigorous

In the early-morning hours of November 9, 1960, Richard Nixon all but conceded the election to John Kennedy from Republican Party headquarters at the Ambassador Hotel in Los Angeles. Pat campaigned tirelessly for her husband. "Now I'll never get to be first lady," she moaned.

First Lady Mamie Eisenhower, sixty-four, sneeringly referred to her successor, Jackie Kennedy, thirty-one, as "the college girl." After JFK won the 1960 election, Mamie reluctantly invited Jackie, still recovering from a C-section for the birth of John F. Kennedy Jr., for the traditional private tour of the White House. Jackie was promised a wheelchair, but Mamie never offered her one, and by the end of the visit Jackie was pale and exhausted.

From left to right: Pat Nixon, Mamie Eisenhower, Lady Bird Johnson, and Jackie Kennedy watch as President Kennedy delivers his inaugural address on January 20, 1961. Pat was vengeful after her husband's brutal defeat and even suggested a recount.

Jackie Kennedy loved being a mother and had a sense of fun rarely seen by the public. "Let's go kiss the wind," she would whisper to her daughter, Caroline, before they ran outside to play on the White House lawn. Here she and President Kennedy play with their children, Caroline and John F. Kennedy Jr., in the White House nursery after a joint birthday party. *Below:* Caroline, seated at the center of the table wearing a red headband, and her classmates celebrate Halloween in the White House kindergarten that Jackie created.

Vice President Lyndon Johnson takes the oath of office aboard Air Force One on a tarmac in Dallas on November 22, 1963, after President Kennedy's assassination. Lady Bird *(left)* could never convince Jackie *(right)*, her husband's blood still staining her dress, to return to the White House, and was hurt that Jackie came back only at Pat Nixon's request. But the two women were united by history and forged a deep, lifelong bond.

Chief Usher J. B. West, Lady Bird Johnson (carrying a portrait of President Johnson's mentor, House Speaker Sam Rayburn) and the Johnsons' youngest daughter, Luci (with beagles Him and Her), move into the White House after President Kennedy's assassination. Lady Bird lamented, "People see the living and wish for the dead."

Lady Bird Johnson, who was so shy that she took public speaking classes when her husband was in Congress, became the first first lady to make a solo campaign trip when she toured eight southern states on her whistle-stop train tour in 1964.

Pat Nixon *(middle)* learned how to be first lady by watching Mamie Eisenhower *(left)* when her husband served as vice president in the Eisenhower administration in the 1950s. But by the time Richard Nixon was elected president in 1968, Mamie's old-fashioned approach seemed out of place. "Life and history have not been fair to Pat Nixon. Period," says Connie Stuart, Pat's former chief of staff and press secretary. Pat's daughter Julie is on the right.

Left: Pat—derided in the press as "Plastic Pat"—stirs the crowd at the 1972 Republican National Convention in Miami Beach. (Ronald Reagan stands behind her in a white jacket). *Right:* The Nixons have a quiet family dinner in the second-floor Family Dining Room on election night in 1972.

Left: Pat Nixon takes her East Wing staff on a trip to Mount Vernon aboard the presidential yacht, the *Sequoia*. *Right:* Pat Nixon's 1973 surprise birthday party in the White House movie theater. Pat sits casually on the floor with her social secretary, Lucy Winchester, on the right and her director of correspondence, Gwen King, seated, wearing green.

Pat kisses Betty Ford, who would suddenly succeed her as first lady after President Nixon resigned. "My heavens, they've even rolled out the red carpet for us, isn't that something," a bitter Pat told Betty. "You'll see so many of those. . . . You'll get so you hate them."

First Lady Betty Ford gives a tour of the Fords' bedroom to Lady Bird Johnson and her family the day before she had a mastectomy. Not wanting to ruin their visit, she never told Lady Bird about the surgery. The only clue is the black suitcase at the foot of the bed that Betty had packed for the hospital.

The day before she left the White House, Betty Ford used her training as a Martha Graham dancer to jump up on the Cabinet Room table, where seats were often reserved for men only. A Ford family friend says President Ford "about fell off his chair" when he saw the photo for the first time.

Above: Rosalynn Carter hugs her husband, Jimmy, on election night, November 2, 1976. *Below:* The Carters have their weekly lunch in the Oval Office. "Whatever secrets there were," Carter's vice president, Walter Mondale, said, "she knew about all of them."

Lady Bird Johnson, who outlived her husband by thirty-four years, was the grande dame of the first ladies. She forged deep and lasting friendships with other first ladies, including Barbara Bush, with whom she is laughing at the 1981 dedication of the Gerald R. Ford Presidential Library, and with Hillary Clinton, whose husband she would later call upon for a political favor.

Rosalynn Carter, Lady Bird Johnson, and Betty Ford sat on rocking chairs at Lady Bird's Texas ranch in 1987. The unexpected sight of three former first ladies thrilled tourists driving by. "I have never seen so many camera lenses; it was just like a sea of windows filled with black circles," said an aide to Lady Bird. Lady Bird and Betty were so close that Lady Bird kept a small framed photo of Betty in her bedroom until her death.

four- or five-month-old little girl," she later recalled, with no hint of shame or regret. "It was the big outside world, and for once I was sort of the center of attention. I must say I enjoyed it." While her husband was back in his Texas district, Lady Bird stayed in Washington with her daughter and wrote to him: "Lynda is too active for my peace of mind, and she fell off the bed today." Years later, in a *Good Housekeeping* interview that she did with Betty Ford and Rosalynn Carter, Lady Bird was asked whether a woman's greatest influence is as a mother, especially a mother of sons. She sidestepped the question and replied, "It's a big plus that men have come to share in the lives of their children, in such necessary things as feeding them, changing their diapers, tending to them when they're sick." Once men began seeing the workload of motherhood, they would have greater respect for what women have been doing for centuries, she said.

After their father had decided not to seek reelection, Lynda and Luci Johnson were clearly upset during the pre-inaugural coffee with the Nixons in the Red Room. Their father seemed heartbroken. The sound of Vietnam protesters chanting, "Hey, hey, LBJ, how many kids did you kill today?" across the street in Lafayette Square had grown louder and louder over the years. Butler George Hannie once heard Johnson discussing Vietnam with aide Joe Califano. "Our kids are dying over there," he said. "We have to do something."

Nash Castro worked for the National Park Service and had collaborated with Lady Bird on her beautification project. Castro says that he and Lady Bird would often meet in the West Sitting Hall for working lunches and the First Lady would "wrestle up" hamburgers for them. But on at least one occasion the chants from the protesters across the street were too loud for them to carry on a conversation, so they moved to the Queens' Bedroom. But even there they could hear the angry voices. "Let's not hear any more of that," she said. "Let's move somewhere else." Finally, they ended up finishing their work in the Lincoln Bedroom. Chief Usher J. B. West recalls hearing Lady Bird whistling to herself as she walked along the deep, wide hallways of the mansion. She learned to build a cocoon of calm around herself over the years, one that made life with Lyndon and life in the White House more tolerable. "She had an escape valve," West says, "some secret little room inside her mind that she could adjourn to when things got tense."

Castro remembered the day before Johnson announced that he wouldn't be running for a second term as president. He was taking a quiet drive with Lady Bird, who had adopted beautification as her signature program, to see magnolia trees in a park near the White House. She spotted a patch of barren land and asked, "Nash, when are we going to beautify this rectangle?" "Well before your second term ends, Mrs. Johnson." She stared and stared at her good friend for so long that he started to get embarrassed. "We'll see," she said finally, knowing that she could not reveal a secret only she and a close circle of family knew: there would be no second term. After her husband's announcement, she was sitting in the backseat of a car with their social secretary, Bess Abell, as they were being driven out of the White House's Northwest Gate just as the sun was setting. "Oh, Mrs. Johnson, are you going to miss all this?" Abell asked her. Lady Bird replied, "Yes, like a front tooth. But there's nothing in the world that would make me pay the price of another ticket of admission."

Unlike the Ford children, who were secretly happy that their father lost because they believed the strain of a second term shortens presidents' lives, the Johnson daughters knew it would be hard for their father to live a more private life. Luci and Lynda wept during Nixon's inauguration at the Capitol and had to leave to go to the restroom to cry privately. President Johnson retired to the Texas White House and lived only four more years, until he died of a heart attack in 1973 at age sixty-four.

WATCHING YOUR CHILDREN suffer for choices you and your husband made is extraordinarily painful. The Nixons were a very close family. "The women's libbers are not going to like what I'm going to say now, they're not going to like it at all," President Nixon said, long after his resignation. "Her [Pat Nixon's] greatest legacy are her children. She's been a magnificent mother. . . . Patricia and Julie are remarkable young ladies. I was away a lot and she certainly gets the credit for that." The Nixons developed a sort of bunker mentality, hunkering down during Watergate and the Vietnam War protests. Julie and Tricia Nixon worshipped their father. Once, Tricia called the White House in the evening to say that she was in the middle of a political argument with someone and she needed to talk to her father to get the facts. "Dick was out swimming," Pat recalled. "The poor man got out of the pool and took the phone to answer her questions. Tricia called back later to say, 'I won. Thanks a lot.'" Pat said the President was happy for the call for two reasons: she thanked him, she wanted the facts, and she wanted to win. "That's three reasons, I guess."

Tricia Nixon learned quickly how constraining life in the White House would be when, on the night of her father's first inauguration, the twenty-two-year-old went to the family's quarters on the second floor after the inaugural parade and put her hand on the doorknob of her new room and heard a voice: "Do not try to open the doors. They are locked." A Secret Service agent emerged from the shadows and opened the door for her.

The Nixons would soon learn to find their escape at Camp David, the rural presidential retreat in Maryland sixty-two miles north of Washington, where they took long walks and enjoyed a sense of privacy. The barbed-wire and high-voltage electric fences made it so secure that Secret Service agents did not have to trail them quite so closely, which was a relief. Pat often declined trips to their Winter White House compound in Key Biscayne, Florida, because Secret Service officers would get into the water whenever they did and the Nixons felt that their voices had to be kept low so that no agents could listen in on their conversations. Pat would sometimes ask agents to carry scuba gear when they walked along the beach with the family so that they would not look so obvious.

Of course the White House is a magical place that offers surreal experiences almost daily for the families who live there. Tricia remembers watching as Americans Neil Armstrong and Edwin "Buzz" Aldrin became the first people to walk on the moon on July 20, 1969. "I remember being in the West Sitting Hall with my mother and sister and if you know what that's like you can look out of the window and see the Oval Office, so we actually watched the TV but we also watched the Oval Office so we could see my father speaking to the astronauts on the moon both in the Oval Office and on TV."

Both Tricia and Julie were married and spending the holiday at their homes with their husbands during the Christmas of 1972, when President Nixon started the biggest bombing campaign against North Vietnam, dropping more than 20,000 tons of explosives. This decision weighed heavily on the President, and because it was the first Christmas without either of their daughters it was a painful time for him and for the First Lady. Secret Service agents surrounded their Key Biscayne home as security threats grew. When Pat suggested they open presents on Christmas morning to lighten the mood, the President grumbled gloomily, "Later." The presents were sent back to Washington untouched.

The Watergate investigation dragged on for more than two years, and by the winter and spring of 1974, it was totally eclipsing the presidency. The Nixons sought refuge with their daughters. At least twice a week the President and the First Lady visited Julie and her husband, David Eisenhower, at their white-brick house on Armat Drive in Bethesda, Maryland, about a half hour outside Washington. The Nixons brought dinner prepared by the White House chefs and the family settled into a familiar routine of pre-dinner drinks on the suburban house's glassed-in porch. Before dinner, the President would light the fire and Pat would try to cheer him up by pointing out what flowers were in bloom, doing anything she could to avoid the suffocating tension in the room. At the height of the Watergate investigation, the President talked wistfully about the early days when he and Pat first started dating. For the President's son-in-law David the routine was especially painful because as a student at George Washington University Law School he overheard his professors and other students who knew people on the Senate Watergate Committee talking about the incriminating evidence against his father-in-law. He was often silent during these dinners, not knowing what to say.

Pat was a devoted mother and wife, and the West Wing staff cut off her newspapers in a patronizing effort to shield her from the painful headlines. It was heart-wrenching for her to see her daughters face angry protesters who blamed their father for mishandling the war in Vietnam and for bombing Cambodia, and how Julie, in particular, stood up for her father during the two years of bitter debate surrounding the Watergate break-in. The Nixon daughters occasionally confided in the residence staffers, the butlers, maids, and doormen who they felt were the only people who did not judge them. "You see beyond politics, you see beyond the story, you see the true person," Tricia said. In the elevator with Doorman Preston Bruce, Julie would ask him, with tears in her eyes, "How can they say such awful things about my father?" "Never mind," he told her. "Ignore all that. You know politics. It'll all come out right in the end." As the scandal raged on Julie confronted her father for being despondent and not realizing how much her mother was trying to do to help him. "It's hard for her, too," she told him. In a biography she wrote about her mother, Julie admitted feeling a pang of guilt as she remembered how she vented her frustrations to Pat about criticism of her father. "She had so many concerns and adjustments of her own, and to see her daughter under stress was surely the greatest strain of all."

Because her sister, Tricia, was private and her mother too beleaguered, it was Julie who came to her father's defense so often in the press, and it was Julie whom her parents leaned on most heavily. At times her mother seemed to want to reverse their roles. Julie had long helped her mother escape the confines of the White House by taking long walks with her on Roosevelt Island, a small, densely wooded island in the Potomac River about a ten-minute drive from the White House. After dinner they sometimes took walks together in downtown Washington near the executive mansion, in a neighborhood that was largely deserted at night at that time because people thought it was too dangerous. Pat wore a scarf to cover her blond hair during their long walks.

Julie's valiant attempts to help calm her mother did not end after her parents left Washington. A few weeks before her father was set to testify before a special grand jury on Watergate in June 1975, Julie called her mother. "Why don't you come out here [to visit us in California]?" Pat asked her. Julie told her that David was studying for his second-year law school exams and she needed to stay in Washington to be with him. "You have only one person to take care of there but two broken people here," Pat said.

Pat was devastated by Bob Woodward and Carl Bernstein's book *The Final Days*, which described the Nixons' marriage as loveless and alleged that she was a heavy drinker. She tried to get a copy of it but her husband was adamant that she not read it. Finally, she borrowed a copy from one of his secretaries and that same day she suffered a stroke. The President blamed the book for her stroke but, in truth, the decades of being a political spouse and the humiliation of watching her husband resign were stressful enough. David Eisenhower said in a 1973 interview, "She [Pat] is a shoulder to everyone—but whose shoulder does she lean on?" In the White House, Pat hardly ever canceled events, but she became more and more anxious as Watergate dragged on. Before Nixon's resignation, Pat's anxiety increased. In the elevator on her way to meet visitors she asked Doorman Preston Bruce, "Bruce, do you think these people will be friendly?" He tried to put her at ease: "They seem *very* friendly, Mrs. Nixon."

In the spring of 1970, at the height of the antiwar protests, when the President sent American troops into Cambodia and four students at Ohio's Kent State University were killed by members of the Ohio National Guard, the President agonized over whether to go to Julie's graduation from Smith College. She did not want him to go and was willing to miss it herself if it meant the ceremony would be turned into a giant protest against her father. The White House knew that antiwar activists Jerry Rubin, Rennie Davis, and others were organizing anti-Nixon demonstrations around the event. Julie wrote a note to Nixon's adviser John Ehrlichman at the end of April, asking her father not to come. "I truly think the day will be a disaster if he comes," she wrote. "The temper up here is ugly." She mentioned a rally with thousands of people chanting "Fuck Julie and David Eisenhower." The head of Julie's Secret Service detail warned her against attending her own graduation and David against attending his. Antiwar organizers said they could bring upwards of two hundred thousand people to campus if President Nixon showed up. The President decided not to attend. On June 6, the Nixons had a private family party at Camp David and President Nixon was in an unusually upbeat mood, toasting his daughter, but Pat was quiet. She knew the small dinner could not make up for Julie having to miss her college graduation because of the public life her husband had chosen, a life that she grudgingly accepted.

It wasn't only the Vietnam War that weighed heavily on her husband. During Watergate, Pat watched helplessly as he became more and more despondent. Nixon could be found late at night wandering the halls of the White House and talking to portraits of the presidents before him. His family was concerned that he might commit suicide. "You fellows, in your business," the President said to his chief of staff, the four-star General Alexander Haig, "you have a way of handling problems like this. Somebody leaves a pistol in the drawer." After one speech in which he defended his handling of Watergate, Pat, Tricia, David, and the President's private secretary Rose Mary Woods answered phones while he retreated to the Lincoln Sitting Room, his favorite hiding place in the mansion. There he sat by the fire and cranked up the air-conditioning. "I hope I don't wake up in the morning," he mumbled.

But Julie refused to give in. At the top of her calendar for October 26, 1973, she wrote: "Fight, fight, fight." On May 11, 1974, she stood in her father's place during a press conference, desperate to defend him. "He is stronger now than he ever has been in his determination to see this through." A reporter said that he was not sure what she was doing there in place of her father, "since in our system we do not hold the sins of the fathers against the following generations." Julie replied, "I have seen what my father has gone through, and I am so proud of him that I would never be afraid to come out here. . . . I am not trying to answer questions for him. I am just trying to pray for enough courage to meet his courage." Julie's husband, David, worried that she was getting too involved. As hard as it was to watch, Pat wanted her daughter to support the family. Pat confronted David: "Why aren't you giving Julie support?"

Before President Nixon resigned in August 1974, he went to Camp David and asked his family not to come with him. But the next morning, when he walked into the living room of Aspen Lodge, the President's cabin on the sprawling retreat, he was surprised to see Tricia sitting there. She and David and Julie had been up almost all night and had decided that one of them had to go and offer the President support. Tricia had arrived at Camp David with a Secret Service escort early that foggy morning to tell him how much she and the family loved him, and to encourage him to answer the public cry that his advisers, Haldeman and Ehrlichman, had to go. (Even the residence staff disliked the duo, Butler Herman Thompson said: "There was something about Haldeman and Ehrlichman that you could look at them and you knew that they would never have respect for a person like you.") The President asked Tricia to stay all day and keep him company, but she knew she had to leave him alone to make the decision.

Pat's daughters were entirely consumed by Watergate. Just days before their father announced his resignation Julie wrote him a note: "Dear Daddy, I love you. Whatever you do I will support. I am very proud of you. Please wait a week or even ten days before you make this decision. Go through the fire just a little bit longer. You are so strong!"

———

THE WHITE HOUSE is a wonderland for children: Sasha and Malia Obama invite friends over and have sleepovers on air mattresses in the third-floor Solarium; Chelsea Clinton sunbathed on the window ledge of her bedroom until members of the press told the chief usher and he demanded that she come down; the Johnson daughters used the Solarium as a teenage hideaway complete with a soda fountain; all the children eventually discover the secret stairway that connects the second and third floors. The Ford children wore jeans and put their feet up on furniture until their mother admonished them, "Don't put your feet up there! That's Jefferson's table." Betty insisted on manners once they got to the White House. She wanted her family to step up to the level of the White House, not to bring the White House standards down. She spoke as honestly about the trials of motherhood as Lady Bird had. "God bless nursery schools," she wrote in her memoir. "I must say it was a joy to have half a day without two little boys running around pulling out all the pots and pans." Because of her husband's travel as a congressman, Betty had been left to raise their four children—including three rowdy boys—alone, sometimes for more than half the year. Ford's long absences were inexcusable, said Bonnie Angelo, a reporter who covered the Fords for *Time* magazine. "She was really boxed in and she was not a spirit that was intended to be boxed in," Angelo said of Betty. In the last year that Ford was House minority leader, he attended some two hundred political events and was away from home 258 days. "I couldn't say, 'Wait till your father comes home,'" Betty recalled. "Their father wasn't going to come home for maybe a week." It was Betty who took the kids to the dentist, to doctor's visits, to football practice. Ford aide Robert Hartmann eventually caved to pressure from Betty to curtail her husband's schedule when he became vice president. "We have to look at this differently now," Hartmann told the schedulers. The sheer exhaustion of the daily routine weighed heavily on Betty, and later she would say in an interview with *Good Housekeeping* that she hoped men would begin to share the workload in greater numbers with their wives. Like many political wives of the era, she was "more often political widow than political wife," said journalist Cokie Roberts. And like many stay-at-home mothers, Betty went through periods of loneliness and bitterness.

The Fords never had to endure a bruising campaign to get to the White House. Ford was selected by President Nixon to replace the disgraced Vice President Spiro Agnew, who was forced to resign because of tax evasion charges. In fact, Ford had only ever stood for election in Michigan's Ionia and Kent counties. When the family moved into the White House Betty could not understand why the maids and butlers were so quiet around her. She thought they might not like her. She found out that Pat Nixon had preferred that they stay in the background. When she redecorated the Oval Office she told her press secretary, Sheila Rabb Weidenfeld, that she wanted to replace the blue and gold colors because they "seemed to reflect a kind of Imperial Presidency." She redecorated with darker earth tones and even added houseplants.

Susan Ford recalled that her family was truly like middle-class families around the country: "My parents, when we were kids, if you picked a fight, you fought your fight. They would not go in and break up a fight between us kids. If somebody got hurt that was different." The Ford kids wore clothes from Sears and JCPenney. "When you've got four kids and you've got to put four kids through college you have to save your pennies when you can." The first time Susan got a Lord & Taylor dress was when her dad became Vice President. The Fords did not even have a separate dining room table at their Alexandria house, so the kids would cram next to each other at the kitchen table where there was a lazy Susan. The three boys always grabbed the food before it went around the second time to Susan, who was the only girl and the youngest. Susan says that when Jack was a teenager, he would pick fights with his mother. "There was no father there to say, 'Jack Ford, stop that.'" Susan would end up going to her mother after one of their fights at dinner in an effort to calm her down, and her brother Mike would go up to Jack's bedroom and tell him that he needed to apologize. Betty made no secret of her unhappiness at having to raise the children without a father much of the time. The future president felt guilty about his long absences and would try to make it up to her by buying her jewelry. But his time was what she wanted most.

———

IT IS IMPOSSIBLE to completely shelter a child who grows up in the White House. Nine-year-old Amy Carter took one look at the reporters lined up to watch her leave the executive mansion to go to her first day of school at Thaddeus Stevens Elementary and asked, "Mom, do we still have to be nice to them?" The press swarmed around the Carters' car as they arrived at the school with Amy looking miserable. President Carter had been on the school board in Georgia and the Carters remembered how, when schools were desegregated, people took their children out and sent them to private schools. It was important for them that Amy be exposed to people from different economic and racial backgrounds. "We decided to try to promote the public schools," Rosalynn said in an interview. "The kids that she went to school with were mostly the sons and daughters of the staff that worked for us. I think there were twenty-eight different languages in her class."

Though Amy ate hot dogs and beans for lunch, just like her classmates, she was clearly different. Her bedroom at the White House had once been Caroline Kennedy's, and she did her homework at Eleanor Roosevelt's old desk. During her first week of school her teacher made her stay inside the classroom with her Secret Service agents during recess because the other students were all crowding around her on the playground. She was so unhappy with the arrangement that they soon let her play outside. The school set up a special office for her two Secret Service agents so they could stay out of sight. Amy was the Carters' fourth child and their only daughter, and Rosalynn insists that life in the White House felt normal to her. "It was what she knew because she was three when we moved to the Governor's Mansion."

At the Governor's Mansion in Georgia there was even less privacy, Rosalynn said. There, the only way to get to the kitchen was to go through the tourists. Once, Rosalynn said, she had a momentary lapse and "stepped out in my bathrobe" in front of a crowd of visitors. Public life was the only life Amy had ever known. "Everybody made a big fuss over the baby when they saw her, she got to where she'd just walk straight through and look straight ahead. . . . I remember when she went to school the first day in Washington everybody was so distressed because Amy looked so lonely. That was just her normal life." Soon the other kids got used to Amy and she would bring home friends like Claudia Sanchez, whose father was a cook at the Chilean Embassy. They had sleepovers in the Lincoln Bedroom and listened for President Lincoln's ghost. They even slept outside in a tree house on the South Lawn on balmy summer nights.

Rosalynn said that it helped that they brought Amy's nanny, Mary Prince, with them to the White House. Rosalynn first met Prince when she was a prisoner brought to work at the Governor's Mansion through a trustee program. Prince was serving a life sentence for murder. ("I was in the wrong place at the wrong time," Prince says. "She was totally innocent," Rosalynn said in an interview.) Prince was twenty-seven years old when she began working at the Governor's Mansion taking care of three-year-old Amy. The two played endless games of hide-and-seek, tickled each other, and climbed trees. At bedtime, Prince rubbed Amy's back and helped her fall asleep. Sometimes she would lie down with her and sing "Swing Low, Sweet Chariot." When Carter's term as governor ended in 1975 and the family moved back to Plains, it seemed Prince's Cinderella story was over, too, and she returned to prison.

But Rosalynn did not forget her, even after becoming the wife of the Democratic nominee for president, and visited Prince at the Fulton County Jail and the Atlanta Work Release Center, where Prince worked as a cook. When the Carters moved into the White House, even though Prince was not eligible for parole for another three months, she traveled to Washington for the inauguration and spent two nights in the White House. She went to an inaugural ball wearing a gown she had sewn from velvet given to her by her fellow female prisoners. Right before she left to go back to Georgia, the new First Lady asked her, "How would you like to work in this big old place?" One letter from the Carters to the Georgia prison officials, and Mary was free to work as Amy's nanny. An unusual agreement was made for President Carter to serve as her parole officer. Prince moved into a bedroom on the third floor and was paid $6,004 a year. To this day, Mary still takes care of the Carters and lives three blocks away from them. She even helped Amy when she became a mother. "If anybody gets sick or needs her she's always there," Rosalynn said of her longtime friend. "We couldn't travel and do the things we're doing now without Mary taking care of things back home."

In the White House, Mary helped make Amy's life more predictable. President Carter woke up every day at 6:00 a.m. (two glasses of orange juice were always on his bedside table when he awoke) and was in the Oval Office by 6:30 a.m. Before he left their bedroom, Carter would put one of the glasses of juice on Rosalynn's bedside table. Rosalynn, like so many mothers, would wake up their daughter and run her bath, then turn on the Suzuki violin tape of the song she was being taught. Rosalynn remembers a time when Amy was supposed to attend a White House reception for a conservation program for children set up by the Department of Energy. Hundreds of children were waiting to see her on the South Lawn, but she had just had her braces tightened that morning and her teeth hurt so much that she was crying. Rosalynn brought Amy to see the White House physician, Dr. William Lukash, who put drops in her eyes so that it would not look like she had been crying when she went outside to make her appearance. Amy often got sick of making such an effort, and in public she would reach a limit after giving several autographs, so it was decided that she would not give any. Sometimes, when people would recognize her in public, she would pretend the closest Secret Service agent was her father.

Prince started taking swimming lessons because Amy loved to swim and the nanny wanted to be prepared. One early evening she walked by the White House swimming pool, where Rosalynn was doing laps. "Come on in!" the First Lady said playfully. "I don't have a bathing suit," Mary told her. "Just dive in in your uniform!" So she kicked off her shoes and jumped in in her white pantsuit and showed the First Lady what she had learned in her swimming classes. "I think that was the most fun time that I really had. Just me and the First Lady together out there swimming."

Mary insisted that Amy was never spoiled. "She was always an independent little girl and she's an independent woman. . . . She was not a spoiled brat, she really never tried to get her way. She was just a young kid having fun." But reporters were appalled when Amy brought a book to a state dinner. As Rosalynn explains, "The reason was, we were married twenty-one years when Amy was born. And she was born in '67 and Jimmy was elected governor in '70. And she got to where she didn't want to go with us because all she did was go listen to political speeches. And so we started letting her take a book or take a coloring book just to make her want to go. And she, being a child growing up with adults, she learned to be just alone in her own little world no matter where she was." At President Carter's inauguration a family friend who had been Amy's teacher in Plains was able to fish a book out of Amy's coat pocket before they descended the stairs of the Capitol to take their seats. Amy had planned to keep it handy in case she was bored during her father's inaugural address.

———

NOT ALL FIRST families had uncomplicated relationships with their children. After undergoing a mastectomy in 1987, Nancy Reagan got a phone call from the last person she was expecting to hear from: her daughter, Patti Davis. Patti was an outspoken Democrat who had not voted for her father in the 1980 presidential election, and she had not spoken with her mother in two years. Patti called her only after Nancy's brother urged her to. It was an awkward conversation. "I'm sorry," Patti told Nancy, whose voice, she said, sounded weak. "If you decide to have reconstruction I know several good plastic surgeons in Los Angeles."

There was a long pause. "I don't want to have more surgery," Nancy told her.

"Oh, well, I just thought—if you decided down the line . . ." Patti's voice trailed off. Nancy was offended and said later, "I longed to hear something more comforting about what I had just gone through."

Ten days later, in another blow, Nancy's mother died. Patti did not go to her own grandmother's funeral—she said she had travel plans that she could not change. Nancy's assistant, Jane Erkenbeck, is still upset at the way Patti treated her mother during such a difficult time. "No call, no card, no flowers—nothing." Erkenbeck was the one who had to tell Nancy that Patti would not be attending the funeral. "She was sad. . . . Patti missed many wonderful opportunities with her parents being President and First Lady." Nancy's office issued a statement that said Patti's decision not to attend her grandmother's funeral was "another crack in an already broken heart."

But the relationship between the Reagans and their children had been strained almost from the start. Nancy dedicated her memoir, *My Turn*, "To Ronnie, who always understood. And to my children, who I hope will understand." Patti resented her parents' closeness and how it got in the way of their relationship with their children. "Ronald and Nancy Reagan are two halves of a circle," she said, "together, they are complete, and their children float outside." She said that her mother was physically abusive and her father was emotionally distant. Her brother, Ron, had a better relationship with them but butted heads with them over politics.

Maureen Reagan, who was the first child of Ronald Reagan and his first wife, Jane Wyman, and Michael Reagan, who was their adopted son, were treated like outsiders by Nancy, Patti said. After their father was shot in a 1981 assassination attempt, they sat in stony silence on the flight to Washington, realizing how little they all knew each other. They had not called each other when they heard the news and Nancy had not called them.

Patti visited the White House only a handful of times when her father was President. "I realized that my parents had brought with them the same hushed atmosphere that always waited beyond the front door of our home. . . . My mother's footsteps were louder than my father's, more determined." When news of her overnight stay at a hotel with celebrity Kris Kristofferson somehow reached her mother, who must have found out from the Secret Service agents who were assigned to watch Patti's every move, Nancy was vicious. "I realize you have a long history of promiscuity but your father is President now and I think you could manage to be considerate of that fact."

BARBARA BUSH, WHO passed away in April 2018, was the first woman since Abigail Adams to be both the wife and the mother of U.S. presidents. Barbara was also in the delicate position of being the mother of two sons with presidential ambitions. Worthington White, a six-foot-two former tackle at Virginia Tech who worked as a White House usher from 1980 to 2012, rarely becomes emotional. But when he talks about seeing Barbara Bush and her family, he gets misty-eyed. The fiercely devoted mother, grandmother, and great-grandmother was celebrating her elder son's second inauguration as president in 2005 with most of their large family at a brunch in the second-floor Family Dining Room. She was also in the odd position of comforting her other son, Jeb, who was governor of Florida at the time. White saw Barbara standing in the hallway outside the Queens' Bedroom and the Lincoln Bedroom with her husband, President George H. W. Bush; Jeb and Jeb's wife, Columba. Barbara looked concerned, with tears welling up in her eyes as she talked to Jeb and his wife. Here she was, with one son celebrating a second presidential victory down the hall and another son going through a political crisis.

The Bushes had been shocked when Jeb lost his first run for governor in Florida in 1994, the same year that his brother, George W., won the governorship in Texas. A stunned President Bush told the press at the time, "The joy is in Texas, but our hearts are in Florida." Jeb asked his mother after his defeat, "How long is it going to hurt?" She recalled that that conversation "killed me." Barbara and George H. W. Bush were at Jeb's side when he ran again in 1998 and won. George W. also ran again in Texas that year and won in a landslide, but it is clear whom the Bushes thought they needed to be with that election night.

Though it is not certain what they were discussing on that day in 2005, the Terri Schiavo case was raging in Florida. Jeb had become deeply involved in the emotional battle that was consuming the country over whether to remove Schiavo's feeding tube. She had been in a persistent vegetative state for fifteen years. He got the legislature to pass "Terri's Law" ordering that the feeding tube remain, but the Florida Supreme Court struck down the law as unconstitutional. Bush's lawyer appealed for a hearing in the U.S. Supreme Court but four days later the Court announced it would not hear the case, clearing the way for Schiavo's husband, Michael, to order the removal of the feeding tube. Barbara was telling Jeb that he had accomplished so much and had many more accomplishments ahead of him. "She was giving him emotional support, almost as if he had lost a big fight," White recalled. "It touches me all these years later."

Five decades earlier, Barbara had faced every mother's nightmare when their second child, three-year-old daughter Robin, was diagnosed with leukemia. The Bushes' son Jeb was only a few weeks old when Robin woke up one morning in 1953 and told her mother, "I don't know what to do this morning. I may go out and lie on the grass and watch the cars go by, or I might just stay in bed." When the Bushes brought Robin to see their doctor to find out why she was so tired, they were told she had the highest white blood cell count the doctor had ever seen. When they asked what they could do, they were told to take her home and in three weeks she would be gone. They would not let that happen without a fight, and the very next day they took Robin to New York and left George W. and his baby brother Jeb with friends.

In the end it was Barbara who stayed in New York with her sick daughter while George H. W. Bush flew back and forth to Midland, Texas, where he had just started a new business. Robin was given aggressive treatment by doctors at Memorial–Sloan Kettering hospital, which gave her seven more months to live but only after painful bone marrow tests and blood transfusions. Barbara became friends with other parents who were keeping vigil for their children, exposing her to people from different walks of life, such as one woman who had to commute every day on the bus from the Bronx to be by her son Joey's bedside, unlike Barbara, who stayed at her in-laws' elegant apartment on Sutton Place. "I loved that courageous lady, and I loved Joey. God bless him," Barbara wrote in her memoir. Barbara taped photos of Robin's brothers on her headboard at the hospital. Robin called her big brother George "superman."

People didn't know very much about leukemia then, and

some of the Bushes' friends were afraid it was contagious. It was Barbara who was by Robin's side, holding her hands and combing her hair during her last days. She never cried in front of her daughter and told anyone who came to visit, including her husband and her mother-in-law, that they were not allowed to cry in front of her, either. She did not want her daughter to know how sick she was. "George and his mother are so softhearted, I had to order them out of the hospital room most of the time," Barbara says. When he became emotional George H. W. Bush would excuse himself and tell his daughter that he had to go to the restroom. He and Barbara wondered if Robin thought "he had the weakest bladder in the world" because he left so often. Barbara recalled, "He just had the most tender heart." She was only twenty-eight years old when she had to make a quick decision: perform a scary operation to stop her daughter's internal bleeding or let her die. She could not reach her husband as he traveled to New York, so she decided to let the doctors operate. Robin never made it out of that operation and died just before her fourth birthday. "I saw that little body, I saw her spirit go," Barbara says. Both parents held her one last time.

Barbara had been unbelievably stoic throughout her daughter's battle with leukemia, but when she sat in an upstairs bedroom at her in-laws' house and heard guests gathering to attend her daughter's memorial service she allowed herself to give in to her grief. "For one who allowed no tears before her death, I fell apart," she recalled. "And time after time during the next six months, George would put me together again." Their friends tried to make them feel better, but really there was nothing they could say. Barbara was furious when she found one friend actually practicing her most grave expressions in the mirror before she went in to see her. "At least it wasn't your firstborn and a boy at that," the visitor said callously. When Barbara exploded in anger about such insensitivity, her husband helped her. "George pointed out that it wasn't easy for them and that I should be patient," she remembered. "He was right. I just needed somebody to blame." For a long time no one would speak of Robin, and that made Barbara even more upset. It was Robin's older brother George W. who started to mention her casually. Once, at a football game, he told his father that he wished he were Robin. When his father asked him why, he answered, "I bet she can see the game better from up there than we can here." Barbara relied on her elder son to cheer her up and help relieve her unbearable sadness. One day she heard him tell a friend that he couldn't go play outside because he had to stay inside and keep his mother company. It was then that she knew she had to try to move on for the sake of her children. "I was thinking, 'Well, I'm being there for him,'" Barbara said later. "But the truth was he was being there for me."

The Bushes donated Robin's body to scientific research, and they are happy to see that so much progress has been made on leukemia. "Robin to me is a joy. She's like an angel to me, and she's not a sadness or a sorrow," Barbara said, remembering "those little fat arms around my neck." George H. W. Bush has told family members that when he passes away Robin will be the first person he expects to see. His wife was sure of it. But it was never easy to talk about Robin, and when the subject came up Barbara said, "We're all fine now," clearly wanting to move on from the topic.

───────

HILLARY SAW MORE of her daughter in the White House than ever before. When she was working as a law partner at the Rose Law Firm in Little Rock, Arkansas, and Bill was governor, they had a series of live-in babysitters who were on call twenty-four hours a day, seven days a week. When Chelsea asked for her mother as a toddler, she would learn to answer her own questions with "Mommy go make 'peech." In the 1992 presidential campaign Hillary did homework with her daughter by fax and talked to her every night on the phone from her hotel room. Once they were in the White House, the Clintons turned a second-floor Butler's Pantry into an eat-in kitchen so that they could occasionally eat together informally around a small square table. One night when Chelsea was sick, Hillary said she knew then that they had made the right decision to put in the small kitchen. "I went to make her some scrambled eggs and, you know, everybody went crazy. Oh, we'll bring an omelet from downstairs. I said no, I just want to make some scrambled eggs and applesauce and feed her what I would feed her if we were living anywhere else in America." The Fords' son Steve said that he felt sorry for Chelsea being an only child growing up in the giant house alone under the glare of the media spotlight. He wrote her a note giving her advice: befriend your Secret Service agents. When Barbara Bush gave Hillary a tour of the residence she recommended that Hillary bring a cousin or friend of Chelsea to live with her for a year to keep her company.

Clinton aides say Hillary has a warm, maternal side. Hillary's aide Shirley Sagawa started working at the White House weeks after she gave birth to her first child. She got the call from Hillary's chief of staff, Melanne Verveer, asking if she could join Clinton's team and it was a job she could not pass up. Before she lined up child care, she came into her office, which was adjacent to Hillary's in the West Wing, with her son in a stroller. (She jokes now that he was probably one of the only babies who had to go through a metal detector.) "He had just woken up from a nap and was just howling, and all of a sudden she's standing in my door and there's the baby crying." Sagawa, who was on an important call, was sure that Hillary would tell her that it wasn't working out, but instead she took Sagawa's son and walked him around the halls of the West Wing to calm him down while his mother finished the call. Sagawa says Hillary gave her some advice: spend time with your child when he's little. "When they're little they're always around and you can talk to them when you want to talk to them. When they're older, if you're not around them very much, you may miss the time when they're ready to open up to you in the car about what's bothering them . . . because it's on their agenda, and not yours." Hillary always wanted to be around Chelsea as much as her schedule would allow, taking family bike rides along the Chesapeake & Ohio Canal in Washington and attending school fund-raisers. Chelsea may not have really needed her help with homework, but Hillary often offered it, just to spend time with her at the end of the day.

Even though Hillary tried to protect Chelsea from becoming spoiled, it wasn't always possible. When they were in the Arkansas Governor's Mansion the Clintons' lives changed and they began to have more in common with celebrities than with friends from their former lives. Today, in Little Rock, a fifteen-minute drive east on President Clinton Avenue takes you from the Hillary Rodham Clinton Children's Library straight to Bill and Hillary Clinton National Airport. Mary Ann Campbell, a friend of Hillary's from Little Rock, remembers having lunch with her and their friend actress Mary Steenburgen. Hillary told them a story about Chelsea, who was in grade school at the time when her father was governor. Chelsea was playing with another child but started fighting about a game and said, "If you don't do that, then I'm going to have my daddy call the National Guard on you." Hillary overheard her and was horrified. She told Chelsea, "You can't say that!"

By almost all accounts, Hillary and Bill raised a remarkably unspoiled daughter who was quick to write thank-you notes to White House residence staffers for things like pretty flower arrangements in her room. At a birthday dinner in Jackson Hole, Wyoming, for one of Hillary's aides, Chelsea was given a commemorative Smokey Bear doll from a National Park Service worker. Chelsea would not leave until she got the name and address of the person who gave it to her so she could send a thank-you note.

———

MOTHERHOOD UNITES ALL of these women, no matter how different they are. Michelle Obama and Hillary Clinton do not have much in common. Friends say that Michelle never wanted to be a public person and that she signed up for eight years and cannot wait for them to end. That is clearly not the case for Hillary, who is trying for a second time to get back into the White House. One thing they do have in common is their deep relationship with their mothers and their own commitment to being good mothers.

"It hurt so much when I lost my mother, I know how it feels," Hillary told a friend whose mother had recently passed away. "I will *never* get over it." In a 2015 interview with ABC News, Hillary got emotional when she mentioned her mother, Dorothy Rodham, who died in 2011. Dorothy grew up in poverty and at eight years old she was sent from Chicago to California to live with her grandparents after her parents divorced. "She told me every day you've got to get up and fight for what you believe in, no matter how hard it is. I think about her a lot, I miss her a lot. I wish she were here with me."

Michelle has a strong relationship with her mother, Marian Robinson, whom she credits with helping her family stay grounded in the White House. She says she felt like a single parent when her husband was elected to the Illinois State Senate. He was typically home in Chicago only from Thursday night until Monday afternoon: the rest of the week he was in Springfield. "At times it can be wearing, because you're on twenty-four/seven. Part of what we've had to figure out is what kind of support do I need to make my life less hectic? I'd like the support to come from Dad, but when it can't, I just really need the support. It doesn't really matter whether it's him or not as long as our kids are happy and they feel like they are connected to him. So I have to get over the fact that it's not him. It's Mom, friends, babysitters."

Unlike Hillary, whose infamous cookie comment offended stay-at-home mothers, Michelle frames her struggles with work-life balance and motherhood in a more subtle way by urging women to prioritize their own happiness. She admits that there were times when she felt lonely. "I am sitting there with a new baby, angry, tired, and out of shape. The baby is up for that four o'clock feeding. And my husband is lying there, sleeping. That's when it struck [me] that if I wasn't there, he would eventually have to wake up [and take care of the girls]. It worked. I would get home from the gym, and the girls would be up and fed. That was something I had to do for me."

When she interviewed for her job at the University of Chicago Medical Center she was on maternity leave and still breast-feeding her newborn daughter. She didn't have a babysitter so she took her daughter to the interview. "Sasha slept through it, thank goodness." Michelle's longtime Chicago hairstylist Michael "Rahni" Flowers said that she's like her mother, who is a firm disciplinarian. "All they have to do is give you that eye—it will turn you into stone, it will stop you in your tracks." There's always a bowl of candy at the front of the hair salon, and instead of grabbing a handful, like most kids, Sasha and Malia would always ask first, "Mom, is it okay if I have a piece of candy?" Like any mom, she would sometimes have to bring her two daughters with her when she was getting her hair done. When they were really little, she would let other ladies hold them while she was getting her hair washed, but once she got under the dryer she'd hold the baby on her lap. "It was such a beautiful thing," Flowers says, "and that's the life she gave up."

Former White House Chief Usher Admiral Stephen Rochon remembers that on his birthday, Malia came into the Usher's Office followed by her mother, who was carrying a birthday cake for him. The Obama girls were unfailingly polite, Rochon says. "Malia would be heading upstairs to the residence and I'd ask, 'How was your day?' and she'd reply, 'How was *your* day?'" At their Chicago home, Michelle had rules that are for the upstairs bedrooms, where more silliness is allowed, and rules for the downstairs, where grown-ups congregate. Even in the White House she allows her daughters only one hour of television a day, and only after homework is done.

When it comes to parenting, Michelle admires Hillary's ability to raise Chelsea and her demands for privacy for her only child. "You can tell from one conversation with Chelsea that she's a mature, decent, well-balanced young lady. [The Clintons] did something right," she said. Michelle made it clear to her husband's advisers that she expected to have a family dinner most nights at 6:30 p.m., and she and her girls are rarely ever seen in the West Wing. They see their father much more now than before when he was in the Senate and commuting between Chicago and Washington, or while he was going back and forth from Chicago to Springfield. "Being in the White House has made our family life more 'normal' than it's ever been," the President wrote in a column for *More* magazine. "To our surprise, moving to the White House was really the first time since the girls were born that we've been able to gather as a family almost every night."

Michelle has kept a strict rule in the White House: the second and third floors are the family area. The Obamas are the first first family to turn off the lights in the living quarters themselves. "She treats it just as if it were her house," says Usher Worthington White. "She doesn't need anybody going up and turning the lights off for her, she wants privacy." Before the Obamas, at night an usher would drop off a folder of work from the West Wing for the President on the reading table on the backside of a sofa, outside his bedroom. The folder was clearly in view when he and his wife walked out of their bedroom—the President's papers were to the left and the First Lady's were always to the right. Michelle did not like that system because it implies that there is always business going on, even in the most intimate parts of the residence. She issued a mandate that all of her husband's work material goes in his office in the Treaty Room because that's where business is conducted. Reading material for her from the East Wing is placed in an ante office. It's a small change, but it represents a whole different way of thinking: she wants everyone on staff to know that this is the family's home, not an extension of the Oval Office.

She misses being able to spend time with her girls outside the White House without being swarmed by photographers and reporters. A close Obama aide has a child around the age of one of the Obamas' daughters. During soccer season, the First Lady teased him that he would probably be tied up all weekend doing carpools. "Yeah, probably," he said with a shrug. "I'm sure you don't miss it." She replied, "Oh, you'd be surprised."

Marian Robinson lives in a suite on the third floor, and not long after she moved in she called the Usher's Office asking to be served the food the staff eats; she was quickly growing tired of the elaborate meals the chef conjures up to impress the first family. She had not wanted to move and give up her life in her hometown of Chicago—she had just joined a running club for senior citizens and had won her first track meet—and she agreed only after Michelle made the case that it was the best way to keep Sasha and Malia grounded. "They're dragging me with them," she said in a 2009 interview, "and I'm not comfortable with that. But I'm doing exactly what you do. You do what needs to be done." Because she has successfully avoided the spotlight, she remains relatively anonymous. She takes the girls to school in an unmarked SUV and occasionally leaves the White House to go shopping. When they first moved into the White House, President Obama, bemused, said that his mother-in-law "just walks out the gate and goes over to CVS and starts doing her shopping." But as the years have dragged on, Marian feels increasingly isolated.

"Ma'am, I'm going to get my wife to get you out for a while, to get some fresh air," Head Butler George Hannie told Marian one morning when he served her breakfast.

"I'd love to," she told him. So his wife, Shirley, took Michelle's mother to a suburban mall for lunch. Shirley wouldn't say which mall because she worries that it could make it harder for Marian to leave the confines of the White House if people knew where she goes.

"I'm sure it's lonely," Shirley said. "They have their schedule being first family; there are downtimes for her."

The First Lady is maternal toward trusted staffers, especially the young ones like Reggie Love, who was twenty-four when he began working for Obama in the Senate in 2006. "Strong and beautiful—reminds me of my mom," Love says of her. Before Love left in 2011 to go to business school, Michelle teased him about finding a girlfriend and settling down. During the 2008 campaign she would approach staffers and ask, "What's going on with you?" "You eating okay?" When there's a tragedy in a young staffer's family, she often checks on them. Bill Burton was national press secretary during Obama's first presidential campaign and then was deputy press secretary in the White House, and he remembers the thrill of traveling in 2008 with Michelle, before she grew tired of the road. He traveled to New Hampshire with her and her press secretary, Katie McCormick Lelyveld, and remembers the forty-minute drive in the rental van from the airport to the first event and how she wrote her entire speech on eight pages of legal pad paper in longhand. But she didn't end up using it. "When we got to the event she gave the entire speech without notes and spoke in these perfectly formed sentences and paragraphs and wowed the crowd." They bounced around New Hampshire the rest of the day and stopped at a McDonald's, where the soon-to-be First Lady got a Filet-O-Fish sandwich. ("I'll never forget it because who gets the fish at McDonald's?" Burton said, laughing.) They ended up being snowed in at the airport that night for several hours. So they sat at the small airport cafeteria and shared a pizza, and Michelle drank wine while he had a beer. "It was one of those really lovely days on the campaign trail that you see in the movies. Since ninety percent of the days are not like that, you appreciate those days."

V

Supporting Actors

★

Somebody else can have Madison Avenue. I'll take Bird.

—LBJ ON HIS WIFE'S EXTRAORDINARY POLITICAL
SAVVY

First ladies support their husbands, and that includes acting as sources of reassurance and normalcy during times of tragedy, as Lady Bird Johnson did after President Kennedy's assassination and as Laura Bush did after 9/11. They can speak to grieving mothers and wives in a more personal way than their husbands can. They often put their own ambitions and desires aside for the sake of their husbands' presidencies. Even when they want to do something as small and seemingly inconsequential as replace a member of the White House residence staff, they seek the President's approval. They are co-stars on a national stage where their every move is scrutinized and they cannot do a thing without considering how it will affect the presidency. In all cases it is doubtful that their husbands would have been elected had it not been for them.

Lady Bird Johnson loved to read, but she developed macular degeneration in her old age and could no longer read easily. Her devoted staff, made up of a handful of women, some of whom had been with her in the White House, took turns reading to her. Shirley James was Lady Bird's executive assistant and was with her when she passed away at ninety-four years old on July 11, 2007. Years earlier, James was preparing Lady Bird for a retrospective interview she had agreed to do about the year 1968. The two sat quietly together at the Johnsons' Texas ranch and James read aloud the parts of Lady Bird's diary that were about the assassinations of Robert Kennedy and Martin Luther King Jr. James fought back tears as she read Lady Bird's entry from the day Robert Kennedy was killed. "Nineteen sixty-eight was a hell of a year," James said, shaking her head as tears rolled down her cheeks. When she looked up, she was surprised to see Lady Bird, who rarely cried, also in tears. "Yes," Lady Bird said softly, "It was a hell of a year." In an entry from her diary on the day Robert Kennedy was shot, Lady Bird wrote, "There was an air of unreality about the whole thing—a nightmare quality. It couldn't be. You dreamed it. It had happened before."

She knew all too well what had happened before, when President Kennedy was murdered on November 22, 1963, and her life changed forever. No modern first lady has ever had to handle such a violent transition as Lady Bird Johnson did. Unlike her predecessors, Lady Bird moved into a White House in mourning. Her social secretary, Bess Abell, remembered just how jarring the transition was: "Instead of coming in with the excitement and the thrill of an inauguration, we moved into a house that was covered with black crepe on all the chandeliers and the columns."

The new First Lady often lamented the impossible position her family was suddenly thrust into. In her diary she wrote, "If Lyndon could pull all the stars out of the skies and make a necklace for Jackie Kennedy he would do it." Lady Bird was in the motorcade with the Kennedys, and on the flight back from Dallas, as President Kennedy's casket sat in the plane's corridor, she approached a dazed Jackie. "We never even wanted to be vice president," she told her. "Now, dear God, it's come to this." When the media began pelting her press secretary, Liz Carpenter, with questions about when Jackie and her two children would be moving out of the White House, Lady Bird was furious. "I would to God I could serve Mrs. Kennedy's comfort; I can at least serve her convenience," she told Carpenter.

Lady Bird was adamantly opposed to the plan to move her family into the White House on December 7, 1963, because it fell on the anniversary of Pearl Harbor. "The only argument I ever recall witnessing my parents having—I didn't actually witness it, I was eavesdropping—I heard raised voices and some expression of anger between my parents," Luci Johnson said. "It was my mother, who was always so respectful and deferential, and my father, who was always honoring my mother deeply. My father was saying, 'We have to move December seventh, Bird.' My mother said, 'Lyndon, any day but that. *Any* day but that.'" Lady Bird was "begging for an alternative," her daughter recalled. Ultimately, she lost the fight.

Lady Bird had a complicated relationship with Jackie, whose youth and jaw-dropping beauty she could not match. A newspaper editor from Texas told her, "You poor thing having to follow Jackie Kennedy." "Don't pity me," she said. "Grieve for Mrs. Kennedy; she lost her husband. I still have my Lyndon." What she couldn't match in appearance she made up for in dedication and stamina. Because Jackie was pregnant with John-John, then-Senator John Kennedy had asked Lady Bird to take on a defining role in the 1960 campaign. She was proud of her southern roots (she regularly peppered sentences with phrases like "He was as full of ideas as a pomegranate is of seed") and she was a natural on the campaign trail. She never complained and always sought to shield her husband. When she was campaigning with LBJ and the Kennedys, she got a call telling her that her father, whom she adored, had developed blood poisoning in one of his legs and that the leg would have to be amputated the next day. Her entire body flinched when she answered the phone, but she quickly straightened up. "What time will they operate?" she asked her father's doctor. "I will be there." She didn't tell LBJ right away because he was getting dressed for an event and was dealing with several political problems. She waited until he was in good spirits, put her hand calmly on his shoulder, and said, "Daddy's going to have to be operated on in the morning, and I will have to leave and be there." Johnson sighed deeply and nodded, and the two of them went through the campaign events they had lined up for the rest of that evening. Lady Bird summoned her extraordinary self-discipline to push her private pain from her mind and get back to work.

When she became First Lady, she eagerly took on an exhausting schedule. She told Chief Usher J. B. West, "My husband comes first, the girls second, and I will be satisfied with what's left." Doorman Preston Bruce, who started at the White House at the beginning of President Eisenhower's first term, would stand in the doorway of the sweeping Entrance Hall and watch her with amusement. "I never saw her take a moment for herself all the time she was at the White House." During the 1960 campaign, she traveled 35,000 miles, visited eleven states, and went to about 150 events during one two-month span. During just five days she gave forty-five speeches. "Lady Bird carried Texas for us," Robert Kennedy said at the time. Once her husband became President Kennedy's vice president, she spent much of her time being a pinch hitter and doing the photo ops and events that

Jackie Kennedy didn't want to do. Lady Bird took Jackie's place more than fifty times, filling in for her while Jackie did one of her signature PBOs, her own acronym for "the polite brush-off." Jackie's staff came to refer to Lady Bird as "Saint Bird" for saving them from embarrassment again and again.

Bess Abell, who had two young children when she was the Johnsons' social secretary, remembers how much the Johnsons entertained and how hard they, and everyone on their staffs, worked. Before formal dinners, after all the guests were seated, Abell would sneak into the Usher's Office and read bedtime stories to her sons over the phone. "Some people think that was unforgivable," she laughed, but it was a job and a friendship that both she and Lady Bird would not have traded for anything. In 1968, when Lady Bird's husband announced his decision not to seek the presidency again, Lady Bird said, "We need to make every minute, every day, every hour between now and next January twentieth count."

Lady Bird had been a gifted student in high school, but she was so painfully shy that she purposefully answered some questions incorrectly on exams so that she wouldn't have to speak as valedictorian or salutatorian at graduation. But through the years her confidence grew, and she attended the University of Texas, where she earned a double bachelor's degree in history and journalism at a time when few women would have dreamed of going to college. Her father was the richest man in their small East Texas town, and her mother, who died when she was five years old, was from a wealthy Alabama family. When LBJ decided to run for Congress, his bride took ten thousand dollars of her inheritance to help get him there.

She had wanted to become a newspaper reporter, but soon after she met young congressional aide Lyndon Baines Johnson, she traded in her plans for this larger-than-life character, whom she called "electric." She said she felt "like a moth drawn to a flame." He proposed the day after they met but she was unsure. The two exchanged more than ninety letters sent between Washington, D.C., where Johnson was working for Texas Congressman Richard Kleberg, and her home in Karnack, Texas. "We either do it now, or we never will," he wrote to her. Days later, he showed up at Bird's doorstep with a $2.50 ring from Sears, Roebuck and refused to leave without her acquiescence. They married on November 17, 1934, when she was twenty-one years old and he was twenty-six. It was less than three months from the day they first met.

Even though Lady Bird helped get him elected to every office he ran for, by supporting him financially or emotionally, LBJ sometimes treated her with outright contempt. He made other couples blush when he harangued her in public, comparing her with other women he found more beautiful. At parties he would yell at her to get him another slice of pie, or tell her to change her "funny-looking shoes." He did not even bother informing her about his first run for Congress until he announced it publicly. "See you later, Bird," he'd bark the minute any political conversation came up—her cue to leave the room immediately. He hated the color purple and would tell his wife not to wear it, and to stop wearing "saddlebag" fabrics. ("He likes the things that show the shape of your figure, if you have one to show," says Abell.) LBJ's drinking sometimes got out of hand and Lady Bird would occasionally ask the White House butlers to cut his Cutty Sark whiskey with water. Johnson's adviser Joe Califano said Lady Bird was the best thing that ever happened to LBJ. "She helped him when he was down; he was essentially a manic depressive, up and down; she leveled it out for him."

As LBJ's political star rose, Lady Bird became more and more sure of herself, slowly transforming from a shy bookworm into a political force and a cunning businesswoman who (against her husband's wishes) invested $17,000 of her inheritance in a small media company that by the time they got to the White House was worth $9 million (roughly $68 million in today's dollars). Lady Bird vividly remembered when they first made a profit—eighteen dollars—on her investment in August 1944. She began taking an active role in politics in 1941, after he lost his first bid for the Senate and returned to the House. While he was on active duty in the navy during World War II, she managed his legislative office.

Lyndon Johnson smoked nearly sixty cigarettes a day and suffered an almost-fatal heart attack in 1955 while in the Senate. It was then that he began to see her as a lifeline, and he pleaded with her to stay by his bedside the entire time he was in the hospital. Like the dutiful wife that she was, she returned home only twice during those five weeks to see their eleven-year-old and eight-year-old daughters. "Her priority was always him," said the Johnsons' social secretary, Bess Abell. "Those two girls, they could take care of themselves." The ordeal softened LBJ's treatment of Lady Bird. After his brush with death he let her listen in on policy discussions and asked her how she thought certain decisions would play to the American public. She changed, too, in part because of her new position in her husband's world. In the mid-1950s, she started to critique LBJ, sometimes even handing him notes during public speeches that said things like "That's enough" when she thought he was going on too long. Occasionally, when he did not heed her advice, she physically pulled on his jacket lapel to get him to sit down.

In the White House, Lady Bird had each day planned out ahead of time and worked diligently in her "office," the cream-colored bedroom where she studied speeches and dictated letters. Sometimes she escaped to the blue-and-white Queens' Sitting Room to work on projects like Head Start and organize monthly luncheons dubbed "Women Do-ers," which gathered high-powered businesswomen together. She's best remembered for the Highway Beautification Act, signed by her husband on October 22, 1965, and nicknamed "Lady Bird's Bill," which called for limiting billboards and landscaping and planting flowers along the nation's highways. What is less known is that she influenced almost all of the nearly two hundred laws having to do with the environment during her husband's administration. She fought to protect California's redwood trees and to preserve the breathtaking beauty of the Grand Canyon. She was one of the country's earliest and most famous environmentalists, and she believed that there was something sacred about nature's beauty that must be cherished and preserved. "Where flowers bloom, so does hope," she'd say.

She was kind to the staff. Electrician Bill Cliber remembers Secret Service agents approaching him after the birth of his son. They asked him which hospital his wife was at because the First Lady wanted to send flowers. "No," he said, shaking his head as tears filled his eyes. "The First Lady went and got flowers and she took them to her and gave them to my wife in the hospital." When Cliber thanked her later, Lady Bird told him that it was the easiest thing she ever had to do as First Lady.

In 1964, the stakes were even higher than they had been in 1960, and her husband told her he needed her help to win the presidency. She became the first first lady to go on the campaign trail without the President at her side when she traveled 1,628 miles across eight southern states on her "Lady Bird Special," making forty-seven speeches to half a million people on the historic whistle-stop train tour. It was the fall of 1964 and her husband was in trouble in the South because, months earlier, he had pushed Congress to pass the Civil Rights Act of 1964, which overturned the so-called Jim Crow segregation laws. Some southerners felt that their way of life was being threatened. Lady Bird, who grew up in a small town in East Texas, was the administration's emissary to the South. In a slow and deliberate voice, she urged southerners to accept desegregation or else watch their economy crumble. Referring to her Texas accent an aide said, "They may not believe what you're saying, but they sure will understand the way you're saying it!" She told her staff, "Don't give me easy towns. Anyone can get into Atlanta—it's the new, modern South. Let me take the tough ones." She insisted on calling the senators and governors of each state that she visited, Democrat or Republican, to tell them of her arrival and to ask them to hop onto the train with her. It was a clever move that helped endear her to her husband's fiercest critics. "I don't think I'll have many takers," she admitted. "But it's only polite to ask."

Tens of thousands of people lined the tracks at railroad stations in small towns across the rural South. There were death threats and angry hecklers who held up signs that read "Black Bird. Go Home." Aides noticed that her southern accent got more and more pronounced as they traveled farther and farther south. Her message to those who considered the Civil Rights Act a betrayal: "There is, in this Southland, more love than hate." She spoke from the platform of the caboose and would sometimes calmly raise a white-gloved hand to try to calm the protesters. At one stop she told the angry crowd shouting racial epithets that their words were "not from the good people of South Carolina but from the state of confusion." Johnson's aide Bill Moyers remembers hearing from an advance man who called from the road almost in tears. "As long as I live," he said, trying not to cry, "I will thank God I was here today, so that I can tell my children that courage makes a difference." In Columbia, South Carolina, a group of young men shouted, "We want Barry [LBJ's Republican opponent, Barry Goldwater]! We want Barry!" Without losing her composure, the First Lady turned to them and said: "My friends, in this country we are entitled to many viewpoints. You are entitled to yours. But right now, I'm entitled to mine." The crowd roared with approval. When Louisiana Congressman Hale Boggs grew so angry with the hecklers that he told the First Lady that he wanted to make a statement on her behalf, she called him into her private train car. "I can handle any ugly moment," she told him. Lady Bird refused to call off the trip even when Secret Service agents told her that it would be necessary to sweep the railroad tracks for bombs. (An extra engine traveled fifteen minutes ahead of her train for this very reason.)

The Carters of Georgia shared the Johnsons' southern roots, and Lillian Carter, President Carter's mother, was a county chairman for Lyndon Johnson in Americus, Georgia, during the 1964 campaign. "Nobody else would take [the job]," said Rosalynn Carter, who was the only other first lady who could truly understand what Lady Bird went through during that southern swing. People wrote racial slurs with soap on Lillian's car parked outside campaign headquarters and tied her radio antenna in a knot. "Our boys would go to school with Democratic buttons on, Lyndon Johnson buttons on, and literally get beat up," President Carter recalled. "Their clothes would be torn."

Even amid all the hate, Lady Bird had fun traveling through the South and the train was full of laughter. On board were pretty, young hostesses wearing blue uniforms and handing out "All the Way with LBJ" buttons. For the 225 members of the traveling press who rode in the nineteen-car caravan there was a daily happy hour from 4 to 5 p.m. complete with food from the region: ham and biscuits in Virginia, shrimp and avocado dip in Florida. The two dining cars were open at all hours and offered dishes like "LBJ steak platter—Please specify: raring to go, middle of the road, or all-the-way." Johnson carried most of the South in November and won the election. "All those women that were on that train trip, if they weren't feminists before the train trip I'm sure they were afterwards," Bess Abell said with a smile. Lady Bird called the trip "the most dramatic four days in my life, the most exhausting, the most fulfilling."

Lady Bird had evolved from a woman who was totally removed from politics to an indispensable adviser to her husband in the White House. Over the years LBJ described her as "the brains and money of this family." When President Johnson was mired in self-doubt before the 1964 election, she did more than win votes for him: she boosted him up. "Beloved—You are as brave a man as Harry Truman—or FDR—or Lincoln. You can go on to find some peace, some achievement amidst all the pain," she wrote to him in a letter, adding that she wasn't afraid of "losing money or defeat." This kind of unflinching strength is typical of all the modern first ladies, who view the support of their husbands as part of their job descriptions. "I know you are brave as any of the thirty-five [Johnson was sworn in as the thirty-sixth president]," she wrote.

She was used to LBJ's eccentric demands, including his insistence on an impossibly forceful shower in every house they ever lived in, and a telephone always within reach. When President Nixon was elected, he had fifty telephone lines removed from the presidential bedroom. When Betty Ford was giving a tour of the second floor to her new press secretary, she pointed to about ten electrical outlets over the sink in the President's bathroom.

"I understand Johnson ordered these one day in a moment of frenzy when the one existing outlet did not work." Well before he became president, LBJ was on the phone so often that he demanded that one be permanently placed underneath a shaded tree in the backyard of the family's Austin home. When Lady Bird went into labor with their first daughter, Lynda, LBJ had to be yanked off the phone during one of his interminable calls.

One phone call between Lady Bird and the President on October 14, 1964, shows that she was truly her husband's moral compass. Weeks before the presidential election, their longtime friend and political adviser since 1939, Walter Jenkins, was arrested on what was then called a homosexual morals charge in a YMCA men's room a few blocks from the White House. Because of the scandal, Lady Bird knew that Jenkins could not continue to work for her husband's administration, but she did not want to set him and his family adrift.

In a call to her husband she suggested that they offer Jenkins the number-two job at the Austin television station they owned. "I wouldn't do anything along that line now," the President said, urging her to let Jenkins and his wife, who was a dear friend of theirs, know, through an aide, that Jenkins would not have any trouble finding work. After a long pause Lady Bird said firmly, "I don't think that's right. . . . When questioned, and I will be questioned, I'm going to say that this is incredible for a man that I've known all these years, a devout Catholic, the father of six children, a happily married husband. It can only be a period of nervous breakdown." Johnson cut her off and begged her not to say anything publicly. "If we don't express some support to him I think that we will lose the entire love and devotion of all the people who have been with us," she told him. It's only then that the President told her to meet with his advisers about issuing a statement, but when she told him that she already had (she was often one step ahead of him) he still resisted. She kept pushing for a public statement of support, but Johnson said, "The average farmer just can't understand your knowing it and approving it or condoning it."

The call ends with Lady Bird stroking her husband's ego in a sweet lyrical voice and then telling him that she is going to put out a statement, whether he likes it or not. "My poor darling, my heart breaks for you, too."

"I know it, honey," he says.

"You're a brave good guy and if you read where I've said some things in Walter's support they'll be along the lines that I've just said to you." Her statement came out before the President's.

Larry Temple, who served as special counsel to President Johnson, says "there was nobody closer during my time to LBJ than Lady Bird Johnson. Absolutely no one whose advice, whose counsel, whose judgment he sought and took more than Lady Bird Johnson." Temple was as close to their relationship as one could get; among his responsibilities was briefing the President in their bedroom at seven thirty every morning. LBJ and Lady Bird would both still be in their pajamas in bed, but the President would have been on the phone for a long time by then. Temple knew when Lady Bird was out of town to be extra careful with the President. "If she were gone, and occasionally she'd go to New York to see a play with a friend, he'd be like a caged animal."

She was his trusted adviser. The two of them would have breakfast together in his bedroom and he would listen to her intently. She even graded his speeches. "She graded him and he expected to sit there and listen to it because he felt that she had no alternative agenda except his best interest and she would tell him what he needed to hear whether he wanted to hear it or not," the Johnsons' daughter Luci says. "Did he like it? No." She laughs and says that her mother was "that one person who's going to tell him if there's spinach in his teeth so he has a chance to get to a mirror and get it out." Lady Bird was her husband's best friend. "I think he thought he was a better man because he had someone who loved him that much," Luci says.

In a phone call on March 7, 1964, after he gave a news conference, Lady Bird asked her husband, "You want to listen for about one minute to my critique, or would you rather wait until tonight?" "Yes, ma'am," he replied. "I'm willing now." Her takeaway: he spoke too fast and looked down too often. He needed to study the text before he got onstage and read with more passion, "I'd say it was a good B-plus." Moments before the shocking 1968 nationally televised address in which President Johnson announced he would not seek another term, the First Lady rushed to his desk in the Oval Office and handed him a note: "Remember—pacing and drama."

For many years, long after his death, Lady Bird was a constant presence at her husband's presidential library. There are audio speakers in the re-creation of President Johnson's Oval Office, and she could hear his voice echo up and down the halls. "I often wondered how hard that must be on her to hear his voice," her friend and former assistant Betty Tilson said. "I think she was comforted by it. She used to talk about him quite a bit. . . . She used to say how she wished he could have seen the fine young women Luci and Lynda had become." In a January 13, 1999, letter Lady Bird told her friend Betty Ford how much she had missed her husband over the holidays, when their grandchildren and "great-grands" came to visit. "Lyndon would have loved it, and no doubt, would have stirred it up some more!"

MODERN FIRST LADIES set their own dreams aside to support their husbands' ambitions. But in the case of Hillary Clinton, she took a temporary detour to help her husband, but she never abandoned her own plans. She would not be content playing the role of supporting actor her entire life.

How Bill and Hillary met says so much about their relationship and Hillary's undeniable self-confidence. They were both studying one night in the Yale Law School library, and Bill spent much of the time staring at Hillary. She was sitting at the opposite end of the library, wearing oversize glasses and no makeup. He was stunned as he watched her walk toward him. "Look, if you're going to keep staring at me, then I'm going to keep looking back," Hillary said, "and I think we ought to know each other's names. I'm Hillary Rodham." Bill recalls being "dumbstruck" and unable to remember his own name.

Hillary knew from the moment they met that Bill wanted to be president. He was quick to tell friends of his aspiration, and she fell in love with him and his ambition. She stayed an extra year at Yale to be with him, rather than graduate with her own class (she was one of twenty-seven women in her class). After a whirlwind courtship, Bill proposed three times before Hillary said yes. In an interview, Hillary said she was "terrified" about marrying Bill because she worried that her identity would get "lost in the wake of Bill's force-of-nature personality."

Hillary grew up in Park Ridge, Illinois, a middle-class suburb of Chicago, and she seemed destined to move to a big city and join a law firm or run for office herself. But she knew that, to be with Bill, she would have to move with him to his home state of Arkansas, where he was planning to run for Congress. And unlike Bill, who grew up with an eccentric mother and an abusive stepfather, Hillary was from a stable home. Her friends told her that she would be squandering her own astounding potential— they wanted her to delve into politics herself instead of playing the traditional role of the supportive wife. "I was disappointed when they married," says Betsey Wright, a longtime friend of the Clintons who was Bill's chief of staff when he was governor and later worked on his 1992 presidential campaign. But in the struggle between her head and her heart, Hillary's heart won out. Once Hillary decided to move to Arkansas there was no turning back. "I think I knew at some level that I would be very cowardly and foolish to walk away from that relationship," she said. In 1974, after working on the House Judiciary Committee's impeachment investigation of President Nixon, Hillary moved to Fayetteville, Arkansas. They married in 1975 in the living room of their first house.

Hillary became the second woman to join the University of Arkansas Law School faculty. Bill also taught classes at the university while he ran for Congress and, according to students who took classes with each of them, Hillary was the better teacher. She was rigorous and disciplined while Bill earned a reputation for being the easier grader.

Bill ran for Congress in 1974 and lost, but he was elected attorney general in 1976 and the Clintons moved to Little Rock. Hillary kept her maiden name and joined the prestigious Rose Law Firm, where she specialized in children's rights cases, and Bill geared up to run for governor. Hillary's refusal to change her last name became a growing liability after Clinton was elected governor in 1978. After the election, he was asked by an Associated Press reporter about Hillary's decision to keep "Rodham." "She decided to do that when she was nine, long before women's lib came along," Bill answered defensively. "People wouldn't mind if they knew how old-fashioned she was in every conceivable way." Bill's Little Rock friend Guy Campbell could not understand why Hillary would not take her husband's last name. Finally, at dinner with the Clintons one night, Guy leaned into Hillary and said, "All right, Hillary, I just want to know, why didn't you take your husband's name?"

"Look, my law practice was already established with the name as it was," she said, fixing her gaze at him sincerely, and adding sweetly, "But really, I just love my daddy so much." In the 1980 election, Clinton's Republican opponent, Frank White, told voters as often as possible that his wife was "Mrs. Frank White." White won the election. When Cragg Hines, then the Washington bureau chief of the *Houston Chronicle*, asked Bill's mother, Virginia Kelley, what she thought of Hillary when she first met her, she paused and said, "Damn Yankee, I guess!" Virginia blamed Hillary for her son's 1980 loss, saying that half of the voters in Arkansas, most of whom were socially conservative, thought that the Clintons were unmarried and were living in sin in the Governor's Mansion. "The only time she got weepy was when she talked about Bill Clinton losing in 1980," Hines recalled. "This was something that wasn't supposed to happen."

When Clinton announced in February 1982 that he was seeking the governorship again, Hillary began to be referred to as "Mrs. Bill Clinton." She dyed her hair and got contact lenses, determined that she would not be the reason for another defeat. "I'll be Mrs. Bill Clinton," she told reporters in 1982, the day her husband announced his bid to get back into the Governor's Mansion. "I suspect people will be getting tired of hearing from Mrs. Bill Clinton." From 1983 to 1992, when Bill was elected president, Hillary was mostly referred to as Hillary Clinton. But when the Clintons got to the White House and Hillary was put in charge of the health-care overhaul, she used Hillary Rodham Clinton. She never legally changed her name from Hillary Rodham.

Hillary sparred with the southerners, particularly the men, who made fun of her feminism and even of her appearance, yet she knew there was no point arguing with them. As the first lady of Arkansas, Hillary was sometimes asked to host fund-raisers, some even involving the incongruous sight of her modeling clothes. At one fund-raiser Hillary had her makeup done professionally and modeled a cashmere sweater. Guy Campbell went backstage and said, "Hillary, I can't believe it, tonight you resemble a woman." Hillary smiled through her annoyance and said, "Only you, Guy Campbell, would say something like that to me."

Bill often told staffers to run their new ideas past his wife, and he put her in charge of his efforts to reform Arkansas public schools, which were almost at the bottom in national rankings. Hillary cofounded the Arkansas Advocates for Children and Families and helped get funding for early education, and she worked on reforming the juvenile justice system. As an associate and then a partner at the Rose Law Firm, she earned more than three times what her husband did.

She never stopped being Bill's fiercest defender, and in May 1990, when her husband was running for his fifth term as Arkansas governor, she stood in the crowd in the state capitol's rotunda as Tom McRae, his challenger in the Democratic primary, held a press conference. When McRae attacked Bill for refusing to debate him, a determined voice called out: "Tom, who was the one person who didn't show up in Springdale? Give me a break! I mean, I think that we oughta get the record straight. . . ." Hillary emerged from the crowd and walked toward McRae as the television cameras shifted their focus from him to her. "Many of the reports you issued," she charged, waving a sheaf of papers in her hand, "not only praised the governor on his environmental record, but his education record and his economic record!" At the end of the press conference a local reporter wrapped up his live shot by saying, "Hillary Clinton showed again that she may be the best debater in the family." She had saved Bill from what could have been a devastating defeat, and by doing so she had brought him one step closer to the presidency.

In the White House, the Clintons had a complicated relationship that played out every day in front of the residence staff. They stayed up late and entertained celebrities with invitations to stay the night in the Lincoln Bedroom. (The Clintons had so many guests in the White House that residence staffers kept a list of them in their shirt pockets in case Hillary stopped them to ask who they were hosting on any given evening.) They never seemed to stop working. They quizzed staffers to find out what people outside the Beltway thought and they talked politics constantly, even on vacation. In Martha's Vineyard, Hillary told a reporter, "I was cutting Bill's grapefruit this morning and we had the best idea we ever had about day care, and all of a sudden there's this flapping at the window and it's a seagull—a seagull at our window!"

The Clintons also had heated arguments and long, stony silences. During a movie screening in 1994 in the White House theater, the Clintons' interior decorator, Kaki Hockersmith, who lived off and on at the White House for years, warned a guest, "Things are really dark around here; they may even leave early tonight." White House Florist Ronn Payne remembers coming up the service elevator one day with a cart to pick up old floral arrangements and seeing two butlers standing outside the West Sitting Hall listening as the Clintons fought. The butlers motioned him over to them and put their fingers to their lips, "Shhh." Suddenly,

Payne heard the First Lady shout, "Goddamn bastard!" And a heavy object slammed against the floor.

But there were sweet moments, too, and Hillary tried to help lighten the mood for her husband in the White House. She asked Head Housekeeper Christine Limerick to convert the room at the end of the hall—Room 330 on the third floor—into a music room for President Clinton as a surprise Christmas present. The room was painted and refurbished and outfitted with music stands, stereo equipment, speakers, and his saxophone collection. Limerick wrapped the entry door on Christmas Eve and Hillary led Bill to the room early Christmas morning. It was one of the rare moments when the Clintons were not working.

———

SOMETIMES BEING A supportive partner in the White House means being a firm taskmaster and a consistent, strong presence during times of tragedy. There is a depth and complexity to Laura Bush that few ever get to see. Laura says that her mother-in-law, Barbara, is much more "acerbic" than she is, but when Laura was in the White House she had a harder edge than Barbara ever did. When President George W. Bush asked for something, his staff moved as fast as they could. When Laura Bush had a request, everyone ran.

Laura was a prim and proper first lady and she was often not amused by the casual atmosphere in the West Wing. After the West Wing was redecorated, Laura walked through the new press room and lower press office. One of the twentysomething press assistants had a bunch of pictures pinned to the wall above her desk. Laura walked by, glanced at her space, and shook her head disapprovingly. "This is the White House, *not* a sorority," she said. A few minutes later, the photos were down. Usher Worthington

White remembers how angry Laura was when residence staffers lost the keys to her daughter Jenna's car twice. Jenna parked her car on the South Grounds, but sometimes the car had to be moved, either because the President would be making a statement outdoors, where the car would be visible in the camera shot, or because a last-minute guest was arriving and room needed to be made for the motorcade. Laura was always very calm and controlled but when she came into the Usher's Office to find out what had happened the second time her daughter's keys were lost, she was livid when she discovered that a staffer had accidentally dropped them into a storm drain. Her hands were shaking and her tone was curt: they were not inconveniencing her, they were inconveniencing her daughter, which was far worse in her mind. Staffers finally decided to place spare copies of Jenna's keys in a safe in the Usher's Office.

Laura did not miss a thing, White says. One day, shortly after he was made the usher in charge of housekeeping, the phone in the Usher's Office blinked "Family Table," indicating it was a call coming from the family breakfast table upstairs. It was the First Lady asking him to meet her at the President's elevator right away. Laura quickly congratulated him on his new position and summoned him toward her. They walked into the East Sitting Hall, in between the Queens' Bedroom and the Lincoln Bedroom, where she pointed to a small leak. "It has been like this for nine months," she said. "I want it fixed."

It's remarkable that Laura, a shy librarian who married her husband on the condition that she would *never* have to make a political speech on his behalf, would become so comfortable giving orders in the White House. Laura was thirty-one and had already spent a decade working as an elementary school teacher and a librarian before she started dating George W. Bush, who really is her opposite in so many ways. She smoothed the edges of her husband's brash personality. On the campaign plane she would tell him, "Rein it in, Bubba," when he was holding court in front of reporters. Around the residence she would admonish him with a delicate "Bushieee" (her voice lowering at the end) when he was out of line. And he helped her heal from the shame of a car accident, in which she accidentally ran a stop sign and killed one of her best friends when she was seventeen. She felt so guilty that she never told their daughters—they found out only when their father was governor of Texas and someone on their protective detail mentioned it, assuming they already knew.

Laura could never have known back in Midland, Texas, where she was born and raised, that she would one day have to help shepherd the country during the worst terrorist attack since Pearl Harbor. It was the residence staffers, who serve from one administration to the next, regardless of political party, who helped Laura feel she could go on after September 11, 2001. "We knew we were going to be there [in the White House], and we were confident that we would be safe, but on the other hand they [White House staffers] could have chosen another job or just said, 'You know, this is just too much stress now. I'd rather go on,'" Laura said in an interview. "And they didn't, none of them did."

Veteran White House reporter Ann Compton says she remembers being at a private lunch with the First Lady when Laura told her that, in the terrifying hours after the terrorist attacks, she almost burst into tears when her Secret Service agent told her that all of the former first families were secure. "She hadn't even thought about the ripple effect," Compton said. Susan Ford's two daughters attended Southern Methodist University and called their mother in a panic on September 11. Susan contacted one of the Secret Service agents who had been on her detail when she was living in the White House and who lived near SMU, and he and his wife took her daughters in for several days. One daughter told her professor before leaving, "I know this may sound strange to you but my grandfather was President Gerald Ford and I have to leave." When Laura Bush heard the story her eyes filled with tears; the bond these families share with the Secret Service and with each other runs deep.

Six days after 9/11, Laura Bush was sent to Shanksville, Pennsylvania, as one of several administration officials dispatched to deal with the crisis. Hundreds of family members of the forty passengers and crew of the hijacked United Airlines Flight 93 gathered in the desolate field, where a crater was still smoldering from the impact of the crash. It was the only one of the four hijacked planes that did not reach its intended target, because of the heroism of the passengers and crew who tried to regain control of the plane from the hijackers. A White House aide, who had been at the event site for hours before Laura arrived, said the audience seemed reassured when they saw her. "When she showed up, it felt different, it felt better," he recalled. "People can believe what she says, they feel like they can cry on her shoulder and she can be strong for them." Aides say that she is at her best in intimate settings, when the cameras are not on. Her visit to Shanksville was emotional. She had private meetings with family members who wanted to know what she and her husband could do to help them recover from their immense loss. "America is learning the names, but you know the people," she told the audience, many of whom were crying in disbelief. "And you are the ones they thought of in the last moments of life. You're the ones they called, and prayed to see again. You are the ones they loved."

Laura told her staff that she wanted to visit all fifty states as First Lady, and by the end only one state was left: North Dakota.

Laura's chief of staff, Anita McBride, recalled accompanying Laura to her last event, a potluck dinner in a church basement in North Dakota. "It was as middle America as you can imagine— the casseroles, the paper napkins—maybe a hundred people, all women dressed up." Suddenly, a woman got up and started singing "God Bless America," and Laura Bush, who had seen the pain of 9/11 family members and wounded soldiers at Walter Reed Army Medical Center, began to cry. It was one of the only times she allowed herself to become visibly emotional, at a small potluck dinner in North Dakota that marked the end of her eight-year journey as First Lady.

VI

East Wing vs. West Wing

★

*We don't **have** to do anything.*

—Michelle Obama to her advisers after the
2008 election

The old-fashioned East Wing versus West Wing battle of the sexes has been a prominent feature of every modern White House. In the Kennedy White House it was Jackie's formidable social secretary, Letitia Baldrige, in one corner and White House Press Secretary Pierre Salinger in the other. When Baldrige would walk between the West Wing and the East Wing by the White House swimming pool, President Kennedy would occasionally call out to her as he was doing laps. "Now what's with the East Wing? What are your problems today?" While JFK was amused by the drama, he usually took the side of the East Wing. Baldrige knew how to use Jackie's proximity to power to get what she wanted. "If Pierre went against the specific instructions of JBK (Jacqueline Bouvier Kennedy) I would get hell from Jackie, [so] I'd tattle on Pierre to the President, and the President went to bat for me against Pierre." Jackie was ultimately in control.

During the Ford administration, Betty's press secretary, Sheila

Rabb Weidenfeld, saw the East Wing as the heart and the West Wing as the head. "They were responsible for policy; we interpreted it by daily living, by example." When she interviewed Maria Downs to be her new social secretary Betty asked her, "Could you go to bat against them [the President's aides in the West Wing]?" Betty had watched helplessly as West Wing aides tried to take control over the guest lists for state dinners during the brief time that she did not have a social secretary.

Michelle Obama wants to maintain complete control of her image. One former adviser to the First Lady said that she wants every event to have a "clear electoral purpose," and that "every time that she was used in any capacity, . . . it had to be connected to strategy." Michelle had been a reluctant campaigner and has been a reluctant First Lady at times, the staffer says.

In the Obama White House, tension between the West Wing and the quiet second-floor office of the First Lady in the East Wing is still brewing. During the transition, after her husband was elected but before his inauguration, Michelle gathered her small staff in the transition headquarters and told them, "We don't *have* to do anything." Anything that they decided to do, she said, must be done "really, really well." She had to be "value-added" or else she would not do anything. Every event must have a goal and casual suggestions were not welcome; instead every idea should be carefully considered, every downside explored, before it was even presented to her. All of that meant that she expected her schedule to be planned weeks in advance, even though the President's schedule is more ad hoc and sometimes planned hours in advance, depending on global events. Her plan when she entered the White House was to work only two or three days a week and devote the rest of her time to her daughters. A former West Wing staffer made it clear that Michelle has the final word and that any attempts to overschedule her, or to do something spontaneous, were not wise: "You knew what the limitations were."

Once she commits to doing something, however, aides say Michelle spends hours and sometimes days personally preparing and editing her speeches. Her staff will have a lectern moved into her office so that she can practice them. What she most enjoys is speaking to young inner-city girls to whom she can be an inspiration. "Nothing in my life's path ever would have predicted that I would be standing here as the first African American First Lady," she tells them, her voice swelling with emotion. "I wasn't raised with wealth or resources or any social standing to speak of."

Michelle Obama is on her fourth social secretary after the departure of the first man and first openly gay social secretary, Jeremy Bernard. Four months after becoming First Lady, Michelle replaced Chief of Staff Jackie Norris, who ran the President's successful Iowa operation, with her old friend Susan Sher. At the end of 2010 she replaced Sher with Tina Tchen, a lawyer who worked in the White House Office of Public Engagement. The turnover in her office is higher than in most of her predecessors'—Laura Bush and Hillary Clinton each had two chiefs of staff over their eight years as first lady.

Michelle speaks bluntly. She is willing to be a good sport, but she made it clear from the beginning that she does not appreciate other people speaking on her behalf and making promises that she would show up at events, without first consulting her. She was particularly angry when the President's then–Chief of Staff Rahm Emanuel made commitments on her behalf. "Rahm has frayed relationships with everyone. I don't think anybody has an uncomplicated, warm relationship with him," a former Obama administration staffer said. When Michelle was being overscheduled she told the President's aides: "Stop this right now." Michelle's backers in the White House say they felt as though Emanuel was using her and that it was not fair to punish her and ask her to campaign more than other first ladies simply because she was popular.

Michelle's relationship with her husband's first press secretary, Robert Gibbs, was no better than it was with Emanuel. According to a former White House official with personal knowledge of the dynamic, Michelle thought Gibbs was brash and a know-it-all from the beginning, and she worried that he was more concerned with Obama the candidate than Obama the man. Gibbs was one of Obama's few advisers who were vocal in their criticism of the East Wing. He was allegedly worried about Michelle's decision in 2009 to hire decorator Michael Smith, who, unbeknownst to the First Lady, had been in charge of the $1.2 million redecoration of ousted Merrill Lynch CEO John Thain's office. Thain's outlandishly expensive trash can ($1,200) and even more absurdly priced rug ($87,000) became synonymous with Wall Street greed during the financial crisis, and Gibbs worried about the public backlash. But the First Lady argued that she was only trying to make the private quarters more comfortable for their daughters and that they would not be using taxpayer dollars. The President agreed with Gibbs, and while Smith was not fired he was asked to order less expensive items from stores like Anthropologie. Michelle resented her every decision being scrutinized by her husband's advisers.

———

THE OBAMA EAST Wing is far more traditional than the Clinton East Wing. In the Clinton administration, Maggie Williams became the first person to serve both as chief of staff to the First Lady and as an assistant to the President. Many members of Hillary's staff worked in the West Wing and the Eisenhower

Executive Office Building (formerly the Old Executive Office Building) instead of in the East Wing. Hillary's decision to take up an office in the West Wing rankled some administration officials. "It got out pretty quickly that Susan Thomases [a close friend of Hillary's who worked on Clinton's 1992 presidential campaign] had a yardstick and was over at the West Wing and the Old Executive Office Building measuring offices and deciding who is going to sit where," said Roy Neel, who served as Al Gore's vice presidential campaign manager and later as President Clinton's deputy chief of staff. "That pissed off everybody." Hillary even told her successor, Laura Bush, that, if she could turn back time, she would not have had an office in the West Wing. After health-care reform failed she rarely used it anyway, she said. Hillary's aides told Laura's staff that once it had been done, undoing the controversial office arrangement would have raised too many questions. There was never any debate about whether Michelle Obama wanted to play a role in the West Wing—she made it crystal clear from the start that she did not want to follow in Hillary Clinton's footsteps. All communication with the West Wing is done through Michelle's chief of staff, Tina Tchen. "It is quite unusual for the First Lady to have any interaction with the West Wing staff, unless she's getting briefed on something. For the most part she doesn't come over there," said former Obama communications director Anita Dunn. "Maybe she was there once because we were doing a photo shoot. Besides that she never came over there. She just didn't."

Whereas Hillary fought for her team to have access to information, Michelle is not as involved. "The notion of sitting around the table with a set of policy advisers—no offense—makes me yawn," Michelle said. "I like creating stuff." Michelle does not want to be told about the day-to-day issues consuming the West

Wing because she says she is not making policy. Her "Let's Move!" campaign to end childhood obesity has been her signature effort and has been relatively uncontroversial (though it has riled some critics who argue that she is acting like the food police and rigidly dictating what children should be eating).

Because Michelle does not stand up for her staff as much as Hillary did, they sometimes get steamrollered by the West Wing. Emanuel excluded the First Lady's chief of staff, Jackie Norris, from the all-important 7:30 a.m. West Wing planning meeting. Norris says that the West Wing made a strategic miscalculation by not sharing more information. The President's advisers were consumed with fixing the economy during the recession, and they considered things that the East Wing was dealing with, like handling the logistics of getting the Obama girls to school, to be trivial. "There's equal parts blame to go around," Norris says. "There's blame on me, there's blame on him [Rahm], there's blame on the team, because I think together we would have been better."

The White House is full of type A staffers who want to be part of the inner ring, as close to power as possible. Knowledge is the currency in Washington, and something as small as knowing two hours ahead of time that an event is going to happen is powerful because information is doled out to such a select group of people. Staffers in the Obama East Wing are often the last to know about the President's schedule and are often treated like second-class citizens. There is a meeting of the press staff in the morning and a wrap-up meeting at the end of the day, separate from the morning staff meeting led by the President's chief of staff. Michelle Obama's aides would almost always be in those morning press meetings but sometimes they were left out of the end-of-the-day meetings. The East Wing began to be referred to as "Guam" by staffers because it was often on the outside ring of the circle, the furthest from the center.

The one figure who is central to decision making in both wings is Valerie Jarrett. Jarrett is the Obamas' best friend, and because of that she's defensive and protective of both of them. Each of the first families becomes a commodity, and Jarrett is the CEO of Obama Inc. Both Obamas have gone to Jarrett to discuss their plans after they leave the White House. In Jarrett the Obamas have something that the Clintons did not have, and that's someone who can act as a conduit between the West Wing and the East Wing. No staffer ever wants to get between the president and his wife, but Jarrett can. Jarrett occupies the second-floor office in the West Wing that once belonged to Hillary Clinton and, later, George W. Bush's adviser Karl Rove. Even the closest staffers, like David Axelrod, who was a top Obama campaign strategist and then adviser in the White House, are still considered "staff," but Valerie is almost like a "third principal," aides say. She is "their everything," according to one former Michelle Obama adviser who agreed to speak candidly on the condition of anonymity. Jarrett is part of the Obama family and is one of the only staffers routinely invited to the private residence. She occupies a unique position, being equally close to the President and to the First Lady. She tells friends she will stay until the end, and "turn the lights off in the White House."

If one thing binds the often dueling West Wing and East Wing staffs, it's their resentment of Jarrett, who many believe gets in the way of the relationship they have with their bosses. Jarrett can get messages to the President and the First Lady and undermine decisions already agreed upon on a staff level. "It's harder to see how decisions are getting made; sometimes Valerie inherently makes decisions or makes recommendations based on what she thinks the President or First Lady will want and that can be a struggle for people," says one former aide to the First Lady. "They'd rather understand the logic and the framework."

No MODERN FIRST LADY had a more fraught relationship with her husband's advisers than Pat Nixon. It was so bad that when Betty Ford became first lady she said, "They're not going to lead me around like they did Pat." H. R. "Bob" Haldeman was Nixon's chief of staff and tried to have complete control over every part of the White House, including the First Lady's office and the residence staff. Haldeman and the President's counsel and assistant for domestic affairs, John Ehrlichman, took it upon themselves to reorganize the office of the First Lady and combined the posts of staff director and press secretary. The President himself even insisted on overseeing the delicate seating arrangements at state dinners, usually in the purview of the First Lady's office, and he wanted to weigh in on the musical entertainment and what was being served.

When Pat's director of correspondence, Gwen King, found Haldeman and Ehrlichman looking in cubbyholes and peering over people's desks in her East Wing office, she was worried. Not long after that she got a memo telling her that she would be reporting to someone in the West Wing, instead of the East Wing. When she told the First Lady, Pat was furious. The very next morning King got a call from the First Lady, who said, "Business as usual." She had won this battle—King would be reporting to Pat's chief of staff—but she would lose many more.

To the First Lady's face Haldeman was unfailingly courteous, but behind closed doors he referred to her derisively. Joni Stevens, who worked for special counsel and political strategist Harry Dent in the Nixon White House, remembered another staffer gesturing to Haldeman and asking, "Do you know who that is?" "No, I don't," Stevens replied. "That's God. Or at least he thinks he is." Haldeman's control was so complete that Stevens was once asked to report to the Old Executive Office Building next to the White House at 4:30 a.m. to type a top-secret report, based on results of a particular primary election, that was going to be sent to the President. A uniformed division Secret Service agent stood guard at the door while she typed, and absolutely no one other than Stevens and a handful of advisers was allowed in the room. She never found out why that seemingly innocent primary election was so important.

On January 8, 1970, Haldeman wrote in his diary, "P [President Nixon] called me back up with Bebe [Bebe Rebozo, Nixon's best friend] about problem of personal household staff, lousy food of wrong kind, etc. Wants me to solve it." Even though it was the First Lady's job to approve the menus each week, the President was having his chief of staff, and not his wife, tell the White House chef what to do. When given the chance Pat knew exactly what to tell the chef: "No lamb. Dick doesn't like lamb, he had too much lamb in the Pacific [during the war] and he does not want lamb." But the President's requests were even more specific: no French or California white, "only Moselle or Rhine, Johannesburg, only Bordeaux red or *very* good light French Burgundy," Haldeman told the chef. White House Doorman Preston Bruce remembered when Haldeman announced that no one would be allowed to stand in the hall outside the State Dining Room during state dinners—not even the Secret Service. It had been a perk of the job for the butlers to listen to the toasts from the hallway. Haldeman's office also sent out a memo reminding the residence staff not to ask for a photo or autograph of the President or his family. If they did, they would be fired immediately. "We all felt this was a cheap little shot," said Bruce. "We knew better than to approach the President with such requests."

The Nixons' social secretary, Lucy Winchester, said that she could always count on Haldeman to critique social events put on by the East Wing, and that once, when she fought back and told him that he did not know what he was talking about, he looked at her in "utter fury." "You and Mrs. Nixon say 'West Wing' in the same voice you would say 'left wing,'" he said, red in the face. "You don't even think I know which knife to lick first." Occasionally, he'd ask Winchester to fire residence staffers, but she always refused. At just five feet, one and a half inches she would straighten up and get very tall and tell him, "Listen here, you don't know anything so let me tell you about this man and what you need to know and what you haven't bothered to find out." Haldeman threatened to fire her when she mentioned inviting the Johnsons' social secretary, Bess Abell, and Lady Bird's press secretary, Liz Carpenter, to the Navy Mess, which is usually reserved for the White House staff. "We spent too much time and effort trying to get those people out of the White House!" Haldeman bellowed. (Winchester wanted to show them what redecorating they had done, even though she was growing concerned that the White House was becoming ridiculously threadbare. She carried a pair of small scissors in a little beaded evening bag that she had for state dinners and would run around and cut the "whiskers" off furniture where the fabric had worn through.) Pat Nixon felt the West Wing pressure. "My mother was frequently exasperated by the indifference she encountered in Haldeman and some of his aides," Julie Nixon Eisenhower wrote in her biography of her mother. "But she had spent so many years around power that she took with a grain of salt how it changed people."

Pat was aware of Haldeman's growing influence, and she

hated his constant videotaping of formal White House events. She wanted to maintain some sense of privacy and was frustrated at every turn. Pat was upset when she discovered that Haldeman had unilaterally approved Johnny Cash's request to record a concert at the White House and call it *Johnny Cash at the White House*. She vetoed the idea, viewing it as disrespectful because it echoed his famous recording at Folsom Prison. Yet, by that point in 1970, the White House did feel like a prison to her. Haldeman helped redesign Air Force One so that the large staff section was directly behind the President's office and before the First Lady's sitting room. The family had liked to gather in the presidential lounge that had been next to the presidential suite. With the redesign, every time a family member wanted to go to the lounge, she or he would have to walk through the staff compartment, where Haldeman would inevitably be sitting keeping tabs on who was visiting the President and for how long. Pat let her displeasure be known after the first flight from Andrews Air Force Base to "La Casa Pacifica," the Nixons' beachfront mansion in San Clemente, California, where they went to escape the pressures of Washington. Eventually the plane was returned to its original design, with a suite of rooms for the President and his family at the front of the plane, at a cost of approximately $750,000.

The President's advisers never understood Pat Nixon's public power. She became the first wife of a president to lead a United Nations delegation overseas when she went to Liberian President William R. Tolbert Jr.'s inauguration in 1972; her trip was a huge media success, but no one in the President's office congratulated her. Nixon's aide Charles Colson wrote a memo to the President that said, "As you know we have tried for three years to project 'color' about you, to portray the human side of the President. . . . Mrs. Nixon has now broken through where we have failed." But somehow that message was never conveyed to her and she felt undervalued. She was able to put people at ease in a way her husband never could. Once, a group of women from the Appalachian Mountains came to visit the White House and presented the First Lady with a cherry-tree quilt they had made for her. Some of them were weeping openly because they were so nervous and intimidated by the imposing surroundings. Pat entered the Diplomatic Reception Room on the ground floor of the White House, where they were gathered, and walked around the room, giving each guest a hug.

Chinese leaders wanted Pat to join her husband on his groundbreaking 1972 trip to China, the first visit ever by a sitting president to mainland China. But the men in the West Wing did not see the point. "He [Chinese Premier Zhou Enlai] wants Mrs. Nixon, he wants her on the trip," National Security Adviser Henry Kissinger told the President. "If she goes, she goes solely as a prop," Haldeman said, oblivious to the powerful image of an American First Lady visiting Chinese schools, factories, and hospitals and interacting with the Chinese people in a way the President could not. A hug between the First Lady and a Chinese child splashed across front pages could do as much to help diplomatic relations as high-level back-channel talks between diplomats. After it was settled that she would accompany her husband, Pat was told that she could take one person with her. "Mrs. Nixon said she wouldn't go if she couldn't take her hairdresser," an aide recalled, laughing. Indeed, her hairstylist, Rita de Santis from the Elizabeth Arden Salon in Washington, was her traveling companion on the historic trip. They had fun together and even developed their own hand signals to communicate in their hotel suites, knowing the Chinese had them bugged. When later asked how the President could not see the political pluses of taking his wife, Pat's chief of staff and press secretary, Connie Stuart, replied, "You can't be president of the United States unless you think you're the most important person in the world. You are more important than your wife. Period. I'm not so sure that the President was even happy that she came along, it was one more encumbrance, it meant more Secret Service, it meant another car." Pat, though, was happy Zhou Enlai pushed for her to go. She enjoyed being a part of history.

Zhou took a liking to the First Lady and at one banquet they discussed her visit to the Beijing Zoo, where she saw the giant pandas. When she reached for a container of Panda cigarettes, which had a drawing of two pandas on it, she turned to him and said, "Aren't they cute?"

Zhou replied, "I'll give you some."

"Cigarettes?" she asked him, confused.

"No, pandas." Two giant pandas were soon sent to the Washington National Zoo and became a sensation.

On the plane ride back from China, the First Lady told reporters, "People are the same the world over. I think they're [the Chinese] good people. It all depends on the leadership." Her image as "Plastic Pat" was partly a by-product of being cast aside by the President's West Wing, led by a small cadre of men, including the President, who never understood her power.

Pat Nixon was the ultimate political wife, with decades of training, and that may have been her problem. Rosalynn Carter's press secretary, Mary Hoyt, said she had heard that Pat Nixon's press secretary called her "the principal." "I always thought that was a little bit chilly." *New York Times* reporter Tom Wicker noted her ability to sit through speeches she had heard dozens of times as her husband was running for Congress, the Senate, and the presidency "with an only slightly glazed expression of awe and admiration." Polly Dranov, who covered Pat Nixon for the Newhouse News Service, remembers how relaxed and chatty she could be with the female reporters who were covering her, and how that changed on a dime. "She had mic fright and camera fright. As soon as those lights went on, she froze." Once, traveling with a chatty group of female reporters, Pat stopped talking as soon as one of them turned on a tape recorder. "She was very, very observant," East Wing staffer Joni Stevens says, "and she always made you feel like you were the only person in the room." That was the friendly Irish Pat Ryan sneaking through, with no West Wing staffers around to stop her. During a trip to Africa, *Time* reporter Bonnie Angelo says that she saw "Pat Nixon" return to the fun-loving woman she was and emerge as "Pat Ryan." "Pat Nixon was left somewhere flying over the middle of the Atlantic," she said. "I thought she was a special person and was being misused."

Pat was pretty, slim, and graceful, and she often came across like a delicate china doll. Her social secretary, Lucy Winchester, remembered that, like all first ladies, she had a side to her that very few people ever saw. Winchester always tried to make her boss laugh and would bring tabloid newspapers into the White House and send them up in a folder to Mrs. Nixon. Pat would devour them and send them back with a note, "Burn before reading!" She instructed Winchester to get rid of any trace of them so that the press would not find out about her guilty pleasure. Once Pat told Winchester, "I shared them with Dick and he thought they were hilarious!" Another time Winchester, who loved to play practical jokes, used a blow-up doll to surprise members of the Daughters of the American Revolution who were touring the White House. She knocked on the First Lady's door before the group arrived, knowing that she would be ready on time with every hair in place. When Pat answered, she saw the twinkle in Winchester's eye and the strange doll and said, "What have you done *this* time?!"

"Let's put her in the Queens' bathtub!" Winchester suggested. "We were sobbing with laughter, she was holding one end and I was holding the other, marching her down the hall and there was a startled policeman there at the end of the hall and we put her in the bathtub," Winchester said, laughing at the memory of this carefully controlled woman who claimed that she liked to iron her husband's clothes to relieve stress, and who always wore sensible shoes and kept her skirt length at least two inches below the knee, lugging this doll down the hallway of the White House. They were howling with laughter until suddenly Pat froze and said, "They're going to think it's me!" And that made them laugh even harder.

Pat and her social secretary could tease each other in a way that only close friends can. After several state dinners, Pat asked Winchester, a Kentucky native, "Lucy, is this too much for you, a farm girl? Meeting all the kings of the world?"

"Oh, Mrs. Nixon, you were a farm girl so you understand this: feeding kings and feeding cattle are pretty much the same thing. Feed them what they like, don't make loud noises or sudden gestures, and clean up afterwards."

Winchester's young daughter, also named Lucy, was given some toads and frogs as pets. "You know what frogs eat, don't you?" the First Lady asked Winchester, not seeming a bit horrified. She always kept a flyswatter nearby on the shelf of her sitting room closet. ("She had a deadly sure swing," her daughter Julie said.) For several weeks, until Winchester took the frogs and toads back to live with her mother in Kentucky, the First Lady sent down a red-tagged envelope in interoffice mail that was full of dead flies that she had swatted for Winchester's daughter. "The White House is full of cluster flies, as old houses are," Winchester said. The First Lady included a note: "Lucy, dear, I hope these help solve your feeding problem."

These lighter moments are overshadowed by the darker ones. The Nixons had a complicated marriage, and when asked, Connie Stuart says she never saw them argue: "Mrs. Nixon would never be seen arguing in public, are you kidding?" Pat was treated so shabbily at times by her husband that Nixon's media adviser Roger Ailes wrote Haldeman a memo on May 4, 1970, advising the President to "talk to her and smile at her." One event went particularly badly. "At one point," Ailes wrote, "he walked off in a different direction. Mrs. Nixon wasn't looking and had to run to catch up." In the margins of the long memo Haldeman wrote, "Good," "Absolutely," and "Right!" but for this particular suggestion he told Ailes flatly: "You tell him." Pat's press secretary, Helen Smith, says that Haldeman thought the President "would do well to dump her," and rumors of an impending divorce after they left the White House were circulated by West Wing aides. Nixon's private secretary, Rose Mary Woods, was close to Pat and would stick up for her during debates with Haldeman and Ehrlichman. But Pat was still often ignored. During a press conference with women reporters in honor of his wife's birthday, the President was asked what woman he most admired. "Well, Mrs. Charles de Gaulle," he said after a long, awkward silence. Yet Pat was getting more than five hundred letters a week, most of them supportive, at the height of Watergate. Pat had stood by him during the 1952 presidential election, when, as Eisenhower's running mate, he was accused of accepting an unethical expense fund, charges he responded to with his famous Checkers speech. And she stood by him after his 1960 defeat when he ran against John Kennedy for president, and she did not waver after his defeat in the 1962 California governor's race.

Being pushed aside, coupled with increasingly busy schedules, damaged the Nixons' relationship and created tension among their staffs. "Unfortunately," Ehrlichman said, "the Nixon family usually left it up to the staff to fight out these jurisdictional battles, and that allowed unnecessary animosities to develop." A triangle was formed. Pat would sit down with her husband in the residence over dinner and tell him, "Dick, there's something wrong down there and we've got to fix it!" Then the President would turn to Haldeman and tell him, "Bob, there's something wrong over there. Pat says there are some problems. Now we've got to fix them." They went around and around in the triangle, the First Lady and Haldeman growing increasingly frustrated with each other. Connie Stuart was installed by Haldeman to be the First Lady's press secretary and chief of staff so that the triangle could be a square: the First Lady to the President, the President to Haldeman, Haldeman to Stuart, Stuart to the First Lady. Haldeman wanted Stuart to give him warning before the First Lady went to the President with something.

Shortly after she started working for the First Lady in 1969, Stuart got a call from Haldeman telling her that the President wanted to see her. She found President Nixon eating his usual cottage cheese and pineapple for lunch in the small sitting room off the Oval Office. He asked her to sit down and for a half hour told her how important Pat was, and how she deserved good press. "Get your hands on everything you can to read about her, so that you get to know her as quickly as possible." He told Stuart that she was an amazing woman who had accomplished a great deal in her life. Before Stuart left him, he added, "Make sure you don't become a lightning rod," acknowledging the tension he knew was constantly consuming the East and West Wings of his White House.

Stuart was married to a West Wing staffer, and Haldeman considered her an ally in his ongoing war with the East Wing. "To him the East Wing was a problem and if I could keep the lid on it, I was his friend," she said. "The real adversarial relationship in the White House is the men against the women." Haldeman's plan did not work. Stuart got a call one morning from Haldeman saying, "The President doesn't like his lettuce." "So?" she said. "Well, you've got to do something about the lettuce, it's not fresh enough." "Bob, what am I going to do about the lettuce?" "I don't know how, but get it fresher." That's how it worked, she said: the President yelled at Haldeman and Haldeman yelled at her.

Feminist author and activist Gloria Steinem accompanied the Nixons on a ten-day campaign swing in hopes of getting an interview with the President for *New York* magazine. She was disappointed when she was given access to the First Lady only, but was surprised to discover that she "liked her [Pat] much better after this interview than before." At first she was disappointed by Pat's guarded answers, including her answer to what woman in history she most admired and would most want to resemble herself. Pat's answer, "Mrs. Eisenhower," was unconvincing to Steinem, and she pushed her to explain why she admired Mamie. Steinem says that after the two very different women sat through a long, awkward pause, "the dam broke." In a slow and deliberate voice, Pat revealed her resentment of Steinem, the tone of her questions, and her entire generation. "I never had time to think about things like that, who I wanted to be, or who I admired, or to have ideas. I never had time to dream about being anyone else. I had to work. My parents died when I was a teenager, and I had to work my way through college." She talked about an older couple whom she drove in their Packard cross-country so that she could make extra money to put herself through school, and how she had to fix their car when it was overheating in the desert and when the brakes gave out in the mountains. "I worked in a bank while Dick was in the service. Oh, I could have sat for those months doing nothing like everybody else, but I worked in the bank and talked with people and learned about all their funny little customs. Now, I have friends in all the countries of the world. I haven't just sat back and thought of myself or my ideas or what I wanted to do. Oh no, I've stayed interested in people. I've kept working." Then she gestured toward her folder bursting with letters and said the minute she has a free moment she makes sure to answer every last one of them. "Nobody gets by without a personal note," she continued. "I don't have time to worry about who I admire or who I identify with. I've never had it easy. I'm not like all you. . . ." Her voice trailed off and almost instantaneously she returned to her guarded self and acted as if nothing had happened. She patted Steinem's arm and said, "I've really enjoyed our talk. Take care!" Steinem was stunned, but Pat's brief flash of anger helped make her seem human.

When Pat ticked off the list of jobs she had held over the years, she left out her work as a technician in a hospital in upstate New York that treated patients with tuberculosis. Those were the most "haunting" six months of her life, she said. "They weren't supposed to do it, but some of the young patients would sneak away to go bobsledding and I went with them." When asked if she was afraid of catching the disease from them she said, "I never had the least fear of that. And it almost seemed that they believed they might contract good health from me."

While in the White House, Pat received hundreds of letters

every week (sometimes more than a thousand a week) and prided herself on reading almost every one. She did not want anyone who took the time to write to her to receive a form letter with a signature from an auto pen. She sat at her desk in the residence for four to five hours every day answering letters, often after dinner. Her office would send a pile of letters in brown expandable accordion folders, sometimes as many as five or six a day, to the second-floor residence. Each of Pat's signed letters was set aside to let the blue ink dry. When her head of correspondence arrived back at her office at eight thirty the next morning, the folders would be placed neatly on her desk. The only way that the women of the East Wing knew for sure that the President was resigning was when the folders stopped being returned. Pat did not open any letters during those painful final days.

First ladies get heart-wrenching requests, including letters from parents begging for help for their sick children. Several children were admitted to the National Institutes of Health because of Pat. One family wrote to the First Lady saying that their young daughter, who was very sick, needed heart surgery. An aide to the First Lady telephoned the American Heart Association and gave them the name and address of the little girl and told them that it was an emergency. Less than three months later Pat got a note from the little girl's parents thanking her for saving their daughter's life: "It may have been only a coincidence that shortly after your letter was received the problem was resolved in such an easy and a smooth succession of events. But we want to think that there was more to it than that." Pat set aside especially touching or funny notes, including one titled "I am the wife of President Nixon," written by a fifth grader from Elmont, New York. "Every time I make a speech I get a sore throat. When I go traveling with my husband we have to stand up for hours and my feet are killing me. My back aches from sleeping in so many different hotels. When I'm in bed trying to rest I hear the body guards standing outside my door. I wish I could be an ordinary house-wife and wear sneakers and blue jeans." Pat wrote back saying how happy she was to be First Lady, but in a note to an aide she said: "I have kept her letter. She hits the spot!"

Pat considered answering mail part of her job as first lady, and she did not want anyone to challenge it. Once, Ehrlichman asked for a meeting with Pat and quickly discovered how much quiet power she wielded. They met in the late afternoon in the elegant Yellow Oval Room on the second floor of the mansion, overlook-ing the South Lawn. "Perhaps you feel the need of someone to talk to—even to share problems with. There's the mail, for ex-ample. I would be glad to try to ease that burden," Ehrlichman said. At the mention of the mail Pat tensed up and knew exactly why he had come: to keep tabs on her and eventually control her correspondence. "I have an obligation to all the people who cared enough to write me," she told him. "I might be slow and old-fashioned, but I believe everyone deserves a personal answer and a personal signature." When he told her she would never have the time to answer every letter, she simply nodded once. The subject was closed.

Before he left, Ehrlichman told her that he was worried that she had grown too thin: "In the same way that you owe your cor-respondents your personal attention, you owe your family and friends the best care you can give yourself." He said she should call his wife, whom she was friendly with, if she wanted to talk to someone. But the First Lady did not offer any reaction at all. Ehrlichman said he was readying himself for tears or for anger, but her cold stare shook him to the core. He had been sent to talk to her by the President and by Haldeman, and as he sneaked out of the room, barely remembering to say goodbye, he realized he had absolutely nothing to report. This was a woman who was in complete control. It was a fierce battle between the East and West Wings because Mrs. Nixon was putting up a fight.

In interviews she often said she was never tired, and on the campaign trail she would sometimes make do with only a banana until dinner. But she never complained about being hungry. She had taken charge of her family's household after her mother died when she was a young girl and could not afford to be tired or hungry. "I don't get ill," she told one reporter. "The girls [her daughters, Tricia and Julie] say that there's no point in telling me if they don't feel well. They'll get no encouragement from me." She once went so far as to say, "Even if I were dying, I wouldn't let anyone know."

Like most first ladies, she was more liberal than her husband and was pro-choice and supported the Equal Rights Amendment. In a rare moment of candor, she told a group of women reporters that she was pushing her husband to nominate a woman to the Supreme Court for the first time. "Don't you worry," she said, "I'm talking it up." The President asked Attorney General John Mitchell to offer a list of qualified women and he seriously considered nominating a California Supreme Court associate, but decided against it. After weeks of consideration he announced his decision to appoint William Rehnquist and Lewis Powell to fill the two vacancies. When Nixon made the announcement Haldeman told him gushingly that he had "scored another ten-strike."

"Well, probably so, except for my wife, but boy is she mad." The silence at the dinner table that evening was broken by an angry Pat. She had gone out on a limb and spoken publicly, urging him to nominate a woman. Now letters flew in sympathizing with her about how her husband had "let her down." "Women in 1971," she told him, "need the recognition that a female member of the Supreme Court would bring them." The president sighed heavily and said, "We tried to do the best we could, Pat."

———

BETTY FORD, WHO replaced Pat so suddenly after President Nixon's resignation, was unusual because she publicly challenged her husband's decisions and made statements that sent his male political advisers into a frenzy. Her 1975 interview on *60 Minutes* with Morley Safer shocked the nation. She said that all of her children had experimented with marijuana, and she said that if she were a teenager she would probably try marijuana herself. She also admitted to seeing a psychiatrist, and she revealed that she was pro-choice. When Safer asked how she would feel if the Fords' eighteen-year-old daughter, Susan, confessed to having an affair, she said, "Well, I wouldn't be surprised. I would think she's a perfectly normal human being, like all young girls." There was an uproar as hate mail piled up in the First Lady's correspondence office and angry callers jammed the White House telephone lines.

Not long after the *60 Minutes* interview Betty doubled down with an interview for *McCall's* magazine in which she said that she wanted to have sex with her husband "as often as possible," and that she was "working on getting a woman on the Supreme Court." But soon the hate mail was outweighed by the number of fan letters from people happy to finally see a first lady express her own opinions, and the *60 Minutes* interview is now featured at President Ford's presidential library, along with exhibits devoted to Betty's outspokenness. *Time* reporter Bonnie Angelo summed up Betty's candor when she said, "She had not really been a captive of the political spotlight. Part of it was because she was always home with the children. So she didn't have the edges all worn smooth."

Ford had never faced a fierce primary before he got to the White House, and his family was not used to being on display. Betty was more outspoken and less willing to bite her tongue, even during the 1976 presidential campaign. Ford's advisers were not pleased. Once, when President Ford was meeting with his staff right before the kickoff of the campaign, one of his political strategists carefully brought up the "problem" of his wife. "Mr. President, we're so close to getting into the campaign, we love your wife, but do you think there's any chance you might be able to speak to her and just sort of politely ask her if she could tone it down until the campaign is over?" Ford looked around the table at each of his advisers and said, "My wife's office is right down that hall and I know she's in it right now. If anybody at this meeting would like to get up and talk to her you're more than welcome." No one took him up on his offer.

The Fords brought a casual warmth to the residence, even allowing their teenage daughter to roller-skate in the East Room and wear jeans on the State Floor, where the most formal and public rooms are located. Betty wanted to get to know the residence staff. Carpenter Milton Frame was impressed by her approachable manner. "I do recall that Mrs. Ford, she would invite you to sit down and have a cup of tea," he said fondly. She also enjoyed teasing the staff. During a tour of the private quarters, her press secretary, Sheila Rabb Weidenfeld, noticed a flower vase with the figures of two angels, with their hands almost touching. A cigarette was perched perfectly between them. "Oh, that," the First Lady said, laughing. "I put it there. That's just my way of testing whether the maids have cleaned the room!"

She was fun-loving and never really changed from the

outspoken Alexandria, Virginia, housewife she had been before becoming first lady and before then being the wife of the vice president. More than any other first family, the Fords brought a middle-class sensibility to the White House. One Saturday night, Butler James Jeffries was told to stop washing dishes and go upstairs to the second floor to help Betty with something. When he got upstairs, Betty asked, "Where are the butlers?" She was looking for the full-time butlers.

"They just went downstairs. I can go get them for you," he told her, pushing the elevator button to go back down.

"All I need is a man," she called to him, impatiently, from the Family Dining Room.

He laughs with a wink. "I said to myself, *Wait a minute, what is this lady getting me into?* So I went to see what she wanted and all she wanted me to do was take the nineteen-inch television into the bedroom!"

VII

The Good Wife

★

Strength and dignity are her clothing,
and she laughs at the time to come.
She opens her mouth with wisdom,
and the teaching of kindness is on her tongue.
She looks well to the ways of her household
and does not eat the bread of idleness.
Her children rise up and call her blessed;
her husband also, and he praises her:
"Many women have done excellently,
but you surpass them all."

—PROVERBS 31:25–29

Your mother is very sick, and she had to go to a psychiatrist.
—THE FORD CHILDREN'S NANNY, CLARA POWELL,
AFTER THEIR MOTHER, BETTY FORD, SUFFERED A
BREAKDOWN

Jackie Kennedy had always felt like "the worst liability" to her husband: she was too rich, she was too beautiful, she had an almost comically breathy voice, and she was often pregnant during the height of his campaigning, so she could not join him.

The President would get upset at her when the press wrote about her extravagant spending and her wealthy pedigree (she was educated at Miss Porter's, Vassar, and the Sorbonne, and she was the product of a broken high-class marriage), and her sister Lee's 1959 marriage to Polish Prince Stanislas Radziwill did not help. "I'm sorry for you that I'm such a dud," she told him. (Her husband's tastes were less highfalutin—she'd joke that the only music he really enjoyed was "Hail to the Chief.") But soon she started seeing the crowds turn up during the 1960 presidential campaign just to see her, and letters poured in asking her about her clothes and how to replicate her hairstyle. On their way to the inaugural balls, President Kennedy told their driver to turn on the lights inside their car "so that people can see Jackie." Kennedy family friend William Walton remembers, "We made her sit forward so that they could see her."

In the spring of 1961, less than six months after the President took office, the Kennedys went to Europe, where he famously said, "I do not think it altogether inappropriate to introduce myself. . . . I am the man who accompanied Jacqueline Kennedy to Paris, and I have enjoyed it." Jackie thrilled the crowds, with half a million people lining the streets chanting "Vive Zhack-ee" and "Kenne-dee." She spoke what French President Charles de Gaulle called her "low, slow" and flawless French. De Gaulle told the President that his Francophile wife "knew more French history than most French women." (Jackie hired French chef René Verdon from New York's famed Carlyle Hotel to take over the White House kitchen from navy stewards and caterers. She was the first first lady to insist that state dinner menus be written in French.)

Jackie could not help being aware of her own popularity and was sometimes generous with it. In Vienna, she stood on a balcony as a crowd of five thousand people below cheered "Jack-ee!" and she deftly pulled the dowdy and overlooked Nina Khrushchev, wife of Soviet Premier Nikita Khrushchev, outside with her and the chants morphed into "Jack-ee! Ni-na!" Nina reached for Jackie's white-gloved hand and held it high in hers, in a salute to the crowd. By the time they left the palace, Nina got an almost equal share of the applause. French cultural minister and author André Malraux was initially skeptical about the young American president and his wife, but Jackie won him over after an elaborate dinner she threw at the White House in his honor. At the end of the evening she got what she had been dreaming of when Malraux whispered to her softly, "Je vais vous envoyer *La Joconde*" ("I will send you the *Mona Lisa*"). Leonardo da Vinci's masterpiece was lent to the United States for the first and only time ever, all because of Jackie.

Jackie developed the first official White House guidebook as a way to raise money for redecorating (it sold an astounding half a million copies within ten months of publication). Nash Castro, who helped with the redecoration, recalls sitting with her during one of many meetings in the Yellow Oval Room of the residence as she went through every page of the book for two hours, making suggestions to editors along the way. She was far from her glamorous self in a loose housedress and loafers with no socks. Castro remembers one meeting ending at 6 p.m. Jackie's hair was undone and she had no makeup on. The next morning he woke up to a front-page photo in the *Washington Post* of her looking gorgeous at a state dinner the night before.

It seems that Jackie adopted an obsession with appearances and with perfecting the furnishings of the White House as a way of stifling a deep sadness that must have come from knowing about her husband's constant cheating. White House usher

Nelson Pierce remembered how involved Jackie was in the aesthetics of the mansion. "Mr. Pierce, I need some help!" she would often yell down. "I'd like to move this sofa over here," she said one day. Pierce asked whether she wanted him to see if one of the doormen was free to help, but she said no. "You pick up one end and I'll pick up the other." That night they moved the sofa to three different locations in the West Sitting Hall before she finally decided where she wanted it.

The President often seemed amused by his wife's obsession. White House Electrician Larry Bush remembers standing on a six-foot-tall ladder installing two gold sconces by the fireplace in the Red Room when the President walked in at the moment he began cutting into the gorgeous red twill satin walls. "Larry," he said, "what in the world are you doing?" "Your wife wants these gold sconces. . . ." Bush said. The President smiled, shook his head, and watched for a moment or two before he went back to his office.

Hundreds of pages of exhaustive handwritten memos reveal how much Jackie truly cared about the history of the White House and the preservation of its priceless antiques, and she succeeded in turning it into a living museum. "All these people come to see the White House and they see practically nothing that dates back before 1948 [when the White House was last restored during President Truman's administration]," she said in an interview with *Life* magazine in 1961. "Every boy who comes here should see things that develop his sense of history. For the girls, the house should look beautiful and lived-in. They should see what a fire in the fireplace and pretty flowers can do for a house." She hated the word "redecorate" and insisted that she was on a scholarly mission of "restoring" the mansion. While some of her personal memos— asking the household staff to bring down "our pathetic group of lamps" so that she could examine them, or to "take down the two hideous mirrors over the sofa" in the East Sitting Hall—seem elitist, they show her intensity and passion for making the White House more beautiful for every American. "The sun is going to fade the walls and curtains in the green, blue and red rooms—so the minute the tours are over, could you have the blinds drawn," she told Chief Usher J. B. West in one memo. "Also in the Blue Room make sure the braid on the curtains is turned in . . . if the braid faces out it will get sunburned."

Looking at her personal memos, however, it seems her quest for perfection would never be fulfilled: there was always more furniture to be ordered, more artwork to be swapped out or rearranged. She stood next to Electrician Larry Bush as he worked to arrange lighting for paintings depicting Native American life by George Catlin that she had acquired. Bush was lying underneath a piano in the room, trying to take measurements and decide where the spotlights should go. He went to fish a pen and paper from his pocket to write down some notes and was embarrassed to discover that he didn't have either. "I'll run and get my steno pad," she told him. He dictated notes to her of what he would need for the lighting and she suggested exactly where she wanted the spotlights to go. "A little to the left," she told him, motioning with her hand.

Her restoration of the White House was described in detail in the wildly popular hour-long CBS Television tour broadcast on Valentine's Day, February 14, 1962. *A Tour of the White House* was the first time television cameras were allowed inside the White House, and it was shot with eight television cameras over the course of almost seven hours in one day. "She was a brilliant woman. I wrote a script of what the questions might be, but she was so far ahead of me that she didn't need it," says CBS producer

Perry Wolff. Wolff went into the shoot with three color-coded scripts: one if Jackie was just interviewed, another if she was going to show photos, and the third if she was going to do a tour. "But she threw my script away; she was ready."

Jackie never buckled under the pressure but between takes "she smoked all the time," Wolff recalled. "She kept missing the ashtray and flicking the ashes onto the expensive silk covering of the bench she was sitting on. I knew there was tension there." That night she had dinner with columnist Joseph Alsop and his wife, Susan Mary Alsop. Later, when she and President Kennedy watched clips from the taping, the President was so impressed with her performance that he asked CBS if the crew could re-shoot his segment the next morning so that he could match hers.

In a letter to the Kennedys' friend William Walton, Jackie wrote, "My life here which I dreaded & which at first over-whelmed me—is now under control and the happiest time I have ever known—not for the position—but for the closeness of one's family. . . . The last thing I expected to find in the W. House." Behind the scenes she was a skilled caretaker of her fragile husband, who suffered from severe back pain and other medical problems. In a memo to the President's White House doctor she reminds him to use Johnson's Back Plasters, sent from Kennedy's mother. "He used one yesterday and liked it very much. It, obvi-ously, isn't a cure—but, it makes the sore spot feel warm which is better than just having it ache." She gets into every detail and when she asks the doctor to order more plasters she even gives him the price: forty-three cents each. She ends the note by asking him to send some mineral oil and talcum powder to the Presi-dent's valet, George Thomas, because he needs those to make sure his skin isn't irritated when he takes the plaster off.

Above all else, Jackie wanted her husband to be happy. On

particularly hard days, when she knew he was grappling with a major issue, she would leave him hand-drawn cartoons and do one of her hilarious impersonations of world leaders or his advisers. She always wanted the children to be on their best behavior when they saw their father after work, and she committed herself to making life in the residence a "climate of affection and comfort and détente." She organized small dinners with their closest friends and would wait as late as 6 p.m. to have the President's personal secretary, Evelyn Lincoln, phone in the invitations, because she often would not know if her husband would be in the mood for company until then. Every two weeks or so she would organize more elaborate dinners where guests danced to an orchestra in the elegant and intimate Blue Room until 3 a.m. She took care of her husband's every need; in a memo dated April 2, 1963, sent to Chief Usher West, she asks him to inquire with the Smithsonian Institution to find a woodcarver who could make a copy of the President's ornate Oval Office desk to be displayed in his library. In another she tells him that the President doesn't like the "muddy colors" of the rug in the Cabinet Room and asks that the curtains in the Oval be less "draped" and less "feminine." She even brought in his favorite foods, such as Joe's Stone Crabs from Miami.

Once she told her friend, the historian Arthur Schlesinger Jr., that she made what she considered the terrible mistake of asking her husband about what was happening in Vietnam. "Oh, my God, kid," Kennedy said, using a term of endearment that understandably rankled Jackie, "I've had that, you know, on me all day. Don't remind me of that all over again." The President had just taken his daily swim and was in his "happy evening mood," and she was consumed with guilt for even bringing the topic up. If she wanted to know what was going on, he told her, she should ask his national security adviser, McGeorge Bundy, to let her see all the cables. She read the weekly CIA summary as well as the India-Pakistan cables, mostly because she enjoyed the witty writing of Kennedy's ambassador to India, old friend and scholar John Kenneth Galbraith.

One thing she was never curious about was the details of her husband's cheating, though she certainly knew what was happening. But she had a sense of humor about him being a flirt. Early in their marriage, she was visiting Jack in the hospital where he was staying because of his bad back. Before the visit she went out to dinner with friends and the beautiful actress Grace Kelly was there. When Jackie got up to leave, Kelly said, "You know, I always wanted to meet Senator Kennedy." Jackie replied, "Will you come back with me to the hospital and meet him now?" Jack had complained that the nurses were older and not very attractive, so Jackie asked Kelly to put on a nurse's cap and uniform and tell Kennedy that she was his new night nurse. For a few minutes he didn't know who it was but then he exploded in laughter.

But the President committed constant betrayals, including having trysts with women as young as nineteen who were working in the White House. Jackie had a decision to make: look the other way or risk losing everything. Not long before Kennedy's inauguration, Jackie wrote a note to journalist and author Fletcher Knebel. "I would describe Jack as rather like me in that his life is an iceberg," she wrote. "The public life is above the water—& the private life is submerged." Her own father had cheated routinely on her mother, and she had come to accept it as the norm. A week after their tenth wedding anniversary Jackie wrote a letter to their friend Charles Bartlett, who had introduced them years earlier. She told him that without Jack her life would have "all been a wasteland, and I would have known it every step of the way."

But it was hard looking the other way all the time. One woman, named Mimi Alford, was a college freshman when she began a sexual relationship with the President. She and other young women were interns in the press office and soon became involved in relationships with Kennedy and some of his aides. "The thing that amazed me so was that these two or three girls were great friends and bosom buddies and gathered in corners and whispered and giggled, and there seemed to be no jealousy between them, and this was all one great big happy party and they didn't seem to resent any interest that the President or any other men might have in any of the girls," recalled Kennedy press aide Barbara Gamarekian. "It was a marvelous example of sharing, which I found very difficult to understand as a woman!" Kennedy's cheating was an open secret with reporters, who made offhand remarks about it, but it was considered off-limits to serious journalists.

Jackie was no fool. She sought out a doctor, who was a friend and neighbor of Robert Kennedy, to talk about the bouts of depression her husband's cheating had brought on. Once, when she was giving a reporter friend of hers from *Paris Match* a tour of the White House, she went to the vestibule of the Oval Office to say hello to the President's secretary, Evelyn Lincoln. She noticed one woman who was said to be having an affair with her husband sitting quietly nearby, probably petrified. Jackie turned to her friend and said, in French, "This is the girl who supposedly is sleeping with my husband." (Decades later, when Diane Sawyer asked Caroline Kennedy if her mother ever spoke about JFK's betrayals, Caroline said uncomfortably, "I wouldn't be her daughter if I would share all that.")

Jackie was always an individual. When the President came to her with letters criticizing her for wearing shorts that were too short, she simply said, "But they're not too short," and he would let it go. He did suggest that she wear hats instead of the scarves that made her look like a movie star. In an interview with the JFK Library, Jackie's mother, Janet Lee Bouvier Auchincloss, revealed advice she surely gave her daughter when she was first lady. "I do really think that you have to keep your own identity or you just become exactly like Mrs. Coolidge or exactly like Mrs. Eisenhower or exactly like Mrs. Truman. I think you must try somehow—within bounds there are certain things that obviously you can't do when you are very much in the public eye. I think Jackie, on the whole, was right to do what she thought was right or natural to her."

―――――

JACKIE SPOKE IN a childlike whisper of a voice (Kennedy's sisters called her "the Deb" behind her back), but she was tough as nails and would cut people off if she felt they had betrayed her. She delicately crafted the image of Camelot after persuading her friend journalist Theodore H. White to refer to the Kennedy years as Camelot—a magical time that was too good to last—in *Life* magazine. "Only bitter men write history," she told White. "Jack's life had more to do with myth, magic, legend, saga and story than with political theory or political science." She was terrified that her husband's dreams and accomplishments would be forgotten. In the days following the assassination she asked President Johnson to rename the Florida space center, Cape Canaveral, after her husband. Within an hour, Johnson had it done. She did not want her contributions to be forgotten, either, and she wrote an eleven-page memo listing the treasures she had brought to the White House and had it sent to Lady Bird before she moved out.

Jackie summoned White to the Kennedy compound in

Hyannis Port on Cape Cod in Massachusetts just a week after her husband's murder and delivered an incredibly compelling four-hour narrative of their tenure in the White House. According to handwritten notes White took during the interview, Jackie told him, "I'm not going to be the widow Kennedy in public; when this is all over I'm going to crawl into the deepest retirement there is." Jackie painted a vivid picture of those frightening moments after her husband was shot, when she cradled him in her arms as they raced to Dallas's Parkland Memorial Hospital. "Jack, Jack, can you hear me? I love you, Jack." When they finally got to the hospital (the short ride felt interminable) Jackie's beloved Secret Service agent, Clint Hill, pleaded with her to allow them to get the President out of the car. But she didn't want anyone to see him like that, with his brains exposed and blood everywhere.

"Mrs. Kennedy," Hill said. "Please let us help the President." But she would not let go of her husband.

"Please, Mrs. Kennedy," he begged her. "Please let us get him into the hospital." When she didn't answer he instinctively knew the problem and took off his jacket and placed it over the President's head. It was only then that she let go.

She insisted on going in to see her husband before they closed the casket in the hospital, and a police officer helped her pull off her stained white gloves that were stiffened with his blood. She put her simple bloodstained gold wedding band on his finger and kissed his hand. Later, she regretted the decision and felt she had nothing left of him, so one of Kennedy's most trusted aides called the morgue and got the ring back. "This is the closest thing I have to a memory of him," she told White as she quietly twisted it around her finger. "He bought it in a hurry in Newport just before we were married. It wasn't even engraved to me when he gave it to me. I had to put the date in later."

She carefully edited White's thousand-word essay, which ran in *Life*'s December 6 issue. She talked about the "magic" of her husband's presidency and how they would listen to the Lerner and Loewe Broadway musical *Camelot* before going to sleep. "I'd get out of bed at night and play it for him when it was so cold getting out of bed," she said, using the "old Victrola" in the dressing room between their two bedrooms to soothe him to sleep. His favorite lines came at the end: "Don't let it be forgot, that once there was a spot, for one brief shining moment, that was known as Camelot."

Jackie, like most of the other first ladies, was the fiercest protector of her husband's legacy. She held epic grudges against any of his detractors, or anyone who questioned the mysterious perfection of those thousand days. She never spoke again to their close friend the *Washington Post* editor Ben Bradlee after his book *Conversations with Kennedy* was published in 1975 because she felt that the book was too intimate. She selected historian William Manchester to write the definitive account of her husband's assassination and gave him unprecedented access, spending hours with him recounting her most personal memories of her husband's death. But she was furious when she saw the final product, *Death of a President*, and demanded that his publisher, Harper & Row, and *Look* magazine, which was set to run an excerpt of the book, make hundreds of changes. "The worst thing in my life was trying to get all those things of Mr. Manchester's out of his book," Jackie said. "I did my oral history with him in an evening and alone, and it's rather hard to stop when the floodgates open." She failed in her attempts to make sure that Manchester did not receive any of the profits, but he was hospitalized for a nervous breakdown because of the stress of the legal battle.

Jackie was similarly furious when, in 1978, she signed the

deed of gift on her oral history interview for the LBJ Library and almost immediately Hugh Sidey of *Time* magazine got hold of it and wrote a column on it. Soon other organizations were clamoring for it and for duplicate copies of the tape of the interview. The tape and the transcript were to be made available unless the donor objected, and since Jackie had signed over the deed to the library no one was at fault. Still, she was angry and had her lawyer insist that the transcript and tape be removed from the research room until she and the library could work on a new agreement. Lady Bird wrote to Jackie on August 3, 1978, acting like a concerned mother: "Library staff members have explained to me how the routine of the Archives regulations could result in the unfortunate exploitation of your interview. Nonetheless, I feel that steps could have been taken, and should have, to be more protective of you. You have had to endure so much in the public eye, I hate for us to be even the distant agent for unpleasant publicity for you." Lady Bird would never stop feeling protective of Jackie.

PAT NIXON GREW up on a small truck farm in Artesia, California, about twenty miles southeast of Los Angeles. She lost her mother to cancer when she was twelve. After her mother's death she took over the household chores, including the laborious task of doing the laundry, which involved building a fire in an outdoor brick fireplace and lifting the clothes with long sticks from cauldrons of boiling water into cold water and hanging the heavy wet clothes on a line to dry. (Even in the White House, with a staff of almost one hundred, she insisted on washing her own underwear and nightgowns and doing her own packing for trips.)

She told her daughter Julie, "When my mother died I just took responsibility for my life." She also took care of her two older brothers and her father before his death from silicosis, or miner's disease, five years after her mother's passing. By the age of seventeen, Pat was an orphan. She was determined to get a college degree and worked her way through the University of Southern California as a telephone operator and a bit actor in movies. She graduated cum laude in 1937. When she worked at a bank she was robbed at gunpoint; even then she calmly studied the robber's face and identified him to police. She met Richard Nixon when they both tried out for parts in a local production of *The Dark Tower* in 1938. She was earning $190 a month teaching shorthand and typing at a high school in Whittier, California, and he was a young lawyer in town who had just graduated from Duke University School of Law, where he was nicknamed "Gloomy Gus."

Nixon fell in love with Pat at first sight and proposed to her the day they met, but he had to court her for two years until she agreed to marry him. He was so infatuated that he even occasionally drove her to Los Angeles to meet other men for dates just so that he could spend time with her in the car. Her letters to him were friendly and decidedly unromantic. She began one 1938 letter with "Hi-ho, Hi-ho! How does it go?" and invited Nixon over so she could "burn a hamburger" for him. His notes to her reveal a deep love that may have lessened over the years but was strong at first. "Every day and every night I want to see you and be with you. Yet I have no feeling of selfish ownership or jealousy. In fact I should always want you to live just as you wanted—because if you didn't then you would change and wouldn't be you," he wrote in a voice that is hard to picture as Richard Nixon's. "Let's go for a long ride Sundays; let's go to the mountains weekends; let's read books in front of fires; most of all let's really grow together and find the happiness we know is ours." They married on June 21, 1940, in a Quaker ceremony in Riverside, California.

Pat was twenty-eight and Dick was twenty-seven. After several years in the navy during World War II, Nixon decided to run for Congress. Pat became his office manager and spent the rest of her life supporting his political ambitions, even though it was not the life she had ever wanted for herself or for her family.

Richard Nixon's youngest and last surviving brother, Ed, remembers those early days and how Pat, whom he had met in 1939 when he was nine and she was twenty-seven, took him under her wing. He told her that he wanted to see what the beach was like and she said, "Well, let's go see!" The Nixons were a working-class family who all worked at the family-owned grocery store and gas station in Whittier, and Ed says they never had time for anything but work. At the beach, Ed says, "I remember her running, she could almost run as fast as me, and that was something for a girl. . . . She wanted me to see the other side of life."

Pat's White House chief of staff and press secretary, Connie Stuart, says Pat did not want to be first lady in 1968; she wanted to be first lady in 1960, when her husband lost to John Kennedy. Pat was so upset by that defeat that it would be the only time photos show her crying. In fact, she sobbed after her husband all but conceded the election to Kennedy in the ballroom at the Ambassador Hotel in Los Angeles. She tried to hide from the cameras as she walked with her husband to their fifth-floor suite. Unable to hold it in any longer, she left his side and darted out ahead of him and ran to her bedroom so she could close the door and mourn the loss alone. She had worked hard on the campaign trail and she tried desperately to fight back bitter tears: "Now I'll never get to be first lady."

Pat was all the more stung by the narrow loss because her husband had been so kind to Kennedy; they shared memories of their time as junior senators and of the times when Nixon visited him as Kennedy was recovering from a back operation that nearly killed him in 1954. Jackie even wrote Nixon a note thanking him for his help while her husband was sick: "I don't think there is anyone in the world he thinks more highly of than he does you—and this is just another proof of how incredible you are." But during the heat of the 1960 campaign, the gloves were off and Pat was deeply hurt. Years later, when they were finally in the White House and Watergate was consuming her husband's presidency, she wondered aloud why no one in the media crucified Kennedy for stealing that election, citing the speculation that Chicago Mayor Richard J. Daley had stolen Illinois's twenty-seven Electoral College votes for Kennedy. (Kennedy won the bitter 1960 election by just 300,000 votes, or less than one-half of 1 percent of the total vote.) *Why had no one investigated the Kennedys for voter fraud when her own family was subjected to so much scrutiny?*

Nixon had promised Pat that he would not run again after he lost his 1962 comeback campaign for governor of California, famously blasting the press with this parting message: "You don't have Nixon to kick around anymore."

Pat was relieved. Her happiest years were after that 1962 defeat, when the family moved to New York and retreated to private life and Nixon worked as a lawyer. Jackie's reply to a condolence note that the Nixons had sent her after Kennedy's assassination in 1963 must have made Pat question whether her husband should ever return to politics. "We never value life enough when we have it," Jackie wrote. "I know how you must feel—so long on the path—so closely missing the greatest prize—and now for you the question comes up again—and you must commit all your and your family's hopes and efforts again. . . . If it does not work out as you have hoped for so long—please be consoled by what you already have—your life and your family."

Pat was not eager to enter the fray again in 1968. By the time they actually got to the White House in January 1969, the Vietnam War was raging and the feminist movement was in full force. As the wife of President Eisenhower's vice president, Pat had been trained at the knee of Mamie Eisenhower, the quintessential 1950s political wife, and she would have been an excellent first lady in the 1950s and early 1960s. "Life and history have not been fair to Pat Nixon. Period," Connie Stuart says. On the eve of Richard Nixon's first inauguration, Pat was asked if she had wanted her husband to get into politics. "No," she said. "I did not. Politics was not what I would have chosen for him because, after all, you don't see as much of your husband as you would like and it's a hard life."

Jackie wrote to Pat again after Nixon's victory. The handwritten card was delivered by messenger from Jackie's 5,300-square-foot New York apartment at 1040 Fifth Avenue to the Nixons' apartment at 810 Fifth Avenue (the most famous First Lady and the incoming First Lady lived just twenty-three blocks away from each other). In the letter Jackie congratulated Pat but added ominously, "You are such a close family that I know you will be able to be happy in spite of the pressures and the absence of privacy." Firmly believing their time had passed and wishing that her husband had given up politics, the exhausted Pat ate dinner alone before the inaugural balls while her family had a decadent steak meal served on china in the Family Dining Room. "I don't want any dinner," she said. "You've got to eat something, Pat," her husband told her. She relented and asked for a bowl of cottage cheese in her room (which sent the kitchen staff into a frenzy when they discovered that they did not have any cottage cheese on hand and someone had to race out to a local supermarket). Pat was in no mood to celebrate.

But she took her job seriously. She traveled more than one

hundred thousand miles as First Lady, visiting more foreign countries (seventy-eight) than any before her. Her foreign travels included the Nixons' historic visit to China in 1972 and a trip to Peru in 1970, when she led a major humanitarian effort, bringing tons of donated food, clothing, and medical supplies to tens of thousands of people devastated by an earthquake. She became the first first lady since Eleanor Roosevelt to travel to a combat zone when she visited wounded American soldiers in South Vietnam in 1969. She flew from the Saigon airport to the Presidential Palace in a helicopter that made dramatic nearly vertical takeoffs and landings to avoid sniper fire. Her Secret Service agents were armed with machine guns and shoulder belts loaded with cartridges. During a visit to an orphanage with 774 children, fighter jets and circling helicopters nearly drowned out her conversations with the children.

The protests over the war in the fall of 1969 were so large that the President called in hundreds of army troops to Washington to defend the White House. There were days when the window shades had to be drawn and the bomb shelter under the East Wing was used as an official command center where communications were kept open with the military in case National Guard troops were needed. The Nixons' social secretary, Lucy Winchester, had unknowingly scheduled the annual Senate Ladies Luncheon at the height of Vietnam War protests in May 1971. Streets around the White House were clogged as two hundred thousand demonstrators flooded the city. Winchester says that when she was leaving work protesters would leap on her car and spit on her windshield.

"Are you sure you want to do this? We can cancel this," she told the First Lady.

"Absolutely not," Pat replied—she had chaired the group when her husband was vice president. "The senators have no idea what we put up with all day long, every day. They are so sheltered. If their wives have to come to town, they will see what we are up against and they will tell their husbands." She told Winchester to spend the night before in a guest room on the third floor and not to forget her party dress. "I will not have you be held up in the morning by all those bad actors. The luncheon goes on."

Though she never publicly crumbled, Watergate took a terrible toll on Pat Nixon's health as she lost more and more sleep and felt that she needed to put on a brave face. She also lost weight and rumors of her drinking began to circulate, though her loyal aides beat them back, saying that she enjoyed an occasional highball and a cigarette at the end of a long day. "Watergate is the only crisis that ever got me down," Pat told her daughter Julie. "It is just constant. And I know I will never live to see the vindication." In a letter from the Eisenhowers' home in Gettysburg, Pennsylvania, Mamie wrote, "Pat Dear—This is not an engraved invitation but I would love to have you come up here when the President goes away—you could rest, walk, read, and gossip with me—know please everything would be on the QT." She signed the note "Love, Mamie E" and never once mentioned Watergate, but the implication that she knew Pat needed a place to escape is clear.

Pat strongly objected to her husband's decision to release transcripts of secretly recorded tapes of conversations relating to Watergate. She said they should be destroyed (preferably burned), and she was hurt that her husband never asked for her opinion before they were released. The tapes, she told her close friend Helene Drown, should be treated like "private love letters" meant for "one person alone." She was fiercely loyal to her husband, whom she had stood by for nearly thirty years of political life.

House Minority Leader John J. Rhodes, a Republican, told a group of reporters at a breakfast session that the President should consider resigning in order to avoid impeachment. "If Nixon comes to conclude that he can no longer be effective as president, he will do something about it," Rhodes said. "If he should resign, I would accept it." In fact, resignation, he said, "would probably be beneficial" to the party.

Rhodes came face-to-face with Pat Nixon in a receiving line at a party on Capitol Hill that evening.

"How are you, Mrs. Nixon?" he asked her.

As a photographer asked them to smile for a picture she said, through pursed lips, "Oh, yes. Let's smile as if we liked each other."

"Mrs. Nixon," Rhodes replied, "it isn't the way you heard it."

"Yeah," she said coolly, "that's what they all say."

In the spring and summer of 1974, before her husband's resignation, she spent most of her time in her pale yellow bedroom on the second floor of the residence, a prisoner of the White House. She still answered as many letters as she could, looking out onto a magnificent view of the National Mall. She also read books about friendship and love, and around 11 a.m. she would order a coffee and chef's salad or soup to be served at 1 p.m. Often the coffee would be the only thing she touched on the tray. Things got so tense that the butlers rushed to serve the Nixons dinner because once they sat down there was a deafening silence in the Family Dining Room that made five minutes seem like an hour. But there were times when the President tried in vain to lighten the mood. He suddenly looked at his wife one morning, focusing on her for the first time that day, and said, "My, that's a pretty suit you have on, Pat, you really look nice. I like that." She replied, a little sharply, "Oh, Dick, I've had this suit for years. You've seen this before. You know this isn't new."

On Valentine's Day in 1974, six months before the President's resignation, the Nixons had a rare dinner out at Trader Vic's, not far from the White House. UPI reporter Helen Thomas and CBS reporter Lesley Stahl found out that they would be there and got a table nearby. The Nixons brought along the President's best friend, Bebe Rebozo, and when they got up to leave Thomas and Stahl pushed to get ahead of them and ask them questions. The two reporters thought they would be getting a scoop, but as soon as the Nixons stepped outside, microphones and cameras were shoved in their faces by reporters who had been staking out the restaurant. Stahl and Thomas found themselves pushed aside as everyone clamored to ask the President about Watergate. When Thomas glanced to her left she saw that someone else had also been left behind: Pat Nixon. "How are you?" Thomas asked her. "Helen," the First Lady said, her eyes filling with tears, "can you believe that with all the troubles Dick has had, all the pressures he's been under, he would do this for me?" Thomas was speechless—she thought the President owed his loyal wife much more than just a dinner date.

In early August President Nixon told his family of his decision to resign and they pushed him to reconsider. But even they recognized the deep hole he was in when the so-called smoking gun transcript was released revealing a June 23, 1972, meeting between the President and Haldeman proving his culpability in the cover-up of the Watergate break-in. "This was the final blow, the final nail in the coffin," Nixon told former aide Frank Gannon in a 1983 video. "Although you don't need another nail if you're already in the coffin—which we were." On August 7, a congressional delegation led by Republican Senator Barry Goldwater told the President that he would not survive an impeachment vote. That night, Nixon decided he finally had to resign. Pat began packing and worked through most of the night; there was no use trying to sleep anyway. She would stand by him through it all. "With us sometimes," the President reflected, "you don't have to say it publicly, or even privately. Things unspoken say it more strongly."

They left the White House on August 9, 1974, and spent months in self-imposed exile at their home in San Clemente, California. When the former President was in the hospital because of a blood clot in his lung, Pat brought him McDonald's hamburgers and the two huddled together and watched reruns of *Bonanza*, a TV show they had never had time to watch before. So much had changed in their lives. The helicopter landing pad at their home was turned into a makeshift volleyball court and weeds started to take over the small golf course on their property. They were used to being completely surrounded by aides who acted as buffers between them, and it was the first time since their first political campaign in 1946 that they were truly alone with each other. Julie says that she and her sister, Tricia, saw "that they both survived because when my father felt defeated, Mother upheld him, and when she was spiritless, he rallied to comfort her. We never saw them give in to despair at the same time." Nixon would encourage his wife to eat more at dinner—"try the delicious squash from the garden"—and she'd leave a gardenia on his pillow at night.

———

BETTY FORD HAD dealt with debilitating pain from a pinched nerve after tripping over a stool in the family's den in their Alexandria, Virginia, home. She was also racked by arthritis. Her addiction to painkillers began in 1964 when she was prescribed medication for her neck, and those prescriptions multiplied when her doctor gave her pills for everything: for pain, for anxiety, to help her sleep. She was taking as many as twenty pills a day and often mixing them with alcohol, a potentially deadly combination that she began to depend on when she was raising her four children in their suburban home. It was a dependence that her husband did not want to admit to himself.

It was clear to some of the women in the East Wing that the First Lady had a serious problem. One of her East Wing staffers, along with a navy nurse who traveled with Betty, approached the White House physician, Dr. William Lukash, and told him they were concerned about the seven or eight bottles of pills, including pain medicine, that the First Lady traveled with. "We believe Mrs. Ford is taking too much medication," they said. He stared back at them: "Which medical school did you go to?"

Like so many women of her generation, Betty struggled to be the perfect housewife. She felt the heavy responsibility of raising children alone in the suburbs and keeping up appearances for her husband, his work colleagues, and their friends. But behind the scenes, Susan Ford recalled witnessing her mother buckle under the weight of it all and break down in the Fords' bedroom. Susan was eight years old and her congressman father was on the presidential yacht, the *Sequoia*, with President Johnson. She found her mother alone and sobbing. She ran to get their nanny, Clara, who called Ford and told him he needed to come home. Clara told the children, "Your mother is very sick, and she had to go to a psychiatrist." Susan Ford remembered not being able to process that at her young age. "I didn't know what I was supposed to do, where I was supposed to go. I was scared that mother might fall apart in front of my friends."

Betty kept her painful secret private during her time in the White House. Finally, on a Saturday morning in 1978, after the glare of the White House years was gone and the Fords had retired to Rancho Mirage near Palm Springs, California, her addiction was hard to ignore. For decades President Ford had looked the other way and refused to acknowledge it. The family staged an intervention at Susan Ford's insistence. Betty was thinking of calling her son Mike and his wife, Gayle, who lived in Pittsburgh, when the doorbell rang and Mike walked in. Suddenly she found herself sitting on the living room couch with her children sitting in chairs in a semicircle around her. Betty was stunned. "They went from one to another saying how I had let them down, how I had disappointed them. And, of course, this just was cutting to me. I was so hurt. I felt I had spent my whole life devoted to them, and they were telling me I was failing them."

They confronted her with the mornings when she had forgotten what they had told her the night before because she had had too much to drink. They went over the times when they had to turn to Clara when they were growing up because their mother wasn't acting like herself. Her son Jack said he avoided bringing friends home because he was never sure whether she would be slurring her words or not. Mike and Gayle told her they wanted her to be healthy for her grandchildren. Steve talked about a weekend not long before when he and his girlfriend had made dinner but Betty refused to come to the table and eat with them when they asked her to. "You just sat in front of the TV and you had one drink, two drinks, three drinks. You hurt me." She felt humiliated and strangely alone, and she burst into tears. "It'll be a day we'll never forget, but let me say this very affirmatively: it was the only thing that saved Betty's life," President Ford said.

Betty had trouble admitting that she was an alcoholic but she acknowledged her dependence on pills and partly blamed the doctors who had been overmedicating her for so many years. "It was easier to give a woman tranquilizers and get rid of her than to sit and listen to her." In 1978, two days after she turned sixty, Betty entered Long Beach Naval Hospital's alcohol and drug rehabilitation unit. When she went to drop off her things, she was astounded to discover four beds in her room. She said she would not sign in unless she was given her own room. "If you insist on a private room, I will have all these ladies move out," said Captain Joe Pursch, a navy doctor. "No, no, I won't have that," she told him, and within an hour she was moved in and a statement was being read to reporters.

It took Betty several days in treatment to acknowledge that she was not only dependent on pills, but also an alcoholic. "You're trying to hide behind your husband," Pursch said. "Why don't you ask him if it would embarrass him if you say you're an alcoholic?" She began to cry and her husband took her hand in his and said, "There will be no embarrassment to me. You go ahead and say what should be said." She sobbed uncontrollably and that night, lying in bed, she wrote a statement revealing the whole truth for the first time. "I have found that I am not only addicted to the medications I have been taking for my arthritis, but also to alcohol." Every evening the Fords would have a drink before dinner, but when Betty left treatment President Ford gave up his Jack Daniel's Silver and replaced it with club soda with lime. Betty had supported him through all those years; now it was his turn to support her.

After President Ford's death in 2006, Betty was depressed and was having trouble coping with life alone. Ford was the first president to reference his wife in his inaugural address when he said, "I am indebted to no man, and only to one woman." When Betty stayed at Blair House during her husband's state funeral she cried herself to sleep each night. (President George W. Bush was in office, and he told a staffer who was planning the funeral, "Whatever they need, we'll do.") "Do you think this is going okay?" Betty asked her assistant Ann Cullen. "I've got to tell you," Cullen replied, "I think you are doing absolutely a magnificent job." Betty started to cry and said, "Well, I have to because I'm doing it for him." President Bush, who was to escort Betty down the long aisle to her seat at Washington's National Cathedral at the state funeral, asked her if she wanted to use her wheelchair. She was eighty-eight years old and frail, and would have to endure days of national mourning and ceremonies, but she refused. She told friends, "I just did what my husband would have wanted me to."

When she was at President Ford's burial site at his museum in Grand Rapids, Michigan (Ford's presidential library is in Ann Arbor), her family kept asking her if she wanted to use her wheelchair, but again, she refused. She had walked along the river with President Ford near the exact spot where he was to be buried, and she wanted to make the walk with him one last time. With everyone worried about her health, all she could think about was her husband and the deep love they shared for more than fifty-eight years of marriage. She insisted on making the long walk from the car to the burial site, and told anyone who objected, "This is the last time I'll make this walk." After the funeral, she kept white Christmas lights plugged in year-round on an olive tree in front of their house. She did it, she told friends and family, so that her husband could see her from heaven and know that she was all right. When the Fords' personal chef, Lorraine Ornelas, saw Betty after her husband's death, they sat on the edge of the Fords' bed and Betty pushed a photo of her late husband closer to the edge of the nightstand toward them. "There he is," she said wistfully. "I just want to go be with my boyfriend," she told her children. "I don't know why I'm still here, I don't want to be here. I'm ready to go."

—————

LIKE PAT NIXON, Rosalynn Carter acted as a mother figure early on in her life. She knew aching loss as a young girl when her father, Edgar, died in 1940 when she was only thirteen. Wilburn Edgar Smith was a cotton and peanut farmer and a mechanic and he was a strict disciplinarian. But at the end of the day, he loved getting down on the floor and roughhousing with his brood of four children. "We had as much as anybody else in town and so we didn't realize we were poor," she said. Rosalynn helped milk cows and her father would flavor the milk with vanilla or chocolate and sell it at five cents a bottle. She also pruned watermelons and put arsenic on cotton to combat the boll weevil beetles that destroyed crops. During harvesttime, she picked cotton and harvested peanuts by pulling them up from under the ground and shaking the dirt off them. When her father died of leukemia at age forty-four, her whole life changed and she had to help her mother, Allie Smith, who was only thirty-four years old. Rosalynn's mother recalled the painful day when her husband gathered the children together to tell them he wasn't going to get better. He told his small children—the youngest was just four years old when he died—that he wanted them to look after their mother. "They all started screaming," Rosalynn's mother said. "Of course, I started crying, too." Rosalynn recalled, "My mother depended on me to help her with the smaller children. I worked in a beauty shop in Plains for a while but, looking back, I didn't help her nearly as much as I should have." She did the cooking, laundry, and cleaning so that her mother could go to work at the post office and support their family.

Rosalynn threw herself into her schoolwork. She was her school's valedictorian, and in seventh grade she got five dollars from a man in town who said he would give the cash reward (which is the equivalent of approximately eighty-five dollars today) to the student with the highest grade point average because he didn't pass the seventh grade.

It is not surprising that Rosalynn crossed paths with Jimmy Carter, who also grew up in Plains, Georgia, a small town with dirt roads and a population of fewer than seven hundred people. They grew up at a time when a bag of candy cost a nickel and everyone in town knew each other. The closest movie theater was in Americus, about ten miles away, which meant if they went, they would go for the whole day. There were nine girls and six boys in Rosalynn's high school class. She was on the basketball team, and because her school was so small the girls on the team became cheerleaders after they played.

Rosalynn's mother was a true southern lady (during the births of her four children she said, "I tried to be as quiet as I could"), and she raised Rosalynn to be a feminine, shy little girl who liked to play with dolls. "Some children get out and get so dirty, but she was right neat and all," her mother recalled.

Rosalynn and Jimmy met through Jimmy's sister, Ruth, who was Rosalynn's closest friend. Jimmy's mother, Lillian (a tart-tongued woman affectionately referred to as "Miss Lillian" by almost everybody), was a nurse in town and was helping to care for Rosalynn's father during the year and a half that he was sick before he passed away. Lillian knew that Rosalynn's mother had four children to care for, so she would occasionally bring Rosalynn home with her to stay at their house after she took care of her father. Rosalynn's mother sometimes asked her to go get the doctor when her father could not take the pain any longer. Once, Rosalynn ran to the doctor to get the medicine herself instead of waiting for him to come. She ran so hard and so fast that she was out of breath by the time she got to his house and couldn't tell him what was wrong, so he took her back home in his car. "It was a terrible time," Rosalynn's mother recalled.

Like Lyndon and Lady Bird Johnson, Rosalynn and Jimmy did not know each other well before they got married, but they wrote to each other every day while he was at the U.S. Naval Academy in Annapolis, Maryland, and she was at Georgia Southwestern College. They were married in 1946 in a small ceremony with no attendants, when Rosalynn was eighteen and Jimmy was twenty-one. By then they were both itching to leave Plains. "When we got married I think I was kin to everybody that Jimmy wasn't," Rosalynn said. "Once we got married, we were kin to everybody in town." Rosalynn became a navy wife and gave birth to three sons while Jimmy was away at sea. They moved around the country, from bases in Virginia to Hawaii to Connecticut. Each of their three sons was born in a different state, and Rosalynn raised them and kept track of all the family's bills, a job she maintains today. She made most of her children's clothes and all of her own. (Years later, when she was in the White House, she brought a sewing machine with her, which she kept in her dressing room and used to do quick repairs on dresses for herself and for their daughter, Amy.) Jimmy was accepted into an elite nuclear submarine program but turned it down after his father died so they could return to Plains in 1953 to look after the family's peanut farm. But he didn't bother to consult his wife about the decision, and about relocating the family yet again after his seven years as a naval officer. Rosalynn was so furious that she refused to talk to him during their entire trip from where they were living at the time, in Schenectady, New York, to Plains. "I didn't particularly want to come back. I thought I was seeing the world," Rosalynn said. After that, Carter learned his lesson: to always consult his wife on major decisions.

Back home in Plains, Rosalynn helped run the peanut farm and raised her family there. She remembers arriving in Plains shortly before the landmark Supreme Court case *Brown v. Board of Education,* in which the Court decided unanimously that racial segregation in public schools violated the Fourteenth Amendment. "It was a hard time for us," Rosalynn said, since some of their neighbors treated them badly because of their support for integration. "I remember going to church when people wouldn't speak to you, you're kind of outcasts." Sometimes, when they pulled up at a gas station, nobody would come out to fill up their car.

Soon Jimmy began his first political campaign. In 1962 he won election to the Georgia Senate, and in 1970 he was elected governor of Georgia. By the time he announced his presidential campaign in December 1974, Rosalynn was a seasoned politician herself. She would number her husband's jokes so that he wouldn't repeat any to the same group, she typed thank-you notes to people her husband met on the campaign trail, and she even started taking memory classes to remember faces and names. Rosalynn worked tirelessly and stayed up until the early hours of the morning rehearsing campaign speeches.

Carter ran for president against Gerald Ford in 1976 as a Washington outsider. Before he won the Democratic nomination, he had a group of Georgia volunteers, known as the Peanut Brigade, who campaigned door-to-door for him. Rosalynn hit the road with a vengeance, and when she arrived in a small town she would scope out the tallest antennae and head straight there to the local television and radio stations to offer herself up for an interview. Some of the stations were so small that they had only one employee, who usually had no idea who Jimmy Carter was. Rosalynn came prepared with a list of five or six questions she wanted asked. Nine times out of ten, she said, the station used the questions she suggested. "I was getting my message across."

Carter won a narrow victory over President Ford in 1976, capturing just 51 percent of the popular vote and 297 electoral votes (Ford won 241 electoral votes). After his inauguration, Carter, who was a Baptist Sunday school teacher, banned hard liquor from being served at White House formal dinners. Because he thought it was too pompous, he insisted that "Hail to the Chief" no longer be played, a tradition that dated back to 1829. He took the oath of office wearing a $175 business suit from Georgia, pledged to cut back on chauffeured cars for staff members, and sold the presidential yacht, the *Sequoia*, in his effort to be a citizen-president.

After her husband was elected, Rosalynn sometimes felt intimidated. She remembers how mortified she was when Henry Kissinger, who was President Ford's secretary of state, came to brief Carter in Plains before the inauguration, and she went to get Kissinger a glass of water. It was a Tweety Bird glass from *Looney Tunes*. She thought, *When I get to the White House, I'll serve him with crystal.*

Jimmy and Rosalynn ignored security concerns and broke with tradition when they decided to walk hand in hand with their daughter Amy down Pennsylvania Avenue after the inauguration ceremony. It was part of their mutual desire to connect with people and move away from what they saw as President Nixon's imperial presidency. Rosalynn even wore the same ensemble to the inaugural balls in 1977—a gold-embroidered sleeveless coat over a blue chiffon dress—that she wore to her husband's inauguration as governor in 1971. Two of the Carters' sons and their families, Jimmy Carter's mother, and his brother Billy all lived in the residence part-time. Rosalynn had to contend with an eccentric and hard-drinking mother-in-law who paid butlers to walk to Connecticut Avenue to buy her a bottle of Jack Daniel's from a liquor store because her son kept such a watchful eye on her. (An aide remembers her saying, "Okay, now that Jimmy's gone, you want a drink?") The President's younger brother Billy was involved in several scandals while his big brother was President, and he loved his beer. "I didn't know he drank until I saw him sober one time," said a Carter family friend.

Jimmy Carter was the first American president to be born in a hospital, and in many ways his wife helped modernize the office of the First Lady. As a young girl, Rosalynn had watched Eleanor Roosevelt wield an enormous amount of power and influence as First Lady. Rosalynn was the first first lady to use her own office in the East Wing, and she became the first first lady to hire a chief of staff whose government salary and rank were equal to the President's chief of staff. Full-time positions in the East Wing grew by almost 20 percent under her stewardship. In order to get to work efficiently every day and not be distracted by the tourists who visited the White House from 8 a.m. to noon, Rosalynn took a secret passageway through the basement underneath the mansion, passing large laundry rooms, the Plumber's Shop, and the bomb shelter, and coming up through a stairway that led straight to her offices in the East Wing. The steam pipes running in the basement ceiling made the route especially welcome on cold days. "With Jimmy's energy conservation program, it was the only really warm place in the White House," she joked.

Rosalynn had an official lunch with her husband in the Oval Office every Wednesday, a highly unusual arrangement that followed the tradition of the President and Vice President's weekly lunches. The ritual came about because Rosalynn had pressing issues to discuss, including their personal finances and their children, as well as the policy issues she cared deeply about. When the President stepped off the elevator on the second floor at night he dreaded seeing her because he knew she would come at him with an onslaught of questions and suggestions. Once he proposed a weekly lunch, she began to organize her thoughts and put important notes in a brown leather folder that she brought with her each week. By the time it was Wednesday the folder was completely stuffed. Sometimes she would bring up personnel issues—she lobbied intensely to have her husband fire Joe Califano, the secretary of health, education, and welfare. "My reasons were purely political," she said. "I felt Jimmy could find someone who would do the job just as well and keep a lower profile." She was much more political than her husband and would often argue passionately with him about postponing certain decisions and announcements until after his reelection, including parts of the Mideast peace agreement and federal budget cuts that would affect the Democratic constituency in New York City a week before the New York State primary. "Can't you wait a week?" she pushed him. He had a stock reply to her pleas, which only angered her more because it sounded so pompous: "I'll never do anything to hurt my country."

Jerry Rafshoon, who was one of the President's top three advisers, turned to Rosalynn if they couldn't convince the President of something. He said pollster Pat Caddell did the same. If Caddell was worried about something that Rafshoon and other aides were pushing, he would tell Rosalynn, "These guys screwed up, they're my friends, but they're wrong," Rafshoon said. "Then she would get on Jimmy and he would get on us." Sometimes Caddell would have dinner with the Carters alone. Rafshoon says that he could always tell the next day because the President would walk into the Oval Office with bloodshot eyes because the First Lady had been trying to convince him of something that Caddell had told her. "She's had him all night," he and Chief of Staff Hamilton Jordan would joke.

During the 1976 campaign the press called Rosalynn the "steel magnolia" because she masked her own sharp intellect under a veneer of southern femininity. (She did not mind the nickname and said, "Steel is tough and magnolia is southern.") She was an active first lady who, during her first fourteen months, visited eighteen countries and twenty-seven U.S. cities, made fifteen major speeches, and held twenty-two press conferences, according to a study by the *Washington Star*. She clearly loved every minute of it and was thrilled when the President asked her to take a twelve-thousand-mile journey to visit seven countries in Latin America, where she pushed leaders on human rights and nuclear nonproliferation. She joined Israeli Prime Minister Menachem Begin and Egyptian President Anwar Sadat at Camp David. She was there for much of the thirteen-day summit at the secluded, 134-acre retreat in Maryland's Catoctin Mountains, where they reached a historic agreement in September 1978. "I was there for most of it and I saw her being deeply involved in the process," said Carter's vice president, Walter Mondale. In her autobiography, Rosalynn wrote about "our experiences" with Sadat and Begin and says, "We had found the two men to be very different." Rosalynn was her husband's confidante, she was perceptive, and she was able to see things that the President could not. "He's not observing when people are lying to him, or kissing his ass, and she is," Rafshoon said.

Rosalynn took almost two hundred typed pages of notes during the summit. When she could not sit in on meetings, the moment the President walked in the door she asked him, "What happened?" She went through the ups and downs and the false starts and stops during the momentous series of meetings. She knows her husband better than anyone else and wrote in her notes: "When Jimmy's pondering, he gets quiet, and there's a vein in his temple that I can see pounding. Tonight it was pounding, and neither of us could eat much as the sun set on our third day." (Rosalynn had helped smooth the path of negotiations by hosting Sadat and his wife, Jehan, during a visit to Camp David in February 1978, seven months before the Camp David negotiations began. The Carters and the Sadats had taken snowmobile rides on the grounds of the beautiful presidential retreat and Rosalynn had made sure that Sadat's favorite hot mint tea was always available.) Among the best days of Jimmy Carter's presidency was Monday, September 18, 1978. While Sadat and Begin watched from the balcony, Carter briefed a joint session of Congress on the success of the summit and had to stop twenty-five times for applause. Rosalynn sat between the two leaders wearing a pretty blue blazer and matching skirt. Few people ever knew just how important she was to the negotiations and that she was there through every turn.

The most controversial thing that Rosalynn did as first lady was to attend Cabinet meetings, something no other first lady had done, at least not to public knowledge. She said she needed to know what was happening so that she could tell the American people. "I never, of course, liked the criticism, but I didn't pay any attention to it," Rosalynn said in an interview. "I had learned that you were going to be criticized for whatever you did, so why not do what you wanted to do." Other women do not blame her. Ann Romney, married to Mitt Romney, who ran for president in 2008 and was the Republican nominee in 2012, says, "Frankly, I'd love to [go to Cabinet meetings]. Who wouldn't?"

President Carter said he had no problem with his wife attending the high-level gatherings. Jerry Rafshoon said it was to be expected because the Carters talked to each other about absolutely everything. "Whatever secrets there were," Vice President Mondale said, "she knew about all of them." That kind of intimacy can be unnerving, even for longtime aides. Rafshoon says, "They used to read the Bible in Spanish. Hamilton and I would really get worried when we'd be in a meeting with the Carters and if the subject was a little bit touchy, if we were advocating something, all of a sudden they'd start speaking to each other in Spanish." Neither Rafshoon nor Hamilton spoke Spanish. (Herbert Hoover and his wife, Lou, both spoke Chinese after living in China for several years, and shared the same intimacy—they would whisper in Chinese to each other when they wanted to have a private conversation during receiving lines at the White House.)

The first Cabinet meeting Rosalynn went to was on February 28, 1978. She sat next to Veterans Administration head Max Cleland near the door and occasionally took notes. President Carter says that no one else paid much attention to her. But he knew. "I was constantly aware that my wife was watching me," he said. By attending such high-level meetings Rosalynn left herself open to criticism in a way that Nancy Reagan, who wielded as much power as Rosalynn, would never allow. (Nancy said she would have been "embarrassed" to attend a Cabinet meeting, yet in fact she helped select members of her husband's Cabinet and was a critical part of her husband's political career, including his two terms as governor of California.)

It was a few months after President Carter's inauguration when he asked Rosalynn to go on a special mission for him. He said he was too consumed with the energy crisis and the Middle East peace process to go himself. The trip to Central and South America during the first two weeks of June 1977 was not devoted to typical visits for a first lady to schools and hospitals. This time

Rosalynn was being sent to deliver a very serious message on human rights to the leaders of Costa Rica, Ecuador, Colombia, and Venezuela. Critics in Congress and the press were furious—one *Newsweek* reporter said a first lady should be given such a weighty foreign policy assignment only if some way could be found to hold her accountable if something went wrong. Rosalynn was determined to be taken seriously and spent two months preparing for the precedent-breaking trip, with countless briefings from the State Department. She brushed up on her Spanish with lessons with Gay Vance, the wife of Secretary of State Cyrus Vance, three mornings a week in the White House Solarium. During meetings with leaders she took notes and then wrote long memos to the President and the State Department. It was not an easy visit. When she met with the president of Costa Rica, he invited his wife to join them and she worried that he had assumed the visit was purely social. "No matter what I asked him, he would answer to the men in our party," she said. "I was determined to get his attention and to have my say, and finally, when I opened my notebook and continued to address questions directly to him, he began to respond to me." Eventually, one by one, she began to win over different South American leaders, most of whom were not used to talking to a woman about policy. They began to realize that she had a direct line to the President and that it would be far more effective to communicate with her than with any member of his Cabinet.

Like any shrewd politician, she knew that on her trip she would be peppered at press conferences with questions about the latest controversy, including one involving a U.S. financier accused of fraud who was seeking refuge in Costa Rica. But she was a step ahead of the press corps: "I had anticipated this before leaving Washington and had refrained from being briefed about him so

I could legitimately claim ignorance of the situation." When she came back to Washington she briefed the Senate Foreign Relations Committee.

Her signature issue was mental health, an issue that dominates the news decades later. She had a distant cousin who suffered from mental illness when Rosalynn was a young girl, and she remembered running and hiding when she heard him coming down the streets of their small town singing at the top of his lungs. Years later she felt ashamed at how she had treated him, and she devoted much of her time in the White House to advocating for better care for the mentally ill. She wanted mental illness to be treated like any physical illness. One month after taking office, President Carter created the Mental Health Commission. On the day the committee was announced, Rosalynn told the press that she had just gotten a note that very morning informing her that the Department of Justice prohibits the president from appointing a close relative, such as a wife, to a civilian position. Up until then she was planning to chair the commission. "There is, however, no problem with you being designated as honorary chairperson," she said, amid laughter from reporters. "So I'm going to be a *very* active honorary chairperson." She was upset that the press overlooked the commission's work to cover sexier stories, like the Carters' edict banning hard liquor from state dinners. She delved into the committee's work, and she helped draft a bill that provided more funding for the treatment and prevention of mental illness and was submitted to Congress in 1979. She was the second first lady (Eleanor Roosevelt was the first, when she testified on behalf of coal miners) to testify before Congress. She was constantly talking with Congressman Henry Waxman and Senator Ted Kennedy, the chairmen of the House and Senate committees handling the legislation, even as Kennedy was mounting a challenge to her husband during the 1980 primary. The bill passed and the Mental Health Systems Act was signed into law by President Carter in October 1980. But when President Reagan came into office he cut most of the funding for the legislation. "I felt betrayed," Rosalynn said. "It was one of the greatest disappointments in my life." Now, when she sees mental health discussed as such an important issue, she's frustrated. Rosalynn's director of projects in the White House, Katherine Cade, says that on a number of occasions in private meetings Rosalynn has said that if the recommendations of her commission had been implemented thirty years ago, it might not be such a crisis now.

———

THE HARDEST PERIOD of the Carter presidency was during the Iran hostage crisis, which consumed the last 444 days of her husband's presidency. On November 4, 1979, Islamic revolutionaries stormed the U.S. Embassy in Tehran and took more than sixty Americans hostage. The hostage takers, who were mostly students, said that the American hostages would not be released until the shah, an exiled former Iranian leader who had sought treatment for cancer in the United States, was sent back to Iran so that he could stand trial. The revolutionaries said the shah was "anti-Islamic" and they accused him of stealing billions of dollars. Rosalynn admitted that she wanted to send the shah back to Iran so that the hostages would be released, but she knew he would most likely have been killed. "I never stopped wishing we hadn't let him come into the country in the first place. I wished Jimmy had followed his first instincts. But when the shah became ill, it was the right thing to do, and I suppose we always have to do 'the right thing.'" The bulk of the campaigning in 1980, when Carter ran against Ronald Reagan, fell to Rosalynn because the President decided to stay in the White House to handle the crisis. She checked in several times a day from the campaign trail, and when she could not speak with her husband she talked directly with National Security Adviser Zbigniew Brzezinski, who even initiated meetings with her to discuss how to handle the crisis. "I kept her abreast because I knew she would be discussing those issues with the President."

When the Carters left the White House in January 1981, they returned to Plains and embarked on the longest and most ambitious post-presidency in American history. Despite all of his accomplishments, Jimmy Carter says, in all of his ninety-one years he is proudest of marrying Rosalynn. "That's the pinnacle of my life."

———

LIKE BETTY FORD, whose father was an alcoholic who died in an apparent suicide when she was just sixteen years old, Nancy Reagan had a painful relationship with her father, who left her mother a few months after she was born. Her mother, Edith, was a Broadway actress who got a divorce from Nancy's father and passed along her own incredible determination to her daughter. When she arrived at the hospital to give birth to Nancy and was told there were no rooms available, Edith said, "No rooms? Then I guess I'll have to lie right down on the floor of this lobby and have my baby here!" Edith sent a two-year-old Nancy to live with her sister and brother-in-law in Bethesda, Maryland, outside Washington, D.C., so that she could pursue her acting career. Nancy's six-year abandonment haunted her forever. When she was five years old she got double pneumonia. *If I had a little girl*, Nancy said to herself, *I'd certainly be there if she was ever sick.*

When Nancy was seven years old, her mother married a prominent surgeon named Loyal Davis, and Nancy moved with

Edith to live in Chicago. Edith gave up acting and devoted herself to promoting her husband's career. The family lived on the city's wealthy Gold Coast in a fourteenth-floor apartment on Lake Shore Drive. Nancy begged Loyal to adopt her but he resisted because her biological father was still alive. But she was determined, and by age sixteen she was officially Loyal's daughter. As with her mother, once Nancy had her sights set on something it was going to happen. Once she decided Ronald Reagan would be her husband, Nancy won him over by going to his Los Angeles horse ranch on weekends and helping him with the decidedly unglamorous task of painting the pickets on his fence.

Nancy so appreciated the unconditional love she received from her husband that she fiercely protected him from anyone who she felt did not have his best interests at heart. The men in the West Wing were absolutely afraid of crossing her. The West Wing staff called Nancy "Evita" (after Argentina's first lady Eva Perón) and "The Missus" behind her back. "At the end of the day, first ladies are going to bed with the president each night and may say, 'I really want you to do this for me,'" said a staffer. "And then he will likely say yes."

In a letter Lady Bird sent to Nancy on November 9, 1994, five years after Ronald Reagan left office, Lady Bird refers to an interview Nancy gave to Charlie Rose a few weeks before at the 92nd Street Y in New York. In that interview Nancy skewered Oliver North, who was the Republican Senate candidate in Virginia at the time. When Rose asked her about North she said, "Ollie North—oh, I'll be happy to tell you about Ollie North," pausing for laughter and applause. "He lied to my husband and lied about my husband—kept things from him he should not have kept from him. And that's what I think of Ollie North." She was referring to North's central role in the Iran-Contra affair, when the Reagan administration admitted to selling arms to Iran in violation of an embargo in exchange for the release of hostages, and to using the proceeds of those sales to fund the Contra rebels in Nicaragua. "The last time you and I talked, we were discussing giving or not giving interviews," Lady Bird wrote. "I feel I know exactly why you did it—because he [Oliver North] tried to hurt your husband—my reaction would be to feel like striking back. But I can't resist telling you, Nancy, that the 'fall-out' of your interview was a most wonderful surprise and help for me and mine!" In a strange twist, Nancy Reagan, the most well-known Republican woman at the time, helped Lady Bird's son-in-law, Democratic Virginia Senator Charles Robb, in his reelection bid because Oliver North was his opponent. Nancy's comments helped destroy North's political career, and Robb won the election.

Nancy was especially furious about the way her husband's chief of staff, Don Regan, was handling the Iran-Contra scandal. Nancy prodded her husband to get out and make a public statement and fire the people responsible, something he had always resisted. But once President Reagan took his wife's advice and spoke publicly about the scandal and acknowledged his mistakes, his popularity surged. Nancy helped push out National Security Advisers Richard Allen and William Clark, Secretary of the Interior James Watt, and Secretary of Health and Human Services Margaret Heckler. But Don Regan was the best-known casualty of her anger. Two years after becoming her husband's chief of staff, he was fired. Reagan's first chief of staff, James Baker, explains Regan's departure simply: "He did not take care to make sure that he had one-half of the team [Nancy] on his side, which was a fundamental mistake."

Nancy thought Regan was pushing her husband in all the wrong ways. She worried about Reagan's 1987 State of the Union address, which came just three weeks after he had prostate surgery. ("He doesn't need to work full-time," she told Regan, "he can work out of the residence.") She was not the only one who did not think Regan was up to the job. Vice President George H. W. Bush told the First Lady, "You've really got to do something about Donald Regan."

"*I've* got to do something? What about *you?*" she said.

"Oh, no, no, no. It's not in my job description." Firing high-level presidential aides was not technically in her job description, either, but, she said, "It landed on my watch." If no one else was going to take charge then she would. She deftly arranged for her husband to meet with former Democratic National Committee chairman Robert Strauss, whose opinion the President respected, and who also wanted Regan gone. Strauss's advice helped bolster Nancy's argument and Regan was soon out.

Later she said Regan had overstepped in other ways, even trying to monitor the President's phone calls. There was no doubt in her mind that he had to go after he hung up on her twice. "You might have been able to get away with it once, but not twice!" the Reagans' son, Ron, said. "That was really the end of Don Regan. That's not something you're going to do to my mother."

In her memoir, Nancy, a self-described worrier, wrote, "In my next life, I'd like to come back as Ronald Reagan. If he worries, you'd never know it. . . . I seem to do the worrying for both of us." Before President Reagan left for a trip, Nancy would give him a three-by-five card with reminders: *5 p.m.: Take medication; 6 p.m.: Dinner; 9 p.m.: Brush teeth; 9:30 p.m.: Bedtime.* After his surgery for an enlarged prostate in 1987 she reminded him, "Honey, stop talking, go take your bath." George Hannie, who was a White House butler, says Nancy would watch the President get ready for press conferences in the Rose Garden from the window in the West Sitting Hall, and she would let everyone know if she thought his jacket was not quite right. "Here, go bring him this one," she'd say, handing a butler a different jacket. Once there was hardly any time before the news conference was set to begin, and the butler did not want to bother the President, but he dutifully raced to the Rose Garden. No one wanted to disappoint Mrs. Reagan.

Reagan's adviser Michael Deaver remembered one hilarious visit to an Episcopal church near Middleburg, Virginia, during the 1980 presidential campaign. After making sure the sermon would be suitable and nothing would catch the Reagans off guard, he agreed that they would attend an eleven o'clock service. The Reagans were stunned, however, when they were invited, along with the rest of the congregation, to the front of the church to take Communion. Nancy had a look of panic on her face, and as they walked up the church aisle she whispered, "Mike! Are those people drinking out of the same cup?" At the Reagans' church in Los Angeles, Bel Air Presbyterian, small glasses of grape juice and squares of bread were passed between the aisles, so the Reagans really had no idea what to do. Deaver told Nancy that she could simply dip the wafer into the cup, but when she did, it fell in. Reagan followed his wife's lead and dropped his wafer in the wine. Nancy was mortified, but as her husband stepped out into the midday sun he had a smile on his face, confident that all had gone well. It was Nancy who was left to worry about whether the press would notice that the Reagans had no idea how to take Communion.

Nancy was most concerned about who was advising her husband, and she had final say. The First Lady wanted James Baker, a more moderate Republican, to be chief of staff in her husband's first term, even though her husband wanted the more conservative Edwin Meese. Baker got the job. "I would never have been in the Reagan White House had it not been for Nancy Reagan,

I'm quite confident of that," Baker admits. Baker picked Deaver, a close confidant of Nancy, as his deputy, a smart decision that showed he knew just how important it was to have the First Lady in his corner. Nancy worked to make sure that her husband was surrounded by aides who were loyal, and she favored moderates because she knew that he would have to work with the Democratic-controlled Congress and that moderates would have a better chance of getting deals done. Reagan political consultant Stuart Spencer says, "She made decisions on who was going to be around him from the campaign to the [California] governor's office to the White House. That was her role." She was at almost every campaign meeting, and she cultivated wealthy California friends who she knew could help her husband's gubernatorial campaign and, later, his presidential campaign. "I talk to people, they tell me things. And if something is about to become a problem I'm not above calling a staff person and asking about it," Nancy said at a 1987 luncheon at the American Newspaper Publishers Association convention in New York City. "I'm a woman who loves her husband and I make no apologies for looking out for his personal and political welfare."

She even had a hand in foreign policy. She felt that it was important for the United States to open up a dialogue with the Soviet Union. She thought that National Security Adviser William Clark was too much of a hard-liner when it came to the Soviet Union. She was constantly talking to Secretary of State George Shultz, a moderate, and she eventually pushed Clark out. "Ronnie thought," she hastened to add, "as did I, that there had to be a breakthrough. . . . Well, I didn't just sit back. I was talking to people."

In September 1984 the President invited Soviet foreign minister Andrei Gromyko to the White House. Nancy swept in, wearing one of her signature bright red dresses. The men were having sherry before lunch. "Does your husband believe in peace?" Gromyko asked her.

"Of course," she said.

"Well then, whisper it in his ear every night."

"I will, and I'll also whisper it in your ear." She wanted to make an impression that would get back to the Kremlin.

It was Nancy who was always looking for signs of disloyalty among her husband's political aides, and it was Nancy who scanned the crowd as her husband spoke to see who was paying him the proper respect. At the Italian-American Federation dinner in Washington with Democratic rival Walter Mondale, Nancy said, "When it was Ronnie's turn to speak, I noticed that Mondale didn't applaud—not even once." During his 1984 reelection campaign, Reagan had a disastrous debate with Mondale and Nancy demanded answers. When her husband told her that he'd felt "brutalized" by the grueling debate prep, which included a full-dress rehearsal in the Old Executive Office Building complete with lights and cameras and about thirty staffers pelting him with suggestions, she was furious. "I was upset because I thought they'd gone about it all wrong. And they had. They overloaded him."

The Reagans' son Ron said that his father was impossible not to like. "You can dislike his policies or something he said, but him personally, he was very, very difficult to dislike." Nancy, on the other hand, was a "pricklier personality" and he watched as his mother became a magnet for criticism that should have been directed at his father. If people disagreed with the President they vented their frustration by labeling the First Lady as a ruthless, vapid, control freak. Ron said he's not sure if his mother took on this burden consciously or not, but by doing so she shielded her husband from lots of pain and took it upon herself to be the lightning rod for his administration. Ronald Reagan desperately wanted everyone to like him and, of course, everyone likes to be liked, but Nancy was willing to sacrifice that admiration to be her husband's ultimate protector. And she paid the price: in a December 1981 Gallup poll, she had the highest disapproval rating—26 percent—of any modern first lady.

————

HILLARY CLINTON'S DEFINITION of being a good wife was very different from her predecessors', and was more transactional. She did not want to just sit in on Cabinet meetings—she wanted to speak up during Cabinet meetings. At first she wanted to be her husband's domestic policy chief, but the President's pollster, Stan Greenberg, convinced them that it would be disastrously unpopular. The President's own secretary of health and human services, Donna Shalala, and Treasury secretary, Lloyd Bentsen, warned Clinton against appointing Hillary to head up the Task Force on National Health Care Reform to usher in the biggest social program since President Roosevelt's creation of Social Security. Hillary led a massive, bureaucratic team to come up with a plan for a new health insurance system that would keep costs down and expand coverage. It would be her job to sell the plan to lawmakers and business leaders. Alarms sounded in the West Wing when the President announced his wife's appointment just five days after the inauguration. But the President knew how badly she wanted to tackle the issue and he felt he had to give her the important assignment after she stood by him during the allegations that he had had an affair with Gennifer Flowers. (Flowers claimed she had a twelve-year affair with Clinton in Arkansas; years later he would admit to one occasion in 1977.)

Clearly his advisers were correct and Hillary's interpretation of the role of first lady was not meshing with what most Americans wanted. A Gallup poll found that after the 1993 inauguration Hillary was viewed favorably by 67 percent of Americans. By July 1994, only 48 percent rated her favorably, with a large number saying she had overstepped by having an office in the West Wing. She invited a group of female reporters to lunch at the White House and asked them how she could soften her image. "I am surprised at the way people seem to perceive me," she said to the group, which included Marian Burros of the *New York Times* and Cindy Adams of the *New York Post*. "Sometimes I read stories and hear things about me and I go 'ugh.' I wouldn't like her either. It's so unlike what I think I am or what my friends think I am." When Burros wrote a story—"Hillary Clinton Asks Help in Finding a Softer Image"—that appeared on the front page of the *New York Times*, Hillary was furious and demanded an apology, arguing that the lunch was supposed to be off the record. "I was dumbfounded," Burros said. "There was nothing unflattering in that piece. On the contrary. I had taped the whole thing, including where she gave us permission to quote her." Hillary's need for control eclipsed the story and became late-night news fodder.

She wanted to play a major role in policy decisions, but when her health-care plan failed to get approval from Congress and Democrats suffered a disastrous loss in the 1994 midterm elections, she decided to leave Washington as often as she could. She had a "two-hundred-mile limit," according to veteran ABC reporter Ann Compton, who covered the Clintons. In Washington Hillary was very unapproachable, but the farther out of town she got the more accessible she became. Hillary loved going on foreign trips, especially when she traveled with Chelsea. The press had lots of personal time with her on those trips when they sat around and really talked, almost always off the record. "The minute we

The Reagans kissing under the mistletoe in 1987. These women are their husbands' greatest confidantes and their fiercest protectors. "My life began with Ronnie," Nancy said.

Barbara Bush's husband served as vice president to Ronald Reagan for eight years, but she was rarely invited to the private living quarters of the White House. When a scathing biography of Nancy Reagan was published, Barbara quickly snapped it up and slapped another book jacket on it so that no one would know what she was reading.

Hillary Clinton is the only first lady to run for office herself. Before then she was completely devoted to her husband's political career, yelling, "Give me a break!" during a press conference held by one of his opponents when Clinton was running for his fifth term as governor of Arkansas. Here she campaigns for her husband ahead of the 1992 presidential election.

First Lady Barbara Bush *(left)* welcomes her successor, Hillary Clinton, for a tour of the White House on November 19, 1992. Barbara would never forgive Hillary for deeply personal attacks made during the campaign against her husband, President George H. W. Bush.

From left to right: Ted Kennedy (standing), Jackie Kennedy (wearing a striped shirt and sunglasses), Hillary Clinton (in a straw hat and sunglasses), and Bill Clinton on a cruise along the coast of Martha's Vineyard in August 1993. Hillary idolized Jackie and asked her for advice on raising children in the White House. Jackie told her, "You're going to have to put your foot down."

Six first ladies gathered to raise funds for the National Botanical Garden in May 1994. *From left to right:* Nancy Reagan, Lady Bird Johnson, Hillary Clinton, Rosalynn Carter, Betty Ford, and Barbara Bush.

From left to right: Rosalynn Carter, Hillary Clinton, Betty Ford, Barbara Bush, Nancy Reagan, and Lady Bird Johnson at the dedication of the George H. W. Bush Presidential Library on November 6, 1997, in College Station, Texas.

Former White House Head Butler George Hannie remembers how quiet Hillary Clinton was when she was consumed with worry about the Monica Lewinsky scandal. Here Hillary watches as her husband speaks on the day the House of Representatives voted to impeach him on charges of perjury and obstruction of justice.

At the end of Lady Bird Johnson's 2007 funeral, the University of Texas band played their school spirit song, "The Eyes of Texas," and native Texan and UT alumna Laura Bush gave the "Hook 'em Horns" sign. Laura's mother-in-law, former First Lady Barbara Bush, smiles along with Susan Ford *(right)*. Caroline Kennedy, head bowed, stands to the left of Barbara Bush. *Front row, from left to right:* Nancy Reagan, Rosalynn and Jimmy Carter, Laura Bush, and Bill and Hillary Clinton.

Laura Bush, a Republican, and Michelle Obama, a Democrat, are closer than Michelle is with Hillary Clinton. During the 2008 presidential campaign, Laura defended Michelle when she came under criticism, and the two have since praised each other's work as first ladies.

Hillary, then secretary of state, talks with Michelle Obama at an awards ceremony at the State Department in 2010. The two are not close, in part because of bad blood left over from the bruising 2008 Democratic primaries, but also because they are fundamentally very different women.

From left to right: Rosalynn Carter, Michelle Obama, Hillary Clinton, George W. Bush, and Nancy Reagan attend Betty Ford's 2011 funeral. After President Ford's death in 2006, Betty told her children, "I just want to go be with my boyfriend."

Michelle Obama is counting down the days until she can leave the confines of the White House. In 2011, she took a rare trip to a suburban Target department store in Alexandria, Virginia, where an Associated Press photographer shot photos of her. Michelle's first chief of staff, Jackie Norris, says, "I think there were a lot of people saying no to her in the beginning. . . . That's pretty hard when you first come into an environment and have so many restrictions put on you and such high scrutiny."

Michelle Obama grew up in a working-class family on Chicago's South Side and she's most comfortable talking to young boys and girls with backgrounds like her own. "Don't ever scale back your dreams," she told students graduating in 2010 from Anacostia High School, considered one of the worst schools in Washington, D.C. And she's known for her hugs. Here she bear-hugs a young girl at an event in the White House's East Room on April 22, 2015.

Michelle Obama came into the White House describing herself as "mom-in-chief," and her devotion to the Obamas' two young daughters has remained her top priority. When their father's term ends, Sasha will be a sophomore in high school and Malia will be in college. *Above:* The Obamas sit for a family portrait in 2009 in the Green Room of the White House. Sasha has her arm around her father, and Malia has her arms around her mother. *Left:* The Obamas in 2015 in the Rose Garden. Malia is on the left, and Sasha is on the right, posing with their Portuguese water dogs, Sunny and Bo.

In 2013, Michelle Obama, Laura Bush, Hillary Clinton, Barbara Bush, and Rosalynn Carter gathered for the opening of the George W. Bush Presidential Center in Dallas. These remarkable women, who are sometimes political rivals, will always be united as part of the uniquely American sisterhood of first ladies.

Melania Trump appears with her husband, Donald Trump, shortly before he won the Republican presidential nomination. She is the latest woman to take on the challenging role of First Lady.

Less than forty-eight hours after the most divisive campaign in modern history, First Lady Michelle Obama invited incoming First Lady Melania Trump for tea in the Yellow Oval Room in the White House residence. The two women were carrying on a tradition that was started decades ago and is a small but integral part of the country's peaceful transition from one administration to the next.

came home the political walls went back up," Compton recalled. These glimpses of an unguarded Hillary were so sought after that reporters clamored to get on the foreign trips. On her first trip overseas, according to her then–press secretary, Neel Lattimore, there was so much interest that he had to bring reporters to the luggage compartment and ask them to take some of their things off the plane because the plane was too heavy. (The excess luggage was put on a separate support plane.)

While Hillary was still First Lady she decided to run for the Senate, and things were better around the White House as the fighting with Bill over the Monica Lewinsky affair subsided. "She would have hit him with a frying pan if one had been handed to her," says Hillary's friend Susan Thomases, "but I don't think she ever in her mind imagined leaving him or divorcing him." Members of Hillary's inner circle say that the idea of running for the Senate came from New York congressman Charlie Rangel, but it's clear that no matter who brought it up first she didn't need much convincing. President Clinton was pushing her behind the scenes to run—he knew that he owed her that much at least. In a 1999 interview with *Talk* magazine Rangel said, "He [Clinton] was the one who asked the most questions about how she could win. You could see the guilt written all over his face. Any man would do anything to get out of the doghouse he was in." When Hillary first told Thomases about her idea, her friend said that she did not want to see her battered in a campaign. "Then it became clear to me that this was something she really wanted to do, and she convinced me that it was very important for her that she herself have validation by the voters." During those final months as First Lady, when she was looking at floral arrangements for formal dinners, Hillary's mind was clearly elsewhere. "You could feel there was some disconnect. Sometimes she'd sigh, 'I've got to hurry, I have to be somewhere,'" said White House Florist Bob Scanlan. She was thinking of bigger things.

Hillary had fought for her husband during the Senate impeachment trial. She helped win him the support of the Democratic caucus by arguing before its members as dispassionately as possible that what he had done was wrong but not impeachable. "You all may be mad at Bill Clinton. Certainly, I'm not happy about what my husband did. But impeachment is not the answer," she told them. "Too much is at stake here for us to be distracted from what really matters." Some members left with tears in their eyes.

On the same day that the Senate was voting against impeachment, Hillary was meeting with New York politico Harold Ickes, who had been her husband's deputy chief of staff, to plot her run for the Senate. She bristled at the thought of being known as the "former first lady" for the rest of her life. She had used her star power to help salvage her husband's presidency under humiliating circumstances, and now it was her turn. "After eight years with a title but no portfolio," she said, "I was now 'senator-elect.'" Ironically, years later, Hillary was asked what TV show she enjoyed watching when she took a break from the presidential campaign. Her reply: *The Good Wife*.

VIII

Bad Blood

★

When Michelle Obama views the Clintons, I don't want to say
she's looking down her nose at them—but she kind of is.
—FORMER OBAMA ADMINISTRATION AIDE

During the 1960 presidential election, Republican President Dwight Eisenhower supported Richard Nixon, his vice president, and made his aversion to the young John Kennedy clear when he derided him as "the boy." When Kennedy won the election, Eisenhower took it as a personal blow. The enmity was mutual. Kennedy's friend Charles Spalding said that Kennedy thought of Eisenhower as "being a nonpresident" who was not "totally aware of his powers."

More than any other first lady—with the exception of Hillary Clinton—Mamie Eisenhower hated to leave the White House. She had never spent so much time with her husband as she had when he was President. He'd been the Supreme Commander of Allied Forces in Europe during World War II and was often overseas. And at age sixty-four Mamie resented her replacement, whom she sneeringly referred to as "the college girl." Jacqueline Bouvier Kennedy's beauty and cutting-edge style would soon eclipse the middle-class and ultrafeminine shirtwaist dresses, pearl chokers, and short bangs of Mrs. Eisenhower.

The outgoing first lady traditionally gives her successor a walk-through of the White House's private living quarters on the second and third floors. The press was clamoring to find out the date when Jackie would get her private tour, just like the tour Lou Hoover had given Eleanor Roosevelt, and Bess Truman had given Mamie. Jackie had never seen the second floor, and as late as mid-November no one had any idea when she would get a look. Time was of the essence as Jackie was pregnant and her due date was fast approaching. During a November 22, 1960, press conference the Kennedys' vivacious social secretary, Letitia Baldrige, told reporters, "The invitation has not been extended yet, but we hope it will be."

Jackie had been told by the White House that she would be getting an invitation in mid-November, but Mamie clearly had no interest in making a big announcement or a show of public affection to her young and beautiful successor. Mamie was in control and she intended to relish her position. Finally, the invitation was formally extended through Mamie's secretary to Jackie's secretary for a visit on December 9. The call came a few days before November 25, when Jackie delivered her son John-John by C-section, and it was a much more formal invitation than the personal call Bess Truman had made inviting Mamie to the residence after the 1952 presidential election. The much-anticipated meeting was not revealed to reporters until five minutes after Jackie had arrived.

Before the visit, Jackie's Secret Service agent called Chief Usher J. B. West, who ran the residence, advising him to have a wheelchair and a staffer to push it readily available, since Jackie was still weak from the C-section. When West told Mamie, she replied, "Oh, dear. I wanted to take her around alone." Mamie suggested

that a wheelchair be ready but not made available unless Jackie asked for it.

Exhausted and pale, Jackie arrived alone at noon on the ninth, a little more than a month before her husband's inauguration. She was dressed in a dark coat, black fur hat, and black gloves. West led her through the imposing Diplomatic Reception Room and into an elevator to the second-floor residence, where Mamie was standing regally in the hallway.

"Mrs. Kennedy," West said, introducing the new First Lady. Mamie extended a cool hand toward Jackie but never stepped forward, forcing Jackie to walk slowly toward her. The First Lady was not going to make it easy for the woman who was dethroning her. "I turned and left them, and waited in my office for a call for the wheelchair," West recalled. "A call that never came." After some time, two buzzers rang in the Usher's Office, the signal that Mamie and Jackie were coming down the elevator. The tour had lasted an hour and ten minutes, and Mamie showed Jackie some thirty rooms. As the First Lady walked over to a Chrysler limousine that would take her to her usual card game, Jackie slowly and quietly made her way to her three-year-old station wagon. "I saw pain darken her face," West said. There had been no wheelchair, that much was clear. The next morning West and Maître d' Charles Ficklin went to Mamie's bedroom for their daily meeting. The First Lady sat, propped up by pillows against her pink headboard, picking at her breakfast. There was even a pink bow in her hair. She lowered her voice and said, "There certainly are going to be some changes made around here!"

After her White House tour, Jackie went to meet her family at the airport for a flight to the Kennedy estate in Palm Beach. Ever the politician, she lied to reporters and told them how kind Mamie had been to have a wheelchair available for her, but that she had chosen to walk. When a reporter asked Jackie what color

she planned to paint John-John's nursery, she laughed: "Don't ask such silly questions." She had much more than the nursery on her mind. She was carrying copies of the entire White House floor plan and spent much of the planned vacation before the inauguration outlining how she wanted to change each and every room.

Two months later, when Jackie was comfortably installed as the new First Lady, she turned to West and asked, "Did you know that my doctor ordered a wheelchair the day I first went around the White House?"

"Yes, I did," he replied.

She was puzzled. "Then why didn't you have it for me? I was so exhausted after marching around the house for two hours that I had to go back to bed for two whole weeks!" West told her that Mamie had asked him to have it placed behind a closet door next to the elevator in case she needed it. But Mamie never mentioned it to her guest. Jackie laughed and said, "I was too scared of Mrs. Eisenhower to ask."

———

PAT NIXON WAS so humiliated by her husband's 1960 defeat to John Kennedy that she did not want him to concede the election too soon, and she even demanded a recount. There were hurt feelings on Jackie's side as well. During the campaign, when Jackie was accused of spending thirty thousand dollars a year on her clothes and going on shopping sprees in Paris, she shot back, "I couldn't spend that much unless I wore sable underwear." She added cattily, "I'm sure I spend less than Mrs. Nixon on clothes." Jackie later said that she was grateful that her husband didn't make her "get a little frizzy permanent and be like Pat Nixon."

Oddly enough, Pat and Jackie first met when Jackie was the "Inquiring Camera Girl" for the *Washington Times-Herald* before her

marriage to JFK. She was paid $42.50 per week and she lugged a ten-pound Graflex camera around Washington; her short columns featured chatty interviews. In one column, Jackie asked six housewives, "Do you think that Mamie Eisenhower's bangs will become a nation-wide fad?" She asked Pat Nixon, when she was the wife of the vice president, "Who will be Washington's No. 1 hostess now that the Republicans are back in power?" Pat shrewdly replied, "Why, Mrs. Eisenhower, of course." Jackie even interviewed six-year-old Tricia Nixon for her column. Three days after Eisenhower was first elected, Jackie went to the new Vice President's house on Tilden Street in Washington and asked Tricia, "What do you think of Senator Nixon now?" The little girl replied, heartbreakingly, "He's always away. If he's famous, why can't he stay home?" Jackie's boss at the newspaper teased her when she told him that she was quitting her job and getting married to then-Senator John Kennedy. "Don't you think he's a little too elderly for you?" Jackie was then twenty-four years old and Jack was thirty-six.

Because Nixon was Eisenhower's vice president, the Kennedys had to come face-to-face with their defeated challengers the morning of the inauguration for the ceremonial coffee at the White House. "I remember," Jackie recalled, "sitting on the sofa next to Mrs. Nixon, who looked really pretty that day. You could see she could really be rather New York chic when she wanted." Mamie Eisenhower got one final dig in as she, Jackie, and New Hampshire Senator Styles Bridges, who was responsible for part of the inaugural ceremony, waited in the car. President Eisenhower and President-elect Kennedy walked by in their black top hats and Mamie exclaimed, "Look at Ike in his top hat. He looks just like Paddy the Irishman!" Mamie no doubt referred to the caricature of an Irishman on purpose as the nation's first Irish Catholic president was on his way to being inaugurated.

JACKIE AND HER successor, Lady Bird Johnson, had a complicated relationship. When LBJ was her husband's vice president she got to know Lady Bird well. Jackie said that she had never seen someone so eager to do her husband's bidding. Lady Bird, she moaned, "would crawl down Pennsylvania Avenue over splintered glass for Lyndon." In a conversation with her friend, the historian Arthur Schlesinger Jr., Jackie compared Lady Bird to a "trained hunting dog" when she saw her taking notes for her husband. In her oral history for Johnson's presidential library, Jackie recounts the same episode but with a different spin, saying how "impressed" she was with Lady Bird jotting down names of important people in the Kennedys' Hyannis Port living room after Johnson was picked as Kennedy's running mate. In this retelling, Lady Bird had a small spiral notepad balanced on her lap as she sat and chatted with Jackie and her sister, Lee, in one part of the living room as the men sat on the opposite side talking shop. LBJ would occasionally call out, "Bird, do you know so-and-so's number?" She would always have it on hand. "Yet she would be sitting with us, looking so calm," Jackie mused. "I was very impressed by that."

Part of what complicated their relationship was the 1960 campaign, when Johnson and Kennedy were fighting for the Democratic nomination. In the heat of the campaign Jackie called Lyndon Johnson "Senator Cornpone" and Lady Bird "Mrs. Pork Chop." Lady Bird, however, admired Jackie and was a bit threatened by her, and LBJ had a terrible relationship with Jackie's brother-in-law Robert Kennedy. Johnson's adviser Joe Califano says the Kennedys and the Johnsons were "street fighters on opposite sides of the street." Johnson certainly felt that most of President Kennedy's aides disliked him; he told Social Secretary Bess Abell, "I've got one friend in the White House and fortunately his name is Jack Kennedy." In a series of oral history interviews Jackie did after JFK's assassination, she said that while her husband was not planning on dropping Johnson from the ticket in 1964, he told her, "Oh, God, can you ever imagine what would happen to the country if Lyndon was president?" Shortly before his death, Kennedy had begun talking with his brother Robert about how to thwart Johnson from running for president in 1968.

In the White House, Jackie was mortified when Lady Bird told her that she didn't know who Pablo Casals was. Jackie had invited Casals, who was widely regarded as the world's greatest cellist, to perform at a state dinner. But Lady Bird never pretended to be anything other than what she was, the daughter of the most prominent man in their small East Texas town. "Goodness knows," she laughed, "I didn't know a fauteuil from a *bergère*." The Johnsons were deeply hurt by the Kennedys' treatment, and, after LBJ became president, the East Wing staff was self-conscious about organizing any event that would fit the stereotype. "I would have loved to have had a square dance in the East Room for a visitor from abroad—American folk dancing—but I just didn't feel that we could get away with it," Abell said, still remembering the strained atmosphere.

The nearly twenty-year age gap between Jackie and Lady Bird did not help. Lady Bird invited Jackie to meet about a dozen other senators' wives after Kennedy was elected to Congress. At the small tea, Lady Bird recalled, Jackie struck her as a "bird of beautiful plumage among all of us little grey wrens." Jackie was a source of fascination for Lady Bird, who would always remember how Jackie pronounced her name: "Lay-dee Bird." But Lady Bird was often awkward around Jackie. She tried to comfort her on Air Force Once as they flew back from Dallas on November 22, 1963, but her immediate comment after the President's assassination was thoughtless. "I don't know what to say," Lady Bird told a shell-shocked Jackie. "What wounds me most of all is that this should happen in my beloved state of Texas." Jackie did not respond but just sat there, motionless, caked in her husband's blood. When Lady Bird offered to send someone into the private bedroom on Air Force One to help Jackie change out of her bloodstained suit, Jackie vehemently refused. "I want them to see what they have done to Jack."

Lady Bird made it clear that she did not want to rush Jackie out of the White House. But much of their interaction was stilted and formal. "I was not an intimate of Mrs. Kennedy, by any means," Lady Bird said. "Lyndon actually saw more of her because she was a very appealing woman. I remember when she wanted to get something done, she was absolutely the most graceful person. At the same time, I felt she could also be a difficult opponent." Jackie did not vote in the 1964 presidential election, when Johnson ran against Republican Barry Goldwater, because, she said, "Jack would have been alive for that vote." At the time of the election, she had just moved to New York and was still registered in Massachusetts, and she could have easily voted by absentee ballot. But she refused. She never even sent Johnson a telegram congratulating him on his victory because she felt that her husband should have been the one sitting in the Oval Office. Jackie said that she had heard that President Johnson was hurt that she did not vote. "I'd never voted until I was married to Jack," she said. "I thought, 'I'm not going to vote for any [other person], because this vote would have been his.'" Even Robert Kennedy, who hated President Johnson, pressured Jackie to vote, knowing what a media firestorm it would be if word got out that she had not voted. Jackie held her ground and told him, "I don't care what you say, I'm not going to."

Luci Johnson said that after the assassination her mother was worried that the "economically endowed" people whom Jackie convinced to join the White House Fine Arts Committee, which she established within a month of becoming first lady, would leave without Jackie at the helm. She also worried that Kennedy aides, many of whom had tangled with her unpredictable and wildly emotional husband when he was Vice President, would leave when LBJ needed them most. Lady Bird had the Johnsons' family cook, Zephyr Wright, bake dozens of loaves of bread, and Lady Bird marched up and down the halls of the White House pushing a grocery cart full of warm homemade bread wrapped in aluminum foil, each loaf tied with a tidy ribbon. She went into every single office and thanked aides for supporting the President and Mrs. Kennedy and asked that they continue their support for her husband.

When it came time for her to transition out of the White House, Lady Bird was handing the baton to someone she knew well. Lady Bird and Pat Nixon had known each other for years because their husbands served in Congress at the same time and they both loyally attended the Senate Ladies Luncheons. After the 1968 election, Lady Bird gave Pat and her daughter Tricia a tour of the private quarters of the White House. She apologized for the stains left by their dogs and told Pat that she had not bothered to change the once-white carpet because she assumed they would want to choose a new carpet themselves. (Pat told her daughters that she wished Lady Bird had done at least a little upkeep.) Lady Bird was generous and even opened closet doors in each of the bedrooms. She had been reluctant to change any of Jackie Kennedy's décor, knowing that changes could spark a public relations nightmare, so the house had grown threadbare from the five years of the Johnsons' expansive entertaining and the seven million tourists who had walked through.

Even though Lady Bird and Pat were friendly, the ride to the Capitol for the swearing-in ceremony was still full of long pauses and stilted small talk. "I'm so happy it didn't sleet today," Lady Bird said. Pat replied, "We might get lucky and have no rain." A car packed with Secret Service agents separated them from the car their husbands shared. Lady Bird and Pat had made the same trip eight years earlier, when Pat was leaving Washington as the wife of the Vice President and Lady Bird was taking her place. Their small talk was cordial but Lady Bird's feelings about President Nixon and her loyalty to the Democratic Party were clear in her critique of the forty-five-minute inauguration ceremony. "It was low-keyed, restrained, grave, it seemed to me," she wrote in her diary. "Perhaps the times set the mood. None of the youthful ebullience, the poetic brilliance of the Kennedy Inauguration, nor the robust, roaring Jacksonian quality of ours." Lady Bird was touched when she boarded the plane with her husband to go home to Texas and found a large bunch of yellow roses from the Nixons at her seat. She dutifully sent Pat a thank-you note five days later from the Johnsons' Texas ranch: "What a dear and thoughtful gesture!" She knew better than anyone else the challenges that lay ahead of the Nixons.

Once she was First Lady, Pat learned the hard way why Lady Bird had not changed anything in the residence. During the last month of the Johnson administration, the Committee for the Preservation of the White House, with Lady Bird presiding, had decided to replace a wooden mantel from the Lincoln Bedroom with a historic late-eighteenth-century marble mantel. There was a public outcry when news broke that the mantel being replaced was the one on which Jackie had placed a tender inscription: "In this room lived John Fitzgerald Kennedy with his wife, Jacqueline, during the 2 years, 10 months and 2 days he was President of the United States." Headlines blared, "Pat Nixon Removes Jackie's Handiwork." The decision had been made during the Johnson administration, but it was not carried out until the Nixons moved into the White House, so Pat bore the brunt of the criticism. First ladies must tread carefully when it comes to replacing any part of Camelot. Years later, Betty Ford made the bold decision to remove antique wallpaper Jackie had picked out that depicted a Revolutionary War battle scene. It had hung in the Family Dining Room on the second floor, and Betty remarked with her customary honesty, "It's really very difficult to sit there eating and watching all these people shooting each other and bleeding."

———

When Ronald Reagan challenged President Gerald Ford in an audacious bid for the Republican nomination in 1976, the party was torn. There had been subtle signs before Reagan announced his attempt at a palace coup, as when Ronald and Nancy walked in front of the Fords at an event, leaving Ford's political aides aghast. In a dramatic scene at the Republican National Convention, which was split down the middle, Betty Ford and Nancy Reagan sat across the hall from each other, and dueling rounds of applause erupted from the crowd. Nancy was upset that she was assigned a skybox while Betty, who was First Lady, was given a seat on the floor. On the second night of the convention Nancy felt upstaged by Betty, especially when she started dancing with Tony Orlando to "Tie a Yellow Ribbon Round the Ole Oak Tree" at the same time the crowd was applauding Nancy; everyone's attention immediately turned to Betty. The two never really got along. "Mrs. Ford did not admire Nancy Reagan," a close aide to Betty Ford said. Betty was particularly upset when she found out that Nancy was not supporting the Equal Rights Amendment. "I couldn't understand how a woman who had had a professional life could show so little interest in working women," Betty said in an interview at the end of the convention. "I just think when Nancy met Ronnie, that was it as far as her own life was concerned. She just fell apart at the seams." Betty refused to call Nancy and apologize, even when Betty's press secretary, Sheila Rabb Weidenfeld, pressed her to. "You've got to call and say that's just not the case, that you never said that." But Betty held her ground; that was what she thought and she wasn't about to apologize for it.

———

SUSAN PORTER ROSE, who handled correspondence and scheduling for Pat Nixon, coordinated scheduling for Betty Ford, and worked as Barbara Bush's chief of staff when Barbara was second and then first lady, says there is a natural inclination for politicians to guard their hard-won turf once they are in the White House. Political party does not matter, she said; you can dislike someone in your own party. "They're fiercely *themselves*. . . . I think when you're president, if there are other people who've been president or first lady or are aspiring to be, they don't want other people thinking about being president while they're there."

When Sarah Weddington traveled to the Johnson ranch in Texas to interview Lady Bird Johnson, Betty Ford, and Rosalynn Carter for a 1988 *Good Housekeeping* story, she found three former first ladies who were like old friends. The three women had banded together to fight for passage of the Equal Rights Amendment (which was defeated), and they had all attended the 1977 National Women's Conference in Houston, the first and only national women's conference sponsored by the federal government. Each one of them knew the sting of defeat: Rosalynn and Betty had cried bitter tears when their husbands lost, and Lady Bird had struggled with her husband's decision not to seek reelection. Lady Bird had showed up herself to pick up Betty and Rosalynn at the airport to spend the weekend at her Texas ranch, where Lady Bird pointed out different animals and the flowers she loved best. Weddington remembers being on the plane with Betty and Rosalynn flying home. She and Betty started talking about how hard it was for the Fords to leave the White House. "No matter who follows you, you know they didn't deserve to be there," Betty said. Rosalynn overheard their conversation, but instead of being offended—since she was the woman who followed Betty as first lady—she chimed in, "Betty, you are so right!"

Though the Fords and the Carters became close after the White House, initially Betty Ford was furious when her husband lost to Jimmy Carter. Like so many other first ladies, she bore the grudge for the entire family. After watching Rosalynn do an interview on a morning news show during the bitter 1976 campaign, Betty told an aide, "Rosalynn Carter looks tired. . . . She has a way of smiling while sticking a knife in your back. There's a saccharine quality to her." In early December 1976, after Carter had won the election, the Fords invited the Carters to the White House for the traditional tour. The Carters were staying at Blair House, the formal guesthouse across the street on Pennsylvania Avenue, when Rosalynn got a call from Betty's assistant saying that the First Lady was not feeling well and that the meeting would have to be canceled. Rosalynn did not realize at the time that Betty was dealing with addiction. On that day in December, after two and a half years as First Lady, Betty Ford was fragile.

Not long afterward another call came through. "Everyone thinks it would be better if you came this afternoon," a Ford aide told Rosalynn. Then another call came to say the First Lady still was not well enough for a meeting. The next in the flurry of calls was from

Jimmy Carter himself, telling his wife that she should come and that if she did not come it would become a news story. So Rosalynn put on a brown-and-blue wool dress, which she had bought for the occasion, and had a quick but friendly enough tour with Betty Ford.

David Hume Kennerly was President Ford's White House photographer and a close Ford family friend. He remembers waiting for the Carters to arrive for that first visit after they won the election. He recalls Betty not wanting to go greet them. She whispered to her husband as they waited at the door of the White House, "I really don't want to do this." He said, "You've got to do it, we have to be good sports here." (Privately, though, President Ford griped, "I can't believe I lost to a peanut farmer.") Kennerly said he could understand Betty's reaction. "Most people don't like getting their ass kicked; you don't get real warm and fuzzy about the people who did it to you."

President Ford was able to put his hurt feelings aside more easily than his wife—he even offered Jimmy Carter the use of the private office next to the Oval Office if he needed it for briefings before his inauguration. Carter declined. "To this day Cheney [Dick Cheney, who was Ford's chief of staff] doesn't like Carter. A lot of people took it [the loss] personally, it was very emotional," Kennerly said. "I think what Carter did was really hurting her [Betty's] husband and she didn't take it lightly." Eventually, though, Betty grieved the loss (Susan Ford actually referred to it as "grieving") and recovered, and by the time the Fords left she decided to have some fun. On her last full day in the White House Betty said goodbye to her husband's West Wing staff. As she was walking back to the residence she passed the empty Cabinet Room and thought, *You know, I've always wanted to dance on the Cabinet Room table.* She had a willing accomplice in the twenty-nine-year-old Kennerly.

"I think I want to do this," she told him.

"Well, nobody's around," he said, as he readied his camera.

"I took off my shoes, hopped up there, and struck a pose," she recalled, bringing her experience as a Martha Graham dancer to one of the most powerful rooms in the world. She was a little embarrassed by the photo, so she had it restricted in the archives at her husband's presidential library for nearly two decades before Kennerly published it in a book in 1995. He remembers that when President Ford saw it for the first time, "He about fell off his chair." Ford looked at his wife and said, "Well, Betty, you never told me you did that."

"There are a lot of things I haven't told you, Jerry!'"

ROSALYNN CARTER ADMITS that she still feels the sting of her husband's loss to Ronald Reagan in 1980. She ends her autobiography, *First Lady from Plains*, with: "I'd like people to know that we were right, that what Jimmy Carter was doing was best for our country, and that people made a mistake by not voting for him." She lets her own personal ambition show. "Our loss at the polls is the biggest single reason I'd like to be back in the White House. I don't like to lose." The worst moment for President Carter was not when he found out that he had lost the election; it was breaking the news to his wife. "Don't say anything to Rosalynn yet," Carter instructed his staff. "Let me tell her." Rosalynn simply refused to believe the lopsided verdict. "I was in such denial," she admitted years later. "It was impossible for me to believe that anybody could have looked at the facts and voted for Reagan."

There was bad blood between the Carters and the Reagans long before Election Day. During the campaign the Reagans' son, Ron, accused President Carter of "having the morals of a snake" who "would have sold his mother to get reelected." Ron said that he made the comments because he resented Carter for implying that his father was "a racist and a warmonger." Reflecting on it now, he says, "You're competing, it's a very personal kind of competition. It's not sports, you're not on a tennis court, you're competing with, in the best-case scenario, with your ideas and your character so it can get very personal during a campaign." Rosalynn grew even angrier when rumors circulated that Nancy Reagan wanted the Carters to move out a few weeks before the inauguration and live in Blair House, across the street from the White House, so that she could begin redecorating the family's private quarters. Rosalynn said that Nancy called her to deny reports that she wanted them out. "I don't know whether she said she was sorry or not," Rosalynn said. "She just said she did not make those statements."

White House Florist Ronn Payne says that between the election and President Reagan's inauguration, every time he went to the family's private living quarters he could hear at least one member of Carter's extended family crying. Rosalynn remembered how agonizing were those weeks between the election and the inauguration. "You lose the election on November 4, and then you're just ready to go home." It may have been the enormity of the loss—Carter won just 41 percent of the vote—that made it that much harder to take. The morning after the election, Carter's communications director, Jerry Rafshoon, went to visit the President, who was sitting with tears in his eyes in the Oval Office. "Forty-one million, six hundred thousand people don't like me," Carter said. His best friend and chief adviser, Rosalynn, admits she was "bitter enough for both of us." Even years later, in a 1999 interview with the *New York Times*, Rosalynn said, "My biggest regret in life was that Jimmy was defeated."

When it came time for Rosalynn to give Nancy her first tour of the residence, she dutifully walked her through the second and third floors, describing as they strolled through the Yellow Oval Room her efforts to showcase American paintings. But she was not at all enthusiastic, and she abruptly cut the tour short without showing Nancy the presidential bedroom and study. "The chill in her manner matched the chill in the room," Nancy recalled. (Jimmy Carter insisted on keeping the White House a cool 65 degrees during the day and a downright chilly 55 degrees at night because of the energy crisis. White House staffers often typed with gloves on, and a maid even picked up a pair of long underwear for Rosalynn when she went to buy some for herself.)

The tension at President Reagan's inauguration was amplified by the Iran hostage crisis. The Iranians had finally decided to release the hostages but they kept the planes with the returning Americans waiting on the runway so that they would not clear Iranian airspace until after Ronald Reagan became President at noon. Rosalynn was furious and saw it as one final dig at her husband. After the traditional coffee with the incoming president and his wife in the Blue Room, both the Carters and the Reagans left for the Capitol and the swearing-in ceremony. Barbara Bush, who was the wife of the incoming vice president, remembered being kept waiting by Rosalynn as she said goodbye to the residence staff. Barbara and Nancy Reagan felt they were standing around for forty-five minutes with nothing to do. "We won't drag it out like this," Barbara whispered to Nancy at the time. But Barbara said that when she had to leave the White House twelve years later, she could understand why Rosalynn acted the way she did.

Rosalynn says she felt "very smug" knowing, as she made chit-chat with Nancy Reagan, that fifty-two American hostages were coming home after being held in Iran for well over a year. But she knew that most people would assume that Reagan had gotten them released. Walter Mondale, Carter's vice president, said, "The Reagans were not very good at handing out compliments to others. That was not their strong suit." Nancy remembered how awkward the ride to the Capitol was with Rosalynn and how thankful she was that House Minority Leader John Rhodes was there to make conversation. "Rosalynn just looked out the window and didn't say a word. I didn't know *what* to say, so I kept quiet, too. Fortunately, it's a short ride."

Nearly a year after the 1980 presidential election, the wounds between Nancy and Rosalynn were still fresh. When Egyptian President Anwar Sadat was assassinated by Islamic extremists during a military parade in Cairo in 1981, the Secret Service decided that neither President Reagan (who had barely survived an assassination attempt just six months before) nor Vice President George H. W. Bush should attend Sadat's funeral. In an unprecedented show of support for the U.S. ally, President Nixon, President Ford, and President Carter agreed to attend in Reagan's place. Rosalynn Carter accompanied her husband because she had developed a close friendship with Sadat and his wife, Jehan, while they were working on the Camp David peace treaty. President Reagan's assistant Kathleen Osborne remembers how surprised everyone was to see Rosalynn, the only first lady among the three presidents. "I don't know if it was just understood or it was made clear that it was just the former presidents, but she showed up, and they didn't know what to do. I guess she decided to go, which is fine, but it would have been nice if somebody had told us." Hundreds of staffers gathered on the South Lawn and watched as the former presidents and the former first lady stepped off the helicopter and walked across the sweeping White House grounds to meet with the Reagans. What no one could see was the look on Barbara Bush's face as she peered through heavy silk drapes from a window in the White House, taking in the scene on the lawn with a wry smile. "It all rather amused me," she said. "I don't really think they liked each other very much."

———

THE CARTERS AND the Clintons would seem like natural allies: both former presidents are southern-born Baptists, and they are the only two Democrats to have won the presidency between 1964 and 2004. Rosalynn Carter and Hillary Clinton challenged tradition and sought a place at the table in high-level meetings. Rosalynn, like Hillary, was even asked to run for the Senate by her party after her husband's defeat. The Clintons were early Carter supporters when Carter ran for president in 1976, and when Bill Clinton was governor of Arkansas he stood by Carter and did not support Senator Ted Kennedy in his efforts to win the 1980 Democratic nomination. But the relationship between the Carters and the Clintons eventually disintegrated. It is so bad now that the Carters privately hoped that Elizabeth Warren, a liberal senator from Massachusetts who is a leading critic of Wall Street, would challenge Hillary Clinton for the Democratic nomination in 2016. If Clinton wins the election they would like to see Warren challenge her in 2020.

When President Carter was campaign chairman of the Democratic National Committee in 1974, he went to Little Rock to help "this kid Billy Clinton who was running for Congress." Clinton, as usual, was forty-five minutes late. Carter aide Jerry Rafshoon was waiting at the hotel with Carter's trusted staffers, Hamilton Jordan and Jody Powell. "What the hell are you doing? You're late!" Rafshoon said. Carter is never late, an attribute Rafshoon credits to his years at the U.S. Naval Academy.

Even though that first meeting did not go according to plan, the Carters and the Clintons were firmly in each other's corners. But Hillary soon began to annoy the Carters' inner circle. She went to Carter's Atlanta campaign headquarters wearing no makeup and her trademark thick glasses, and told Jordan that she wanted to handle Illinois because she was from Chicago. He laughed at her. "You think you can handle Mayor Daley?" Jordan asked her mockingly, convinced that the hard-edged mayor with working-class Irish roots would have no interest in meeting with this self-proclaimed feminist with an Ivy League pedigree. "I can handle him," she said. But Jordan refused and instead gave her a much less weighty assignment and sent her to Indiana.

The biggest blow to their relationship came in May 1980 when Carter sent eighteen thousand Cuban refugees to be interned at Fort Chaffee in Arkansas. Several hundred broke out and yelled "Libertad! Libertad!" through the streets, sparking a political disaster for Clinton, who was then Arkansas's governor. When Clinton called to talk to President Carter, he was punted to a midlevel aide. Eventually Carter promised not to send any more refugees to Fort Chaffee, but he broke his promise when, during his run for reelection and three months before Clinton was up for reelection, Carter moved all the refugees that he had sent to more important political states (like Pennsylvania) back to Arkansas. Clinton was convinced that Carter's decision cost him the election. "There was a big political price to pay for supporting his President," Hillary Clinton wrote in her memoir.

When Clinton ran for president he did not see any use in cozying up to the one-term Democrat, whom many perceived as a failure, and Carter's requests to discuss foreign policy with the newly elected President were never answered. Carter vented his frustration in a *New York Times* interview shortly after Clinton's inauguration. In the interview he said he was "very disappointed" that the Clintons had decided to send Chelsea to the Sidwell Friends private school, instead of to a Washington, D.C., public school, as the Carters had done with their young daughter, Amy. He also got in a dig about the Clintons' visit to Georgia the summer before to help Carter build houses for Habitat for Humanity. "He was obviously not an experienced carpenter," Carter said dismissively. The Carter camp's real vitriol is reserved for Hillary though. In a 2001 *Wall Street* journal op-ed, Carter's former chief of staff, Hamilton Jordan, wrote: "Instead of leaving him for his public betrayal, Hillary Clinton exploited her public image of a wronged but loyal spouse to create a new persona for herself and win election to the Senate. The Clintons are not a couple but a business partnership, not based on love or even greed but on shared ambitions."

While the Clintons were in the White House, Rosalynn saw Hillary only a handful of times, once at President Nixon's funeral. "This is embarrassing," Rosalynn said, squirming, when asked how often she'd seen Hillary since she became first lady. Rosalynn understood the politics behind their distance: "When they first went to Washington, he [Bill Clinton] was a southern governor," she said. "And Jimmy had not been reelected. And I think they wanted to detach themselves a little from that. And I can understand that." Rosalynn recognizes the distance between herself and her Democratic successors—Hillary Clinton and Michelle Obama—who don't often seek her advice. First ladies, she says, are "bound together by having had the experience of living in the White House and all that involves," but, she adds, "I'm not sure we would call the relationship among first ladies a sisterhood. About the only time we are ever together is when a new presidential library is established or for a funeral."

———

NANCY REAGAN CERTAINLY did not offer to leave the White House early when it was her turn to move out. She and Barbara Bush had such a caustic relationship when George H. W. Bush was Reagan's vice president that Barbara had very little idea what the residence looked like when she moved in. During the eight years that Barbara Bush was second lady she was rarely invited to the family quarters. Barbara said the chief usher came to the Vice President's residence to show her pictures of the rooms on the second and third floors of the White House. "I really didn't know anything about the upstairs at the White House to speak of and he told me different things. I then marked things that were to go to the White House because most of our things went to Maine [their summer home in Kennebunkport]."

In his private diary, President George H. W. Bush put it bluntly when he wrote in a 1988 entry, "Nancy does not like Barbara." Nancy, he said, was jealous of his wife. "She feels that Barbara has the very things that she, Nancy, doesn't have, and that she'll never be in Barbara's class." There was no official tour of the residence until January 11, only nine days before the Bushes were to move in. And it was brief and unsatisfying. The animosity was mutual. When a negative biography of Nancy Reagan was published, Barbara snapped it up but slapped on another book jacket so that no one would know what she was reading. When Barbara visited a San Antonio clinic as first lady in 1992, a recovering drug addict handed her a photo of himself and asked her to autograph it with Nancy's antidrug motto, "Just say no." Barbara simply signed her name.

Nancy Reagan had her own friends, and Barbara had hers. Barbara was from an old patrician family—she grew up in Rye, New York, and is related to President Franklin Pierce—and she could not have approved of Nancy's obvious grasp for power and of her movie star friends. Nancy Reagan's assistant Jane Erkenbeck was reticent when asked to describe their relationship. They had, after all, eight years to get to know each other. "I'm not going to go into that," she said, pausing a moment. "She was there because her husband was vice president. Mrs. Reagan was there because her husband was president. The men had a very good relationship, saw each other a lot. . . . If your husband and my husband were law partners and they were friends and they see each other all the time, of course that doesn't mean that you and I have to be good friends." Nancy once paused when a reporter asked for her opinion of Barbara. "Well, I never got to know her very well," she said.

Barbara had a way of connecting with people as First Lady and was nicknamed "the National Treasure" by her husband's aides. She became everyone's favorite grandmother: loving, self-deprecating, and, above all, compassionate. She cultivated an image as the anti-Nancy, oblivious to her hair or what she was wearing. On the eve of her husband's inauguration Barbara said, "My mail tells me that a lot of fat, white-haired, wrinkled ladies are tickled pink. I mean, look at me—if I can be a success, so can they." The 1987 visit of Soviet leader Mikhail Gorbachev and his wife, Raisa, marked the first time a Soviet leader had come to Washington since Nikita Khrushchev in 1959, and the Gorbachevs' arrival ceremony at the White House was watched by the world. Barbara recorded in her diary that she wore "a very Republican cloth coat and Nancy wore her mink." Barbara was not putting on an act, says Joni Stevens, who worked in the Military Office across the hall from the First Lady's office. At the head of the stairs are the men's room and the ladies' room, and in between them were two giant photographs of Barbara Bush and George

H. W. Bush (the photos, known as "jumbos," are scattered along the walls of the West Wing and the East Wing and change periodically). A couple of days after the Bushes moved into the White House, Stevens ran into Barbara at the top of the stairs as she was going into the ladies' room. "Who is that wrinkled white-haired lady?" Barbara asked, pointing to her photo. Barbara looked at her Secret Service agent and he just started laughing.

Barbara and Nancy were from the same political party, but they had such different personalities that they had closer friendships with Democrats. Barbara became close to Democrat Lady Bird Johnson, and Nancy had enormous respect for Democrat Jackie Kennedy. Even when Barbara tried to be nice to Nancy it backfired. During the only debate between Reagan and Carter before the 1980 election, Barbara and her husband sat with Nancy in the auditorium. "I think [Reagan] looks so much better than Carter," Barbara whispered. "His makeup is better." Nancy replied dismissively, "Ronnie *never* wears makeup." Nancy readily admitted that she did not care for George H. W. Bush when her husband picked him as his running mate; Bush had run against Reagan in the Republican primaries and had criticized his policies. "George's use of the phrase 'voodoo economics' to describe Ronnie's proposed tax cuts still rankled," Nancy wrote in her memoir.

Nancy was a perfectionist and had very particular ideas of how she wanted the White House to look. She was also constantly sizing people up. For the Gorbachevs' visit, White House Florist Ronn Payne recalls when the First Lady and her social secretary came into the Flower Shop on the ground floor and told the florists, "We want to blow [Raisa's] socks off." Payne said, "We changed every single flower in the house three times in one day: for the morning arrival, for the afternoon lunch, and for the state dinner. Every single flower, three times, every one." Nancy and

Raisa also did not get along. During their first meeting over coffee the two sat with their interpreters. Jane Erkenbeck recalled a couple of times when Raisa spoke in English. "She was just trying to humiliate the First Lady: 'I can speak English as well as Russian. You cannot speak Russian.' That set the tone." Barbara described the animosity between the two first ladies as a "chemical thing." Barbara had a better relationship with Raisa than Nancy did, and Raisa even asked her why she thought Nancy did not like her. Barbara was hard-pressed to answer.

Nancy was a First Lady who was often hard to please and sometimes seemed to be looking for slights. Head Housekeeper Christine Limerick avoids saying anything negative about her former bosses, but one incident involving the Reagans' personal belongings caused her to leave the White House for five years before Barbara Bush asked her to return. Christine had gotten along with Nancy and even talked with her about her love life (the First Lady considered herself a born matchmaker and was thrilled when Christine told her she was getting married to White House Electrician Robert Limerick). The Reagans had "an incredible amount of stuff and that's because they don't have to clean," Limerick said, with a wry smile. If any of Nancy's collectibles—including about twenty-five small hand-painted porcelain Limoges boxes, silver frames, and expensive perfume bottles—was put back in the wrong place after a cleaning, Limerick would hear about it. "At the beginning of their administration," Limerick recalled, "there were several items that were broken: one by Housekeeping, one by the Secret Service, and one by the Operations Department." Nancy blamed Limerick and yelled at her with such venom that Chief Usher Rex Scouten had to come to Limerick's defense. Nancy was so angry, she had Limerick pack up most of the keepsakes that she kept in the private living quarters and put them away for several months, until things calmed down. Limerick decided then that she needed a break from the White House. The hushed voices in the corridors of the executive mansion during the Reagan years were no surprise to the Reagans' children, who knew how much their mother valued order and respect for material objects. "Things rarely got broken in our house; Kool-Aid wasn't spilled on couches, chocolate wasn't smeared on draperies. Fabergé eggs and antique china vases were safe from us," said the Reagans' daughter, Patti Davis, referring to herself and her younger brother, Ron.

Time could not heal old wounds between Nancy and Barbara. Barbara was fuming when, as first lady, she reviewed the guest list for the 1989 unveiling of the Reagans' official portraits at the White House. Nancy had commandeered the list and once again had taken control. "She was angry. She felt that they were imposing on her," said former White House Usher Chris Emery, who was close with Barbara. "*She* was the first lady, it was *her* White House and they were telling her what to do. It was like they were still in charge." Just before President George H. W. Bush left office, he awarded President Reagan the Presidential Medal of Freedom. Nancy called Dick Cheney, who was Bush's secretary of defense and a friend of the Reagans, to make sure he would be at the East Room ceremony; she told Cheney that they needed allies there. Nancy obviously did not consider the Bushes to be on their side. "Nancy apparently never even said thank you to Barbara," President Bush recalled in his diary.

Ron Reagan wrote a scathing op-ed in *Esquire* about President George W. Bush three months after Bush and his father spoke at President Reagan's 2004 funeral. Nancy called Barbara Bush to apologize but it was not enough; there was too much bad blood between them. Nancy stayed at the White House at the invitation of George and Laura Bush, and during Bush's presidency she urged him, mostly through emissaries, to support embryonic stem-cell research as a potential tool for treating Alzheimer's disease, which had afflicted her husband. But Bush restricted federal financing for the experimental procedures that required the use of cells from a human embryo. Nancy said she thought she brought it up directly with him once, "and then I didn't anymore."

———

BARBARA BUSH HAD more in common with Nancy Reagan than she might like to think: they both worried much more than their husbands did, and neither cared half as much as her husband did about what people thought of her. Barbara, like Nancy, was the chief disciplinarian and grudge holder for her family. President Bush told reporters, "Look out, the silver fox is really mad at you," referring to his wife. George W. Bush told a reporter that his mother "can smell a phony a mile away."

Weeks before the President left office the Bushes were in Moscow, where he was signing a nuclear treaty. Reporter Cragg Hines had just filed an unflattering story about Bush's loss to Clinton. The "silver fox" was not happy. Hines was with a group of traveling reporters who were giddily taking photographs in the Kremlin when he saw Barbara approaching them from the top of the stairwell. Hines had begun covering Bush in 1964, when Bush made an unsuccessful bid for the Senate, and felt comfortable enough with Barbara to approach her. "Mrs. Bush, can I take a picture with you?" She glared at him. "Not with *you*, bub," she replied.

Barbara, like Nancy, expressed opinions about her husband's team of advisers. She was not happy with his decision to name Dan Quayle, a forty-one-year-old senator from Indiana, as his running mate. Bush had kept many of his top aides in the dark until the last minute. Barbara sided with longtime Bush allies who were unhappy with the choice and who resented not being part of the decision-making process. Once they were in the White House, the Bushes and the Quayles had a strained relationship. Quayle was ridiculed in the press for gaffes, like when he went to a Trenton, New Jersey, school and a student was asked to write "potato" on a blackboard and he urged him to add an "e" at the end.

Barbara never warmed up to Quayle's wife, Marilyn, who is more than twenty years younger than her. A friend of Marilyn said that getting invited to a state dinner was like "pulling teeth" for the Vice President and his wife. But the relationship between the Vice President's wife and the President's wife is almost always fraught, and it can resemble the relationship between a daughter-in-law and a mother-in-law. Barbara made it clear when she did not want Marilyn talking about a particular issue or going to a certain event. "Barbara Bush had been the student of Nancy Reagan for eight years. She thought Marilyn should suck it up," Marilyn's friend said.

The two vice presidential candidates in the 1992 campaign, Al Gore and Dan Quayle, enrolled their daughters at Washington's elite all-girls' National Cathedral School. Kristin Gore, Sarah Gore, and Corinne Quayle were at the school at the same time and were the school's three star lacrosse players. "Marilyn Quayle told me those girls clung together, they protected each other, they shut out the political world, the campaign," said former ABC News White House correspondent Ann Compton. Marilyn Quayle's former chief of staff, Marguerite Sullivan, said that the life of a second lady is very different from the life of a first lady. They have many of the trappings of the office, including Secret Service protection, and almost none of the luxuries. "If you want to go somewhere you have the same security apparatus as the first lady, but you either go on commercial airlines or you get somebody to donate a plane." It is considered a cardinal sin for the second lady to outshine the first lady; there is an understanding in Washington that vice presidents cannot help their running mates get elected, but they can certainly hurt their chances, and the same is true of vice presidential wives. During a campaign, the wives of the vice presidential nominees are sent to parts of the country that are considered second or third tier and are not crucial for an electoral victory.

Laura Bush and Lynne Cheney, the wife of George W. Bush's vice president, Dick Cheney, were friendly but they were not close. Lynne never thought that her husband would become vice president—she told a friend how relieved she was that he was on the committee to select Bush's running mate: she thought this would ensure that he himself was out of the running. Bush campaign advisers agreed that Lynne was a better speaker than Laura, but it was decided during the 2000 campaign that she should be used sparingly so that she did not outshine Laura.

Sullivan says that the President and his wife and the Vice President and his wife are like knights in medieval times. "The knights have their own entourage and they come together and then separate and do their own thing." There is no going rogue for second ladies—they have to be part of the apparatus, the behemoth that is a presidential campaign, and they must play the role they have been assigned to play. Barbara Bush made sure that Marilyn Quayle never forgot that.

As First Lady, Barbara Bush had only one real brush with controversy. ("Short of ax murder," says former Bush spokeswoman Sheila Tate, "I think she could get away with anything. She's so benign.") In 1990 she was invited to deliver the keynote address at the graduation ceremony at the all-women's Wellesley College in Massachusetts. One hundred and fifty students signed a petition saying they were "outraged" by the decision to have Barbara speak because, they said, she was famous only because of the man she married. (Barbara had dropped out of Smith after her freshman year, intent on focusing all of her attention on Bush.) Soon the storm blew over, but Barbara would not be made a fool of—before she made the speech, she called two of the Wellesley students who were leading the protest so she could "twist the knife in a little" and embarrass them, an aide said. In her speech Barbara said that women should always put family before their careers.

Behind the scenes, Barbara was a protective wife and mother. (In 1984 she famously called her husband's rival, Democratic vice presidential nominee Geraldine Ferraro, "that four-million-dollar—I can't say it, but it rhymes with rich.") Barbara stood by her husband through two terms in Congress and through stints as UN ambassador, GOP chairman, U.S. envoy to China, and CIA director. She devoted her life to her family and like Betty Ford she raised their six children largely alone. She struggled with depression, she said, partly because "women's lib had made me feel that my life had been wasted." She represented a different generation than her successor Hillary Clinton, who was a proud feminist and a baby boomer. During the 1992 campaign Hillary was asked for her response to Barbara's speech at Wellesley, Hillary's alma mater, and gave a restrained answer: *"Personally,* I believe that a woman should put her family and her relationships—which are really at the root of who you are and how you relate to the world—at the top of your priority list. I don't believe that I, or Barbara Bush, should tell all women that's what they have to put first. . . . What we have to get away from is the idea that there's only one right choice."

Barbara worshipped her husband and put his needs above her own every time. George Herbert Walker Bush's brother Jonathan said of the Bushes' courtship: "She was wild about him. And for George, if anyone wants to be wild about him, it's fine with him." The Bushes moved twenty-nine times during their marriage, eleven times in the first six years. When they were finally settled and putting down roots with their growing family, the nomadic George Bush came home one day, clapped his hands, and told his wife, "We're moving to Odessa [Texas]." Barbara was heartsick. Silent for a moment, she composed herself and looked up adoringly at her husband: "I've always wanted to live in Odessa." She knew that this was George H. W. Bush's essence; he could never stay in one place too long.

Barbara worried about the negative campaign ads put together by Bush advisers Lee Atwater and Roger Ailes in the 1988 presidential campaign. She was concerned about whether they would reflect poorly on her husband. When Ailes walked into the room she announced, with a weary smile, "Here's my bad boy." But when her husband's reelection prospects against Bill Clinton were looking dim in 1992, Barbara told him flatly, "I'm going negative." Barbara was keeping score as she watched Hillary directly attack her husband time and time again. She would not forget how Hillary referred to Bush's four years in office as a "failure of leadership." Suggestions that Hillary, as retribution for all the coverage of Bill's philandering, wanted to expose President George H. W. Bush's alleged affair with a personal aide so infuriated Barbara that it led to a cold war between Barbara and Hillary that still has not thawed.

In a 1992 *Vanity Fair* article, Hillary is quoted saying she had a conversation with a wealthy Atlanta socialite who told her about Bush's alleged affair with a close aide. It's all "apparently well known in Washington," she said slyly. Hillary was referring to Jennifer Fitzgerald, whom Bush was rumored to have had a romantic relationship with for years. "I'm convinced part of it is that the Establishment—regardless of party—sticks together. They're gonna circle the wagons on Jennifer," Hillary said. The Clinton campaign was trying its best to make sure the story of Bush's alleged affair was exposed, and the Bush campaign accused the Clinton campaign of planting the story. "That's definitely playing hardball," Barbara said. Bush wrote in his diary that he and his family were humiliated by the allegations. "I talked to Bar this morning and she was telling me that her friends all had heard these ugly rumors." Barbara invited Cragg Hines, who was then the Washington bureau chief of the *Houston Chronicle*, for an intimate interview in the West Sitting Hall. The First Lady sat demurely in an armchair wearing a pretty lilac suit, but her very serious intentions were clear from the moment Hines walked in. "It was the focus of her day," he recalls with a laugh. She said that any suggestions that her husband had had an affair were "sick" and "ugly." Barbara never mentioned Hillary, but when Hines asked her if this was the lowest point the campaign could sink to, she replied, "It can't get any uglier."

Barbara had the longest memory of anyone in her family, and she can never forgive Hillary. In a 2000 interview, four months before her eldest son was elected president and almost a decade after Hillary first criticized her husband, she said that her daughter-in-law, Laura, would be very different from Hillary because she would "not get into foreign affairs or controversial subjects. . . . I think she would rather make a positive impact on the country." Barbara added passive-aggressively, "I'm not criticizing Mrs. Clinton. But it's like oil and water. We're talking about two different subjects. They're two different people. I think Laura thinks of others." The undercurrent is hard to miss: Laura would not overstep in the same way that Hillary had as first lady, there would be no West Wing office, and there would be no meddling in presidential matters. Barbara has always considered Hillary a politician and therefore fair game. "Governor and Mrs. Clinton had both said that they were going to be a co-presidency," Barbara said during the 1992 campaign.

The friendship between George H. W. Bush and Bill Clinton has not softened the relationship between their wives. The two men became friends when they traveled to South Asia to help the victims of the 2004 tsunami and Bush became a sort of father figure to Clinton. According to former White House officials, it's no coincidence that whenever Bill Clinton is invited to the Bush family's summer home in Kennebunkport, Maine, Hillary has other commitments. "The relationship between Franklin and Eleanor [Roosevelt] sounds rather like the relationship between Bill and Hillary," Barbara wrote in her diary. "Respect for each other, but separate lives. Who knows."

Even when it comes to her daughter-in-law Laura, Barbara's sometimes caustic wit could cause the always-in-control Laura to roll her eyes, or force herself to bite her tongue. The two women gave each other a wide berth when the Bushes were all together at the family compound, but occasionally, when Barbara weighed in with parenting advice, Laura made it clear who was in charge of her daughters. Jenna Bush called her grandmother "the enforcer." The night of George H. W. Bush's inauguration every available space in the White House was taken up with a member of the Bush family. If a grandchild showed up to visit without reading material, Barbara marched him or her down to the White House library to pick out a book. She told her children, "If you're going to spend the night, bring your own sheets!" Once, Butler George Hannie said, a bunch of her grandchildren were having a pool party at the White House. Barbara asked him, "George, what's going on at the pool?"

"Ma'am, they ordered sandwiches to eat by the pool."

"Stop right there," she said. "Take everything to the Solarium. Let them come and get it." Then she walked downstairs to the outdoor pool and got them all out and told them if they wanted to eat they needed to do it inside.

In 2012 Barbara and Laura attended a conference at the LBJ Presidential Library. Library Director Mark Updegrove introduced them. "Laura Bush has graciously allowed me to call her Laura for the evening, so I will be referring to her as Laura and you as Mrs. Bush." Barbara shot him a withering glance and said, "I would certainly hope so." The audience burst into laughter. Ultimately, Barbara and Laura were bound by their shared love of George W. Bush. When Laura was asked at the conference what the biggest misconception of her husband was, she said, "That he was sort of a heedless, cowboy caricature." Barbara cut in, "Don't mention it to me, it makes me so mad." But when Barbara was asked what the biggest misconception of her husband was, she replied, "There was none, he is a saint." For the most part, Laura was "very deferential" to her mother-in-law, said Anita McBride, who was Laura's chief of staff. "She knows that that's Bar."

"Sometimes I'm reminded of things that I've said and I'm mortified," Barbara said when a staffer reminded her of how she had told her husband that he needed to lose weight. But it was that kind of candor that earned Barbara the love of the White House residence staff, whom she teased constantly. She was the same way with the press. On a foreign trip a reporter asked her, "Are you going to be buying pearls in Bahrain?" She looked at the reporter and said, "Not as long as [costume jewelry designer] Kenneth Jay Lane is alive."

EVEN SOME OF Hillary Clinton's closest friends are wary of her seeking the presidency for a second time. They say they do not know why she wants to put herself through all of that again. When she was last in the White House, Hillary went through a four-year investigation by Independent Counsel Kenneth Starr into a myriad of charges, including the Whitewater land deal and "Travelgate," the firing of several longtime White House employees in the Travel Office. Of course the biggest scandal of all was the revelation in January 1998 that her husband had been carrying on an affair with White House intern Monica Lewinsky. When the affair was occurring between November 1995 and March 1997, butlers saw the President and Lewinsky in the family movie theater. They were seen together so often that workers let each other know when they had a so-called Lewinsky sighting. West Wing staffers called Monica "Elvira" because of her dark hair and ample cleavage, reminiscent of TV character Elvira, Mistress of the Dark. Hillary's friends wonder, *Why would she want to be reminded of all of that?*

Hillary has been living in a bubble for decades; she has not driven a car in nearly twenty years, and if she wins the 2016 election, she will have the remarkable distinction of being the first president to have had Secret Service protection for a solid twenty-four years before she ever even got to the White House on her own. The Clintons were the only first family in the twentieth century without a home outside Washington. (In 1999, shortly before leaving the White House, they bought an eleven-room Dutch colonial in Chappaqua, New York, for $1.7 million in preparation for Hillary's run for Senate in the state. Shortly after that, they bought a $2.85 million home near Embassy Row in Washington, D.C. Before those purchases the Clintons had not owned a home for sixteen years.) When they moved into the White House they brought everything they owned with them and stored much of it in a climate-controlled storage facility about eleven miles outside Washington in Riverdale, Maryland; there every piece of furniture that has ever been in the White House is carefully cataloged. But one explanation for her decision to run again is clear, says a member of Hillary's inner circle: it is partly out of vengeance for her 2008 loss to President Obama. "When we all first started talking about the Hillary campaign, we said we can't wait to get him [President Obama] out of there and get back somebody who's going to do something." Obama, this former staffer said, does not have the same dogged work ethic as Hillary does.

Michelle Obama and Laura Bush are held to different standards than Hillary is, according to Hillary's loyal staff. Laura Bush's chief of staff, Andi Ball, worked closely with Hillary's then–deputy chief of staff, Melanne Verveer, through the transition, and they've maintained a very good relationship over time. Shortly after 9/11, Laura Bush became the first first lady to deliver the weekly presidential radio address—she used it to draw attention to human rights abuses against Afghan women. "The fight against terrorism is also a fight for the rights and dignity of women," she said, using the bully pulpit of the presidency to make the case. Verveer was one of the first people to call Ball after Laura's radio address. "Hillary *never* could have done that," she said. "If she had taken the microphone of the presidential podium to deliver an address all hell would have broken loose for Hillary. But people didn't expect it out of Laura Bush." That is probably because it was not something that she was naturally inclined to do. It was her husband's idea and she looked at the statement and put it in her own words. She did not know the impact it would have.

The 2008 presidential campaign left deep and lasting scars on both the Clinton and the Obama camps, and they are still shockingly fresh. One Obama aide said that Michelle would have liked to see Vice President Joe Biden run against Hillary for the 2016 Democratic nomination. She is very close to the Bidens, especially Vice President Biden's wife, Jill, whom she's worked with to advocate for military families. Several high-level advisers in both camps expressed disdain for their former opponents and even shared stories that made the other side look bad. One of Hillary's best friends, Susie Tompkins Buell, who describes herself as "an eddy in a wild river" for Hillary, was defensive when asked whether Hillary regretted having an office in the West Wing. Buell said, "Where is Michelle Obama's office?" (Michelle's office is in the East Wing.)

Working for a Clinton, or a Bush, or an Obama, is like working for a major corporation. Staffers come to identify themselves closely with the politician they serve. Some of these aides would lie down on a train track for the president and the first lady. They often hold grudges far longer than the president and first lady do. On the eve of the 2008 New Hampshire primary, after she finished third in the Iowa caucuses, Hillary was asked a question that almost brought her to tears: "How do you do it?" It was a "chick question," said Marianne Pernold, the woman who asked her. She wanted to know how Hillary got up every morning and seemed so put together. Hillary paused for ten seconds and revealed a side of herself that few people ever see. "You know, I have so many opportunities from this country. I just don't want to see us fall backwards, you know?" she said, her voice cracking. She added, "This is very personal for me. It's not just political. It's not just public. I see what's happening, and we have to reverse it." She became the first woman to win a presidential primary with her victory in New Hampshire. Not everyone thought she was being sincere, however. Laura Bush's chief of staff, Anita McBride, remembers watching Hillary answering Pernold's question on the news from her office in the East Wing, and calling Laura in the residence to tell her to turn on the television. "You've *got* to see this," she told her. Even while McBride and other staffers sat with their mouths agape, viewing Hillary's sudden display of emotion as nothing more than a ploy, the sitting First Lady was convinced it was genuine. "You don't understand," Laura told them.

Ahead of the New Hampshire primary, Hillary had said that Martin Luther King Jr. needed President Johnson to pass the Civil Rights Act in order to begin to realize his dream of racial equality. "It took a president to get it done," she said. Critics said she was downplaying King's role in the passage of the legislation. She grew increasingly bitter as more and more of her friends, including Senator Ted Kennedy, who had been a mentor to her in the Senate and part of the family dynasty that she and her husband so revered, publicly expressed their support for Obama. The morning after the primary in South Carolina, where Obama won by twenty-eight points, President Clinton drew fire when, campaigning for his wife, he said, "Jesse Jackson won South Carolina in '84 and '88. Jackson ran a good campaign. And Obama ran a good campaign here." Comparing Obama to Jackson was quickly condemned by African Americans in the state, including the influential former majority whip and key member of the Congressional Black Caucus, Representative Jim Clyburn, who called the former president's behavior "bizarre" and went on television to implore him to "chill."

Bill Clinton's overzealous campaigning for his wife is perhaps a symptom of his own guilt over having put her through so much, since the very start of their life together. Mary Ann Campbell, an old friend of Hillary from Arkansas, remembers a charity roast of Hillary in Little Rock when the Clintons were in the Governor's Mansion. Campbell was assigned the delicate task of roasting Hillary and she made some jokes about Hillary's appearance. "Everybody laughed, except Bill. Hillary just barrel laughed. She knows I like her." When Bill came onstage he said pointedly, glancing sideways at Campbell, "I *like* Hillary's frizzy hair. I *like* her glasses. I *like* Hillary with no makeup." Bill could not stand someone making fun of his wife, just as he could not stand to watch Obama criticize her during the campaign.

Michelle first met Hillary when Hillary was her husband's rival for the 2008 Democratic nomination and, unlike Laura Bush, she would never be able to forget the things that Hillary said about her husband, especially how she mocked his message of hope and change. "I could stand up here and say: let's just get everybody together, let's get unified," Hillary said sarcastically at a campaign stop in Ohio in February 2008. "The sky will open, the light will come down, celestial choirs will be singing, and everyone will know that we should do the right thing, and the world would be perfect."

The Obamas view the Clintons as a political dynasty that came before them. "There's a work functionality to that relationship, not exactly a close personal bond," said one former Obama aide. The Obamas consider themselves far less calculating. Even while Clinton staffers argue strongly that Hillary herself thinks that every first lady has to carve out the job in a way that works best for her and for her family, most of her confidantes say that Michelle Obama has not done enough as first lady. "She gave up a lot of gains," said a former Clinton staffer in a hushed voice.

There is a reason why there were no couples dinners when Hillary was a frequent guest at the Obama White House as secretary of state. By then Hillary was a former senator and fourth in line for the presidency. "I don't think that she [Michelle] ever thought much of the Clintons," says one former Obama adviser. "Even before the presidential race, even before we were really into it, I think that the Obamas' view of the Clintons is that those years were an opportunity squandered. Big things could have been done but there was a lot of nibbling around the edges and a lot of it was consumed by President Clinton's behavior." In a 2007 *Washington Post* story, Michelle refused to say whether she would vote for Hillary if her husband were not in the race. "I would be more concerned at this time with finding the best president for this time, and if it is a woman, that would be a great thing," she said. "Would I naturally be a Hillary supporter if my husband weren't running? I don't know, I'd be looking at the race totally differently. And it's hard for me to see beyond the wonders of my husband."

Shortly before the Obamas moved into the White House, Laura Bush's East Wing aides handed Michelle's staff binders detailing which events were added by which first lady and the different programs Laura had worked on. Laura had been a strong supporter of Save America's Treasures, a program started by Hillary Clinton to help preserve historic sites. Laura's staff was sure that Michelle would feel obligated to support it because Hillary was going to be part of her husband's Cabinet. But Michelle did not feel any such obligation and she did not prioritize the program, which has since lost its funding. In a 2015 interview on *The Late Show with Stephen Colbert*, Colbert asked Michelle, if the next president is a woman, would she leave behind a letter of advice for her husband? Michelle said she would and gave what at first seemed like a safe, non-controversial answer: "I would say, 'Follow your passion, just be you.'" Colbert said quickly, "I think he does," and the audience burst into laughter, the implication being that Bill Clinton has always followed his passions. "I think he would," she replied, smiling broadly at Colbert. "I mean that in the best possible way," Colbert said quickly. "I didn't say . . . I'm just sitting here minding my business," Michelle said, trying to distance herself, raising her hands in the air.

Recent charges of corruption and messy contributions to the Clinton Global Initiative, the family's $2 billion foundation, fuel the animosity between the warring factions. "It fits into this narrative about the Clintons that they come off as just trying to claw their way towards success and money," said a former Obama adviser with close personal knowledge of the dynamic between the two couples. "When Michelle Obama views the Clintons, I don't want to say she's looking down her nose at them—but she kind of is."

Even so, President Obama uses the Clintons' popularity when necessary. It was hard to ignore the difference between the two presidents when they both appeared unexpectedly in the James S. Brady Press Briefing Room in the late afternoon of December 10, 2010. A voice on the loudspeaker was piped into the reporters' booths in the White House and gave a ten-minute warning—no one was prepared for former President Clinton to come out and stand onstage with President Obama. During a half-hour Q&A with reporters, the former president gleefully answered questions and defended President Obama's compromise agreement reached with congressional Republicans to extend tax cuts and unemployment benefits. But Clinton was not about to relinquish the spotlight. "I've been keeping the First Lady waiting for about half an hour, so I'm going to take off," Obama told reporters several minutes into the briefing. "I don't want to make her mad," Clinton said. "Please go," and he stayed for another twenty-three minutes of questions. He seems to want to get back into the White House almost as badly as his wife does.

IX

Keep Calm and Carry On

★

Oh my God, I think I'm going to throw up.
—BETTY FORD, BEFORE MAKING A CAMPAIGN
SPEECH

High office leads to high anxiety, and first families face enormous amounts of pressure. Former White House Maître d' George Hannie remembers how mercurial President Obama could be. "One day he can talk you to death. The next day he can walk past you and he won't say anything. That's why his hair is turning gray, he's having problems." The same is true about the first ladies, he said; they can say hello as they pass staff in the hallway, or they can be so consumed with their own thoughts and private concerns that they keep their eyes fixed straight ahead and don't say a thing. "You know their minds are on something else. It's not them, they're just thinking." Hannie said Hillary Clinton was especially quiet when she was consumed with worry about the Monica Lewinsky scandal. Gwen King, who worked in the Kennedy, Nixon, and Ford administrations, remembered Jackie Kennedy calling one day in a panic from

the residence because she had lost an eighteenth-century historical document that she had been given by a wealthy donor. King
volunteered to go hunting for it and finally found it lodged in a
cubbyhole in a conference room. "She [Jackie] was so grateful, you
would have thought that I was her best friend the way she was
graciously thanking me. The next day I passed her in the hall and
she looked right through me. That was Jacqueline Kennedy."

Lady Bird Johnson was soother-in-chief, spending much of
her time smoothing feathers ruffled by her hot-tempered husband. She was an impeccably well-mannered southern lady
whose husband regularly spoke to aides with the bathroom door
open as he was sitting on the toilet. As a northeasterner, White
House Curator Jim Ketchum, like most of the people working
in the Kennedy White House, was not accustomed to the Johnsons' Texas accent, and he was uncomfortable with the President's brash personality and imposing physicality. "Nobody likes
change," he says.

Lady Bird worked hard to preserve her husband's legacy, and
she always regretted letting one taped conversation out into the
public. In it, the President instructed his tailor to cut his pants
so that he would have more room in the crotch, "down where
your nuts hang," as he put it. "Give me an inch that I can let out
there because they cut me. They're just like riding a wire fence."
During the 1960 campaign Bill Moyers was helping Johnson on
the campaign trail—he would later become his press secretary
when Johnson became president. During the exhausting months
leading up to the election, he slept on the bed in the Johnsons'
basement when they returned from the road for sessions of the
Senate. Moyers missed his wife and their six-month-old son, who
were still in Texas, and Lady Bird could tell. "She would often
come down two flights of stairs to ask if I was doing all right,"

he said. "One night, the Senator and I got home even later and he brought with him some unresolved dispute from the Senate cloakroom. At midnight I could still hear him carrying on as if he was about to purge the Democratic caucus. Pretty soon I heard her footsteps on the stair and I called out, 'Mrs. Johnson, you don't need to come down here, I'm all right.' And she called back, 'Well, I was just coming down to tell you, "I'm all right too."'"

Lady Bird had to face criticism about her husband's policies because the first lady is an easier, more accessible target than the president. On January 18, 1968, she invited a group of women for a luncheon at the White House to discuss how to reduce crime. On the guest list was the famous singer and actress Eartha Kitt, who was in a combative mood. Lady Bird noticed that Kitt did not touch her seafood bisque or her peppermint ice cream at the elegant lunch in the Old Family Dining Room. She did not applaud any of the speakers, either. When Lady Bird asked for questions from the audience, Kitt's hand shot up. She walked toward Lady Bird, stared directly at her, and said, "We send the best of this country off to be shot and maimed. They rebel in the streets. They take pot and they will get high. They don't want to go to school, because they are going to be snatched off from their mothers to be shot in Vietnam." Lady Bird looked back at Kitt, "stare for stare," she later said. Then came the punch to the gut. With her finger pointed at Lady Bird, Kitt said, "You are a mother, too. . . . I have a baby and then you send him off to war." The First Lady's face had lost its color and her voice trembled as she replied, "I cannot identify as much as I should. I have not lived the background that you have, nor can I speak as passionately or as well, but we must keep our eyes and our hearts and our energies fixed on constructive areas and try to do something that will make this a happier, better-educated land." She was not about to raise her voice. Lady Bird, Chief Usher J. B. West noted, "seemed to grow calmer as the world around her became more furious."

Lady Bird had come a long way from the shy Texas girl she once was. In 1959 she began taking speech classes with Hester Provensen at the Capital Speakers' Club to get over her fear of public speaking. Provensen was an institution in Washington and taught two packed classes of wives of senators and congressmen. Class met once a week for nine months, and Lady Bird joined because, she said, "I got real annoyed with myself for being so shy and quiet, and never having anything to say when asked to speak." At the beginning of her husband's political career, Lady Bird hated even standing up and saying something as simple as "Thank you for inviting me to this barbecue." Provensen told her that the people in the audience were just like her, and that helped ease her fears.

Before Provensen's students graduated they had to make a three- to five-minute speech on a subject assigned to them. Topics ranged from "The Plight of the American Indian" to "What I Liked in the Congressional Cookbook." Lady Bird was appropriately assigned "Why Texas Is the Lone Star State." Whenever any of these well-heeled women stammered during their presentation, a penny was dropped into a tin cup. Later, when Lady Bird became first lady, Provensen would be called to the second floor of the White House to help if she was about to give a particularly difficult speech. "I don't remember seeing her nervous, I just remember seeing her practicing and going over her speech cards," Social Secretary Bess Abell said. Lady Bird would become known for her slow, sweet southern drawl, and the way she spoke, her friends and family say, was pure poetry.

Not all the pressures faced by the first ladies involve high policy or giving speeches; some of them are much more private and personal. Nash Castro worked with Lady Bird on her signature beautification program and remembers getting calls from her at 5 p.m. most days asking him to join her on the Truman Balcony. "She would have half a glass of wine mixed with half a glass of water because she was forever watching her weight. I'd have a glass of Scotch and water and there would be a bowl of popcorn between us and we talked about everything." Lady Bird was always on a diet and rarely allowed herself more than a few kernels of popcorn during these informal happy hours. She could not help being wounded by a 1964 *Time* cover story that praised her skills on the campaign trail but said cuttingly, "Her nose is a bit too long, her mouth a bit too wide, her ankles a bit less than trim, and she is not outstanding at clothesmanship." Even Jackie Kennedy, who seemed always to be aware of her beauty, worried that her own hips were too wide. Jackie was so disciplined about her weight—a mere 120 pounds—that if she gained two pounds she fasted for a day, then upped her exercise regimen and limited herself to fruit for days afterward. (Jackie also had an intense beauty regimen that included brushing her hair fifty to one hundred strokes every night and applying skin cream to her eyelashes.) Lady Bird told an aide that she wished she had gotten her nose fixed before she became first lady, but by the time she became a household name, and her appearance was being scrutinized, it would have been too obvious. She felt forever destined to be compared with her predecessor.

The *Time* story was right about one thing: it was true that Lady Bird did not care about high fashion. Bess Abell said she had to convince her to buy dresses that were not off the rack. Lady Bird demurred: "I don't think clothes are that important." She had a limit, however. Before one state dinner, the *Washington Post*'s Katharine Graham arrived wearing the same dress that

Lady Bird had on. Abell ran upstairs to tell the First Lady, who swiftly changed and came down wearing a different gown.

————

GENERAL DON HUGHES, who worked for the Nixons during the vice presidency, was having dinner with them when, almost nine months after Nixon's resignation, the President first learned about the fall of Saigon that marked the end of the Vietnam War. "He showed a great remorse that night," Hughes said. "He said, 'If I had been there those SOBs would never have crossed the DMZ.' He wasn't crying, he was mad; he was mad at himself." Hughes was used to the President's intense flashes of anger, as was Pat. Hughes had been assigned to protect Pat during her husband's 1960 presidential campaign, and though he had served in three wars, "nothing was as draining" as that campaign, he says.

Pat, who had already spent almost eight years as second lady, did not flinch when her husband pledged to campaign in fifty states in 1960. She was willing to do whatever it took, as she watched Democrat John Kennedy move into a two-point lead ahead of her husband. She was almost fifty but she refused to be intimidated by the young, regal Jackie. Richard Nixon was less calm. Once, when they were driving through Iowa, Nixon kicked the seat in front of him, where Hughes was sitting, so hard that Hughes smacked his head on the dashboard. Hughes had to leave the car to cool off. Both Nixons were exhausted after they visited twenty-five states in the two weeks leading up to the first televised presidential debate. Nixon had a 103-degree fever but Pat, who never admitted when she was not feeling well, soldiered on. She clenched her teeth when her husband flew into rages, exhausted because he could not sleep.

She had been through worse. In late November 1957, when

President Eisenhower had a mild stroke, Mamie asked Pat to fill in for her with increasing frequency. Pat was exhausted by the heavy workload, even though she would never allow herself to admit it. Even while Mamie relied on Pat to do her grunt work, just as Jackie would depend on Lady Bird, the Eisenhowers never invited the Nixons to the residence for a party. But they were happy to use them when they needed them.

President Eisenhower asked the Nixons to take an eighteen-day diplomatic trip to South America in the spring of 1958. The point of the trip was to celebrate the inauguration of Arturo Frondizi, the first democratically elected president in Argentina in two decades. The trip was going well until the Nixons arrived at the University of San Marcos in Lima, Peru, where rocks were thrown at them by leftist demonstrators. But the most dramatic episode happened during their stop in Caracas, Venezuela, when the Nixons arrived at the airport and were greeted by protesters who spat on them and threw fruit and garbage at them. On the drive into Caracas, Pat was in the car with Hughes and the foreign minister's wife. In front of them, in a separate car, were Vice President Nixon and the foreign minister. Protesters blocked their route with a vehicle and hundreds of them flooded the streets and attacked both cars, throwing rocks and pipes at them. Pat looked ahead at her husband's car, not knowing if either of them would survive. The foreign minister's wife was sitting next to Pat and began to panic. Pat tried to soothe her, cradling her in her arms like a baby. "I did what I could to help but Mrs. Nixon didn't need it; she calmed her down and comforted her until we got to safety," Hughes recalled, describing that day as the closest he had come to death. A rock struck the Vice President's window and a piece of glass hit the foreign minister's eye and he started to bleed. The demonstrators began rocking the Vice President's car, trying to overturn it. Secret Service agents did not want to draw their guns for fear that would cause more violence. After more than ten minutes, agents were able to use a press car to block traffic and give the Nixons' motorcade a path to speed away and escape to the American Embassy.

The next day the press gathered around the cars, which Nixon insisted be left in full view so that their harrowing journey could be documented. Reporters burst into spontaneous applause when the Nixons left the embassy to attend a government luncheon. Tears welled up in the normally stoic Pat's eyes. Before the Nixons left for home, the governing junta gave Hughes hand grenades for protection. When Pat climbed into the car, she had to delicately maneuver around a grenade that Hughes had accidentally left on the backseat. "I believe this belongs to you," she said as she carefully handed it to him.

The Nixons were welcomed home as heroes. The Eisenhowers met them at Andrews Air Force Base, as did thousands of supporters, half of Congress, and the full Cabinet. Years later, when she was First Lady, Pat found herself surrounded by Soviet security agents at a large Moscow department store as members of the American press clamored to get closer to her and her hostess, the wife of the Soviet foreign minister. Traffic was closed off around the building and the Soviet police began shoving frustrated journalists aside. Pat was at the store's ice cream counter when she noticed Associated Press reporter Saul Pett being pushed against a wall by a burly security guard. "He's with me," she told the guard. "Leave him alone." A skilled politician with decades of training, she pulled Pett close to her and offered him a bite of her vanilla ice cream cone. Pett wrote her a note thanking her for the gesture. "You've been a heckuva good sport," he wrote, "and the ice cream was especially good."

The day before the President announced his resignation, the Nixons' daughter Julie, with tears in her eyes, told her mother that it was all over. Pat never gave up hope, not at any moment during those agonizing months leading up to her husband's August 8, 1974, televised Oval Office address announcing his resignation effective noon the next day. When Julie approached her mother's bedroom, still decorated as it had been when Lady Bird lived there, she found her mother standing in the doorway. "Daddy feels he has to resign," Julie said. "But why?" Pat asked, disbelievingly. Three months before his resignation, the First Lady gave an interview and said that her husband "has never considered resigning and isn't *now*." As late as July 31 she was deciding what china she would order. (She called Curator Clem Conger and told him, "I won't explain, Clem, but don't go ahead with the porcelain. Call it off.") Julie put her arms gently around her mother, afraid that a full embrace would cause them both to break down. The Nixons had weathered other storms together—they had been through eleven major campaigns—and Pat still believed that as a family they would survive this one. Before her husband announced his decision in 1972 to escalate bombing in North Vietnam, she hugged him and said, "Don't worry about anything." She almost always ended meetings with her East Wing staff with a cheerful "Onward and upward!" President Nixon said of his wife years later, "She was a fighter to the last, she was the last to give up." She had publicly defended her husband throughout the Watergate investigation, telling reporters, "The truth sustains me because I have great faith in my husband." Once, when asked by a reporter about her husband's state of mind as Watergate raged on, she waved her arm with her fists clenched and said, "He is in great health, and I love him dearly and I have great faith." Her social secretary, Lucy Winchester, calls Pat a "rock-ribbed woman."

Most members of Pat's East Wing staff were in their mid-twenties or early thirties, and they included Winchester, Director of Correspondence Gwen King, and Susan Porter Rose, who worked on correspondence and scheduling. The trauma of Watergate has bound these women together forever, and many of them still keep in touch. At the time, they were afraid to go out for lunch and encounter protesters in Lafayette Square, so they huddled together and ate in the White House. They were so worried about perception that eight months before the President's resignation, as Watergate dragged on, the First Lady's staffers agonized over a snowman. Before a White House party for the children of diplomats, several of these young women were asked to build a snowman on the South Lawn. Wearing heavy coats over their dresses and skirts, they made the snowman, with the help of groundskeepers who brought over shovels and water to help pack the fluffy snow. After much discussion, they decided that the snowman should be facing away from the White House so that people would not say that the President's snowman had his back to the public. These women knew the pain and tremendous pressure that the First Lady was under, so anytime they received a heartfelt message or an encouraging telephone call, they would pass it along to her. One day the First Lady invited some staffers to go on the presidential yacht, the *Sequoia*. They went down the Potomac River to Mount Vernon, a welcome break from the bunker the White House had become.

The First Lady's staff had found out about Watergate the same way that everyone else did—they read about it in the newspapers. On August 9, 1974, the day he resigned, the President gathered all of the White House staffers in the East Room to say goodbye. The women of the East Wing vowed they would not cry because the First Lady would not want them to. Walking together from the East Wing to the East Room, they all kept their emotions in check, until they hit the Cross Hall, where the Marine Band was playing "You'll Never Walk Alone" from the musical *Carousel*. That undid them, and they walked into the East Room with tears welling up in their eyes. Gwen King remembers the First Lady, standing onstage, ever composed. "I think that I saw a tiny tear," she said. "So I moved over behind somebody; the empathy was just too much for me."

Up until her death, Pat maintained that no one knew the full story of Watergate. Pat's chief of staff and press secretary, Connie Stuart, loves her former boss, and she compares her willful ignorance to that of a woman whose husband has been having a long affair. Pat knew intellectually that her husband had done something wrong, but she did not want to acknowledge it to herself. The President didn't tell his family the whole truth because he didn't want them to carry the burden that he was already carrying, Stuart said. "They're not blind, they can read and they can hear. They're not going to say, 'Daddy, why did you do that?'" Pat became such a loyal defender that she cut out news articles about other presidents who were said to have bugged the White House, including President Franklin Roosevelt, and set them aside. Her close friend Helene Drown said that Pat saw Watergate as an effort by her husband's critics to get their "last pound of flesh."

The residence staff did not know the family was leaving until Pat called downstairs asking for packing boxes. Shortly before the President announced his resignation, Pat's hairdresser, Rita de Santis, finished doing her hair and said happily, "See you tomorrow." Pat hugged de Santis as her eyes filled with tears. She hated the famous photo taken of her family by White House photographer Ollie Atkins in the Solarium on August 7, two days before Nixon left office, because, she said, "Our hearts were breaking and there we are smiling." Nixon said he could tell his wife was upset that evening because when he walked into the Solarium he could see that she was suffering from a terrible pain in her neck—something that happened to her during times of stress. "This time I could see the throbbing. But when she saw me she put on a great act," he recalled in an interview. "She threw her arms around me and she said, 'We're all very proud of you, Daddy.'" The night before Nixon announced his resignation, the First Lady could not sleep. The task of sorting through their furniture, photo albums, books, and clothing all fell on her shoulders.

On the morning of the President's resignation, August 9, 1974, the Nixons were crowded into an elevator on their way to the East Room, where the President would make his emotional goodbye speech to his staff. Pat wore a pink-and-white dress and carried sunglasses with her in case she could not contain her sadness. Nixon's aide Steve Bull began telling them where to stand and where the cameras were when Pat broke in plaintively, "Dick, you can't have it televised." No one had asked her opinion, and it was too late to change anything. The President never thanked Pat in his East Room speech, but her press secretary, Helen Smith, says that might be because "he knew that there is a limit to what Pat can endure—and still keep her head high."

When the incoming President and First Lady, Gerald and Betty Ford, escorted the Nixons from the White House to the waiting helicopter, Pat and Betty clung to each other's arms as they walked four abreast, flanked by two rows of military guards standing at attention. The most famous image from that day is President Nixon doing his trademark double V-for-victory sign as he stood on the steps of Marine One, but the way that Pat and Betty held on to each other on a day that would change the lives of both forever is just as fascinating. Betty Ford's press secretary,

Sheila Rabb Weidenfeld, said, "She [Betty] was very fond of her [Pat] and she felt very sorry for her, because she thought she was a very good person who had a very difficult marriage. She liked her as a person, in fact she liked her very much." On the plane ride to California the Nixons, separated by a partition wall, each sitting alone in his or her own compartment, didn't say a word to each other. And just like that, it was over. Barbara Bush remembered being there with her husband for Ford's swearing in, and how jarring the transition was to witness. "After we waved goodbye to the Nixons the pictures on the wall were all of Jerry Ford's family. We're standing at the helicopter waving goodbye while they changed the pictures."

Not long after the Nixons left Washington, Pat called her old friend Lucy Winchester and said, "I have a problem, I want to cook supper tonight. Dick wants me to fix my meat loaf recipe. The FBI still has my meat loaf recipe, do you remember it?" They couldn't help laughing at the absurdity of it all. Winchester says the FBI took everything for a time, even one of the Nixon daughters' wedding dresses.

On September 8, 1974, a month after Richard Nixon announced his resignation, President Ford granted the disgraced former president a "full, free and absolute" pardon. The Fords' son Steve said that his mother worried about the reaction to the pardon, but his father was thinking of the long-term ramifications for the nation if Watergate dragged on. He said that his parents knew the pardon would cost them support, and possibly the next election. But Betty thought the risk was too high and warned her husband against it. Betty came to resent President Nixon for essentially ruining her husband's chance of winning the White House in his own right. The pardon was the saddest day of Pat's life because it marked her husband's acceptance of defeat. To her, he still had nothing to apologize for. Susan Porter Rose, who worked for Pat and for Betty, said there was no phone call between the two about the pardon. "No, absolutely not. It just wouldn't happen, it wouldn't happen with anybody. . . . Now, had somebody died, they would have called."

Pat Nixon's director of correspondence, Gwen King, went to stay with the Nixons in San Clemente and over dinner and a martini, King started telling the Nixons stories about the presidents she had worked for (she began working at the White House during the Eisenhower administration). Richard Nixon was especially curious about President Johnson, and in the middle of her story King stopped and asked him, "You're not taping this, are you?" The room went quiet and she couldn't believe what she had blurted out. A few seconds went by and Pat burst into laughter. The President laughed, too, and assured her that he was not recording their conversation.

In 1984 Pat declined Secret Service protection (she had had it up until then) because she considered it an unnecessary expense. President Nixon gave up his security detail a year later. Pat retreated into herself and read as many as five books a week. She took to gardening ("I couldn't dig into the White House garden very much. It always had to be on display") and wore through four pairs of heavy gardening gloves as she compulsively tended to their estate in San Clemente, which was situated on a bluff overlooking the Pacific Ocean. She knew how much her husband loved roses, so she made sure to plant some outside the window of his study. Their lives may have been a shambles, but she could make the garden lush and beautiful simply by spending time taking care of it. No amount of time would restore her husband's dignity. Pat reluctantly agreed to pose for her official White House portrait

by Henriette Wyeth Hurd, sister of the renowned artist Andrew
Wyeth. Though she liked the painting, she said, "It makes me
look too sad."

————

SOMETIMES, BEFORE GIVING a speech, Betty Ford was so terrified
that she would confess to her aides, "Oh my God, I think I'm
going to throw up." But when her husband, who was suffering
from laryngitis, could not speak the morning after he was defeated by Jimmy Carter in the 1976 election, it was Betty who read
his concession speech and she did it with grace.

Her courage grew with each passing day that she was in the
White House. One evening, she was about to be given a Bible by
Rabbi Maurice Sage, president of the Jewish National Fund of
America, at a black-tie gala at the New York Hilton, when Sage
collapsed onstage. Betty said it was chaos as people rushed to help
him and when she saw everyone crowding around Sage she went
back to her seat to get out of the way. But as she sat there she felt
uneasy. "I felt someone had to do something," she wrote in her
memoir. "I truly believed that if I could get up there and pray, and
get all these people to pray with me, we might somehow save Dr.
Sage's life." The First Lady took over the microphone as doctors
in the audience of 3,200 and her Secret Service agents rushed to
try to revive the fifty-nine-year-old leader. "We must all pray in
our way," she said, her voice trembling as Sage was being given
oxygen. "It is up to God what will happen. We should all have
faith." She asked those present to bow their heads in prayer. "Dear
Father in Heaven," she recited to the stunned audience. "We ask
thy blessing on this magnificent man. We know you can take care
of him."

When the crowd stood to applaud her, she motioned that they

should sit back down and she said the program should be ended as Sage's life hung in the balance. Sage was pronounced dead at 11 p.m., shortly after arriving at the hospital. This woman, who used to hate public speaking, was able to command the attention of those in that ballroom and keep them calm. The experience of watching Sage die would stay with Betty forever; when she returned to the White House, she was haunted by it.

Betty was also plagued by fear after two assassination attempts were made on President Ford within the span of three weeks. Both attacks occurred in California and they were by the only two women who have ever tried to kill a president. In Sacramento, on September 5, 1975, a Charles Manson groupie named Lynette "Squeaky" Fromme tried to shoot at Ford, but her gun never went off. Seventeen days later, outside San Francisco's St. Francis Hotel, a forty-five-year-old middle-class housewife named Sara Jane Moore fired her gun and narrowly missed hitting the President.

Before these attempts, Betty Ford used to stand on the Truman Balcony to wave goodbye to her husband, watching happily as he walked out on the South Lawn to board Marine One for a trip. After the first attempt on his life, she said, "I couldn't watch him leave without thinking, *What's going to happen this time?* The worry was always there." She told their four children, "Your dad has a really important job and we can't concern him with our fears about his security and his life." Steve Ford says, "We all tried to put on smiley faces." But it weighed heavily on Betty every day. As one White House aide said, "All first ladies live in fear."

The Secret Service insisted that President Ford wear a bulletproof vest, and several were made to match some of his suits. Betty and her children never wanted to know which suits had accompanying vests—they did not want to think about the daily threats that he was facing. President Ford had a wonderful sense of humor, and right after the attempted assassinations he walked into the room where his family was gathered and told his wife, "Betty, those women are lousy shots." It was the perfect thing to say and everyone laughed and was smiling again, at least for that moment.

Gerald Behn was the head of the Secret Service White House detail from 1961 to 1965 and served during Kennedy's assassination. He said that the only way to truly protect the president and his family would be in a dictatorship, where everyone could be kept off the streets when the first family leaves the White House. "But here in this country, well, the president wants to go out; he wants to see the people; the people want to see him."

Even after the first families leave the White House they have threats hanging over them like an endless cloud. Before they left office the Johnsons went to visit the Eisenhowers and Mamie told Lady Bird how upset she was by all the tourists who came to the Eisenhowers' Gettysburg, Pennsylvania, farm. Someone stole a sign, and even though their fence was wired someone— "apparently a psycho case," Mamie said—had walked into their yard. "You'll have all this, too," Mamie told her—hardly a reassuring thought for someone who was leaving the relative comfort and safety of the White House in less than six months.

———

NANCY REAGAN HAD a hard exterior. Residence staffers said that when they were serving the Reagans it felt like serving the king and queen, not the President and the First Lady. When Nancy wanted something she spoke almost exclusively to Chief Usher Rex Scouten, who was the general manager of the residence and after whom she named her Cavalier King Charles spaniel. George

Hannie was one of a half-dozen butlers who worked in the family's private living quarters, and he remembers how nerve-racking it could be serving Nancy Reagan. When she was eating alone, Nancy still wanted a cloth napkin instead of a paper napkin, which would have been fine for some of the other first ladies. "If you had a silver tray, I don't care if you shined it yesterday or an hour before, when you go out there make sure you do it again for Nancy Reagan. She don't miss nothing. Nothing," Hannie said with a laugh. When he first started working on the second floor the other butlers told him, "George, that lady is hard. You won't be able to break her." He replied, "It won't be no problem, give me a couple of months, we'll take care of it." He said he was able to earn her respect just by doing what she asked. "Next thing I know she comes through the White House second floor calling my name. 'I told you, I got her,'" he joked with his colleagues.

Each first lady has had to deal with a tremendous amount of pressure in the White House, and in 1987 Nancy had a succession of events play out in public that would have brought most people to their knees. During a routine mammogram on October 5 a suspicious lesion was discovered, and on October 17 she had her left breast removed. Just ten days later, her beloved mother, Edith Luckett Davis, died. But she could not wallow in her own physical pain from the surgery and emotional pain from her mother's death, because she had to organize a state dinner for the historic visit of Soviet leader Mikhail Gorbachev less than two months later. The visit resulted in the signing of one of the most significant arms control agreements of the Cold War. Through it all Nancy remained composed.

President Reagan's assistant Kathleen Osborne was the first to learn of Nancy's mother's death, and she had all calls to Nancy blocked until she could tell the President, who was in the middle of a television interview in the Oval Office. "I was afraid some-body else would tell her, and knowing him the way I thought I did, I thought he'd want to tell her." Osborne had the President's doctor accompany him upstairs when he went to tell his wife the news. The next day Nancy flew to Arizona, where her mother had lived, with her assistant Jane Erkenbeck and a few aides to sort through her mother's things. She had not yet recovered from her mastectomy. Osborne remembers being on the plane with her and asking what urn she wanted to buy and thinking, *My God, she just had a mastectomy ten days ago and here she is on an airplane, going to Arizona to bury her mother.*

Nancy had been through even worse times. At 2:25 p.m. on March 30, 1981, sixty-nine days into her husband's presidency, John Hinckley Jr. fired a revolver six times at President Reagan after he delivered a speech at the Washington Hilton hotel (which has become so closely identified with the shooting that Wash-ingtonians call it the "Hinckley Hilton"). Nancy learned about the shooting as she was looking at paint colors in the Solarium with Chief Usher Scouten and her interior decorator, Ted Graber. Painter Cletus Clark remembered the moment when the head of the First Lady's Secret Service detail, George Opfer, walked in and motioned Nancy toward him. "The next thing you know, they left. I was still up there trying to mix some paint to match some fabric." The First Lady was told that several people were wounded but that her husband had not been shot, and that there was no need for her to go to the hospital. "George," she said, "I'm going to that hospital. If you don't get me a car, I'm going to walk." A White House limo picked her up at the South Por-tico and brought her to the hospital, where there was absolute mayhem with reporters and curious onlookers flooding the street. The First Lady threatened to jump out of the car and run to the emergency entrance of the gray cinder-block building, but Opfer pleaded with her to wait. Finally, the traffic eased and she ran in. Mike Deaver, the President's deputy chief of staff, met her at the door and said, "He's been hit."

"They told me he wasn't hit," she said, stunned.

"Well, he was. But they say it's not serious."

"Where? Where was he hit?" She demanded answers but Deaver didn't have any. She wanted to see her husband but Deaver said that she couldn't.

"They don't know how it is with us. He has to know I'm here!" she begged. He told her that Reagan's press secretary, James Brady, had been shot in the head and that a Secret Service agent and a Washington, D.C., police officer had also been hit. Deaver led her into an office where she repeated over and over to herself, *They're doing what they can. Stay out of their way. Let the doctors do their work.* Her surgeon stepfather had drilled this into her head. She tried to suppress flashes of herself driving down a Los Angeles highway when she heard that Kennedy had been shot less than twenty years earlier. She would think of Dallas again and again as her husband was in the hospital.

Nurses gave her updates, each more disturbing than the last. She was told twice that they could not find a pulse, and then that the President's left lung had collapsed. Finally, she was allowed to see him and what she saw broke her heart: her husband's new blue pinstripe suit lay in the corner of the room and bandages and blood surrounded his pale body. In an interview for a 2011 PBS documentary thirty years later, Nancy teared up recalling that day. "I've never seen anybody so white. . . . I almost lost him." The President was breathing through an oxygen mask, but when he saw her he took off the mask, his lips caked in dried blood, and whispered, "Honey, I forgot to duck."

When the Reagans' son Ron got to George Washington University Hospital and saw his mother, this political powerhouse, he immediately thought that she seemed so small, and so alone. There were so many advisers, doctors, and police officers wandering around, but she was by herself in those frightening hours following the shooting. "In a moment like that, as the wife of a husband whose life is hanging in the balance, you are very alone," he said. He remembers looking at his father after his mother's mastectomy and thinking the same thing. "You're not a public figure at that point, you're not the President or the First Lady, you're a spouse." Nancy told Ron how frightened she was. "I know, Mom, but hold on." She sat in the waiting room after she escorted her husband in for surgery, and watched as incorrect reports flashed across the TV screen, including a bulletin that Press Secretary Brady had died. But watching television, and even seeing headlines she knew were untrue, provided her some sense of comfort and normalcy. She went to the hospital's chapel, where she met Brady's wife, Sarah, for the first time. "They're strong men," Sarah said. "They'll get through this." The two women, whose husbands were so close to death, held hands and prayed together.

When the Reagans' daughter Patti found her mother in bed the next morning, she was picking at her breakfast and clearly hadn't slept much. Nancy had wanted to stay overnight at the hospital, but her son convinced her not to—it would send the wrong message and would alert the public to just how dire the situation had actually been. Patti kissed her mother on the cheek and sat on the edge of the bed. "He almost died—several times," Nancy said, her voice raspy. "They gave him so much blood. An inch from his heart—that's how close the bullet was. And then when they put the tube down his throat—so scared—he was so scared." But it was Nancy who was the most afraid; she was so deeply in love with this man, she couldn't imagine life without him. When she got back to the White House she went into his closet and got one of his shirts to sleep with. "I just needed to have something of his next to me," she told her daughter, with whom she had fought so fiercely but who now shared her fear and pain. "The bed seemed so empty."

Nancy visited the President at the hospital every day. She brought pictures made by schoolchildren and hung them up on the walls to try to cheer him up. The room was bleak, and even the curtains were nailed shut because of an increasing number of threats on the President's life.

At sixty-nine, Reagan was the oldest man ever to be sworn in as president, and Nancy had always worried about his health, but after the assassination attempt her concerns became all-consuming and she became increasingly involved in the level of protection surrounding her husband. In a CBS interview she told Mike Wallace how worried she was every time he went out in public. "I don't think my heart started again until he came back." She was paralyzed by her fear and referred to the year after the assassination attempt as "the lost year." She became so overprotective that she insisted that her husband come home in the afternoons to the residence and take a nap. If she found him at his desk working, she would tell him, "Horizontal. I want you horizontal." (It became an inside joke around the West Wing, with presidential aides mimicking the First Lady: *I want you horizontal*.") She even brought up Lyndon Johnson to make her point because she knew that he took afternoon naps when he was president.

Nancy began consulting astrologer Joan Quigley as a way of coping, and it helped. She used Quigley's advice to plan her husband's schedule, including the safest times for Air Force One to take off and land. She directed Deputy Chief of Staff Mike Deaver to adjust the President's schedule according to advice from Quigley. She never referred to Quigley by name and called her "my friend." Quigley's recommendations became so important that there was a color-coded calendar (green for good days, red for bad days, yellow for "iffy" days) that the staff could refer to for the best times for the President to travel. (During Barack Obama's first press conference after his election, he was asked if he sought advice from former presidents and said, "I've spoken to all of them that are living. . . . I didn't want to get into a Nancy Reagan thing about doing any séances." Obama called Nancy later that day to apologize for his off-the-cuff remark, and she teased him and referred to Hillary Clinton's relationship with Eleanor Roosevelt: "You've gotten me mixed up with Hillary.")

President Reagan's brush with death seems to have affected his wife far more than it affected him. Richard Allen was Reagan's national security adviser at the time and he had to give Reagan his first national security briefing after the shooting. Allen told his five-year-old daughter, Kimberly, that he would be briefing the President on his first day back in the White House. "Is that right?" she asked. She went off to kindergarten and when she came back she had handmade "get well" cards from everyone in her class. Allen stuck them in his briefing folder, thinking that the President might want to see a couple of them.

"Mr. President, we're having a national security briefing today," Allen said.

"Okay," the President replied, his voice still soft and weak.

"There it is, and you've had your national security briefing. Congratulations, Mr. President."

They both laughed. "Wait a minute, wait a minute, what's that in there?" Reagan asked, pointing to the bulging briefing folder.

"These are cards from the kindergarten class of Oakridge Elementary School in Arlington, Mr. President."

"Let me see them." Allen handed the folder to him and the President looked at each and every card. Allen said there must have been twenty-five of them.

"Which one's your daughter's?" the President asked.

"It's this one." Allen handed him her card that read, "President Reagan, Please get better, Love, Kim Allen." The President asked for a pen and wrote beneath it, "Dear Kim, forgive me for using your card for my answer, but I wanted to let you know how very much I appreciate your good wishes and your lovely card, Love, Ronald Reagan, April 15, 1981."

After the shooting, Nancy no longer resented the constant presence of the Secret Service in their lives. "If it weren't for them, I wouldn't have a husband," she said.

Nancy walled herself off in the White House, especially after the assassination attempt. When her assistant Jane Erkenbeck saw Nancy speak about her husband and his Alzheimer's at the 1996 Republican National Convention, she called her up. It was the first convention that Nancy attended alone, and she was deeply depressed. "It was just wonderful to see you cry like that because that's the real Nancy Reagan and that's the Nancy Reagan no one ever got to see," Erkenbeck told her. Nancy replied, "Well, Jane, when I was in the White House I built a wall around myself. That's the only way I could exist."

Very few people ever get to see that vulnerable side of any first lady, and, unfortunately, that was certainly the case for Nancy. In 2014, decades after the death of White House Doorman Freddie Mayfield, Nancy remembered getting the call that he had passed away and being "shocked and saddened" by the news. She was deeply hurt when the actress Katharine Hepburn, a good friend of her mother's from her acting days, ended their friendship. "I'm terribly busy," Hepburn told Nancy. "And besides, I don't know what we'd have to talk about. After all, you're a staunch Republican and I'm a staunch Democrat." When President Reagan was having his portrait painted by artist Everett Raymond Kinstler, Nancy noticed several paintings of Hepburn on the wall of his studio. "She's my oldest and dearest friend," she told him wistfully. Kinstler offered to call Hepburn, but when he went to hand the phone over to Nancy she pushed it away—intimidated by the star—and said, "No, you talk to her first."

———

First ladies travel around the country and the world and seem to live glamorous lives. But at a moment's notice their Secret Service agents may tell them to duck and run as fast as they can. On a trip to Venice, Italy, after the assassination of Italian Prime Minister Aldo Moro in 1978, Rosalynn Carter and her daughter, Amy, had to wear bulletproof vests. Rosalynn was frustrated because the vest was so bulky and heavy, and it must have been terrifying to watch her young daughter put one on under her small blue windbreaker.

Because so much of the first family's security is cloaked in secrecy, even the first lady does not always know why she is being asked to do certain things. Agents will make strange requests, like having all of the heavy glass ashtrays removed from tables in a banquet hall in Hawaii before the first lady enters, or pushing the furniture on one side of a living room to another in an Iowa farmhouse before the first lady walks in. "I never understood that and wouldn't have known about it if one of my press advance persons hadn't mentioned it on the plane on the way home," Rosalynn mused about the last-minute furniture repositioning in Iowa.

Just weeks after the U.S. bombed Libya in 1986, Nancy Reagan took a trip to Kuala Lumpur in Malaysia, a country with close ties to Libya at the time. A Secret Service officer told Erkenbeck that they were bringing body bags on the plane in case something happened. "I wished for a broken leg or something to keep me off of that trip," Erkenbeck said. After the bombing, hordes of angry Libyans had taken to the streets and shouted, "Down, down USA! Death to all Americans!" Nancy, a constant worrier, went ahead bravely with the trip to globally promote her "Just Say No" antidrug campaign.

Security is an endless concern and it starts well before the White House. After they get their party's nomination—and sometimes earlier—major candidates and their spouses are assigned Secret Service protection. This practice was established after the assassination of Robert Kennedy while he was campaigning in California in 1968.

Agents tell the candidates and their families on the campaign trail that they should lightly touch people's hands and not clasp them, so that no one could lock hands with them and pull them off a platform and into a crowd. If someone hands them a gift or a note, they must hand it to an aide immediately. Once they're in the White House, the only time they are without agents is when they're on the second and third floors. As soon as they step off the elevator from those floors, an agent "picks them up" and escorts them to their office. If they're at Camp David, agents watch them unobtrusively. Once, Rosalynn Carter was enjoying a quiet stroll on the beautiful, leafy grounds of Camp David with her mother.

"Who else is here this weekend?" her mother asked.

"No one," she said.

There was a long pause and her mother looked at her with wide eyes and said, "I know there's somebody else here because someone is following us." She'd heard the rustling leaves behind them. It was Rosalynn's Secret Service agent.

"Just don't look back, Mother, and you'll forget they're here!" Rosalynn told her husband the same thing when he complained about the presidential motorcade, which can include as many as forty cars.

Daryl Wells co-owns Van Cleef hair salon in downtown Chicago, where Michelle Obama had been getting her hair done since she was a high school senior. He remembers the first time she came into the salon after her husband won the Iowa caucuses. Secret Service agents came to the salon an hour before she arrived, to sweep the building and look for exits. "Where's the closest fire department?" they asked Wells. "Why?" "In case a bomb goes off," they told him. While Michelle does not love being trailed by Secret Service agents all the time, she was furious when uninvited guests crashed the Obamas' first state dinner and she understands why they need the protection. "How does this happen? I live here with my girls," former Obama adviser Anita Dunn remembers hearing her say after the gate-crashing incident. Michelle used to sneak out of the White House more, but ever since security lapses occurred in 2011 and 2014 she has ventured out less. "I wouldn't say she sneaks out a lot but you don't need to sneak out a lot to keep your head screwed on straight," said an Obama administration official who spoke on the condition of anonymity. When asked where she goes, the staffer said he couldn't say because it would curtail her freedom even more. He would hate for her to feel even more like a prisoner than she already does.

In 2011 a White House maid was the first person to discover a broken window and a chunk of white concrete on the floor of the Truman Balcony. Because of her discovery the Secret Service investigated and realized that someone had actually fired at least seven bullets at the residence several days before. (The Secret Service knew a shooting had occurred but initially concluded that the shots were fired by rival gangs in a gunfight and were not intended to hit the White House.) Michelle's mother, Marian, and the Obamas' younger daughter, Sasha, were in the residence at the time the shots were fired. The President's top aides decided they would tell the President first and let him tell his wife. But the President was on a trip and the First Lady was home, and she was not happy about being kept in the dark about the incident. She was understandably furious when she heard the news from Assistant Usher Reginald Dickson, who assumed she already knew. When she summoned now-former Secret Service director Mark Sullivan to the White House to discuss the enormous security lapse, she was shouting so loudly she could be heard from the hallway. On September 19, 2014, an even more unbelievable incident happened when a man armed with a knife scaled the White House fence, sprinted across the North Lawn, ran past several Secret Service officers, and made his way into the White House. He ran past the stairway leading to the second floor of the residence and went into the East Room. The intruder was finally tackled by an off-duty agent near the doorway of the Green Room. It was terrifying for the First Lady to think that, had he known the floor plan of the White House better, he could have run up the stairs to the family's inner sanctum on the second floor instead of running into the East Room.

Her family's safety was one of Michelle's biggest concerns when her husband first started talking about running for president. In a 2007 *60 Minutes* interview, Michelle was asked by journalist Steve Kroft if she worried about her husband being shot by "some crazy person with a gun." "I don't lose sleep over it," she said, "because the realities are that, as a black man, Barack can get shot going to the gas station . . . you can't make decisions based on fear and the possibility of what might happen. We just weren't raised that way."

Her family has gotten so used to the constant presence of the agents that daughters Sasha and Malia call them the "secret people." Former Deputy White House Press Secretary Bill Burton says the President's safety weighs heavily on the First Lady's mind. "The first time I went on the helicopter with the President I looked out the window and I saw the two decoy helicopters that were with us." At first Burton marveled at how amazing it was to be part of a helicopter motorcade. "But then comes the realization that there are other helicopters in the air because someone would actually like to kill the person you're sitting next to. So just imagine that that's your husband." He said that thought crossed his mind on every single trip he took with the President around the country. "You can see that he's a guy who knows that he's in mortal danger but he's kind of come to grips with it. He's not going to let that affect him. . . . His fate, in some ways, is not in his hands, and that to him that's not a scary thing, it's just the reality of his life."

Even a simple dinner outdoors is not so simple for the President and the First Lady. "When the President is on the Truman Balcony we serve him behind the columns so nobody can see him," says former Maître d' George Hannie, who served the President and First Lady hundreds of times. "Same for the First Lady. If they're together they're on opposite ends." If there are too many people down around the gate at the far end of the South Lawn, the butlers encourage the President and the First Lady to eat inside. The White House has always been exposed. After Robert Kennedy was killed, Lady Bird and her daughter Lynda sat outside on the Truman Balcony in the early evening, seeking some fresh air on a day that was a painful reminder of JFK's assassination five years earlier. Suddenly Lady Bird was aware of how visible they were from the roof and dining terrace of the nearby Washington Hotel. "Not that I myself ever feel any fear at all," she wrote in her diary. "It is absolutely foreign yet for me, or even really for Lyndon. But maybe neither of the Kennedys felt it either."

Three former residence staffers—Chief Electrician Bill Cliber, Maître d' George Hannie, and Usher Worthington White—say they are deeply concerned about the safety of the Obamas. In an effort to save money, they say, the White House is relying on more and more part-time workers, known as SBAs, an acronym for "service by agreement." These staffers do not have the lengthy full-field security clearance that the full-time staffers have, they say. Investigations into the backgrounds of full-time workers can take up to six months and include in-person visits from agents to their homes to interview their friends and family members, and even to talk with their pastors, to make sure that they would never try to harm the first family. Agents also want to make sure that the prospective employees are not involved with drugs or anything else that could make them a target for blackmail. For a contract worker the vetting can take a few weeks, according to former staffers.

These former residence staffers say they've lost sleep worrying about the growing number of contract workers who are in the same room with the President and the First Lady, and in the kitchen as the full-time staffers prepare meals. White says that everyone blends in when the workers are wearing tuxedos, and so the Secret Service would not know who was full-time and who was there just to help out that night. Full-time staffers like the engineers, electricians, and others who volunteer to help at big events like state dinners keep an eye on the contract workers, but now there are simply not enough full-time staffers who work at these events, White says. Cliber says that full-time staffers have been alarmed by contract workers who ask personal questions about the President and the First Lady. One man who worked in the kitchen washing pans was caught selling drugs and did not return, Cliber said. "If you have a bad element in your life then somebody could use you to accomplish something." At the end of the Bush administration more contractors were hired, and during the Obama administration, according to White and Hannie, it has gotten so that contract workers almost outnumber full-time staffers at state dinners.

Members of the first family always prefer to have people around whom they know personally, partly out of convenience and partly because it makes them feel safe. They have casual conversations with the butlers who work in the family quarters. The first family wants as few people up on the second and third floors of the White House as possible, and the President and the First Lady are comforted by the familiar faces of the butlers and the maids who work there every day. "They're [SBAs] all over the place now," Hannie said. "It's dangerous."

———

As FIRST LADIES, these women are expected to be brave, physically and emotionally. They regularly meet with wounded veterans, the parents of murdered children, and children whose parents have been killed in the line of duty—all without letting their emotions show. Rosalynn Carter remembers one of her first visits to a hospital with mentally handicapped children, and how she could not control her tears. The director took her aside, shut the door, and told her gently, "Mrs. Carter, I've watched you this morning and I have to say one thing. Most mentally retarded people are happy. They do not know that they should be sad. If you are going to help at all, you've got to accept that and get over your tears." First ladies walk a fine line: they need to show their humanity without appearing weak. This is especially the case for Hillary Clinton, who is vying to become the nation's next commander in chief. Lissa Muscatine, who served for many years as a top speechwriter for Hillary when she was first lady and then secretary of state, said that one of the realities of being on the national stage, whether you're a man or a woman, is simple: "You have to be able to chain your emotions."

Muscatine recalls accompanying Hillary on a trip to Romania when she was First Lady; they visited children suffering from terrible diseases. "We went out to this little playground outside and I remember all of us on the staff, probably three or four of us, went to the corner in tears. It was just one of the most horrifying things you've ever seen." When they got back to the motorcade Muscatine asked Hillary, who was wearing sunglasses to hide her tears, "How on earth did you keep it together?" Hillary replied, "I just kept thinking to myself over and over, *This life is so bad for these kids, I have to not cry because crying about their condition would make it worse for them. I just have to not make it worse for them.* So I just kept saying to myself, *Don't make it worse for them. Don't make it worse for them. Keep your stuff together.*" Neel Lattimore, Hillary's press secretary when she was First Lady, remembers a trip to Bangladesh, where Hillary, her chief of staff, Melanne Verveer, and a group of reporters accompanying them got a tour of a hospital for malaria patients. Many of the patients were so sick that they were placed on rubber cots to make it easier to clean them and wastebaskets were at their bedsides in case they had to vomit. "At a certain point, I looked around and it was just me, Melanne, and Mrs. Clinton." The reporters had left because they were overwhelmed by the smell and by so many desperately ill people. "She did not flinch."

President George W. Bush and First Lady Laura Bush regularly went to Walter Reed National Military Medical Center to visit soldiers wounded in Iraq and Afghanistan. They did not bring press with them, but a member of their staff would usually accompany them. Deputy Press Secretary Tony Fratto said, "I never wanted to miss one; as hard as they were and as difficult as they were, you felt you wanted to be there with them." He said the troops gave the President and First Lady strength and that, even when a service member or a family member criticized the President to his face, it was always a trip the President looked forward to. "They have the right to express themselves to the President. But it was amazing how some of the troops could lift him with their encouragement of him as commander in chief." Bush's press secretary, Dana Perino, described how moving it was to see these interactions. During one trip, the President met the parents of a dying soldier and the soldier's mother yelled at him, desperate to know why her son was dying and the Bushes' children were safe. "Her husband tried to calm her and I noticed the President wasn't in a hurry to leave," Perino wrote in her memoir. "He tried offering comfort but then just stood and took it. Like he expected and needed to hear the anguish." On the helicopter ride back to the White House a single tear rolled down the President's cheek. Laura, however, was more solemn and stoic during these gut-wrenching visits. Of the role reversal, an aide noted, "He is more publicly emotional, she was reserved. She never felt comfortable being on public display." But residence staffers and people close to her can tell when she is upset: she quietly fiddles with the pleats in the back of her dress.

———

PRESIDENT OBAMA STARTED every day with a cigarette and ended every night with one until he quit smoking near the end of his first term. A residence staffer used to lead him up to the roof of the White

House, where snipers are stationed and a small greenhouse is located. There the President would have his smoking kit waiting for him. The bundle was prepared by his valet and contained two packs of cigarettes, two packs of matches, and a couple of lighters. Obama always felt an obligation to make a self-deprecating joke about his need to smoke. While his smoking is relatively well known, Laura Bush's urge for a cigarette is not. She dealt with the pressures of being first lady by retiring almost every night to the Treaty Room, a cozy office with a large Victorian chandelier on the second floor across from the Grand Staircase, where she smoked with her husband. Laura smoked cigarettes and President Bush smoked cigars after dinner (a residence staffer even arranged for a humidor specially made in Texas to be installed in a closet off President Bush's bathroom on the second floor). When the door to the Treaty Room was shut everyone on the staff knew that meant they were probably smoking. The Bushes would sit on the couch with the bulletproof glass window open and a fan turned on. Sometimes, when a staffer needed to bring the President an "eyes only" paper to look at and the door was closed, it could be awkward. "My eyes were always on the floor," one staffer said. "I couldn't tell you what they were doing, but the room was always full of smoke."

The residence staff was so concerned about the window being open and about the fact that the President and the First Lady sometimes forgot to shut it when they left the room that the staffers brought it up with the Secret Service. Secret Service agents put a procedure in place to check the window every night. They waited until the Bushes were in bed, and then either an usher or a Secret Service agent would discreetly close the window. By the end of the administration the Bushes had cut down on their smoking and had tried to stop altogether. The first couple did not want to bring the bad habit back with them to Texas.

Ladies, First

★

*It's Heaven not to be bound by a schedule—at least for a few
days—don't you think?*
—LADY BIRD JOHNSON, IN A PRIVATE LETTER TO
BETTY FORD, JULY 31, 1987

First ladies are part of a sisterhood—the world's smallest
and most elite sorority. They live their lives in the fishbowl
of the White House and become symbols of American
womanhood. Behind the scenes, they display incredible courage
and determination under tremendous pressure. Most campaign
hard for their husbands—Barbara Bush was on the campaign
trail for twenty-seven days in one month alone, visiting thirty-
seven cities in sixteen states (and that was just when her husband
was President Reagan's running mate). When Betty Ford left the
White House in 1977, she was crestfallen. She had finally found
her voice and was being forced to leave it all behind after just two
and a half years. Mamie Eisenhower was among that small group
of women who knew what Betty was going through. After President Ford lost the election, Mamie wrote to her, "Words are inad-
equate from your friends but you can always say: 'God I have done

my best,' Amen." When Lady Bird Johnson returned to Texas and found mountains of luggage piled up with no one from the enormous White House staff in sight, she sighed, "The chariot had turned into a pumpkin and all the mice have run away."

Leaving the White House was especially difficult for Jackie Kennedy, who spent the rest of her life struggling with the horror of her husband's murder. In 1968, five years after JFK's assassination, Jackie married the billionaire Greek shipping magnate Aristotle Onassis in a small ceremony on his private island of Skorpios. Their marriage was attacked in the press with headlines blaring "Jackie How Could You?" and "Jack Kennedy Dies Today for a Second Time." Lady Bird Johnson, who was in the motorcade with Jackie in 1963 and who had seen her endure so much heartache, was more sympathetic. In her diary Lady Bird wrote: "Remembering her [Jackie's] eyes when last I had seen her at the funeral of Bobby Kennedy, I thought this complete break with the past might be good for her." Onassis provided Jackie with a retreat from public life and a sense of privacy and security (Onassis had his own speedboats and armed security guards at their private wedding ceremony). But they had a difficult marriage, and when he died in 1975, Jackie was not by his side. After Onassis's death, Jackie worked as a New York book editor at Viking and then at Doubleday, and she began a long relationship with diamond dealer and financier Maurice Tempelsman, who moved into her fifteen-room Fifth Avenue apartment in 1982. (They never married, because Tempelsman, who was separated from his wife, could not get a divorce because she was an Orthodox Jew.) Jackie died of cancer in 1994 at sixty-four years old. Up until shortly before her death, she was working from her New York office—which was crammed with books—three days a week.

Post–White House years were not always easy for Pat Nixon,

either. She had always wanted to be alone with her family and away from public life, but she would forever be haunted by Watergate and her husband's humiliating departure from Washington. In self-imposed exile, Pat spent most of her days obsessively tending to her garden at La Casa Pacifica, their twenty-nine-acre, Spanish-style estate in San Clemente, California, and taking on the hardest jobs, including climbing up on the roof to remove palm fronds—anything to avoid reporters and the gaze of the public. The Nixons moved to New York City in 1980 to be closer to their daughters, after five and a half years in California. Not long after that they bought a home in Saddle River in north New Jersey, where Nixon penned his memoirs and where they spent time with their grand-children. In 1991, when Pat's health was in decline, they moved to a smaller house with an elevator in a gated development in nearby Park Ridge. Pat was eighty-one when she died of lung cancer in 1993. Nixon cried at Pat's funeral and held a handkerchief to his face. Nixon's youngest brother, Ed, remembers how difficult it was. "I had never seen Dick so torn up, he was really out of it," Ed says. "After the ceremony out on the lawn he came inside and spoke to those who were still there—he got front and center like a cheer-leader saying, 'We have to go on now. We'll never forget this lady and what she meant to all of us.'" Nixon died ten months later.

Nancy Reagan had a surprisingly difficult life after the glam-orous years she spent in the White House. She called on the deep and abiding love she had for her husband as she nursed him through a long and heartbreaking goodbye. She passed away a little more than a decade after him. The Fords wrote a letter to the Reagans in 2002 to mark their fiftieth wedding anniver-sary. "Nancy, I can think of no one who so completely embodies St. Paul's admonition that 'love beareth all things, believeth all things, hopeth all things, endureth all things.'"

Sometimes, though, leaving the White House is like being unshackled after serving a long prison term. The endless teas, luncheons, dinners, and photo ops fade away and former first ladies can work on causes they care about. They live remarkably long lives and have often outlived their husbands: Betty Ford was ninety-three when she passed away, Nancy Reagan was ninety-four, and Barbara Bush was ninety-two. Rosalyn Carter is ninety years old. (Bess Truman, who died at ninety-seven, was the longest-living former first lady.)

When President Johnson died of a heart attack on January 22, 1973, he and Lady Bird had been married for thirty-nine years. She lived another thirty-four years, until her death in 2007 at ninety-four. Moody and consumed with how his legacy was being marred by the Vietnam War, in retirement LBJ brooded and said that men in his family typically did not live past sixty-five. He died at sixty-four. After he left the White House, Johnson ignored doctor's orders and began smoking and eating with abandon. On the cold January morning of his death, Lady Bird did not notice anything out of the ordinary and decided to drive into Austin to do some shopping. She received an urgent call on her car telephone from a Secret Service agent at the ranch telling her to return right away. Later, she told an aide, "This time we didn't make it. Lyndon is dead." Lady Bird was composed throughout his funeral; as the Nixons led her to the Rotunda of the Capitol, where her husband's body lay in state, she talked wistfully about all the times she had waited for him at the door of the Senate.

"Mrs. Johnson lived two lives," says her former aide Shirley James, who often refers to the former first lady lovingly as "Mrs. J." "No question, she spread her wings." After devoting almost four decades of her life to her husband's happiness, Lady Bird began to concern herself with her own happiness, traveling and spending time with her grandchildren. President Johnson's wild mood swings and his desire to stay in Texas had made her life more complicated, and while she missed him dearly and spoke of him often in her private letters, she had always wanted to see the world, and after his death she finally could. The Johnsons' social secretary, Bess Abell, says that she once jokingly accused Lady Bird of having a box of three-by-five cards full of things that she wanted to do. "And she did them all."

———

THE FIRST LADY who was in the White House for the shortest amount of time out of all of these ten women is the one who has had the most lasting legacy. After Betty Ford left the White House, she confronted a very modern issue that had once been a very private shame, and she liberated so many others by publicly admitting her addiction to alcohol and pills. Her daughter, Susan, says, "Sometimes I think she gets remembered more than dad does." Ford photographer and family friend David Hume Kennerly says that the Fords' literary agent decided to bundle their 1977 book deal so that no one could look at the amount of money they each got for their memoirs—because it was likely that she would have gotten more. Betty's book, *The Times of My Life*, did outsell her husband's. But President Ford had a sense of humor about it—Betty even gave him a T-shirt for his birthday that read "Bet My Book Outsells Yours." Ford conceded, "She's a lot more interesting than I am!"

The Betty Ford Center was dedicated on October 3, 1982, and is a perfectly manicured oasis on the grounds of the Eisenhower Medical Center, eleven miles southeast of Palm Springs. The center relies on the tenets of the twelve-step program Alcoholics Anonymous, and celebrities, including Elizabeth Taylor and

Chevy Chase, have sought treatment there. But so have people without boldfaced names, and Betty Ford became particularly close to one woman whose life she helped save.

Lorraine Ornelas was in her twenties when she met the Fords in the late 1980s. Ornelas was a chef at the Marriott Desert Springs when her employer staged an intervention and she went to the Betty Ford Center. Ornelas remembers sitting in a circle with a group of patients at the center when Betty Ford walked in. Everyone stood up, except Lorraine. She said she did not recognize the former first lady and at that low point in her life, she did not care. "I was pretty much lost and broken, I had a broken spirit." Betty immediately noticed Lorraine, walked right up to her, stuck out her hand, and said, "Hi, I'm Betty Ford."

Betty had a broken spirit once, too. In 1977 Barbara Walters interviewed the Fords when they were in the White House. Betty's speech was slow and slurred at times, and Walters decided to edit most of it out. Betty's personal assistant, Nancy Chirdon Forster, said the First Lady's staff had asked Walters to postpone the interview, but their pleas "did not seem to matter." A decade later, Betty told Walters how hard it was to come to grips with her addiction. "The word 'alcoholic' to me had a meaning of being disheveled, drunk, all of those things. So how could I be an alcoholic?" The former first lady visited the clinic named in her honor nearly every day.

Shortly after they first met, Betty told Lorraine that she was looking for a personal chef and that Lorraine should drop by the Fords' house for an interview. When Lorraine met with the Fords she felt that, for the first time in years, she had hope for a brighter future. When Lorraine got the job, Betty told her that she would be more than an employee: she would be part of the Fords' large family. Lorraine thought, *Well, that's a nice gesture, but I will be your employee*. But she soon learned that Betty was not exaggerating. Lorraine, who was dyslexic and who had never finished high school, spent every holiday with the Fords for almost seven years and could tell Betty anything. Lorraine says that while Betty had an air of sophistication about her, there was a brokenness there, too. "When it was just her and I in this big house—I was lonely at the time, and I always have that in me. I felt the same from her, that deep down inside she was lonely too," Ornelas recalled. In the beginning, Lorraine was still struggling with her addiction, and after two weeks on the job she took Betty aside and said, "I don't think this is the job for me." But Betty would not give up on her. "Let's just wait two more weeks and see," she said. The weeks turned into years. Lorraine relapsed once while she was with the Fords, and when she told Betty, the former first lady sat her down on the living room couch. "You can fire me if you want," Lorraine said. "Absolutely not," Betty told her, and put her hand on Lorraine's knee. "You never have to be alone."

Betty Ford died at the age of ninety-three, and her July 12, 2011, funeral in Palm Desert, California, was attended by Rosalynn Carter, Nancy Reagan, Hillary Clinton, and Michelle Obama. Presidential historian Richard Norton Smith was one of Betty's eulogists and remembers looking down from the stage to see Rosalynn crying. "Who would have guessed thirty years ago that this is how the story ends," he said, recalling how much bitterness there was after Jimmy Carter beat Gerald Ford in the 1976 presidential election. In her own remarks, Rosalynn spoke lovingly of her onetime rival, a woman with whom she had developed a close friendship. "Her honesty gave to others every single day."

———

THE CARTERS ARE the only post–World War II first couple to return to their original hometown. Since their homecoming to Plains, Georgia, Rosalynn has worked to revitalize the working-class town, revamping the local inn and adding a butterfly garden. But the Carters are most famous for their work with the Carter Center in Atlanta, where they work fifty-one weeks a year (the remaining week they devote to Habitat for Humanity). The Carter Center has a $600 million endowment and oversees elections around the world. The center has also funded treatment for millions of people suffering from diseases and improved the lives of people in more than eighty countries with its work advancing human rights and democracy. Rosalynn has been active in it from its inception. She goes to Africa with her husband a couple of times each year. She gets emotional when she talks about visiting a village where guinea worm, a debilitating disease that in 1986 afflicted an estimated 3.5 million people, has finally been eradicated because of the work of the Carter Center. "It's just so wonderful, just to see the hope on their faces that something good is happening. I didn't mean to get emotional."

Before President Carter announced in August 2015 that he had cancer—surgery to remove a mass from his liver found that cancer had spread to his brain—he was moving at his usual astoundingly energetic pace. Sometimes he was moving so fast that he did not notice that his wife was slowing down. When he announced his diagnosis in a press conference he said, "I was surprisingly at ease, much more than my wife was. But now I think it's in the hands of God and I'll be prepared for anything that comes." In early December 2015, Carter said that the aggressive treatment of the disease had worked and that he was cancer-free.

———

BARBARA BUSH WAS sad to leave the White House for many reasons. One very personal one was knowing that the Clintons were planning to get rid of the horseshoe pit the Bushes had set up next to the swimming pool at the White House. The President and his son Marvin sometimes played there as often as two or three times a week in tournaments against residence staffers. They took the game very seriously and even had tryouts. "You could hear the cling, cling, cling of the horseshoes at lunchtime. . . . It was a wonderful place to live as a home," Barbara recalled. And when President George H. W. Bush's library in College Station, Texas, opened, staffers were invited to come and play horseshoes again at the pit set up outside.

Barbara was one of the happiest ex–first ladies. She enjoyed being a mother and grandmother, and having those "great-grands" that Lady Bird so lovingly talked about. But right after they moved out of the White House, she admitted, she had a difficult time without an army of maids, butlers, and cooks at her disposal. First families can become so out of touch with normal life that, for example, President Reagan quipped that he might not remember how to turn on a lamp after he left the White House. President George H. W. Bush was famously mocked during his 1992 reelection campaign after he marveled at a supermarket scanner. Not long after leaving office, the President took his first trip to a Sam's Club, where he purchased what Barbara deemed "the world's biggest jar of spaghetti sauce and some spaghetti." While he sat down to watch the evening news the former First Lady began to cook—for probably the first time in ages—and accidentally knocked the jar to the floor. She was grateful to discover that night that pizza could be delivered straight to their door.

Barbara was aware of the tremendous power she had, even

twenty years after leaving the White House. When she was asked in 2013 whether her son Jeb should run for president, she said, "We've had enough Bushes" in the White House. Two years later, Jeb announced his candidacy. Jeb's wife, Columba, is shy and consumed by worry about her family's security. (In 2012, Ann Romney was also concerned about the protection of her large family. The Secret Service had already begun talking about adding more people to the staff if her husband, Republican nominee Mitt Romney, had won the election.) Barbara Bush admitted that when Jeb, a seventeen-year-old prep school student, came back from a trip to Mexico and told his family that he had fallen in love with Columba, a Mexican woman who did not speak much English, the patrician Bushes were stunned. "I'm not going to lie to you and say we were thrilled," Barbara recalled.

Before Jeb dropped out of the 2016 presidential race, Laura Bush offered some advice to her sister-in-law. She encouraged Columba to start developing a smart speech and to seek out good and loyal staffers. "Find a way to tell your story," Laura urged. As for what her mother-in-law tells her, Barbara played coy. "She is a tiny, shy woman with a huge heart. I try not to give my daughters-in-law advice, so they will come visit with my sons." But that's not entirely true. Laura says that Barbara did give her one piece of advice that their idol Lady Bird Johnson certainly did not follow. "Never criticize your husband's speeches," Barbara told Laura. "It will only cause arguments."

———

MICHELLE OBAMA IS looking forward to life as a former first lady. Aides say that she will likely focus on causes she cares about and making money through book deals and speaking fees. (Hillary was paid an advance of $8 million for her memoir

Living History.) Advisers say that once they are out of the White House the Obamas will work on issues that particularly affect minorities, like gun violence. The Obamas will have lifetime Secret Service protection if they want it, and the President will get an annual pension of about $200,000. It is likely that the family will move to New York City, but they may wait to relocate there full-time until Sasha finishes high school at Washington's Sidwell Friends School. (When their father's term ends, Sasha will be a sophomore in high school and her sister Malia will be in college.)

Michelle clearly does not share Hillary's childlike feeling of staring at the White House from outside the gates; she cannot wait to break through those gates. The Clintons were so reluctant to move out of the White House and give up the privileges of the presidency that they hosted a series of overnight parties for the staff at Camp David during their last weekend; they stayed up so late the night before George W. Bush's inauguration watching the movie *State and Main* in the White House movie theater that Laura swore she saw the President doze off during her husband's inaugural address. President Clinton confessed to the Bushes on the morning of the inauguration that he had put off packing for so long that, right at the end, "he was packing simply by pulling out drawers and dumping their contents into boxes." The Bushes, however, had packed light, bringing only one chest of drawers and some framed photos; Laura was looking forward to scavenging through the storage facility in Maryland. (Laura would tell Caroline Kennedy that she was using the writing desk that had once occupied her mother's office in the residence.)

There was chaos on the day that the Clintons moved out, and they were later criticized for taking $190,000 worth of china, rugs, televisions, flatware, and other gifts with them when they left. The Clintons agreed to pay $86,000 for the gifts and they sent $28,000 worth of furnishings back to Washington because they mistakenly thought they were personal gifts to them, but in fact they were gifts to the permanent collection of the White House. It was one of the many public scandals of those last few days, including reports that political staffers had vandalized the White House, even removing the "W" key from computer keyboards. The Clintons were not the only ones to bring White House furnishings home, however. Five years after he left office, while redecorating his Houston office, President George H. W. Bush was stunned to discover two bookcases with stickers on the back that read "Property of the White House." The Bushes had a close aide drive the furniture back to Washington in an SUV.

FORMER FIRST LADIES keep their husband's legacies alive through their work with the presidential libraries. Lady Bird Johnson visited every presidential library in existence at the time when she began planning her husband's library and promised that his would outshine them all. Tyler Abell remembers a week he and his wife, Bess, spent at the Johnsons' ranch long after the President had died. Harry Middleton, who was then director of the Johnson Library, had decided it was time to show Lady Bird the courtship letters LBJ had sent her, which library staffers had found in papers donated to the library. Lady Bird could not read because her eyesight had deteriorated, so Middleton read the letters aloud to her. Over the course of the week, Lady Bird and Middleton would go off to the small secluded library at the ranch, and every once in a while the Abells could hear Lady Bird laughing through the closed door. She loved hearing her husband's words again.

No other woman was more devoted to her husband's legacy than Nancy Reagan. A friend of Nancy told her, "You're so lucky, Nancy, because Ronnie left you the library. You have that to work on, and to go to, and, in a sense, to be with him." Her friend was right, Nancy said. "I had never thought of it like that, but it's true. I go to the library or work for the library all the time, because it's Ronnie. I'm working for Ronnie." She made the Reagan Library a cultural and political hub. In the last several presidential elections, she had personally invited each candidate to the pristine library located in Simi Valley, forty-five minutes north of Los Angeles. Before she retired from public life (her last interview before she passed away in 2016 was in July 2009, when she was almost eighty-eight), she helped raise more than $100 million for the library, cultivating wealthy donors and booking famous speakers, including Ted Kennedy and former British Prime Minister Margaret Thatcher. Before she passed away, on the anniversary of President Reagan's death she could be seen sitting alone quietly outside the library at her husband's hilltop gravesite with no one but her Secret Service detail accompanying her.

At her funeral the Reagans' son, Ron, described the deep and private love his parents shared in their more than fifty years of marriage. He seemed to take comfort knowing that they would be buried beside each other. "She will once again lay down beside the man who was the love of her life. The one she loved until the end of her days," he said, his eyes filling with tears. "They will watch the sun drop over the hills in the west, toward the sea. As night falls, they will look out across the valley. My father will tell her that the lights below are jewels. The moon and stars endlessly turn overhead and there they will stay, as they always wished it to be, resting in each other's arms—only each other's arms—until the end of time."

———

THE PERSONAL LEGACIES of these modern first ladies include championing important causes like healthy eating, literacy, drug awareness, and historic and natural preservation, as well as serving as the greatest protectors and confidantes to their husbands. Sometimes they've even decided who should be part of their husbands' Cabinets and helped their husbands develop policy. Whether in the White House or long after they've left, they have tremendous power. Hopefully, they will continue to support each other and to forge deep and long-lasting friendships, empathizing with each other's joys, frustrations, and sorrows. They are bound together by the extraordinary lives they have lived, and they are exceptional in this polarized political climate because their friendships have nothing to do with political party.

Jackie Kennedy made it clear just how grateful she was to Pat Nixon for arranging her family's peaceful and private return to the White House when she wrote, "The day I always dreaded turned out to be one of the most precious ones I have spent with my children." Jackie and Pat were the standard-bearers for opposing political parties—Pat had even suggested a recount when her husband lost to JFK in the 1960 presidental election—and they had very different personalities and interests, but all of that was secondary to the human connection they shared as wives, mothers, and, most uniquely, first ladies.

Melania Trump and Her Place in History

"I would be very traditional. Like Betty Ford or Jackie Kennedy. I would support him."
—MELANIA TRUMP, WHEN ASKED WHAT KIND
OF FIRST LADY SHE WOULD BE

I t has been an incredible year to be studying the influence and impact of the president's spouse. Like everyone else in the United States, and around the world, I have been completely absorbed in this political season. For me it was especially interesting to watch as a former first lady became the first woman to win the nomination of a major political party. And it was incredible to witness Donald Trump's victory, something that none of the polls and almost no one in the media had predicted. Once the nominees were announced I subconsciously began comparing their spouses to the remarkably different women who have been first lady. Would Melania Trump harness the star power of Jackie Kennedy? Would Bill Clinton take on any highly feminized first lady duties, including running the White House residence, or would he be more like his wife and take up an office in the West Wing? One thing has been clear, during this presidential election the role was bound to change forever with either Bill Clinton, the first man who would ever serve as "First Gentleman," or Melania Trump, who will be just as captivating. While I was personally interested in seeing whether a man in the position would change the gendered expectations that define it, in some ways it will be just as compelling to watch how Melania Trump handles the perilous assignment.

Melania may not be changing the gendered stereotypes associated with first ladies—in fact I think she will embrace the most traditional expectations of the position—but she will redefine it in many other ways. She will be the first first lady born outside the United States since Louisa Adams, the wife of John Quincy Adams (Louisa's father was an American, unlike Melania's parents who are both Slovenian), and although Pat Nixon and Betty Ford did some catalogue modeling in their youth, Melania will be the first ex-supermodel to occupy the East Wing. She will also be the first *third* wife of a president (Ronald Reagan is the only other president to have divorced and Nancy Reagan was his second wife).

Melania has said that she would want to follow in the footsteps of "traditional" first ladies like Betty Ford and Jackie Kennedy. But judging by her public statements—of which there have not been many—she would be more traditional than any first lady since Mamie Eisenhower. She has often echoed Mamie, who was emblematic of the times as a 1950s wife and mother and said, "Being a wife is the best career life has to offer a woman." Mamie's predecessor, Bess Truman, said that a first lady's job was to "sit beside her husband and be silent," and she wondered aloud why anyone was interested in her. "You don't need to know me. I'm only the President's wife and the mother of his daughter." Melania's mantra has been similar: "I will support my man," she said. Like Mamie, who proudly announced that she had "only one career, and his name is Ike," Melania has described her marriage to Donald Trump as coming with "a lot of responsibility." She lets Donald have his space; she's not "needy" or "nagging."

As I've written here though, there was nothing conventional about either Betty Ford or Jackie Kennedy, the two first ladies Melania most admires. Betty's striking honesty when she revealed both her breast cancer diagnosis and her addiction to pills and alcohol is far from conventional, and Jackie's solemn vow to stay by her husband's side during the Cuban Missile Crisis, when the threat of nuclear war was greater than it had ever been before, is equally fearless. I cannot find many things Melania would have in common with the outspoken Betty Ford, but there are some similarities with Jackie. Certainly Melania's beauty, elegance, and interest in fashion would make her a natural successor to Jackie Kennedy. During the Trumps visit to the White House less than forty-eight hours after the election—a meeting traditionally held several days or even weeks after the election—Melania wore a black sheath dress reminiscent of Jackie. Jackie was similarly devoted to her husband, who was twelve years her senior (Melania, forty-six, is twenty-four years younger than Donald Trump, who is seventy). Like Jackie, Melania fiercely guards her privacy and the privacy of the Trumps' young son, ten-year-old Barron, and, like Jackie, Melania is fluent in several languages.

But unlike the other women I've studied, Melania is alienated from the close-knit circle of former first ladies because of the bitterness of the campaign. The sense of unspoken civility and sisterhood among them and the empathy that most first ladies have for the candidate's spouse during the campaign—even when that spouse is married to someone from the opposing political party—was strikingly absent during this election because of the personal nature of Donald Trump's charged language. During an interview on a late-night television show then–First Lady Michelle Obama said she had "no sympathy" for the opposing candidate's spouse on the campaign trail. "You have to be in it," Michelle said, in a not-so-subtle dig at Melania. "Bottom line is, if I didn't agree with what Barack was saying, I would not support his run. I stand there proudly and I hope they are too, standing with their spouses proudly. So, no sympathy!" It was Donald Trump's role as the most famous member of the so-called birther movement, which questioned President Obama's citizenship, that most outraged Michelle. "There were those who questioned and continue to question for the past eight years, up through this very day, whether my husband was even born in this country," she said at her first campaign stop for Hillary Clinton, on the same day that Donald Trump acknowledged that Obama was born in the United States. During her passionate remarks, she called Trump "erratic and threatening" without ever using his name. Given the distant relationship between Hillary and Michelle, if it had been any Republican candidate other than Donald Trump, Hillary probably would have received much less support from the Obamas. Michelle is analytical, friends say, and she does not let her emotions take control. She made the calculation to get so involved with the campaign because she thought the stakes were high.

Melania's life has been full of extremes; in many ways her personal story is far more dramatic than that of most first ladies. Long before her $1 million wedding, where she wore a $100,000 Christian Dior gown, and well before she moved into a three-story penthouse in Trump Tower, Melanija Knavs (she changed her name when she began working as a model in Italy) lived in a small factory town called Sevnica, which was then part of communist Yugoslavia and is now part of Slovenia. Communist dictator Josip Tito was president when Melania was born in 1970. She grew up in a nondescript concrete apartment building. A childhood friend recalled how she and Melania would send messages to each other attached on woolen strings strung up between their apartment balconies.

Melania's mother worked as a pattern-maker for a children's clothing manufacturer, and her father was employed as an auto mechanic and car parts salesman and was a member of the local Communist party. Described as sweet and shy by her friends, it seems incredible to think that she would ever get to this point. Her path to meeting billionaire real estate tycoon Donald Trump began at sixteen when she was spotted on the street by a photographer and embarked on a modeling career. She changed her name to Melania Knauss and headed to New York in 1996 to pursue her modeling career. Paolo Zampolli, the head of a modeling agency, introduced Melania to Trump at a 1998 party at the Kit Kat Club in Manhattan and called her "stable and focused."

Melania is married to a man who has very traditional expectations for women. In a 2005 interview with Howard Stern before the birth of their son, Trump said, "I'll supply funds, and she'll take care of the kids." Years later he told Stern, "Melania is a wonderful mother. She takes care of the baby, and I pay all of the costs." For her part, Melania seems to enjoy this arrangement. "We know our roles," she has said. "I didn't want him to change the diapers or put Barron to bed." Unlike Jackie Kennedy, who relied heavily on nanny Maud Shaw to take care of their children, Melania insists that while she has a chef and an assistant, Barron does not have a nanny. "My hands are full with my two boys—my big boy and my little boy!" she often quips. (She sometimes calls Barron "little Donald.") She says that, like his father, Barron prefers suits and is "not a sweatpants child."

There is, of course, a certain irony here since another one of Melania's firsts is being the first first lady to have ever posed nude. In a controversial photo shoot in 2000, Melania posed naked for the cover of *British GQ* wearing handcuffs and sprawled on a bearskin rug aboard her then-boyfriend Donald Trump's Boeing 727. The photo spread was used against Trump during the Republican primary and more risqué photos of Melania surfaced after Trump won the Republican nomination. It makes sense then that Melania has gone out of her way to stress her role as a mother in an effort to make herself less of a sex object and more relatable to women voters. Because of the inherent controversy surrounding her modeling career, she has sought to distance herself from it and it seems to have worked for her. Whatever apolitical issue she takes up will be even less controversial than Michelle Obama's "Let's Move" campaign. She has indicated that she would want to work with children's charities and take on the issue of cyberbullying. Before the election, during her one and only solo campaign appearance, Melania said, "Our culture has gotten too mean and too rough." She did not mention her husband's Twitter wars in which he called Fox News host Megyn Kelly a "bimbo" and told followers to look into an alleged sex tape made by a former Miss Universe contestant who had been critical of him.

Judging by her long absences from the campaign trail—she mostly ceded the spotlight to her stepdaughter Ivanka, who assumed a much bigger role—Melania will be a very private first lady. She was conspicuously absent when Trump announced

Governor Mike Pence of Indiana as his running mate. It marked the first time in modern campaign history that the wife of a presidential candidate has not been there for the public announcement of her husband's running mate. Every candidate's spouse since President Lyndon Johnson has actively sought votes for their husbands in the final days of the campaign. (Jackie Kennedy was pregnant during the 1960 election, giving her the welcome excuse to stay home.) Sometimes wives have been so important to victories that they even campaigned in certain states more than their husbands, as Barbara Bush did in New Hampshire in 1992.

While she prioritizes motherhood, following in the footsteps of her predecessor Michelle Obama, Melania does not seem to share the same sensibility that Michelle has about being a mother. Although Michelle spoke often of putting their daughters first, she also privately expressed her frustration at having to give up a lucrative career in Chicago to be first lady. It seems unlikely that Melania resents putting her career on hold while she raises their son. She has worked outside of the home—in 2010 she designed and sold a line of jewelry on QVC and later developed a skincare line—but she has always made it clear that work was not her primary passion. Barron is the same age as Malia Obama was when her father became president, and Melania will devote herself to getting him settled in his new life, as Michelle did for her two daughters. In the White House Michelle was very concerned with making sure their daughters were not too spoiled by the residence staff and she insisted that they make their own beds and go to the kitchen themselves if they wanted something to eat. Keeping Barron grounded will be a constant challenge for Melania because White House butlers and maids will do anything for the first family.

Underneath Melania's devotion to her husband I suspect she shares an underlying feeling with other first ladies, a sense of sometimes being subservient to and imprisoned by their husbands' overwhelming ambitions. In an interview with the *Washington Post* last April, Donald Trump described his deliberations with his wife ahead of the announcement of his candidacy in June 2015. Melania pleaded with him, "We have such a great life. Why do you want to do this?" He told her, "I sort of have to do it, I think. I really have to do it.... I could do such a great job."

Donald Trump's combative political style has sometimes posed personal problems for Melania. A well-connected Republican, who spoke on the condition of anonymity, told me that it has cost the Trumps friendships, including their relationship with Terry Lundgren, the CEO of Macy's, who stepped down last year, and his wife, Tina Stephan. When Macy's decided to drop Trump's line of ties in 2015 their close friendship was also terminated, the Republican source told me. The decision to end their business relationship was made after Trump's controversial comments about Mexican immigrants, but the Lundgrens did not want to end their friendship with the Trumps. When Macy's later announced that they would be making layoffs and closing more than thirty stores, Trump said in an interview that the company had been "very disloyal" to him. The Trumps have let politics get in the way of friendship, the source said. "I actually don't know anyone who is a true friend to them (anymore)."

The divisiveness of the campaign led to riots in several American cities in the days following the election results. President Obama's invitation to the Trumps to visit the White House less than forty-eight hours after Trump's surprise victory was intended to calm those voters who were deeply disappointed by the outcome. The peaceful transition of power was a priority for Obama and for Trump, and was a continuation of an American tradition upheld no matter how vicious the campaign. And it did get rough as Trump used Bill Clinton's long history of cheating against Hillary in the final months. "In the history of politics," he said at a rally, "Hillary Clinton's husband abused women more than any man that we know of, and Hillary was an enabler and she treated these women horribly. . . . And some of those women were destroyed not by him but by the way that Hillary Clinton treated them after everything went down." At the second presidential debate Trump brought several women who had accused Bill Clinton of inappropriate sexual behavior to a pre-debate press conference and to sit in the audience as his special guests, including Paula Jones and Juanita Broaddrick. "Bill Clinton was abusive to women," Trump said at the no-holds-barred town-hall-style debate as he stood within a few feet of Hillary. "Hillary Clinton attacked those same women and attacked them viciously."

Throughout it all Melania did what candidate's spouses have always done and stood quietly by her husband's side. Even when a shocking and deeply embarrassing tape surfaced revealing extremely lewd comments Trump made about women in 2005, including his bragging about groping women and his failed attempt at seducing a television host, Melania stood by him. "I believe my husband," she said in an interview with CNN days after the story broke. "This was all organized from the opposition. And with the details. . . . Did they ever check the background of these women? They don't have any facts." It was impossible not to draw a parallel to Hillary Clinton's 1992 *60 Minutes* interview in which she was asked about her husband's relationship with Gennifer Flowers. "You know, I'm not sitting here—some little woman standing by my man like

Tammy Wynette," Hillary said. "I'm sitting here because I love him, and I respect him, and I honor what he's been through and what we've been through together."

As first lady that detachment might help shield Melania from the blowback that presidents inevitably get. Susan Porter Rose, who worked in the East Wing for Pat Nixon, Betty Ford, and Barbara Bush, says she remembers Bush in particular "tuning out" what was said about her husband if the headlines became too negative. Nixon's West Wing aides went so far as to make sure that his wife didn't get the newspapers delivered in the White House residence during the final days of Watergate. Melania seems to already possess that habit of self-preservation.

Though Melania will be charting her own course as first lady, she will face the same challenges as the women who came before, clinging to a sense of privacy while living her life on the world's most public stage. She has a hard edge to her and has engaged in her own defense in a way that other first ladies have not. While she has stayed above the political fray she has not shied away from defending herself in court and against the media. She filed a libel suit claiming $150 million in damages against a blogger and the *Daily Mail* for reports that wrongly suggested that she had been an escort. (The *Daily Mail* retracted the story.) The lawsuit is unusual because candidate's spouses, and first ladies, typically do not sue journalists. After an interview she did with *GQ*, she complained on her Facebook page that their story was an example of the "dishonest media and their disingenuous reporting," echoing media criticism that was a hallmark of her husband's campaign.

As a public figure it is impossible to hide from controversy. Her personal website was taken down after reports found no documentation to prove that she graduated from college, which the site had claimed, and she hardly ever tweeted during the campaign. Before her husband announced he was running for president her tweets revealed the lighthearted and privileged life she led as a former supermodel married to a billionaire. A month before Trump announced his candidacy she tweeted a glamorous selfie that read: "Bye! I'm off to my #summer residence #countryside #weekend." The campaign understandably wanted to tamp down the image of a wealthy woman on her way to one of her many homes for vacation. Jackie Kennedy was similarly criticized for being out of touch, specifically for spending too much money on clothes. Before President Kennedy won the election, and before she became an international style icon, Jackie offered her husband an apology: "I'm sorry for you that I'm such a dud."

The most damaging and embarrassing controversy for Melania came during the Republican National Convention when she cribbed parts of her speech from Michelle Obama's 2008 Democratic National Convention address. Eventually a Trump Organization staffer publicly apologized and took the blame for borrowing from Michelle's remarks. In the months after the convention Melania became even more reclusive. When asked for her reaction, Michelle Obama deadpanned: "Yeah, that was tough." Michelle and Melania met for the first time during the traditional tea in the White House residence shortly after Trump won the election. And while the administration released a photo of the two women chatting in the Yellow Oval Room, there were far fewer photos released than had been during the Obamas' meeting with the Bushes after Obama won the 2008 election.

Like most first ladies (with the exception of Betty Ford), if

Melania disagrees with her husband no one would ever know it. A former senior staffer to President George W. Bush said that Melania reminds her of Nancy Reagan: both fiercely defended their husbands during periods of incredible unpopularity. Also, like Nancy, Melania has built a wall around herself that can make her seem cold and removed. Nancy, however, was much more controlling of her husband's image, and unlike Melania, who says she has privately asked Trump to tone down some of his charged language, Nancy very publicly inserted herself into every facet of her husband's work. She had his chief of staff Don Regan fired because, she said, "It landed on my watch." It is hard to imagine Melania getting involved in her husband's personnel decisions. "I chose not to go into politics and policy. Those policies are my husband's job," Melania has insisted.

Aside from litigation, Melania does not seem to engage in the back and forth of politics on any level and she does not want to be part of the story. It has been awkward to watch at times as Donald Trump has railed against illegal immigration, putting Melania as an immigrant herself in the difficult position of defending her husband's controversial stance. The campaign came under criticism for not providing documentation to show how she got a visa and her green card in 2001, though Melania said that she has been "at all times in full compliance" with immigration laws. When asked about her own views on immigration she has defended her husband but not stridently: "You follow the rules," she said. "You follow the law." She is an enigma; it is impossible to know what she really thinks, and that is exactly as she and her husband want it.

Historically, the chief usher, who manages the White House residence, begins trying to learn about the likes and dislikes of the two major party candidates as soon as the nominees are announced, right down to their favorite brand of deodorant and shampoo. Melania will work with the chief usher to run the private quarters of the White House, where the first family resides on the second and third floors. Melania and her staff will be given binders including a layout of the White House, a list of staff with their photographs, and what changes are allowed to be made to the Oval Office. Every president and first lady may redecorate their own private living space on the second and third floors, including their living room, bedroom, study, bathrooms, sitting room, kitchen, and children's quarters. Typically the first family has used the help of an interior designer to redecorate these rooms and the Oval Office. But there are limits to what they can change: structural changes to the mansion and work done in the historic areas on the second and third floors, such as the Yellow Oval Room and the Lincoln and Queens' bedroom, must be approved by the Committee for the Preservation of the White House under the guidance of the office of the curator.

Melania's shy demeanor has intimidated members of the White House residence staff who told me that some permanent staffers are worried about working for the Trumps. Staffers were decidedly more concerned about a Trump victory than a Clinton win. Partly because they told me they knew what to expect from the Clintons, having served them for eight years (three of the six full-time butlers who worked in the residence when the Clintons were last in the White House would have still been there if they had returned, according to one source). A former staffer who spoke on the condition of anonymity because of the sensitivity of the matter (current residence staffers are not supposed to talk to reporters, and former staffers are discouraged from doing so, as well) told me, "As far as I'm concerned, if asked, I would not go back to the White House for Trump, even if they tripled my old pay."

Roland Mesnier was the top pastry chef at the White House and served five presidents from President Jimmy Carter to President George W. Bush, but he said Donald Trump would be entirely different from any president he has ever served. If he were still working at the White House, Mesnier said, he would be "nervous. I think the White House as we know it and the kitchen will be totally different." Mesnier speculated that Melania and Donald might bring in members of their own staff. One thing is clear: the Trumps will certainly be more comfortable being waited on than the Obamas ever were.

ACKNOWLEDGMENTS

They say there's a great woman behind every great man, but it is also true that there's a team of great women behind every great woman. Each of the first ladies is supported by a loyal staff made up mostly of women, and many of them generously shared their stories for this book. Among them were Lady Bird Johnson's social secretary, Bess Abell; Lady Bird's executive assistant Shirley James; Betty Ford's press secretary, Sheila Rabb Weidenfeld; and Betty's personal assistant, Nancy Chirdon Forster. Lissa Muscatine, Melanne Verveer, and Shirley Sagawa worked for Hillary Clinton; Anita McBride was Laura Bush's chief of staff; and Jackie Norris was Michelle Obama's first chief of staff. Susan Porter Rose worked for an astounding three first ladies and I was touched by her clear and undying admiration for each of them. And there were the women who stood behind Pat Nixon during the months leading up to her husband's resignation: Lucy Winchester, Connie Stuart, Joni Stevens, and Gwen King.

My conversations with Rosalynn Carter and Barbara and Laura Bush are what made me to decide to write this book—I wanted to know more about these iconic women and their relationships with one another. I was fortunate to have the opportunity to interview Rosalynn Carter twice, thanks to the indefatigable Jerry Rafshoon and with the help of Melissa Montgomery.

It's been a joy keeping in touch with some of the residence staffers whom I got to know while researching my first book, *The Residence*, including former Usher Worthington White, former Head Housekeeper Christine Limerick, former Chief Usher Stephen Rochon, former Chief Electrician Bill Cliber, and former Maître d' George Hannie and his wife, Shirley. I'm grateful to Luci Johnson, Susan and Steve Ford, and Ron Reagan for sharing stories about their mothers with me. I'm also thankful that Gustavo Paredes agreed to a rare interview with me to share memories of his mother, Providencia, who was one of Jackie Kennedy's closest confidantes.

Without Howard Yoon and Gail Ross at the Ross Yoon Agency I wouldn't get to do this. Howard believed in an idea and took a chance on me when we first met for coffee several years ago. It was then that I told him about an idea I had for a book about the unheralded butlers, maids, florists, cooks, and others who make the White House run every day. He has been my greatest professional ally and a trusted friend ever since. Thanks especially to the incredibly talented and exceedingly kind editor Gail Winston, and to the wonderful Michael Morrison and Jonathan Burnham at HarperCollins. Roger Labrie helped make the book so much better with his crisp and thoughtful edits, Sofia Groopman shepherded the manuscript through expertly, and Robin Bilardello blew me away again with her cover design. And thank you to Tina Andreadis, Kate D'Esmond, and Beth Silfin, who are experts at what they do; and to Cal Morgan and Tim Duggan, who have been with me on different parts of this wild ride.

Julia Livshin is a tenacious researcher who proves the theory that working mothers are the most efficient members of the labor force. I'm also grateful to Shannon Hildenbrand, who culled through letters at President Johnson's Presidential Library; Jonathan Movroydis at the Richard Nixon Foundation; Bob Bostock, a former Nixon aide; John O'Connell and Ken Hafeli at President Ford's Presidential Library; Michael Pinckney at President Reagan's Presidential Library; Ray Kinstler; Walter Mondale; Anita Dunn; Bill Burton; Mary Ann Campbell; and Cragg Hines.

My husband, Brooke, is a tremendously loving father to our two beautiful and hilarious children, Graham and Charlotte, and he is my best friend. I can never thank him enough for being both of those things. My mom, Valerie Andersen, says that she's a good first reader when, in reality, she is so much more. She is a talented—and sometimes ruthless—editor who helped shape this book. My dad, Christopher Andersen, is a brilliant bestselling author who cheers on me and my wonderful little sister, Kelly, every day; he and my mom truly are teammates. And I'm happy to have the friendship and support of Nancy Brower and the Menaquale family.

Most of all, I'm grateful to the first ladies, who are complicated, intelligent women who are interesting precisely because of their imperfection. Working on this book made me appreciate my own female friends so much more. And it made me think about my own mother, who made sacrifices for me and my sister that we will never know about. I've always suspected that she doesn't realize just how awe-inspiring she is. I hope that she knows it now.

BOOK CLUB QUESTIONS
SUGGESTED BY THE AUTHOR

1. First ladies have undefined roles. What are the major expectations the author outlines in the book and how have they changed since Jacqueline Kennedy?
2. Which first lady enjoyed the job the most, and why? The least, and why?
3. Which first ladies became friends and which first ladies never saw eye to eye?
4. How have each of these ten women handled raising children while being in the spotlight?
5. Do you think we need to change any part of the position? For instance, should a first lady be allowed to continue her work in her chosen profession and collect a paycheck, or should she devote her time in the White House to being the president's spouse?

6. One day, when a woman is president, there will likely be a man serving as "first gentleman." How do you think the position will change with a man occupying it?

7. Aside from Hillary Clinton, which of these women had the biggest voice in her husband's administrations and how did she influence policy?

8. Was there a specific message or theme of the book?

9. Was there a chapter or passage that stood out for you?

10. What did you learn from this book that you didn't know before?

11. If you could meet any one of the ten first ladies featured in the book, from Jacqueline Kennedy to Melania Trump, who would you pick and why?

SOURCES AND NOTES

A NOTE ON REPORTING

My research for *First Women* includes interviews with more than two hundred people. These are the residence staffers, high-level political aides, close friends, and family members who know the first ladies best. My candid conversations with three former first ladies—Rosalynn Carter and Barbara and Laura Bush—which I conducted for my first book, *The Residence*, were also crucial to my understanding of these women and helped build the foundation for this book. I was able to interview Rosalynn Carter again for *First Women*. In some situations sources asked not to be named because of the sensitivity of the subject matter, and I respected their wishes. These firsthand interviews, many of which were done in person, were supplemented by research gathered from presidential libraries, including private correspondence between the first ladies that has never been published before; oral histories; exit interviews; and memoirs penned by the first ladies, presidents, and White House staffers.

INTRODUCTION

Interview subjects include Lisa Caputo and Steve Ford. Published material includes Gwen Ifill, "Clinton and Kennedys: In 30 Years, a Full Circle," *New York Times*, August 25, 1993; Mark Leibovich, "Re-Re-Re-Reintroducing

Hillary Clinton: The Meticulously Managed Rollout of a Candidate Whom Voters Think They Know Already," *New York Times*, July 15, 2015; Christopher Andersen, *Bill and Hillary: The Marriage* (New York: William Morrow, 1999).

I. THE POLITICAL WIFE

Interview subjects include Barbara Bush, Rosalynn Carter, Walter Mondale, Christine Limerick, Luci Johnson, Katherine Cade, Sheila Tate, Susan Ford, David Hume Kennerly, Steve Ford, Sheila Rabb Weidenfeld, Gustavo Paredes, Anita Dunn, Bill Burton, Tony Fratto, Shirley and George Hannie, Lissa Muscatine, Anna Fierst, Ron Nessen, Chris Emery, Worthington White, Tony Fratto, Lucy Winchester, Michael "Rahni" Flowers, Nash Castro, Larry Bush, Joni Stevens, Stephen Rochon, Nancy Chirdon Forster, and Jerry Rafshoon. Published material includes Arthur M. Schlesinger Jr., *Jacqueline Kennedy: Historic Conversations on Life with John F. Kennedy* (New York: Hyperion, 2011); the thirtieth episode in the C-SPAN series *First Ladies: Influence and Image*; Radio and Television Report to the American People on the Soviet Arms Buildup in Cuba, October 22, 1962, John F. Kennedy Presidential Library and Museum; letter from Jacqueline Kennedy to Chairman Khrushchev, Volume VI, Kennedy-Khrushchev Exchanges Document 120, U.S. Department of State, Office of the Historian; the oral histories of George Ball, Barbara J. Coleman, Mary Boylan, Charles Spalding, and Dr. Janet Travell can be found at the John F. Kennedy Presidential Library and Museum; "Jacqueline Kennedy in the White House," John F. Kennedy Presidential Library and Museum; Ted Sorensen, *Kennedy: The Classic Biography* (New York: Harper Perennial, 1965); Sarah Weddington, "Three Former First Ladies Speak Out," *Good Housekeeping*, February 1988; Tierney McAfee and Sandra Sobieraj Westfall, "Bill Won't Be Picking White House China: Why Hillary Clinton Won't Leave Traditional First-Lady Duties to Her Husband," *People*, February 3, 2016; Tom Jackman, "Northern Virginia's Slice of Camelot: The Kennedys in Fauquier County, 1961–63," *Washington Post*, November 21, 2013; Clint Hill and Lisa McCubbin, *Mrs. Kennedy and Me* (New York: Gallery Books, 2012); Robert Pear, "Court Rules That First Lady Is 'De Facto' Federal Official," *New York Times*, June 23, 1993; J. B. West, *Upstairs at the White House: My Life with the First Ladies* (New York: Warner Books, 1973); "Hillary Clinton: I Get Inspiration from Eleanor Roosevelt," *Daily News*, October 15, 2007; *The Late Show with Stephen Colbert*, interview with Michelle Obama, September 28, 2015; Lucinda Franks, "The Intimate Hillary," *Talk*, September 1999; Jodi

Kantor, *The Obamas* (New York: Little, Brown, 2012); Hillary Rodham Clinton, *Living History* (New York: Scribner, 2003); Peter Slevin, *Michelle Obama: A Life* (New York: Knopf, 2015); Laura Bush, *Spoken from the Heart* (New York: Scribner, 2010); Lisa Grunwald and Stephen J. Adler, *Women's Letters: America from the Revolutionary War to the Present* (New York: Random House, 2005); Preston Bruce, *From the Door of the White House* (New York: Lothrop, Lee & Shepard Books, 1984); Maurine Beasley, *First Ladies and the Press: The Unfinished Partnership of the Media Age* (Evanston, IL: Northwestern University Press, 2005); Barbara Leaming, *Jacqueline Bouvier Kennedy Onassis* (New York: Thomas Dunne Books, 2014); Kati Marton, *Hidden Power: Presidential Marriages That Shaped Our History* (New York: Anchor Books, 2001); Lady Bird Johnson's Post-Presidential Correspondence with Presidents, VPs, and Their Families, LBJ Library; Sharon W. Linsker, "Letters Signed by First Ladies Supply Insights into the Past," *New York Times*, May 1, 1994; oral histories of Peter Abruzzese, Hugh Sidey, David Gergen, Lilian Fisher, and Sheila Rabb Weidenfeld can be found at the Gerald R. Ford Foundation; Jimmy and Rosalynn Carter Oral History Collection, Series: National Park Service Oral History Interviews, May 11, 1988; Marian Burros, "Hillary Clinton Asks Help in Finding a Softer Image," *New York Times*, January 9, 1995; Betty Ford and Chris Chase, *The Times of My Life* (New York; Harper & Row, 1978); Helen Thomas, *Front Row at the White House: My Life and Times* (New York: Touchstone, 1999); John Robert Greene, *Betty Ford: Candor and Courage in the White House* (Lawrence: University Press of Kansas, 2004); James Cannon, *Gerald R. Ford: An Honorable Life* (Ann Arbor: University of Michigan Press, 2013); Scarlet Neath, "What's the Point of a First Lady?," *Atlantic*, October 6, 2014; Margaret Leslie Davis, *Mona Lisa in Camelot* (New York: Da Capo Press, 2008); *The Starr Report*, submitted by the Office of the Independent Counsel to Congress, September 9, 1998; CNN, "The Rodham Family Biography"; "The 1994 Campaign: Virginia: Mrs. Reagan Denounces Oliver North on Iran Affair," *New York Times*, October 29, 1994; "Nancy Reagan Speaks Out About Obamas, the Bushes, and Her Husband," *Vanity Fair*, June 1, 2009; Traphes Bryant with Frances Spatz Leighton, *Dog Days at the White House* (New York: Macmillan, 1975); Jacqueline Kennedy Onassis Personal Papers, Memos to J. B. West, John F. Kennedy Presidential Library and Museum; Rosalynn Carter, *First Lady from Plains* (Boston: Houghton Mifflin, 1984); Paul Farhi, "Michelle Obama's Target Trip: Critics Take Aim," *Washington Post*, October 2, 2011; Barbara Bush, *A Memoir: Barbara Bush* (New York: Scribner, 1994); Juliet Eilperin, "The New Dynamics of Protecting a President: Most Threats

Against Obama Issued Online," *Washington Post*, October 8, 2014; Hillary Clinton, "Talking It Over," syndicated column, June 4, 1996; Lauren Collins, "The Other Obama," *New Yorker*, March 10, 2008; Eleanor Roosevelt remarks at George Washington University, December 7, 1941; Gail Sheehy, "What Hillary Wants," *Vanity Fair*, May 1992; Gail Sheehy, "Is George Bush Too Nice to Be President?," *Vanity Fair*, February 1987; H. R. Haldeman, *The Haldeman Diaries: Inside the Nixon White House* (New York: G. P. Putnam's Sons, 1994); White House Memos, 1961–64, John F. Kennedy Presidential Library and Museum; Susan Thomases, interview, Miller Center, University of Virginia, President William Jefferson Clinton, Presidential Oral History Project, January 6, 2006; Alastair Granville Forbes's oral history interview can be found at the John F. Kennedy Library and Museum; Kristen Holmes, "Equal Pay for First Ladies Too," CNN.com, April 16, 2015; U.S. Department of Labor, "Women in the Labor Force"; Carl Bernstein, *A Woman in Charge: The Life of Hillary Rodham Clinton* (New York: Vintage Books, 2007); Marjorie Williams, "Barbara's Backlash," *Vanity Fair*, August 1992; Sally Bedell Smith, *Grace and Power: The Private World of the Kennedy White House* (New York: Random House, 2004).

II. SISTERHOOD OF 1600

Interview subjects include Barbara Bush, Rosalynn Carter, Luci Johnson, Jackie Norris, Ann Romney, Laura Bush, Joe Califano, Charles Allen, Susan Ford, Gustavo Paredes, Melanne Verveer, Anita McBride, Lissa Muscatine, Ronn Payne, Steve Ford, Bess Abell, Neel Lattimore, Everett Raymond Kinstler, Sheila Tate, Christine Limerick, George Hannie, Bess and Tyler Abell, Worthington White, Lisa Caputo, Bill Plante, Daryl Wells, Michael "Rahni" Flowers, Bill Burton, Bob Scanlan, Lucy Winchester, Connie Stuart, Joni Stevens, Nash Castro, Ron Reagan, Jerry Rafshoon, Betty Tilson, Larry Bush, Nancy Chirdon Forster. Published material includes Carl Cannon, "Kennedys Share Boat with the Clintons," *Baltimore Sun*, August 25, 1993; Lady Bird's Post-Presidential Correspondence with Presidents, VPs, and Their Families; Betty Ford Letters to Former First Ladies, Gerald and Betty Ford Special Materials, Gerald R. Ford Presidential Library and Museum; Mrs. Bush correspondence with Former First Family: Carter, George H. W. Bush Presidential Library; ABC News, "Laura Bush Praises Hillary's 'Grit and Strength,'" June 9, 2008; 2015 Global Women's Network, George W. Bush Presidential Center, September 22; Gwen Ifill, "Clinton and Kennedys: In 30 Years, a Full Circle," *New York Times*, August 25, 1993; Mark Leibovich, "Re-Re-Re-Reintroducing

Hillary Clinton: The Meticulously Managed Rollout of a Candidate Whom Voters Think They Know Already," *New York Times*, July 15, 2015; Maureen Dowd, "The 1992 Campaign: Campaign Trail; From Nixon, Predictions on the Presidential Race," *New York Times*, February 6, 1992; Hillary Rodham Clinton, *Living History* (New York: Scribner, 2003); Laura Bush, *Spoken from the Heart* (New York: Scribner, 2010); Amy Goldstein, "Part of, but Apart From, It All; Clintons Have Complex Relationship with City," *Washington Post*, January 20, 1997; J. B. West, *Upstairs at the White House: My Life with the First Ladies* (New York: Warner Books, 1973); Sarah Wildman, "Portrait of a Lady," *New Republic*, August 20, 2001; Julie Nixon Eisenhower, *Pat Nixon: The Untold Story* (New York: Simon & Schuster, 2007); Ruth Marcus, "Clinton in Camelot: The Arkansas Traveler, Afloat with the Kennedy Clan," *Washington Post*, August 25, 1993; Peter Slevin, *Michelle Obama: A Life* (New York: Alfred A. Knopf, 2015); Sharon W. Linsker, "Letters Signed by First Ladies Supply Insights into the Past," *New York Times*, May 1, 1994; Gail Sheehy, "Is George Bush Too Nice to Be President?," *Vanity Fair*, February 1987; Barbara Leaming, *Jacqueline Bouvier Kennedy Onassis* (New York: Thomas Dunne Books, an imprint of St. Martin's Press, 2014); Lynn Rosellini, "First Lady Tells Critics: 'I Am Just Being Myself,'" *New York Times*, October 13, 1981; Skip Hollandsworth, "Reading Laura Bush," *Texas Monthly*, November 1996; "Interview: Father Richard T. McSorley, director, Georgetown University Center for Peace Studies," Schiller Institute, *Fidelio* 6, no. 3 (Fall 1997); Jodi Kantor, *The Obamas* (New York: Little, Brown and Company, 2012); letters from President Reagan to Nancy Reagan can be found at the Ronald Reagan Presidential Library; Lady Bird Johnson's oral history interview is available at the LBJ Library; oral histories of Susan Ford, Ann Cullen, and Sheila Rabb Weidenfeld can be found at the Gerald R. Ford Foundation; Bob Colacello, "Nancy Reagan's Solo Role," *Vanity Fair*, July, 2009; Michael Duffy, "10 Questions with Barbara Bush," *Time*, June 15, 2015; Judy Woodruff's interview with Nancy Reagan is featured in the PBS documentary "Nancy Reagan: Role of a Lifetime," February 6, 2011; *Buzzfeed*, "Watch This Rare, Long-Forgotten Interview with Young Hillary Clinton," May 12, 2015; Sumana Chatterjee, "A Powerful Trio Helped Convicted Banker Win Pardon," *Philadelphia Inquirer*, March 9, 2001; Joseph Kahn and Christine Hauser, "China's Leader Makes First White House Visit," *New York Times*, April 20, 2006; Peggy Noonan, "The Reagans and the Kennedys: How They Forged a Friendship That Crossed Party Lines," *Wall Street Journal*, August 28, 2009; Mrs. Jacqueline Kennedy Onassis, Interview, Miller Center, University of

Virginia, President Lyndon Johnson, Presidential Oral History Project, January 11, 1974; Jimmy and Rosalynn Carter Oral History Collection; Series: National Park Service Oral History Interviews, December 8, 1988; Jonathan Van Meter, "Leading by Example: First Lady Michelle Obama," *Vogue*, March 14, 2013; Constance Stuart's oral history is available at the Nixon Presidential Library and Museum; Judy Keen, "Michelle Obama: Campaigning Her Way," *USA Today*, May 11, 2007; Marjorie Williams, "Barbara's Backlash," *Vanity Fair*, August, 1992; Rosemary Ellis, "A Conversation with Michelle Obama," *Good Housekeeping*, September 30, 2008; Anne E. Kornblut, "Michelle Obama's Career Timeout for Now, Weight Shifts in Work-Family Tug of War," *Washington Post*, May 11, 2007; Diane Salvatore, "Barack and Michelle Obama: The Full Interview," *Ladies Home Journal*, August 2008; Will Swift, *Pat and Dick: The Nixons, An Intimate Portrait of a Marriage* (New York: Simon & Schuster, 2014); Hillary Rodham Clinton, *An Invitation to the White House: At Home with History* (New York: Simon & Schuster, 2000); Preston Bruce, *From the Door of the White House* (New York: Lothrop, Lee & Shepard Books, 1984); Jacqueline Kennedy Onassis Personal Papers, Memos to J. B. West, John F. Kennedy Presidential Library and Museum; C-SPAN, "A Conversation with Barbara and Laura Bush," November 15, 2012, http://www.c-span.org/video/?309081-4/conversation-barbara-laura-bush; Helen Thomas, *Front Row at the White House: My Life and Times* (New York: Touchstone, 1999); CBS News, "The Reagans' Long Goodbye: Mike Wallace Interviews Nancy Reagan for *60 Minutes II*," September 24, 2002; Jonathan Weisman, "JFK Jr. visited White House at invitation of Nixon, Reagan: Clinton Claims Corrected in Light of More Accurate Historical Information," *Baltimore Sun*, July 24, 1999; Caroline Kennedy on Pat Nixon for the Richard Nixon Foundation, http://nixonfoundation.org/news-details.php?id=770; Julie Nixon Eisenhower, *Pat Nixon: The Untold Story* (New York: Simon & Schuster, 2007).

III. PROFILES IN COURAGE

Interview subjects include Luci Johnson, Susan and Steve Ford, Nelson Pierce, Nancy Chirdon Forster, Ron Nessen, and Herman Thompson. Oral history interviews with Bonnie Angelo, Ann Cullen, and Guy Swan can be found at the Gerald R. Ford Oral History Project. Published material includes Arthur M. Schlesinger Jr., *Jacqueline Kennedy: Historic Conversations on Life with John F. Kennedy* (New York: Hyperion, 2011); Seymour Hersh, "The Pardon: Nixon, Ford, Haig, and the Transfer of Power," *Atlantic*, August 1983; Clint Hill and Lisa McCubbin, *Mrs. Kennedy and Me* (New York: Gallery Books,

2012); Sarah Weddington, "Three Former First Ladies Speak Out," *Good Housekeeping*, February 1988; Sheila Rabb Weidenfeld, *First Lady's Lady: With the Fords at the White House* (New York: G. P. Putnam's Sons, 1979); Betty Ford and Chris Chase, *The Times of My Life* (New York: Harper & Row, 1978).

IV. MOTHERHOOD

Interview subjects include Rosalynn Carter, Susan and Steve Ford, Mary Prince, Tricia Nixon, Gustavo Paredes, Mary Ann Campbell, Bill Burton, Reggie Love, Jane Erkenbeck, Shirley Sagawa, Daryl Wells, Michael "Rahni" Flowers, Ron Reagan, Bess Abell, Worthington White, George and Shirley Hannie, Larry Bush, Stephen Rochon, and Herman Thompson. Published material includes oral histories from Grace Kelly, Jacqueline P. Hirsh, Leonard Bernstein, Janet Lee Bouvier Auchincloss, Letitia Baldrige, Nash Castro, Maud Shaw, Preston Bruce, Dr. Janet Travell, Christine Camp, Laura Bergquist Knebel, Barbara Gamarekian, and Charles Spalding which can all be found at the John F. Kennedy Presidential Library and Museum; Jacqueline Kennedy Onassis Personal Papers, Pamela Turnure, John F. Kennedy Presidential Library and Museum; Nancy Reagan with William Novak, *My Turn: The Memoirs of Nancy Reagan* (New York: Random House, 1989); Sally Bedell Smith, *Grace and Power: The Private World of the Kennedy White House* (New York: Random House, 2004); Jon Meacham, *Destiny and Power: The American Odyssey of George Herbert Walker Bush* (New York: Random House, 2015); Evgenia Peretz, "How Chelsea Clinton Took Charge of Clintonworld," *Vanity Fair*, September 2015; Barack Obama, "How the Presidency Made Me a Better Father," *More*, July/August 2015; Hillary Rodham Clinton, interview of the First Lady for *House Beautiful*, November 30, 1993, by Marian Burros; Joe Hagen, "Bush in the Wilderness," *New York*, October 14, 2012; George Lardner Jr. and Lois Romano, "Tragedy Created Bush Mother-Son Bond," *Washington Post*, July 26, 1999; Patti Davis, *The Way I See It* (New York: G. P. Putnam's Sons, 1992); Sarah Weddington, "Three Former First Ladies Speak Out," *Good Housekeeping*, February 1988; John Ehrlichman, *Witness to Power: The Nixon Years* (New York: Simon & Schuster, 1982); letter from Jacqueline Kennedy to Father McSorley, August 23, 1968; Barbara Bush, *A Memoir: Barbara Bush* (New York: Scribner, 1994); letters from the private collection of Dolly Lederer Maass; J. B. West, *Upstairs at the White House: My Life with the First Ladies* (New York: Warner Books, 1973); Laura Abernethy, "Michelle Obama's Mother Makes Rare Public Appearance in London," *Guardian*,

June 16, 2015; Sharon W. Linsker, "Letters Signed by First Ladies Supply Insights into the Past," *New York Times*, May 1, 1994; Bob Woodward and Carl Bernstein, *The Final Days* (New York: Simon & Schuster, 1976); "The White House: Moving Out/Moving In," National Archives, January 15, 2009; "Interview: Father Richard T. McSorley," director, Georgetown University Center for Peace Studies, *Fidelio* 6, no. 3 (Fall 1997); Gail Sheehy, "What Hillary Wants," *Vanity Fair*, May 1992; Susan Ford oral history can be found at the Gerald R. Ford Oral History Project; Barbara Leaming, *Jacqueline Bouvier Kennedy Onassis* (New York: Thomas Dunne Books, 2014); Marjorie Williams, "Barbara's Backlash," *Vanity Fair*, August 1992; Preston Bruce, *From the Door of the White House* (New York: Lothrop, Lee & Shepard Books, 1984); Julie Nixon Eisenhower, *Pat Nixon: The Untold Story* (New York: Simon & Schuster, 2007); Jimmy and Rosalynn Carter Oral History Collection, Series: National Park Service Oral History Interviews, December 8, 1988; Rosalynn Carter, *First Lady from Plains* (Boston: Houghton Mifflin, 1984); Jeff Zeleny, "Q&A with Michelle Obama," *Chicago Tribune*, December 24, 2005; Patrick Healy, "New to Campaigning, but No Longer a Novice," *New York Times*, October 27, 2008; Richard Wolffe, "Michelle, on the Move: The First Lady Readies Her Family for Washington," *Newsweek*, November 5, 2008; 2015 Global Women's Network, George W. Bush Presidential Center, September 22, 2015; Rebecca Johnson, "Michelle Obama Interview: I'm Nothing Special," *Telegraph*, July 26, 2008; Gail Sheehy, "Is George Bush Too Nice to Be President?," *Vanity Fair*, February 1987; Nixon-Gannon Interviews, 1983, Walter J. Brown Media Archives & Peabody Awards Collection, University of Georgia Libraries, Athens; Holly Yeager, "The Heart and Mind of Michelle Obama," *O: The Oprah Magazine*, November 2007; Helen Thomas, *Front Row at the White House: My Life and Times* (New York: Touchstone, 1999); Lisa Grunwald and Stephen J. Adler, *Women's Letters: America from the Revolutionary War to the Present* (New York: Random House, 2005); Jan Williams, Jimmy Carter Oral History Collection; Series: National Park Service Oral History Interviews, December 20, 1985; Jessamyn West, "Exclusive: The Unknown Pat Nixon: An Intimate View," *Good Housekeeping*, February 1971; H. R. Haldeman, *The Haldeman Diaries: Inside the Nixon White House* (New York: G. P. Putnam's Sons, 1994).

V. SUPPORTING ACTORS

Interview subjects for this chapter include Laura Bush, Bess and Tyler Abell, Luci Johnson, Joe Califano, Ann Compton, Shirley James, Tony Fratto, Anita

McBride, Christine Limerick, Worthington White, Chris Edwards, Susan Ford, Cragg Hines, Larry Temple, Betty Tilson, and Jerry Rafshoon. Published material includes J. B. West, *Upstairs at the White House: My Life with the First Ladies* (New York: Warner Books, 1973); Preston Bruce, *From the Door of the White House* (New York: Lothrop, Lee & Shepard Books, 1984); Gail Sheehy, "What Hillary Wants," *Vanity Fair*, May 1992; Carl Bernstein, *A Woman in Charge: The Life of Hillary Rodham Clinton* (New York: Vintage Books, 2007); Michael Kelly, "Again: It's Hillary Rodham Clinton. Got That?," *New York Times*, February 14, 1993; Bill Moyer's Eulogy at Lady Bird's Funeral; Sara Rimer, "A Nation Challenged: The Pennsylvania Crash; 44 Victims Are Remembered, and Lauded," *New York Times*, September 18, 2001; LENNY, September 29, 2015, Letter No. 1; Sally Bedell Smith, *Grace and Power: The Private World of the Kennedy White House* (New York: Random House, 2004); Laura Bush, *Spoken from the Heart* (New York: Scribner, 2010); Lady Bird's Post-Presidential Correspondence with Presidents, VPs, and their Families, LBJ Presidential Library and Museum; Enid Nemy, "Obituary: Lady Bird Johnson, 94, Former U.S. First Lady," *New York Times*, July 12, 2007; "Pat Nixon Removes Jackie's Handiwork," *Milwaukee Journal*, September 20, 1969; Liz Carpenter's and Bess Abell's oral histories can be found at the LBJ Library; Lady Bird Johnson's diary, June 5, 1968; Sarah Weddington, "Three Former First Ladies Speak Out," *Good Housekeeping*, February 1988; Jimmy and Rosalynn Carter Oral History Collection; Series: National Park Service Oral History Interviews, May 11, 1988; Lucinda Franks, "The Intimate Hillary," *Talk*, September 1999; Frank Bruni, "For Laura Bush, a Direction She Never Wished to Go In," *New York Times*, July 31, 2000; Skip Hollandsworth, "Reading Laura Bush," *Texas Monthly*, November 1996; Ann Cullen's oral history can be found at the Gerald R. Ford Oral History Project.

VI. EAST WING VS. WEST WING

Interview subjects include Tony Fratto, Connie Stuart, Melanne Verveer, Lissa Muscatine, Joni Stevens, Lucy Winchester, Jackie Norris, Sheila Rabb Weidenfeld, Nash Castro, Steve Ford, Polly Dranov, and Larry D. Hatfield. Published material includes John Ehrlichman, *Witness to Power: The Nixon Years* (New York: Simon & Schuster, 1982); Reid Cherlin, "The Worst Wing: How the East Wing Shrank Michelle Obama," *New Republic*, March 24, 2014; Julie Nixon Eisenhower, *Pat Nixon: The Untold Story* (New York: Simon & Schuster, 2007); H. R. Haldeman, *The Haldeman Diaries: Inside the Nixon White House* (New York: G. P. Putnam's Sons, 1994); Letitia Baldrige's oral history can be found at the John F. Kennedy Presidential Library and Museum; Will Swift, *Pat and Dick: The Nixons: An Intimate Portrait of a Marriage* (New York: Simon & Schuster, 2014); Preston Bruce, *From the Door of the White House* (New York: Lothrop, Lee & Shepard Books, 1984); memo from Roger Ailes to H. R. Haldeman, May 4, 1970, Richard Nixon Presidential Library and Museum; Laura Bush, *Spoken from the Heart* (New York: Scribner, 2010); Roy Neel, interview, Miller Center, University of Virginia, President William Jefferson Clinton, Presidential Oral History Project, November 14, 2002; Helen Smith, "Ordeal! Pat Nixon's Final Days in the White House," *Good Housekeeping*, July 1976; Bonnie Angelo's and Maria Downs's oral histories can be found at the Gerald R. Ford Oral History Project; Helen Thomas, *Front Row at the White House: My Life and Times* (New York: Touchstone Books, 1999); Helen Thomas, "Pat Nixon Answers All Letters to Her," United Press International, December 28, 1971; Lois Romano, "Michelle Obama: White House Rebel," *Newsweek*, June 5, 2011; Sarah Booth Conroy, "First Lady, and Wife First," *Washington Post*, June 28, 1993; Constance Stuart's and Gwendolyn King's oral histories are available at the Nixon Presidential Library and Museum; Trude Feldman, "The Quiet Courage of Pat Nixon," *McCall's*, May 1975.

VII. THE GOOD WIFE

Interview subjects include Rosalynn Carter, Susan Porter Rose, Ann Romney, Walter Mondale, Jerry Rafshoon, Ronn Payne, Katherine Cade, Mary Prince, Ann Compton, Christine Limerick, Connie Stuart, Ed Nixon, Joni Stevens, Bob Bostock, Lynn Langway, Neel Lattimore, Bob Scanlan, and Lucy Winchester. Published material includes J. B. West, *Upstairs at the White House: My Life with the First Ladies* (New York: Warner Books, 1973); White House Memos, 1961–64, John F. Kennedy Presidential Library and Museum; *American Experience: The Kennedys*, PBS; Nixon-Gannon Interviews, 1983, Walter J. Brown Media Archives & Peabody Awards Collection, University of Georgia Libraries, Athens; Susan Thomases, Interview, Miller Center, University of Virginia, President William Jefferson Clinton, Presidential Oral History Project, January 6, 2006; Lucinda Franks, "The Intimate Hillary," *Talk*, September 1999; Hugh Sidey's oral history can be found at the Gerald R. Ford Presidential Library and Museum; Jacqueline Kennedy Onassis Personal Papers, Memos to J. B. West, John F. Kennedy Presidential Library and Museum; oral histories with Mary Hoyt, Allie Smith, Lauren Blanton, and Jan Williams are part of the Jimmy Carter Oral History Collection; Archive of American Television interview with Perry Wolff, http://emmytvlegends.org/interviews/people/perry-wolff#; Theodore H. White personal papers can be found at John F. Kennedy Presidential Library and Museum; oral histories for Nancy Tuckerman and Pamela Turnure can be found at the John F. Kennedy Presidential Library and Museum; Liz Carpenter's oral history can be found at the LBJ Library, August 27, 1969; Bob Woodward, *The Last of the President's Men* (New York: Simon & Schuster, 2015); ABC News special, *Jacqueline Kennedy: In Her Own Words*, September 13, 2011; Jimmy and Rosalynn Carter Oral History Collection; Series: National Park Service Oral History Interviews, May 11, 1988; Michael Hirsh, "The Regrets of Jimmy Carter," *Politico*, August 20, 2015; James Reston, "Kennedy's Victory Won by Close Margin—He Promises Fight for World Freedom—Eisenhower Offers 'Orderly Transition,'" *New York Times*, November 10, 1960; Marian Christy, "Pat Was Trained to Suffer," *Beaver County* (Pa.) *Times*, November 2, 1978; Bob Woodward and Carl Bernstein, *The Final Days* (New York: Simon & Schuster, 1976); Marina Koren, "Jimmy Carter on His Cancer Diagnosis," *Atlantic*, August 20, 2015; Rosalynn Carter, *First Lady from Plains* (Boston: Houghton Mifflin, 1984); Elizabeth Mehren, "Richard Goodwin's Account of a 'Paranoid' L.B.J. Riles Some Ex-Colleagues," *Los Angeles Times*, September 14, 1988; Lisa Grunwald and Stephen J. Adler, *Women's Letters: America from the Revolutionary War to the Present* (New York: Random House, 2005); CBS News, *60 Minutes*, "Jimmy Carter: My Presidency Was a Success," September 16, 2010; Associated Press, "Jackie, Nina, Hit at Vienna," June 5, 1961; Betty Ford and Chris Chase, *The Times of My Life* (New York: Harper & Row, 1978); oral histories of Lorraine Ornelas, Bonnie Angelo, and Susan Ford can be found at the Gerald R. Ford Presidential Library and Museum; Trude Feldman, "The Quiet Courage of Pat Nixon," *McCall's*, May 1975; Jeff Gerth and Don Van Natta Jr., *Her Way: The Hopes and Ambitions of Hillary Rodham Clinton* (New York: Back Nine Books, 2007); oral history interviews with Jimmy and Rosalynn Carter can be found at the Jimmy Carter Presidential Library and Museum; Barbara Gamarekian's oral history can be found at the John F. Kennedy Presidential Library and Museum; Patt Morrison, "Time for a Feminist as First Lady: What Americans Think of Hillary Clinton Is as Much a Verdict on the Role of Women in the '90s as a Judgment of Her Style and Achievement," *Los Angeles Times*, July 14, 1992; Carl Bernstein, *A Woman in Charge: The Life of Hillary Rodham Clinton* (New York: Vintage Books, 2007); Kati Marton, *Hidden Power: Presidential Marriages That Shaped Our History* (New York: Anchor Books, 2001); Marian Burros, "Hillary Clinton Asks Help in Finding a Softer Image," *New York*

Times, January 9, 1995; Lisa Miller, "No More Washington Wives, and It's Our Loss," *Newsweek*, January 3, 2011; Gail Sheehy, "What Hillary Wants," *Vanity Fair*, May 1992; Thurston Clarke, "JFK and Jackie's Secret Life Between the Covers," *Wall Street Journal* blog, July 25, 2013; Clare Crawford, "A Story of Love and Rehabilitation: The Ex-Con in the White House," *People*, March 14, 1977; Will Swift, *Pat and Dick: The Nixons—An Intimate Portrait of a Marriage* (New York: Simon & Schuster, 2014); Helen Thomas, *Front Row at the White House: My Life and Times* (New York: Touchstone Books, 1999); Julie Nixon Eisenhower, *Pat Nixon: The Untold Story* (New York: Simon & Schuster, 2007); Arthur M. Schlesinger Jr., *Jacqueline Kennedy: Historic Conversations on Life with John F. Kennedy* (New York: Hyperion, 2011); Gloria Steinem, *Outrageous Acts and Everyday Rebellions* (New York: Henry Holt, 1983); Jessamyn West, "Exclusive: The Unknown Pat Nixon: An Intimate View," *Good Housekeeping*, February 1971; Richard Nixon–Pat Nixon Courtship Letters, Richard Nixon Foundation; First Ladies Pay Tribute to Pat Nixon, https://www.youtube.com/watch?v=OXl2ngW-JiA, Richard Nixon Foundation; Judith Viorst, "Pat Nixon Is the Ultimate Good Sport," *New York Times*, September 13, 1970; Isabelle Shelton, "Pat Is Pressed," *Evening Star*, September 19, 1972; United Press International, "Release of Tapes Displeased Pat," *Washington Post*, May 20, 1974; Lydia Saad, "Admiration for Hillary Clinton Surges in 1998," Gallup, December 31, 1998; Hillary Rodham Clinton, *Living History* (New York: Scribner, 2003).

VIII. BAD BLOOD

Interview subjects include Barbara Bush, Rosalynn Carter, James Jeffries, Bill Cliber, Shirley Sagawa, Bill Burton, Sheila Rabb Weidenfeld, Susan Porter Rose, Susie Tompkins Buell, Jerry Rafshoon, Anita Dunn, Lissa Muscatine, Mary Ann Campbell, Anita McBride, Joni Stevens, Lise Howe, Ronn Payne, Christine Limerick, Ron Reagan, David Hume Kennerly, Jamal Simmons, George Hannie, Jane Erkenbeck, and Cragg Hines. Sources include Jimmy Carter Presidential Library exit interview with Mary Finch Hoyt; Dorothy McCardle, "Will Mamie Brief Jackie on Home," *Washington Post*, November 13, 1960; Marjorie Williams, "Barbara's Backlash," *Vanity Fair*, August 1992; Associated Press, "First Lady Said Nancy Reagan Called to Deny Wanting Carters Out Early," December 16, 1980; "Reagans' Son, Ron, Blasts Carter," *Eugene Register-Guard*, December 15, 1980; White House Memos, 1961–64, John F. Kennedy Presidential Library and Museum; Arthur M. Schlesinger Jr., *Jacqueline Kennedy: Historic Conversations on Life with John F. Kennedy* (New York:

Hyperion, 2011); J. B. West, *Upstairs at the White House: My Life with the First Ladies* (New York: Warner Books, 1973); Sarah Ellison, "How Hillary Clinton's Loyal Confidants Could Cost Her the Election," *Vanity Fair*, November, 2015; Lady Bird Johnson's Post-Presidential Correspondence with Presidents, VPs, and Their Families; Bess Abell's oral history can be found at the LBJ Library; Chris Chase's oral history can be found at the Gerald R. Ford Foundation; Margaret Leslie Davis, *Mona Lisa in Camelot* (New York: Da Capo Press, 2008); Joan Didion, "Life at Court," *New York Review of Books*, December 21, 1989; Patt Morrison, "Time for a Feminist as First Lady: What Americans Think of Hillary Clinton Is as Much a Verdict on the Role of Women in the '90s as a Judgment of Her Style and Achievement," *Los Angeles Times*, July 14, 1992; Gail Sheehy, "Hillaryland at War," *Vanity Fair*, August 2008; Hillary Rodham Clinton, *Living History* (New York: Scribner, 2003); Judy Woodruff interview with Nancy Reagan featured in the PBS documentary *Nancy Reagan: Role of a Lifetime*, February 6, 2011; Hamilton Jordan, "The First Grifters: Clinton Saw the Pardon Power as Just Another Perk of the Office," *Wall Street Journal*, February 20, 2001; Fox Butterfield, "At Wellesley, a Furor Over Barbara Bush," *New York Times*, May 4, 1990; Jon Meacham, *Destiny and Power: The American Odyssey of George Herbert Walker Bush* (New York: Random House, 2015); Betty Beale, "White House Plans Told: Tish Baldrige Has First Press Conference," *Evening Star*, November 23, 1960; White House Memos, 1961–64, John F. Kennedy Presidential Library and Museum; Cragg Hines, "Queries on Infidelity Infuriate First Lady," *Houston Chronicle*, August 13, 1992; Michael Deaver with Mickey Herskowitz, *Behind the Scenes* (New York: William Morrow, 1988); Barbara Bush, *A Memoir: Barbara Bush* (New York: Scribner, 1994); Gail Sheehy, "What Hillary Wants," *Vanity Fair*, May 1992; Donnie Radcliffe, "Nancy Reagan's Private Obsession; A Tenacious Struggle to Oust Donald Regan from the President's Team," *Washington Post*, February 27, 1987; *Newsweek* staff, "Reagan and Bush: Call It a Snub," March 8, 1992; Gail Sheehy, "Is George Bush Too Nice to Be President?," *Vanity Fair*, February 1987; Charles Spalding's oral history is available at the John F. Kennedy Presidential Library and Museum; Lady Bird Johnson's oral history can be found at the LBJ Library, January 23, 1996; Glenn Thrush, "Clinton's '08 Slaps Still Sting Obama," *Politico*, August 1, 2013; Carroll Kilpatrick and Maxine Cheshire, "The New Tenant Drops By: The Fast-Moving Kennedys Take to Palm Beach Sun," *Washington Post*, December 10, 1960; Elizabeth Mehren and Betty Cuniberti, "Fighting Back: Over the Course of Her Husband's Political Career, Nancy Reagan Has Developed Her Own Mission: To Protect Ronald Reagan, No Matter What," *Los Angeles*

Times Magazine, March 22, 1987; Kati Marton, *Hidden Power: Presidential Marriages That Shaped Our History* (New York: Anchor Books, 2001); Bob Colacello, "Nancy Reagan's Solo Role," *Vanity Fair*, July 2009; Douglas Brinkley, *The Unfinished Presidency: Jimmy Carter's Journey Beyond the White House* (New York: Viking, 1998); Rosalynn Carter, *First Lady from Plains* (Boston: Houghton Mifflin, 1984); Elisabeth Bumiller, "Public Lives: Two First Ladies, So Alike and So Different," *New York Times*, May 12, 1999; Sarah Weddington, *A Question of Choice* (New York: G. P. Putnam Sons, 1992); Patti Davis, *The Way I See It* (New York: G. P. Putnam's Sons, 1992); Mrs. Jacqueline Kennedy Onassis, Interview, Miller Center, University of Virginia, President Lyndon Johnson, Presidential Oral History Project, January 11, 1974; Josh Gerstein, "Emails Show Hillary's Political Sleuthing," *Politico*, September 1, 2015; Nancy Gibbs and Michael Duffy, *The Presidents Club: Inside the World's Most Exclusive Fraternity* (New York: Simon & Schuster, 2012); Jeff Zeleny, "Meet the Woman Who Almost Made Hillary Clinton Cry in 2008," CNN, April 20, 2015; Maurine Beasley, *First Ladies and the Press: The Unfinished Partnership of the Media Age* (Evanston, IL: Northwestern University Press, 2005); "From Inquiring Camera Girl to Next First Lady? Ike's Election Kept Artist Jackie Busy," *Washington Post and Times-Herald*, September 28, 1960; Dorothy McCardle, "Jackie Learned Pat's No. 1 Pick was Mamie," *Washington Post and Times-Herald*, September 30, 1960; Betty Ford and Chris Chase, *The Times of My Life* (New York: Harper & Row, 1978); Kate Andersen and Nick Johnston, "Obama Tax Deal 'Is a Good Bill' Former President Clinton Says," Bloomberg, December 12, 2010; Frank Bruni, "For Laura Bush, a Direction She Never Wished to Go In," *New York Times*, July 31, 2000; Reid Cherlin, "The Worst Wing: How the East Wing Shrank Michelle Obama," *New Republic*, March 24, 2014; Anne E. Kornblut, "Michelle Obama's Career Timeout for Now, Weight Shifts in Work-Family Tug of War," *Washington Post*, May 11, 2007; *The Late Show with Stephen Colbert*, interview with Michelle Obama, September 28, 2015; Diane Salvatore, "Barack and Michelle Obama: The Full Interview," *Ladies' Home Journal*, August 2008; Alessandra Stanley, "Michelle Obama Shows Her Warmer Side on 'The View,'" *New York Times*, June 19, 2008; CBS News, "The Remarkable Mrs. Ford: *60 Minutes* Revisits a Very Candid Interview with the Former First Lady," January 5, 2007.

IX. KEEP CALM AND CARRY ON

Interview subjects include Barbara Bush, Rosalynn Carter, Ann Romney, Reggie Love, Bill Burton, Lissa Muscatine, Tony Fratto, Daryl Wells, Michael

"Rahni" Flowers, George Hannie, Worthington White, Susan and Steve Ford, Nash Castro, Bess Abell, Don Hughes, Wilson Jerman, Jim Ketchum, Cletus Clark, Jane Erkenbeck, Ron Reagan, Lucy Winchester, Chris Edwards, Joni Stevens, Linsey Little, Connie Stuart, Nancy Chirdon Forster, and Everett Raymond Kinstler. Published material includes Nancy Reagan with William Novak, *My Turn: The Memoirs of Nancy Reagan* (New York: Random House, 1989); Constance Stuart's and Gwendolyn King's oral histories are available at the Nixon Presidential Library and Museum; Donnie Radcliffe, "Life as the First Lady's Confidante and 'Protector,'" *Washington Post*, April 14, 1977; Dana Perino, *And the Good News Is: Lessons and Advice from the Bright Side* (New York: Twelve, 2015); CBS News, "Candidate Obama's Sense of Urgency," *60 Minutes*, February 9, 2007; Julie Nixon Eisenhower, *Pat Nixon: The Untold Story* (New York: Simon & Schuster, 2007); Kathleen Osborne, interview, Miller Center, University of Virginia, President Ronald Reagan, Presidential Oral History Project, April 26, 2003; Richard Allen, interview, Miller Center, University of Virginia, President Ronald Reagan, Presidential Oral History Project, May 28, 2002; Michael Deaver, interview, Miller Center, University of Virginia, President Ronald Reagan, Presidential Oral History Project, September 12, 2002; Betty Ford Letters to Former First Ladies, Gerald and Betty Ford Special Materials, Gerald R. Ford Presidential Library and Museum; Lady Bird Johnson diary, June 5, 1968; Associated Press, "President Not Planning to Quit, Mrs. Nixon Says," *Los Angeles Times*, May 11, 1974; Patti Davis, *The Way I See It* (New York: G. P. Putnam's Sons, 1992); Anne Lincoln's and Gerald Behn's oral histories can be found at the John F. Kennedy Presidential Library and Museum; Juliet Eilperin, "The New Dynamics of Protecting a President: Most Threats Against Obama Issued Online," *Washington Post*, October 8, 2014; Judy Woodruff interview with Nancy Reagan featured in the PBS documentary *Nancy Reagan: Role of a Lifetime*, February 6, 2011; Helen Smith, "Ordeal! Pat Nixon's Final Days in the White House," *Good Housekeeping*, July 1976; Lady Bird Johnson diary entry, August 2, 1968; CBS News, "The Reagans' Long Goodbye: Mike Wallace Interviews Nancy Reagan for *60 Minutes II*," September 24, 2002; Trude Feldman, "The Quiet Courage of Pat Nixon," *McCall's*, May 1975; Elizabeth Mehren and Betty Cuniberti, "Fighting Back: Over the Course of Her Husband's Political Career, Nancy Reagan Has Developed Her Own Mission: To Protect Ronald Reagan, No Matter What," *Los Angeles Times Magazine*, March 22, 1987; Kati Marton, *Hidden Power: Presidential Marriages That Shaped Our History* (New York: Anchor Books, 2001); Lady Bird Johnson, *A White House Diary* (New York:

Holt, Rinehart & Winston, 1970); United Press International, "Collapses, Dies, Honoring Betty Ford," *Chicago Tribune*, June 23, 1976; Joan Didion, "Life at Court," *New York Review of Books*, December 21, 1989; Donald T. Regan, *For the Record* (New York: Harcourt Brace Jovanovich, 1988); Bob Colacello, "Nancy Reagan's Solo Role," *Vanity Fair*, July 2009; Betty Cuniberti, "Nancy Reagan's Schedule Ambitious: President, First Lady Off on Separate Paths," *Los Angeles Times*, May 1, 1986; Bernard Weinraub, "Nancy Reagan's Power Is Considered at Peak," *New York Times*, March 3, 1987; Jane Perlez, "Hillary Clinton Visits Romania Children," *New York Times*, July 2, 1996.

EPILOGUE: LADIES, FIRST

Interviews include Barbara Bush, Lorraine Ornelas, Susan Ford, Bess Abell, Nancy Chirdon Forster, Shirley James, and Bill Plante. Published material includes Margaret Truman, *First Ladies: An Intimate Group Portrait of White House Wives* (New York: Random House, 1995); Leo Janos, "The Last Days of the President: LBJ in Retirement," *Atlantic*, July 1973; Michael Beschloss, "In His Final Days, LBJ Agonized Over His Legacy," PBS, December 4, 2012; Hillary Clinton, *An Invitation to the White House: At Home with History* (New York: Simon & Schuster, 2000); Kati Marton, *Hidden Power: Presidential Marriages That Shaped Our History* (New York: Anchor Books, 2001); Barbara Bush, *A Memoir: Barbara Bush* (New York: Scribner, 1994); "Clintons Return White House Furniture," ABC News; Robert McFadden, "Death of a First Lady: The Companion, Quietly at Her Side, Public at the End," *New York Times*, May 24, 1994; Gail Sheehy, "Is George Bush Too Nice to Be President?," *Vanity Fair*, February 1987; Bob Colacello, "Nancy Reagan's Solo Role," *Vanity Fair*, July 2009; Helen Smith, "Ordeal! Pat Nixon's Final Days in the White House," *Good Housekeeping*, July 1976.

AFTERWORD

Julia Ioffe, "Melania Trump On Her Rise, Her Family Secrets, and Her True Political Views: 'Nobody Will Ever Know,'" *GQ*, April 27, 2016; Dragana Jovanovic, "Melania Trump's Childhood Friends Say She'd Make a Great First Lady," ABC News, March 7, 2016; Matt Ford, "Can Melania Trump Win Her Libel Lawsuit?," *The Atlantic*, September 3, 2016; Mary Jordan, "Meet Melania Trump, a New Model for First Lady," the *Washington Post*, September 30, 2015; Kate Andersen Brower, "Why Melania Trump Would Be an Ultra-Traditional First Lady," *Fortune*, May 5, 2016; Ibid., "The Permanent White House Staff Is, Understandably, On Edge About the 2016 Presidential

Race," *Vanity Fair*, April 10, 2016; Andrea Park, "Inside the Small Slovenian Town Where Melania Trump Grew Up Under the Communist Regime," *People*, February 25, 2016.

PHOTO INSERT SOURCES AND CREDITS

Insert one: Getty Images/The LIFE Picture Collection/Hank Walker; Associated Press; Getty Images/The LIFE Picture Collection/George Silk; Cecil Stoughton/White House, courtesy John F. Kennedy Presidential Library and Museum, Boston; Robert Knudsen/White House, courtesy John F. Kennedy Presidential Library and Museum, Boston; Cecil Stoughton/White House, courtesy John F. Kennedy Presidential Library and Museum, Boston; Yoichi Okamoto/White House, courtesy Lyndon B. Johnson Library; courtesy Lyndon B. Johnson Library; Robert L. Knudsen/White House, courtesy Richard Nixon Presidential Library; Byron Schumaker, White House, courtesy Richard Nixon Presidential Library; Oliver Atkins/White House, courtesy Richard Nixon Presidential Library; from the private collection of Joni Stevens; Oliver Atkins/White House, courtesy Richard Nixon Presidential Library; David Hume Kennerly/White House, courtesy Gerald R. Ford Presidential Library; Getty Images/Hulton Archive; Karl Schumacher/White House, courtesy Jimmy Carter Presidential Library and Museum; courtesy George Bush Presidential Library and Museum; courtesy Lyndon B. Johnson Library; from the private collection of Shirley James.

Insert two: Official White House photograph, courtesy Ronn Payne; courtesy Ronald Reagan Presidential Library; Getty Images/New York Daily News Archive; Associated Press/Marcy Nighswander; Getty Images/AFP/David Ake; courtesy Clinton Presidential Library; Getty Images/Hulton Archive/David Hume Kennerly; Associated Press/Susan Walsh; Ralph Barrera, courtesy Austin American-Statesman; Joyce N. Boghosian, courtesy of the George W. Bush Presidential Library and Museum/NARA; Getty Images/Alex Wong; David Hume Kennerly/White House, courtesy Gerald R. Ford Presidential Library; Associated Press/Charles Dharapak; Official White House photograph by Lawrence Jackson; Official White House photograph by Annie Leibovitz; Official White House photograph by Pete Souza; Associated Press/David J. Phillip; Chip Somodevilla/Getty Images; Official White House Photo by Chuck Kennedy.

BIBLIOGRAPHY

Allen, Mike. "Laura Bush: I 'Stood Straighter' After Leaving White House." *Politico*, May 10, 2010.

Andersen, Christopher. *Bill and Hillary: The Marriage.* New York: William Morrow, 1999.

Associated Press. "Husband of Betty Ford's Aide Kills Himself." *Chicago Tribune*, April 12, 1975.

———. "Jackie, Nina, Hit at Vienna." June 5, 1961.

Barrett, Mary Ellin. "Marilyn Quayle: From Ice to Nice." *USA Today Weekend*, November 1–3, 1991.

Beale, Betty. "White House Plans Told: Tish Baldrige Has First Press Conference." *Evening Star*, November 23, 1960.

Beasley, Maurine. *First Ladies and the Press: The Unfinished Partnership of the Media Age.* Evanston, IL: Northwestern University Press, 2005.

Belkin, Lisa. "Bill Clinton as First Gent? He'd Break New Ground—and Maybe a Little China." Yahoo! Politics, June 7, 2015.

Bernstein, Carl. *A Woman in Charge: The Life of Hillary Rodham Clinton.* New York: Vintage Books, 2007.

Beschloss, Michael. "In His Final Days, LBJ Agonized Over His Legacy." PBS, December 4, 2012.

Boyd, Gerald. "Nancy Reagan Maintains Business-as-Usual Poise." *New York Times*, July 16, 1985.

Brinkley, Douglas. *The Unfinished Presidency: Jimmy Carter's Journey Beyond the White House*. New York: Viking, 1998.

Brower, Kate Andersen. "Obama Honors 'Four Patriots' Who Died in Libya Attack." Bloomberg, September 15, 2012.

Brower, Kate Andersen, and Nick Johnston. "Obama Tax Deal 'Is a Good Bill,' Former President Clinton Says." Bloomberg, December 12, 2010.

Bruce, Preston. *From the Door of the White House*. New York: Lothrop, Lee & Shepard Books, 1984.

Bruni, Frank. "For Laura Bush, a Direction She Never Wished to Go In." *New York Times*, July 31, 2000.

Bryant, Traphes, with Frances Spatz Leighton. *Dog Days at the White House*. New York: Macmillan, 1975.

Bumiller, Elisabeth. "Public Lives: Two First Ladies, So Alike and So Different." *New York Times*, May 12, 1999.

Burros, Marian. "Hillary Clinton Asks Help in Finding a Softer Image." *New York Times*, January 9, 1995.

Bush, Barbara. *A Memoir: Barbara Bush*. New York: Scribner, 1994.

Bush, Laura. *Spoken from the Heart*. New York: Scribner, 2010.

Butterfield, Fox. "At Wellesley, a Furor over Barbara Bush." *New York Times*, May 4, 1990.

Calmes, Jackie. "Why Is First Lady Scarce in Campaign? Her Last Name Is Obama." *New York Times*, October 3, 2014.

Cannon, Carl. "Kennedys Share Boat with the Clintons." *Baltimore Sun*, August 25, 1993.

Cannon, James. *Gerald R. Ford: An Honorable Life*. Ann Arbor: University of Michigan Press, 2013.

Carter, Rosalynn. *First Lady from Plains*. Boston: Houghton Mifflin, 1984.

CBS News, *60 Minutes*. "Candidate Obama's Sense of Urgency." February 9, 2007.

CBS News, *60 Minutes II*. "The Reagans' Long Goodbye: Mike Wallace Interviews Nancy Reagan for *60 Minutes II*." September 24, 2002.

Chatterjee, Sumana. "A Powerful Trio Helped Convicted Banker Win Pardon." *Philadelphia Inquirer*, March 9, 2001.

Cherlin, Reid. "The Worst Wing: How the East Wing Shrank Michelle Obama." *New Republic*, March 24, 2014.

Christy, Marian. "Pat Was Trained to Suffer." *Beaver County* (Pa.) *Times*, November 2, 1978.

Clinton, Hillary Rodham. *An Invitation to the White House: At Home with History*. New York: Simon & Schuster, 2000.

———. *Living History*. New York: Scribner, 2003.

———. "Talking It Over." Syndicated column, June 4, 1996.

Cloud, John. "Give 'Em Hillary." *Time*, November 16, 1998.

Colacello, Bob. "Nancy Reagan's Solo Role." *Vanity Fair*, July 2009.

Collins, Amy Fine. "It Had to Be Kenneth." *Vanity Fair*, June 2003.

Collins, Lauren. "The Other Obama." *New Yorker*, March 10, 2008.

Conroy, Sarah Booth. "First Lady, and Wife First." *Washington Post*, June 28, 1993.

Crawford, Clare. "A Story of Love and Rehabilitation: The Ex-Con in the White House." *People*, March 14, 1977.

Cuniberti, Betty. "Nancy Reagan's Schedule Ambitious: President, First Lady Off on Separate Paths." *Los Angeles Times*, May 1, 1986.

Davis, Margaret Leslie. *Mona Lisa in Camelot*. New York: Da Capo Press, 2008.

Davis, Patti. *The Way I See It*. New York: G. P. Putnam's Sons, 1992.

Deaver, Michael, with Mickey Herskowitz. *Behind the Scenes*. New York: William Morrow, 1988.

Didion, Joan. "Life at Court." *New York Review of Books*, December 21, 1989.

Didion, Joan, and John Gregory Dunne. "Pretty Nancy." *Saturday Evening Post*, June 1, 1968.

Dixon, George. "The Ladies Will Be Heard." *Evening Independent*, March 30, 1964.

Duffy, Michael. "10 Questions with Barbara Bush." *Time*, June 15, 2015.

Ehrlichman, John. *Witness to Power: The Nixon Years*. New York: Simon & Schuster, 1982.

Eilperin, Juliet. "The New Dynamics of Protecting a President: Most Threats Against Obama Issued Online." *Washington Post*, October 8, 2014.

Eisenhower, Julie Nixon. *Pat Nixon: The Untold Story*. New York: Simon & Schuster, 2007.

Ellis, Rosemary. "A Conversation with Michelle Obama." *Good Housekeeping*, September 30, 2008.

Ellison, Sarah. "How Hillary Clinton's Loyal Confidants Could Cost Her the Election." *Vanity Fair*, November 2015.

Farhi, Paul. "Michelle Obama's Target Trip: Critics Take Aim." *Washington Post*, October 2, 2011.

Feldman, Trude. "The Quiet Courage of Pat Nixon." *McCall's*, May 1975.

Fields, Alonzo. *My 21 Years in the White House*. New York: Crest Books, 1961.

Ford, Betty, with Chris Chase. *The Times of My Life*. New York: Harper & Row, 1978.

Franks, Lucinda. "The Intimate Hillary." *Talk*, September 1999.

Gamarekian, Barbara. "The Political Husband Is a Rarity No Longer." *New York Times*, November 16, 1981.

Germond, Jack W., and Jules Witcover. "The Election Is More Than Whose Wife Does What." *Baltimore Sun*, August 25, 1992.

Gerstein, Josh. "Emails Show Hillary's Political Sleuthing." *Politico*, September 1, 2015.

Gerth, Jeff, and Don Van Natta Jr. *Her Way: The Hopes and Ambitions of Hillary Rodham Clinton*. New York: Back Nine Books, 2007.

Gibbs, Nancy, and Michael Duffy. "Game of Thrones." *Time*, August 3, 2015.

———. *The Presidents Club: Inside the World's Most Exclusive Fraternity*. New York: Simon & Schuster, 2012.

Gillette, Michael L. *Lady Bird Johnson: An Oral History*. New York: Oxford University Press, 2012.

Goldstein, Amy. "Part of, but Apart from, It All; Clintons Have Complex Relationship with City." *Washington Post*, January 20, 1997.

Greene, John Robert. *Betty Ford: Candor and Courage in the White House*. Lawrence: University Press of Kansas, 2004.

Grunwald, Lisa, and Stephen J. Adler. *Women's Letters: America from the Revolutionary War to the Present*. New York: Random House, 2005.

Hagen, Joe. "Bush in the Wilderness." *New York*, October 14, 2012.

Haldeman, H. R. *The Haldeman Diaries: Inside the Nixon White House*. New York: G. P. Putnam's Sons, 1994.

Harris, John. "Ex-Aides Find 2nd Chance with First Lady." *Washington Post*, September 23, 1999.

Healy, Patrick. "New to Campaigning, but No Longer a Novice." *New York Times*, October 27, 2008.

Henderson, Nia-Malika. "Michelle Obama Warms Up for Campaign Trail." *Washington Post*, October 5, 2010.

Hersh, Seymour. "The Pardon: Nixon, Ford, Haig, and the Transfer of Power." *Atlantic*, August, 1983.

Hill, Clint, and Lisa McCubbin. *Five Days in November*. New York: Gallery Books, 2013.

———. *Mrs. Kennedy and Me*. New York: Gallery Books, 2012.

Hines, Cragg. "Queries on Infidelity Infuriate First Lady." *Houston Chronicle*, August 13, 1992.

Hirsh, Michael. "The Regrets of Jimmy Carter." *Politico*, August 20, 2015.

Hollandsworth, Skip. "Reading Laura Bush." *Texas Monthly*, November 1996.

Holmes, Kristen. "Equal Pay for First Ladies Too." CNN.com, April 16, 2015.

Ifill, Gwen. "Clinton and Kennedys: In 30 Years, a Full Circle." *New York Times*, August 25, 1993.

Isikoff, Michael. "Clinton's Schedules Are Bare." *Newsweek*, March 18, 2008.

Jackman, Tom. "Northern Virginia's Slice of Camelot: The Kennedys in Fauquier County, 1961–63." *Washington Post*, November 21, 2013.

Janos, Leo. "The Last Days of the President: LBJ in Retirement." *Atlantic*, July 1973.

Johnson, Lady Bird. *A White House Diary.* New York: Holt, Rinehart & Winston, 1970.

Johnson, Rebecca. "Michelle Obama Interview: I'm Nothing Special." *Telegraph*, July 26, 2008.

Kahn, Joseph, and Christine Hauser. "China's Leader Makes First White House Visit." *New York Times*, April 20, 2006.

Kantor, Jodi. *The Obamas.* New York: Little, Brown, 2012.

Keen, Judy. "Michelle Obama: Campaigning Her Way." *USA Today*, May 11, 2007.

Kelly, Michael. "Again: It's Hillary Rodham Clinton. Got That?" *New York Times*, February 14, 1993.

Kilpatrick, Carroll, and Maxine Cheshire. "The New Tenant Drops By: The Fast-Moving Kennedys Take to Palm Beach Sun." *Washington Post*, December 10, 1960.

Koren, Marina. "Jimmy Carter on His Cancer Diagnosis." *Atlantic*, August 20, 2015.

Kornblut, Anne E. "Michelle Obama's Career Timeout for Now, Weight Shifts in Work-Family Tug of War." *Washington Post*, May 11, 2007.

Lardner, George, Jr., and Lois Romano. "Tragedy Created Bush Mother-Son Bond." *Washington Post*, July 26, 1999.

Lauter, David. "Mrs. Wonk Goes to Washington: If Hillary Clinton Succeeds, She Could Revolutionize the Role of First Lady. If She Fails, She Could Take the Whole Administration Down with Her." *Los Angeles Times*, May 23, 1993.

Leaming, Barbara. *Jacqueline Bouvier Kennedy Onassis*. New York: Thomas Dunne Books, 2014.

Lee, Carol. "First Lady Embraces Campaign." *Wall Street Journal*, February 11, 2012.

Leibovich, Mark. "Re-Re-Re-Reintroducing Hillary Clinton: The Meticulously Managed Rollout of a Candidate Whom Voters Think They Know Already." *New York Times*, July 15, 2015.

Linsker, Sharon W. "Letters Signed by First Ladies Supply Insights into the Past." *New York Times*, May 1, 1994.

Malone, Noreen. "Senate Wives: Why Is There a President of the Congressional Freshmen Spouses?" *Slate*, March 31, 2011.

Manchester, William. *The Death of a President: November 20–November 25, 1963*. New York: Harper & Row, 1967.

Marcus, Ruth. "Clinton in Camelot: The Arkansas Traveler, Afloat with the Kennedy Clan." *Washington Post*, August 25, 1993.

Marton, Kati. *Hidden Power: Presidential Marriages That Shaped Our History*. New York: Anchor Books, 2001.

McCardle, Dorothy. "From Inquiring Camera Girl to Next First Lady? Ike's Election Kept Artist Jackie Busy." *Washington Post and Times-Herald*, September 28, 1960.

———. "Jackie Learned Pat's No. 1 Pick Was Mamie." *Washington Post and Times-Herald*, September 30, 1960.

———. "Will Mamie Brief Jackie on Home." *Washington Post*, November 13, 1960.

McFadden, Robert D. "Death of a First Lady: The Companion; Quietly at Her Side, Public at the End." *New York Times*, May 24, 1994.

McGrath, Charles. "No End of the Affair." *New York Times*, April 20, 2008.

Meacham, Jon. *Destiny and Power: The American Odyssey of George Herbert Walker Bush*. New York: Random House, 2015.

Mehren, Elizabeth. "Richard Goodwin's Account of a 'Paranoid' L.B.J. Riles Some Ex-Colleagues." *Los Angeles Times*, September 14, 1988.

Mehren, Elizabeth, and Betty Cuniberti. "Fighting Back: Over the Course of Her Husband's Political Career, Nancy Reagan Has Developed Her Own Mission: To Protect Ronald Reagan, No Matter What." *Los Angeles Times Magazine*, March 22, 1987.

Miller, Lisa. "No More Washington Wives, and It's Our Loss." *Newsweek*, January 3, 2011.

Morrison, Patt. "Time for a Feminist as First Lady: What Americans Think of Hillary Clinton Is as Much a Verdict on the Role of Women in the '90s as a Judgment of Her Style and Achievements." *Los Angeles Times*, July 14, 1992.

Neath, Scarlet. "What's the Point of a First Lady?" *Atlantic*, October 6, 2014.

Nemy, Enid. "Obituary: Lady Bird Johnson, 94, Former U.S. First Lady." *New York Times*, July 12, 2007.

New York Times. "The 1994 Campaign, Virginia; Mrs. Reagan Denounces Oliver North on Iran Affair." October 29, 1994.

Noonan, Peggy. "The Reagans and the Kennedys: How They Forged a Friendship That Crossed Party Lines." *Wall Street Journal*, August 28, 2009.

Pear, Robert. "Court Rules That First Lady Is 'De Facto' Federal Official." *New York Times*, June 23, 1993.

Peretz, Evgenia. "How Chelsea Clinton Took Charge of Clintonworld." *Vanity Fair*, September 2015.

Phelps, Timothy M. "How Reagan's Would-Be Assassin Could Go Free; a Well-Behaved John Hinckley May Soon Leave Mental Hospital." *Los Angeles Times*, May 12, 2015.

Quinn, Sally. "Nancy Reagan Looks Back in Anger." *Washington Post*, November 5, 1989.

Radcliffe, Donnie. "Life as the First Lady's Confidante and 'Protector.'" *Washington Post*, April 14, 1977.

————. "Nancy Reagan's Private Obsession; A Tenacious Struggle to Oust Donald Regan from the President's Team." *Washington Post*, February 27, 1987.

Reagan, Nancy, with William Novak. *My Turn: The Memoirs of Nancy Reagan*. New York: Random House, 1989.

Regan, Donald T. *For the Record*. New York: Harcourt Brace Jovanovich, 1988.

Rimer, Sara. "A Nation Challenged: The Pennsylvania Crash; 44 Victims Are Remembered, and Lauded." *New York Times*, September 18, 2001.

Romano, Lois. "Michelle Obama: White House Rebel." *Newsweek*, June 5, 2011.

Rosellini, Lynn. "'Honey, I Forgot to Duck,' Injured Reagan Tells Wife." *New York Times*, March 31, 1981.

Salvatore, Diane. "Barack and Michelle Obama: The Full Interview." *Ladies' Home Journal*, August 2008.

Schlesinger, Arthur M., Jr. *Jacqueline Kennedy: Historic Conversations on Life with John F. Kennedy*. New York: Hyperion, 2011.

Sheehy, Gail. "Hillaryland at War." *Vanity Fair*, August 2008.

———. "Is George Bush Too Nice to Be President?" *Vanity Fair*, February 1987.

———. "What Hillary Wants." *Vanity Fair*, May 1992.

Shelton, Isabelle. "Pat Is Pressed." *Evening Star*, September 19, 1972.

Slevin, Peter. *Michelle Obama: A Life*. New York: Knopf, 2015.

Smith, Helen. "Ordeal! Pat Nixon's Final Days in the White House." *Good Housekeeping*, July 1976.

Smith, Sally Bedell. *Grace and Power: The Private World of the Kennedy White House*. New York: Random House, 2004.

Sorensen, Ted. *Kennedy: The Classic Biography*. New York: HarperPerennial, 1965.

Stanley, Alessandra. "Michelle Obama Shows Her Warmer Side on 'The View.'" *New York Times*, June 19, 2008.

The Starr Report. Submitted by the Office of the Independent Counsel to Congress, September 9, 1998.

Steinem, Gloria. "In Your Heart You Know He's Nixon." *New York*, October 28, 1968.

———. *Outrageous Acts and Everyday Rebellions*. New York: Henry Holt, 1983.

Swift, Will. *Pat and Dick: The Nixons: An Intimate Portrait of a Marriage*. New York: Simon & Schuster, 2014.

Thomas, Helen. *Front Row at the White House: My Life and Times*. New York: Touchstone Books, 1999.

———. "Pat Nixon Answers All Letters to Her." United Press International, December 28, 1971.

Thompson, Bob. "Richard Nixon and the Oobie-Doobie Girl." *Washington Post Magazine*, July 27, 1997.

Thompson, Krissah. "First Lady Embraces Campaign." *Washington Post*, July 26, 2012.

———. "Michelle Obama Out in Full Force for 'Barack's Last Campaign.'" *Washington Post*, November 3, 2014.

Truman, Margaret. *First Ladies: An Intimate Group Portrait of White House Wives*. New York: Random House, 1995.

United Press International. "Collapses, Dies, Honoring Betty Ford." *Chicago Tribune*, June 23, 1976.

———. "Release of Tapes Displeased Pat." *Washington Post*, May 20, 1974.

Van Meter, Jonathan. "Leading by Example: First Lady Michelle Obama." *Vogue*, March 14, 2013.

Venant, Elizabeth. "Nancy's Detractors Take Another Turn." *Los Angeles Times*, November 16, 1989.

Viorst, Judith. "Pat Nixon Is the Ultimate Good Sport." *New York Times*, September 13, 1970.

Weddington, Sarah. "Three Former First Ladies Speak Out." *Good Housekeeping*, February 1988.

Weidenfeld, Sheila Rabb. *First Lady's Lady: With the Fords at the White House*. New York: G. P. Putnam's Sons, 1979.

Weinraub, Bernard. "Nancy Reagan's Power Is Considered at Peak." *New York Times*, March 3, 1987.

Weisman, Jonathan. "JFK Jr. Visited White House at Invitation of Nixon, Reagan: Clinton Claims Corrected in Light of More Accurate Historical Information." *Baltimore Sun*, July 24, 1999.

West, J. B. *Upstairs at the White House: My Life with the First Ladies*. New York: Warner Books, 1973.

West, Jessamyn. "Exclusive: The Unknown Pat Nixon: An Intimate View." *Good Housekeeping*, February 1971.

Wheaton, Sarah. "Clinton's Civil Rights Lesson." *New York Times*, January 7, 2008.

Wildman, Sarah. "Portrait of a Lady." *New Republic*, August 20, 2001.

Williams, Marjorie. "Barbara's Backlash." *Vanity Fair*, August 1992.

Woodward, Bob. *The Last of the President's Men*. New York: Simon & Schuster, 2015.

Woodward, Bob, and Carl Bernstein. *The Final Days*. New York: Simon & Schuster, 1976.

Yeager, Holly. "The Heart and Mind of Michelle Obama." *O: The Oprah Magazine*, November 2007.

Zeleny, Jeff. "Q&A with Michelle Obama." *Chicago Tribune*, December 24, 2005

INDEX

★

KATE ANDERSEN BROWER is the author of the number one *New York Times* bestseller *The Residence: Inside the Private World of the White House.* She spent four years covering the Obama White House for Bloomberg News and is a former CBS News staffer and Fox News producer. She lives outside Washington, D.C., with her husband and their two young children. She can be followed on Twitter: @katebrower.

ALSO BY **KATE ANDERSEN BROWER**

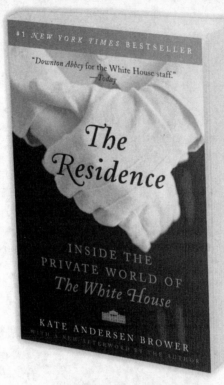

THE RESIDENCE
Inside the Private World of the White House

Available in Paperback and E-book

"A revealing look at life inside the White House...it's *Downton Abbey* for the White House staff." —*The Today Show*

"Absolutely delicious." —*Washington Post*

Using incredible first-person anecdotes from interviews with scores of White House staff members, Brower reveals the intimacy between the First Family and the people who serve them, as well as tension that has shaken the staff over the decades. From the housekeeper and engineer who fell in love while serving President Reagan to Jackie Kennedy's private moment of grief with a beloved staffer after her husband's assassination to the tumultuous days surrounding President Nixon's resignation and President Clinton's impeachment battle, *The Residence* is full of surprising and moving details that illuminate day-to-day life at the White House.